LITERATURE AND HISTORY
OF
AVIATION

LITERATURE AND HISTORY
OF
AVIATION

Advisory Editor: JAMES GILBERT

History of
United States
Naval Aviation

by
Archibald D. Turnbull
and
Clifford L. Lord

ARNO PRESS

A NEW YORK TIMES COMPANY

Reprint Edition 1972 by Arno Press Inc.

Reprinted from a copy in The State Historical Society of Wisconsin Library

LC# 70-169439
ISBN 0-405-03782-1

Literature and History of Aviation
ISBN for complete set: 0-405-03789-9
See last pages of this volume for titles.

Manufactured in the United States of America

73-13776

History of
United States
Naval Aviation

REAR ADMIRAL WILLIAM A. MOFFETT
Chief of the Bureau of Aeronautics, 1921–1933.

History of United States Naval Aviation

by

Archibald D. Turnbull
CAPTAIN, USNR,
DEPUTY DIRECTOR OF NAVAL RECORDS AND HISTORY

and

Clifford L. Lord
LIEUTENANT COMMANDER, USNR,
FORMERLY HEAD OF THE NAVAL AVIATION HISTORY UNIT

NEW HAVEN

YALE UNIVERSITY PRESS

LONDON · GEOFFREY CUMBERLEGE · OXFORD UNIVERSITY PRESS

1949

To the Memory of

REAR ADMIRAL WILLIAM ADGER MOFFETT

SEAMAN   AIRMAN   STATESMAN

Foreword

IN ITS Naval Aviation the United States has a unique weapon, one that really has no counterpart anywhere. This is a primary source of our military strength and the envy of every other military power. The story of the development of Naval Aviation to its present advanced state is well worth study, for it illuminates the means by which we have retained control of the world's seas over which must pass the raw materials of our industrial strength.

This history is not an official history. It does not reflect, and should not be taken as reflecting, the views of the Navy Department. The records of the Department have been made available to the historians with the understanding that they might, and should, report their findings and express whatever conclusions they may have reached.

I believe the results have justified this process, and that military as well as civilian readers will profit from this study.

DAN A. KIMBALL
Assistant Secretary of the Navy for Air

Washington
28 March 1949

Preface

THE PREPARATION of this book was first suggested by the Honorable Artemus L. Gates when Assistant Secretary of the Navy for Air, and the work begun at his instigation has had the sympathetic support of his successors, the Honorable John L. Sullivan and the Honorable John Nicholas Brown. With this strong encouragement, the book has been written ostensibly by two authors, but the names of those who actually helped to write it could not be crowded upon any title page.

It was the foresight of Adm. John Towers, as Chief of the Bureau of Aeronautics, which perceived the need of a Naval Aviation History Unit, and it was he who established it. Flying flag officers who have continued his work, as Deputy Chiefs of Naval Operations, have been Vice Adms. Aubrey W. Fitch, A. W. Radford, D. B. Duncan and John D. Price and the late Adm. Marc A. Mitscher and Vice Adm. J. S. McCain. Chiefs of the Bureau of Aeronautics who have been similarly helpful are Adm. D. C. Ramsey, Vice Adm. H. B. Sallada, and Rear Adm. Alfred M. Pride. In direct supervision of the research have been Capts. W. R. Hollingsworth and E. W. Parish, Jr., Lt. Comdrs. R. J. Monahan and W. T. Amen. Coordination of the work with other historical efforts has been by the Office of Naval History, created in 1944 under Adm. Edward C. Kalbfus, later headed by Rear Adms. Vincent R. Murphy and John B. Heffernan.

It has been a pleasure to meet, in person or by letter, so many who played their parts in bringing aviation in the Navy to its present high place. Some of them have read the manuscript in whole or in part; others, recalling past experiences, have brought to life the personalities of long-gone shipmates and recreated an atmosphere that does not hang over documents, however voluminous. Space permits no detailed account of

their contributions, but to those already named these should
be added: Vice Adms. P. N. L. Bellinger, T. T. Craven,
A. W. Johnson, S. M. Kraus, and E. S. Land; Rear Adms.
F. D. Wagner, A. C. Davis, E. C. Ewen, R. E. Byrd and
A. C. Read; Commodore D. W. Knox; Capts. H. C. Richard-
son, W. McEntee, V. D. Herbster, R. S. Barnaby, F. R. Mc-
Crary, W. S. Diehl, J. W. McElroy, R. R. Paunack and
H. C. Wick; Comdrs. G. C. Sweet and C. W. Mitchell, Jr.;
Lt. Comdr. Nelson Blake; Lt. Gen. R. S. Geiger; Maj. Gens.
P. T. Hill and R. E. Rowell; Brig. Gens. W. O. Brice and
L. H. M. Sanderson; Col. Jarvis Butler and Lt. Col. F. T.
Evans; Drs. J. C. Hunsaker and A. F. Zahm; Messrs. James
C. Fahey, J. B. May, Jr. and Fred Schmitt.

The Naval Aviation History Unit has been indefatigable.
Its present scholarly heads, Dr. Henry M. Dater and Mr.
Adrian O. Van Wyen, themselves the authors of innumerable
authoritative monographs and papers, have shown an in-
exhaustible patience at every step and so inspired the unit to
cooperation that the complete roll must be called: M. C.
Welborn, L. M. Pearson, E. L. Smith, D. M. Foerster, R. M.
Carrigan, D. A. Bergmark, M. B. Chambers, M. E. Jarchow,
M. D. Schwartz, R. C. Weems, J. DuVon, T. A. Miller, R. J.
Doyle, K. K. Weed, C. F. Stanwood, J. E. Jennings, Jr.,
J. P. King, L. H. Hurlbert, W. C. Bryant, K. Hermans,
M. F. Shelley, A. M. Sanchez, W. G. Land, G. Tobias, G. M.
Fennemore, A. F. Vaupel, R. W. Dittmer, W. O. Shanahan,
I. D. Spencer, R. W. July, A. R. Buchanan, G. H. Wright,
R. L. Golden, J. M. Grimes, H. F. Bennett, R. M. Whitney,
D. Daly, A. R. Hilen, Jr., P. E. Garber, P. G. Sullivan, P. E.
Varg, P. N. Cary, F. E. Abbot, R. H. Kelsey, G. McColley.

In one way or another many more have helped. Lt. Comdr.
Shirley Baraw did much to facilitate the preparation of the
manuscript and to iron out mechanical obstacles. Miss Izetta
Winter Robb, experienced as an editor, made many valuable
suggestions, particularly on the chapters dealing with the early
twenties. Dr. Robert G. Albion has been lavish with professional advice. Chief Yeoman R. E. Barton, Miss Eddie
Jane Poindexter, Miss Harriette Baker, Miss Betty Kirkley,

and Miss Shirley Zimmerman have not only typed many pages themselves but also supervised the work of others less skilled, checked names, dates, and facts, and run the endless errands which have been necessary.

Much assistance has been received from personnel of the Navy Department, who have opened their files and offered knowledge come to them through their years of service. Special thanks are owed to Messrs. Carlisle Fliedner, C. A. Burgess, and A. D. Micotti of the Bureau of Aeronautics; to Lieuts. Olive Webb and Harrison Fiddesof, Mrs. Olive Finch, and Mrs. Thelma Barthelmess, all of the Bureau of Naval Personnel. Other keepers of files, with their assistants, have searched long hours for documents and answered innumerable questions. Notable help has been received from Mr. Omar Whaley of the Office of the Chief of Naval Operations, Mrs. P. N. Graves of the Bureau of Aeronautics, and Miss L. I. MacCrindle, Mrs. A. R. Lawrence, and Chief Yeoman B. R. Yantz, all of the Office of Naval Records and Library. Finally, the staffs of the National Archives, the Library of Congress, and the library of the National Advisory Committee for Aeronautics have contributed their specialized knowledge as well as documents and publications from their respective collections.

Given so much assistance of such high quality, there should not be one error in the book. To the charge that there are errors, the authors can plead only that they are human and therefore fallible.

A.D.T.
C.L.L.

Washington, April 1, 1949

Contents

Illustrations

The illustrations except the frontispiece precede Chapter XVIII, page 193.
Official U. S. Navy photographs

Rear Adm. William A. Moffett
First Flight from Any Ship
First Landing on a Ship
Pioneers of Naval Aviation
Directors of Naval Aviation
Naval and Marine Aviators in 1914
Crews of NC Transatlantic Flight, 1919
Early Catapults
USS *Lexington*
USS *Ranger*
USS *Langley*
USS *Wright*
Early Naval Aircraft, 1913–1917
Early Naval Aircraft, 1918–1925
Patrol Aircraft, 1925–1936
Scout-observation Planes, 1926–1940
First Planes to Operate from a Carrier
Carrier Fighters, 1925–1940
Dive Bombers, 1925–1937
Torpedo Planes, 1926–1937
Lighter-than-air Craft

Illustrations

CHAPTER I

Chambers Makes a Start with Curtiss

THEODORE ROOSEVELT, Assistant Secretary of the Navy, sat at his desk in the Navy Department. His calendar marked the date as March 25, 1898, and none knew better than he that war with Spain might come at any moment. Seizing a pencil, he addressed his chief, Secretary Long, in a memorandum that would become historic: "The machine has worked. It seems to me worthwhile for this government to try whether it will not work on a large enough scale to be of use in the event of war."

Beside him at that moment was Charles D. Walcott, director of the Geological Survey and, as was just then of greater importance, a firm believer in Professor Samuel Pierpont Langley. From Walcott had come an enthusiastic account of Langley's "aerodrome" with its 13-foot wingspread, its tiny steam-driven engine, and its total weight of 30 pounds. On May 6, 1896, that model had actually risen into the air and stayed up for about a minute and a half, to cover a distance of 3,000 feet in the first of all flights by a heavier-than-air machine. Listening to Walcott's account Roosevelt, with characteristic perception and vigor, had instantly grasped the possibilities of a full-sized aeroplane, able to carry human beings. Might it become the Big Stick?

Continuing his memorandum, he presently proposed that Comdr. C. H. Davis, head of the Naval Observatory, and some other naval officer of similar scientific attainments be ordered to form a board with two qualified army officers. Let that board call in such civilian authorities as Professor R. H. Thurston of Cornell and Octave Chanute, the expert on gliders who was then president of the American Society of Civil Engineers. After thorough study, let the board make recommendations as to practicability and submit estimates of cost. For this, said Roosevelt, "is well worth doing."

Within the next week Commander Davis and Professor of Mathematics Stimson J. Brown of the Naval Academy held their first meeting with the army representatives, Col. G. W. Davis, Maj. Robert Craig, and Capt. William Crozier. Together they delved into all the records of man's effort to fly, paying particular attention to the reports of such men as Hiram Maxim, Thurston, Chanute, and Alexander Graham Bell, but also listening to many others. They learned that Langley models, with an astonishingly light yet efficient engine, had flown, not once but many times, the distance of a full mile in no more than two minutes. Little by little, they reached "reasonable ground" for believing that a full-sized machine could be built, not only able to carry a grown man for several hours, but also with "carrying capacity so far in excess" of this that it could be used to transport light explosives "to be dropped from an elevation into an enemy's camp or fleet." Summed up, the utility of an aeroplane should fall under three heads: (1) as a means of reconnaissance, or scouting, with capacity to carry an observer; (2) as a means of communication between stations isolated from each other by ordinary means of land and water; (3) as an engine of offense with the capacity of dropping, from a great height, high explosives into a camp or fortification.

The board did not expect Langley's machine to be a "complete and instant success." Modifications and improvements would inevitably be necessary but, even allowing for these, Langley's estimate of $50,000 for experiments appeared reasonable and, by inference at least, the board recommended making that amount available to him. After describing what European nations were already doing along the same line, Commander Davis, transmitting the board's report, wrote: "In view of the great importance which, if successful, it would have in military operations, I do not hesitate to express . . . the general sentiment of the Board in favor of the advisability of continuing the experiments of Professor Langley."

Secretary Long sent the report to the Board of Construction, where sudden death awaited it in this verdict:

The Board has the honor to report that it has considered the within subject, and is of the opinion that such an apparatus as is referred to pertains strictly to the land service and not to the Navy. The question is too intricate for this Board to do justice to, and it respectfully asks to be excused from further consideration of the subject, but believes that it is not expedient at this time for the Navy Department to carry on experiments or furnish money for the purpose.

Could any words better express how little was generally known or even imagined about aviation at the end of the nineteenth century? All military eyes were more than half closed but, in November of this year, after the war with Spain was over, the Army did give Langley $25,000 and, when the Navy declined to match that sum, another $25,000 during the next year. Langley spent $25,000 more of his own, the whole amount going into that series of experiments which ended so spectacularly on December 8, 1903. Maj. Montgomery M. McComb, the War Department's observer, described the events of that day as taking place at the junction of the Potomac and Anacostia rivers, not far from Washington. "The launching car," he reported,

was released at 4:45 P.M. . . . The car was set in motion and the propellers revolved rapidly, the engine working perfectly, but there was something wrong . . . The rear guy-post seemed to drag, bringing the rudder down on the launching ways, and a crashing, rending sound, followed by the collapse of the rear wings, showed that the machine had been wrecked . . . before [it] was free of the ways. [This] deprived the machine of its support in the rear, and it consequently reared up in the front under the action of the motor, assumed a vertical position, and then toppled over . . . falling into the water a few feet in front of the boat. Mr. Manly [the pilot] was pulled out of the wreck uninjured and the wrecked machine was subsequently placed upon the house-boat, and the whole brought back to Washington. From what has been said it will be seen that . . . unfortunate accidents have prevented any test of the apparatus in free flight, and the claim that an engine-driven, man-carrying aerodrome has been constructed lacks the proof which actual flight alone can give.

Since the Navy's sole contribution to that occasion had been an anchor and chain, it escaped the ridicule heaped upon the Army by press and public. It also "escaped" a place in the front rank of aviation development. This was little more than a week before Orville Wright rose into history over the lonely sands of Kittyhawk, the first human being to fly in a motor-driven, heavier-than-air machine.

During the next few years many inventors, of whom the great majority often had little more than vague ideas, approached the Navy Department. Almost invariably, their most earnest plea was for funds to complete experiments with various types of flying machines, ranging from balloons to gliders and back again. Whenever any of these applications got as far as the General Board, that group of high-ranking officers appointed to advise the Secretary of the Navy on all matters of policy, the most frequent comment was to the effect that aviation had "not yet reached sufficient importance to warrant" doing anything definite about it. Sometimes, the ideas submitted received no kinder notice than "Plans and descriptions returned this date."

By 1908, however, the Wrights were no longer the only claimants to successful flight in heavier-than-air machines. Secret trials of other designs, both here and abroad, had been followed by public demonstrations of practicability. The foresight of the so-called "Langley Board" ten years before was proven by the increasing ability of aeroplanes to carry out at least some of the missions suggested by that board. With completed planes available, it remained to be seen whether the Navy would be prepared to spend money upon their possibilities.

On September 17, 1908, observers from the Navy and the Army joined the crowd of civilians on the parade ground at Fort Myer, Virginia, waiting for the Wrights' official trial. For the Navy, the two best-informed observers were Lieut. George C. Sweet, a pioneer in wireless telegraphy who had taken up the study of flying machines, and Naval Constructor William McEntee. Sweet, scheduled to be a passenger on that day's exhibition, had persuaded the Secretary of the Navy, Victor H. Metcalf, to be present to see the flight, but luckily for himself, did not fly. At the last moment his place was taken by Lt. Thomas E. Selfridge, earliest of the Army's flyers and already experienced through participation in civilian tests at Hammondsport, New York, and Baddeck, Nova Scotia. Because Selfridge, under orders to go to St. Joseph, Missouri, to test the Army's first dirigible, would have only that one opportunity to go up with Wright, Sweet at the urging of Alexander Graham Bell and others yielded his turn. Since Sweet was relatively heavy, extra-sized propellers had been fitted for the occasion and as the plane rose these propellers fouled wires leading to the rudder. In the tragic crash that followed, Selfridge was killed, while Sweet lived to become, a year later, the first naval officer in the United States—perhaps in the world—to fly. For the moment, however, the Fort Myer disaster served only to convince the Secretary of the Navy that the day of Naval Aviation was not yet. Nevertheless Sweet, backed by Rear Adm. William S. Cowles, brother-in-law of Theodore Roosevelt and then Chief of the Bureau of Equipment, pushed his recommendation that the Navy begin planning, buying, building, and testing.

What Sweet wanted was a plane, capable of carrying more than one man, so designed that it could be stowed aboard ship and launched from a deck as an air scout. It should make "at least 40 miles an hour, with the possibility of hovering, if such could be accomplished," and be able to rise from or land upon the water. It must carry a "wireless telegraph installation." In Sweet's opinion, all these things were entirely practicable in the existing state of what he termed "aeroitation"; their achievement by adding greatly to the scouting powers of the Fleet and to its means of communication, would materially increase protection against enemy attack. Moreover, said Sweet, since underwater mine fields in Europe had been detected from the air, why might not approaching submarines be discovered in the same way?

Sweet suggested that the Navy buy planes that fulfilled the requirements and place them in the hands of its own personnel, trained as rapidly as might be. At the end of his very important letter, he wrote what would often be recalled:

Attention is invited to the great encouragement being given to inventors of like apparatus abroad, particularly in Germany and France. It is believed that the Department should not be behind in this, as the most practicable flying-machine at present is the invention of a citizen of the United States, and it would seem advisable to lead other navies in this as in the past has been done in other features.

These recommendations were approved by Cowles but conservatism was the naval order of the day, and there is no record of any final action taken upon Sweet's letter. European nations might encourage aviation with men and money; the United States Navy appeared to be willing to await proof of military capabilities and significance. Sweet, still supported by Rear Admiral Cowles and also by Lieut. (later Rear Adm.) Percy W. Foote, nevertheless persisted with his requests and recommendations, especially after the Wrights, in August, 1909, met all the Army's requirements and sold the War Department a plane. The Navy Department's attitude was unshaken by this, by the rise of civilian aero clubs and societies in the United States, by European enthusiasm for the demonstrations of Santos Dumont and the cross-Channel flight of Bleriot, and by the plans for an international "aviation meet" at

Rheims in this same August. The department did, however, consent to send a representative to that meet.

The officer sent was the naval attaché in Paris, Comdr. F. L. Chapin, and there was much of profound interest and importance in the report he submitted. He saw the aeroplane as an established commercial fact, with military possibilities not yet definable but unquestionably great. He proposed that a battleship of the *Connecticut* class be modified to take on her deck one of the Wright's new launching catapults and that auxiliary vessels be constructed with "a floor over the deck-houses"—the first suggestion of a flight deck. Expressing great faith in planes, he thought their value would be particularly high in night attacks upon ships because in the darkness, even at low altitudes, they would not have the vulnerability to rifle fire certain to threaten them in the daytime.

Chapin's report, however, made no strong impression, and in the spring of 1910 Glenn Curtiss got much wider publicity for his speech at a banquet in New York City. The occasion was his successful flight from Albany to New York, to win the *New York World's* $10,000 prize. "The battles of the future," cried Curtiss, "will be fought in the air! The aeroplane will decide the destiny of nations!"

The *World* promptly put Curtiss to the test of "bombing" targets erected near Hammondsport on Lake Keuka. Flying above floats simulating a battleship 500' x 90', he launched eight-inch pieces of inch-and-a-half lead pipe, and on his second day he scored hits from heights averaging 300 feet. To some military observers the tests suggested the possibilities of aircraft as weapons of attack; others were more impressed by the mechanical shortcomings of the plane. Commenting upon these Rear Adm. William W. Kimball, one of the observers, wrote: "These are the aeroplane's present defects for war purposes: Lack of ability to operate in average weather at sea; signalling approach by noise made by motor and propeller; impossibility of controlling heights and speed so as to predict approximate range; difficulty of hitting when working at a height great enough to give the aeroplane a fighting chance of reaching effective range."

Press reports of the Curtiss effort were more enthusiastic. The *World* talked of an aeroplane costing a few thousands but able to destroy a battleship costing many millions, while the *Times* acknowledged a new "menace to the armored fleets of war," comments indicating that the press had started the battleship-aircraft controversy even before the Navy owned a single plane.

Soon after this a plane designed by Congressman Butler Ames of Massachusetts was put aboard the destroyer *Bagley* and given a ten-day test before a naval board. This rather cumbersome design did have lifting power but, as was true in many other experimental types of the period, that power was not great enough to lift a frame sufficiently strong to take the shock of its motor. Such tests, while they gradually increased the Navy Department's interest in aeronautical experiments, left it still unconvinced. Newspaper reports upon the results of civilian "meets" continued enthusiastic; comment by high naval authority remained noncommittal.

This does not mean that all officers were indifferent; on the contrary, many were interested. In this respect aircraft exactly fitted the general pattern of technological advances in the United States, begun about the time of the Civil War in science and in industry, and making their force felt by the Navy about 1880 as steam-driven vessels replaced the picturesque old sailing ships. It is the history of every new weapon that it has first been scorned, then eagerly embraced, and so it was destined to be with aircraft. Their usefulness was doubted by the conservatives, while the liberals at once began to think of them as a new element of sea power. It was fortunate for aviation in the United States that at this moment, the end of September, 1910, a newcomer appeared upon its stage— Capt. Washington Irving Chambers of the Navy.

Widely known as a keen-minded engineer, the captain had been concerned in most of the developments that were remaking the Navy. For the last year, as assistant to the Secretary of the Navy's Aid for Material, his duty had brought him into close association with Rear Admiral Cowles, Lieutenant Sweet, and the handful of other officers who were interested in the possibilities of aircraft; and across his desk flowed a stream of letters from more or less hopeful civilian inventors and enthusiasts. When the head of the United States Aeronautic Reserve, an unofficial organization including inventors, engineers, pilots, journalists, and nonprofessional citizens, wrote to the Navy Department requesting the name of an officer with whom it might correspond, it was natural that Captain Chambers should be directed to keep in touch with the group and to inform himself generally upon progress in aviation outside government circles.

In that autumn of 1910 events were also moving faster inside those circles. Under the direction of Admiral Dewey, whose interest in aeronautics already dated back several years, the General Board of the Navy suggested that the Bureaus of Construction and Repair and of Steam Engineering consider the problem of providing space for aircraft in the plans for the new scouting vessels; a proposal which led to the establishment of an elementary aeronautic organization in the Navy Department. On October 13, 1910, Beekman Winthrop, as Acting Secretary of the Navy, noting Chambers' assignment to the duty of following all developments, directed that each of the two bureaus appoint an officer to study technical questions and to work with the captain. A few days later Naval Constructor William McEntee of Construction and Repair and Lieut. Nathaniel H. Wright of Steam Engineering were duly assigned. Years later, when speaking of this advance, Lieutenant Sweet remarked of Chambers: "Knowing his reputation as a go-getter, I felt that Naval Aviation was underway at last!"

Unfortunately, the captain's appointment had not established him properly. He was not put into a position where he could make any decisions but was merely authorized to offer recommendations to the department, a situation which of necessity made him very cautious. He was not assigned space commensurate with the work upon which he was embarking but found himself, instead, in a dusty room in the old State-War-Navy Building, hidden away among filing cabinets, without clerical help, and not expected to demand greater recognition. Perhaps this explains why he appears not to have "thrown his weight about," as might have been expected of an officer relatively far up the list. From his cubbyhole he wrote many letters to interested civilians, made numerous recommendations to the various bureaus and offices of the department, and talked aviation all day long, but he may have lacked the aggressiveness which might have secured him a more adequate attention. That he did not immediately make a deep impression was not, however, wholly because his work was considered unimportant; it was partly because his own strongest interest was in the scientific, technical elements. More and more he came to devote his time to whatever might help to perfect the machine, leading younger men associated with him to believe that he was not forceful enough in administrative details of practical importance to them, such as arranging for official orders that would cover their expenses in journeying about the country to see new planes or attend exhibitions of civilian flying. This is understandable, but at that early stage of aviation he was right enough in believing that the first essential was a safe, practicable flying machine and that the production of such a machine must precede consideration of what it might be able to accomplish in a naval war. If there are old-timers today who hold that he played the part of hesitant midwife at the birth of the infant, they do not give him due credit for what he did to assist that infant's growth. He was a great help in obtaining the first congressional appropriation, actively interested in the early organization of training and of air operations with the Fleet, and instrumental in establishing the first flying field and aeronautic center. His accomplishments may be summed up under two heads: (1) awakening the general interest of the Navy in flying; (2) constantly stimulating research into the science of aerodynamics, that field in which the Navy's eventual achievements have been so great.

Chambers did get early encouragement from some quarters. The Chief of the Bureau of Steam Engineering, Capt. (later Rear Adm.) Hutch I. Cone, on a hint from Admiral Dewey and that intrepid progressive, Capt. (later Rear Adm.) Bradley A. Fiske, proposed that an aeroplane be bought for the new cruiser *Chester*. Secretary of the Navy George von L. Meyer immediately referred this suggestion to the General Board, thus affording that body the opportunity to reaffirm its belief that the adaptability of aviation to war upon the sea should be thoroughly investigated. With this backing came that of other naval figures such as Rear Adm. Colby M. Chester, Ret., one of the few who had actually "taken a hop," the principal speaker on the subject of military aviation at the Jamestown Exposition in 1907, and later to make a trip to Europe as delegate of the New York Aero Club. All this resulted in the sending of McEntee and Wright to Belmont Park, New York, in October, 1910, to be present at the first American air meet big enough to attract European representatives. A few days later they went to Halethorpe, Maryland, where they met Glenn Curtiss and his star pilot, Eugene Ely. At both places they studied the latest technical advances in structure as well as in motors, and watched men fly through fog, through rain, and through winds of 20-mile velocity. They saw numerous "bombings," and returned to Washington profoundly impressed.

Immediately Captain Chambers proposed that Congress appropriate money to cover "experimental investigation," which should include buying a two-seater plane for each of the new scout cruisers, and also provide for training fields at Annapolis, Charleston, South Carolina, and San Diego. He did not say that aircraft would eliminate battleships but he did say that with this new element of sea power almost anything might happen in the years to come. In whatever did happen, he added, the United States Navy ought to lead the world, and therefore the Navy Department should at once establish a separate office of aeronautics with appropriate staff and adequate authority.

Inevitably, the strongest opposition to any such separate office developed immediately. The Navy Department in general was too accustomed to existing administrative methods and too little air minded to be ready for any radical departure. The bureaus were far too comfortable in their semiautonomy to look with any but the most jaundiced eye at anything that suggested diminution of authority or "cognizance." It would be years before any such office would be even possible and, in the meantime, there were other pressing questions.

Could aeroplanes actually accompany ships at sea? Could they be launched from a deck as well as from the ground or from the surface of the water? If they landed on the surface, how were they to be taken aboard? These were among Chambers' questions and, after unsuccessfully approaching the Wrights, he turned again to Curtiss whom he found always ready to make experiments and as progressive as the Wrights were conservative.

Just at that time came the news that the Hamburg American Steamship Company, abetted by the *New York World*, was planning to have J. A. D. McCurdy, a former Curtiss pilot, attempt a flight from a platform on the liner *Kaiserin Augusta Victoria*. The date set was November 5, 1910, but when bad weather interfered with the preparations a postponement became necessary and it was announced that the liner *Amerika* would be substituted. It was given out that the experiment was designed to improve mail service, but there were not wanting those who suspected that the German Navy was behind the test. Not to be outdone, Chambers, with the active help of Capt. Frank Friday Fletcher, the Secretary's Aid for Material, obtained the use of the cruiser *Birmingham* at Norfolk and set McEntee to building a platform over her deck. Working night and day, McEntee and his men planned to be ready by the 19th of the month and this spurred the steamship men to new efforts. Presently, they announced that they would have the liner *Pennsylvania* ready for the test by the 12th, but through bad luck they met with an accident during their final preparations and thus McCurdy was robbed of his chance to be the first ship-to-shore flier. McEntee had the *Birmingham* ready on the 14th and, although the weather was not favorable, Eugene Ely, whose services Chambers had secured, was not to be stopped. His machine ran down the *Birmingham's* platform, dipped so perilously low that the wheels actually touched the water, rose again—and flew safely to a landing on Willoughby Spit.

All over the world military men and civilians were aroused by this success, and Captain Chambers found a little greater support in the Navy Department for more experiments and for a real program in aeronautics. Suggestions came from several persons working for the Navy outside Washington, such as E. C. Keithley, a mechanic at the New York Navy Yard. He submitted plans for a launching platform to be built on a battleship turret and trained and elevated with the guns, in order that any wind direction might be met without necessitating a change in the ship's course. Rear Adm. E. H. C. Leutze, the colorful commandant of the yard, forwarded the plans as "ingenious," but even Captain Chambers was not prepared to go ahead so rapidly. To him the cruisers, with their relatively longer, clearer quarter-decks, appeared ideal, especially since Ely had demonstrated that it was possible for a plane to take off down-wind. Using the quarter-deck for take-off and for landing would also have the advantage that a pilot who failed to get up quickly or crashed into the water would find himself astern of the ship, rather than ahead of it and in danger of being cut down. Sticking to cruisers, Chambers filed the Keithley plans for future reference and, eventually, it was the British who first brought out the small, turret-borne plane.

Gradual widening of Navy Department interest, particularly such high-level interest as the announced intention of Capt. W. L. Capps, Chief of Construction and Repair, to study foreign progress in aviation during a world tour on which he was starting, encouraged Captain Chambers to repeat his requests that money be appropriated. It was at his suggestion that Lieut. N. H. Wright of the Bureau of Steam Engineering made his recommendations of November 17, 1910, that two planes of each existing American type be purchased; that a flying field be built either at Charleston, South Carolina, or at Pensacola, Florida, to which a station ship should be assigned for experiments; and that at least two officers be trained by experienced civilians to fly each type of plane.

CHAPTER II

Ellyson, Towers, Richardson, and Hunsaker

CHAMBERS wanted money and he let his needs be widely known among civilian enthusiasts. Particularly he wrote his friend Glenn Curtiss, just then planning to build a flying school and an experimental station in southern California. Possibly at Chambers' suggestion, but more probably under his own inspiration, Curtiss, in a fine letter dated November 29, 1910, offered to train an officer in the Curtiss plane at no cost to the Navy Department, an offer which was promptly accepted. This arrangement resulted in the Navy's at last having one officer actually recognized as a student flier, and the man chosen was one whose name appropriately heads the list of sailors who have carried flying to its present high place—Lieut. Theodore G. Ellyson, a Naval Academy classmate of Fleet Admiral Nimitz.

Going out to San Diego, Ellyson immediately began absorbing all that he could from Eugene Ely, who had rejoined Curtiss after an earlier disagreement. Ellyson thus had his part in a whole series of experiments aimed at determining whether planes that were to operate with ships should be fitted with pontoons, to land alongside and be hoisted aboard, or whether they should have wheels and land directly on deck. If the latter, how were they to be prevented from crashing head on into the ship's superstructure? In January, 1911, the attempt was made to answer this last question.

Flying out from the beach on January 18, 1911, Ely landed down-wind on the armored cruiser *Pennsylvania*, to try out the first "arresting gear," a complicated arrangement of 22 lines stretched across a platform on the deck and all fitted at each end with a 50-pound sandbag, added at Ellyson's suggestion. A group of hooks on Ely's plane caught each line in succession, checking his plane and finally bringing it to a halt before it hit the canvas screen erected as an emergency stop across the platform's end.

Taking off from the same platform, Ely flew back ashore, the whole test being so successful that Capt. C. F. Pond, commanding the ship, reported to the department: "I desire to place myself on record as positively assured of the importance of the aeroplane in future naval warfare."

Even though landplanes had been used in the *Birmingham* and *Pennsylvania* tests, Captain Chambers was not yet ready to accept the idea that such planes should be put aboard a new type of ship, the carrier. Not greatly impressed by experiments in France with the *Foudre*, converted into a seaplane tender, he opposed the suggestion that similar experiments be conducted on this side of the Atlantic. Characterizing the new types of vessels as "platform-ships" which were practically "floating garages," he concentrated upon the seaplane itself, particularly the "tractor" type hydro-aeroplane with which Curtiss and Ellyson were experimenting at North Island, California, and which he hoped could be placed aboard already existing types of men-o'-war. He was elated when Curtiss, on February 17, 1911, took such a machine off the water, flew it out to the *Pennsylvania* to land alongside and be hoisted in and out again, then rose from the surface and flew back to the base. Here, in Chambers' opinion, was clear proof that a hydroaeroplane, launched from a ship and landed, for any reason, upon the water, would not be helpless, even if such a landing were made far offshore.

Meanwhile, valuable information on this matter of flying out of sight of land, as well as on the type of plane to use for that work, came as the result of McCurdy's attempt to fly a landplane from Key West to Cuba on January 30. He was underrun by a division of destroyers, led by the *Paulding* under Comdr. (later Rear Adm.) Yates Stirling. This was the first of many history-making flights to be similarly supported by naval vessels. Fourteen miles northeast of Havana, the original goal, a break in the plane's oil system forced McCurdy down upon the sea, to be picked up by the waiting *Paulding*. He was unhurt, but when the plane was hoisted aboard it was found to be too badly damaged for further flight. This was a disappointment because, in preparation for just such a possible forced landing on the water and a relaunching from the ship, a special platform had been built on the *Paulding*. Nevertheless Stirling, impressed by the whole performance, made an enthusiastic report upon it. He noted McCurdy's having been uninjured by the landing and particularly emphasized the point that "Mr. McCurdy could and did steer a compass course" for 100 miles.

This the commander considered to be of great significance to "the future progress of flights across water," and he was right. To fly that far, by compass, for the first time in history was to pass, as it were, another vitally important buoy on the course of Naval Aviation.

McCurdy had hardly made his flight when Curtiss showed more progress in developing a plane that would be restricted neither to the water nor to land. With Ellyson riding on a pontoon, Curtiss made the first passenger-carrying amphibious flight, on February 23, using the same hydroaeroplane in which he had made his earlier flight to the *Pennsylvania*. Almost on the same date Samuel F. Perkins, the kite expert, after succeeding in lifting sandbags, followed this by actually towing human beings through the air, in the persons of two naval officers, Lieut. John Rodgers and Ens. Alexander M. Charlton. Considering all these events, it is understandable that Captain Chambers, in his report of March, 1911, should be enthusiastic:

Ely has proved that an aeroplane can leave a ship and return to it, even with crude preparations. Others have demonstrated that an aeroplane can remain in flight for a long time, from five to eight hours or more, that observations can be made from great altitudes, that photographs can be taken, that reconnaissance can be made, that messages can be sent and received by wireless telegraph, that passengers can be carried, that the aeroplane may be stowed on board in suitably dimensioned crates or boxes and readily assembled for use in less than one hour, and that it is possible to hoist an aeroplane out and in, as you would a ship's boat, to exercise it over smooth water. Mr. Curtiss has also recently demonstrated that it is not necessary for the water to be smooth.

This has all been done within a year and, mostly in a few months since the date on which the Navy first began to take serious notice of the possibilities in aviation.

These remarks emphasized aeroplanes, but the kites had caught the imagination of many officers, including Rear Adm. Chauncey Thomas, Commander in Chief in the Pacific. The possibilities for scouting, tracking, and spotting by kite-borne observers equipped with deck glasses and telephones led to a series of experiments culminating in the kite balloon. An essential feature of these experiments was the towing of targets simulating enemy planes, against which ships must develop proper guns, gun mounts, and shrapnel ammunition. Another feature was the study of observations from aloft as a possible means of detecting approaching torpedoes.

Representative Ernest W. Roberts of Massachusetts was an ardent congressional advocate of such tests and at his suggestion the Secretary of the Navy directed that more of them be held that spring in both the Atlantic and Pacific. Lack of time to spare from other Fleet exercises and maneuvers, however, prevented more complete experiments with aerial targets and ships on opposite or on converging courses, to determine rates of approach, accuracy of the shooting, and the probability of destroying the attacking aircraft. After a study of such tests as were made, the Bureau of Ordnance designed a new antiaircraft one-pounder which, on the one hand, induced among some officers a tendency to overconfidence in the Fleet's security and on the other prompted others to request further experiments.

Captain Chambers, closely watching these results, had used them to persuade Secretary Meyer to convince the House Committee on Naval Affairs that it should recommend $25,000 for the Navy's first planes. The act of March 4, 1911, appropriated that amount and, since it was given directly to the Bureau of Navigation, Chambers, after a few days in the General Board offices where Admiral Dewey gave him desk room, reported to that bureau on April 17, 1911. He was not, as he had hoped and suggested, made head of an independent office of aviation.

Inventors of every kind continued to bombard him with letters, collectively asking for far more money than had been made available. Aware that a real idea might lurk anywhere, he opened and read every letter, then wrote as encouraging an answer as he felt justified in making. Occasionally, however, even he could find no rational answer to "crackpot" letters suggesting such visionary mechanisms as "flying fish" or "ducks." All this correspondence was handled without proper clerical help and with an official support so slight that the Chief of the Bureau of Navigation, on one occasion, actually suggested that Chambers "do the work at home." Instead, he stuck to his small room, crowding it with air-minded visitors and explaining over and over again that any new plane must be more than a blueprint; it must be actually built and must pass all preliminary tests before the Navy could seriously consider buying it.

Most welcome to Chambers at this time was the support he received from Capt. Bradley Fiske. This distinguished officer, dismayed by the dangerous possibility of having to fight Japan for the Philippines with a Fleet far from any United States base, suggested on April 12, 1911, that aircraft might solve this defense problem and proposed four air stations on Luzon, each to support at least 100 planes. Approaching enemy warships and transports could thus, he believed, be driven off if not wholly destroyed. Unfortunately this 30-year look into the future, with Admiral Dewey and some other officers peering interestedly over Fiske's shoulder, was cut short by Rear Admiral Wainwright, who protested: *"Why waste the time of the General Board on wildcat schemes?"* Opportunity's tap on the door of the board had gone unheeded.

Meanwhile Captain Chambers, studying such European progress as the experiments in Britain's National Laboratory, began advocating similar steps in the United States. Before long the American press announced that a research center, to help the inventor and the manufacturer of aircraft, would be established under the Smithsonian Institution and operated by the Bureau of Standards. Formal announcement was to be made on April 27, 1911, at the annual dinner of the Aeronautical Society of New York, to which President Taft had been invited. Interest among civilian enthusiasts ran high but the Bureau of Construction and Repair protested that any such new center would largely duplicate its own Model Basin. Because "the motion of water, effect of stream lines and the theory and mathematics are almost identical whether in water or in air," the bureau considered its own personnel fully competent to undertake the proposed research with its existing equipment. At the same time the Bureau of Steam Engineering drew attention to its own experimental station at Annapolis, "equipped to test all kinds of motors," with apparatus that could be "readily devised for testing propellers of aeroplanes." Submitted by the Secretary of the Navy to the President, these recommendations met the unhappy fate of falling into the hands of Mr. Taft's new Committee on Economy and Efficiency, which drafted an executive order giving the Model Basin the proposed assignment. Secretary Meyer advocated including the Annapolis experimental station and asked the Secretary of War for his suggestions on a plan to combine experimental work by the two departments. The Secretary of War replied that while duplication of effort would admittedly be unfortunate, still each department ought to carry on its separate experiments. He offered his own outline, which went with Secretary

Meyer's to the Committee on Economy and never came back. No executive order was issued. No announcement was made at the New York dinner. For the next 18 months aviation research by the Navy would have to struggle along without what would have been most valuable help.

The Navy Department, however, ordered three planes, which were to be paid for from the $25,000 just appropriated and to be made available in July, 1911. Two were landplanes, one by the Wrights and one by Curtiss, while the third, also by Curtiss, was his new "Triad" amphibian. A clause in the agreements provided that the builder of each plane should train a pilot and a mechanic for it, and this brought new officers and men into Naval Aviation. One officer who reported to the Wrights at Dayton, Ohio, was Lieut. John Rodgers, scion of one of the most famous lines of American seamen and fighters. At the same time Lieut. John H. Towers went to Hammondsport, New York, to join Ellyson and begin the brilliant flying career which made him, in World War II, Chief of the Bureau of Aeronautics; today a four-star admiral and a leading naval figure. Hammondsport was the eastern center of aviation and there Curtiss was bringing together more and more enthusiasts, both military and civilian. Among the latter was John L. Callan, very soon a test pilot and eventually himself an officer, flying in two wars and contributing heavily to the Navy's record.

On the practical side, Chambers' plans for 1911 included the first effort to build an airfield. At Greenbury Point, opposite Annapolis, trees were felled, a swamp was filled in, and, on more solid ground, tent hangars were erected. Chambers proposed that the aviation group, in order to gain "experience in roughing it," should promptly move to the new field. This the group did, but it soon discovered that the cleared space was perilously small for landplanes, that the water near shore was too shallow for hydroaeroplanes, and that the whole establishment was uncomfortably close to the Naval Academy rifle range. These drawbacks resulted in moving the group, in the following year, over to a site nearer the experimental station.

Ellyson was full of enthusiasm and activity. For one thing, he was soon begging Chambers to find more enlisted men who would make electricians and mechanics, men such as those who would later head the list, like Saar, Daniels, Welsh, Wiegand, and Baker in the Curtiss types; like Bronson, Burdon, Rhodes, and Haynes in the Wright types; like Erieson, who "does all the carpenter work and is weeks behind"; like Knapp, who "is kept busy with the boat." As Ellyson saw it, "two good men could learn more here in two weeks . . . than they will pick up in Annapolis in as many months," and unless such men joined the group in advance he feared that the Annapolis authorities would "make us depend upon men detailed from the *Hartford*, and naturally they will not give us the best men." Little by little, as Chambers could get enlisted volunteers for aviation duties, he was meeting Ellyson's pleas.

Even while still at Hammondsport, before the move to Greenbury, lack of enlisted men had not kept Ellyson and Towers from driving ahead with new ideas. Together they designed a dual-control mechanism adapted from the French and, after later modification, destined to become standard for the Navy's training planes. Finding Curtiss ready to try anything, they joined him in innumerable attempts to find some way to launch a hydroaeroplane from a ship which would be better than making the plane take off from the water, a dangerous practice in a seaway. Since it was hardly to be expected that an enemy would agree to delay an action until the water should be smooth, here was a problem of first importance.

In one memorable experiment Ellyson got into a plane balanced by two wires beneath the lower wings and supported by another, heavily greased wire so erected that it inclined down the beach toward the water. He himself described this effort in a letter written to Captain Chambers from Hammondsport on September 7, 1911:

I enclose a rough sketch of the rig we used today in launching the machine from the wire. I am not making an official report of this experiment.

The only changes made in the standard rig of the machine was to fit a groove on the bottom of the boat, one inch wide and one and three quarter inches deep, lined at each end for a distance of three feet with tin, and on the bearing surfaces at each end reinforced with two strips of band iron one-eighth inch thick, and to fit two braces on the after beams of the planes so that the balancing wires would bear on these braces and not on the planes.

The only doubts held as to the success of the experiment before it was tried out was that possibly it would be impossible to get control of the lateral balance of the machine, that is, that it would tip to one side or the other before the machine had gathered sufficient headway for the ailerons to become effective, and if it had started to tip, it would have been impossible to keep the machine from capsizing. This doubt was caused by the fact that once the machine started to tip the balancing wires would become ineffective, as we had found out by experiment. In order to overcome this, a slip rope was placed around each balancing brace and a man tended each line to run with the same after the engine was started to right the machine in case it did not balance. We figured the chances 25 to 1 that it would be successful, but Mr. Curtiss did not want to run the one chance of failure, as the results meant a bad smash or satisfactory results. . . .

[We waited until we had a wind that blew directly up the wire.] The engine was started and run at full speed and then I gave the signal to release the machine. The machine gained headway so rapidly that the people holding the slip ropes could not have used them even if there had been any necessity, but the balance was under perfect control from the start. I held the machine on the wire as long as possible as I wanted to be sure that I had enough headway to rise and not run the risk of the machine partly rising and then falling on the wire outside of the groove. Everything happened so quickly and went off so smoothly that I hardly know what happened except that I did have to use the ailerons, and that the machine was sensitive to their action.

It was evident that so crude a device could not be used aboard ship, especially in rough weather, and that some form of catapult must be devised. This inspired Captain Chambers to seek the help of Lieut. St. Clair Smith from the Naval Gun Factory, and that of Naval Constructor Holden C. Richardson, already an interested observer of aircraft who would soon qualify as a pilot and whose very great scientific abilities would eventually carve a deep mark upon Naval Aviation. With these highly capable assistants, Chambers studied the catapults already tried by the Wrights, the devices used by Chanute for his gliders, and the coiled-spring type once built by Langley. Then with advice from Ellyson the three set to work together and for the next year spent considerable time on a catapult of their own.

Even under all the difficulties of launching, however, the planes of 1911, once they got into the air, were making a creditable showing. John Rodgers flew from Annapolis to Washington and back, with stops at Baltimore and Havre de Grace. On October 11 Towers and Ellyson, in Curtiss' first "convertible landplane-seaplane," left Annapolis for Old Point Comfort. Thirty miles on the way, they came down because the safety wire on the gas tank suspended just behind their heads was carried away. When this had been repaired they went up again, only to be forced down after 20 minutes by the breaking of a bracket on the carburetor. Up again, they stayed up for a half hour, to reach Smith's Point, Virginia, and land with four burnt-out bearings. This meant disassembling the machine and putting it aboard the destroyer *Bailey*. They had, in 85 minutes, flown 79 miles. Other flights at the Annapolis field were made by Ens. V. D. Herbster, recently back from a visit abroad to study French flying. His work was done largely in the Wright's first hydroaeroplane, fitted with the new Burgess pontoons. Most spectacular, however, were the night landings made by Towers, coming down upon the Severn between marker buoys which were actually small boats holding buckets of flaming gasoline.

Meanwhile the Fleet, off the Chesapeake Capes and again off Cape Cod, was shooting both by daylight and by searchlight at huge Perkins box kites, sent up to simulate attacking enemy aircraft. At the very short ranges used, enough hits were scored to please the press and enough near-misses to give many naval men further mistaken notions of the Fleet's invulnerability.

When the old battleship *Texas*, renamed the *San Marcos*, had been converted into a target ship, the Bureau of Construction and Repair proposed that she be bombed by aircraft using live explosives, a suggestion that confronted Captain Chambers with a hard decision. He was well aware that planes, at their current stage of development, would have to approach the ship within what would be easy range for guns quite capable of blowing them to pieces. No existing plane could carry a bomb large enough to do serious damage, even in a direct hit. To make the proposed test under such handicaps might be to confirm opinions that ships were safe from air attack; to refuse would be to suggest that he was afraid of being ridiculed. In the end he chose to risk the second alternative and declined, remarking that such tests must wait until planes could carry 200-pound bombs. If tests of structural strength were immediately desirable, he said they could be made by "dropping bombs from a kite-line." The proposal was laid aside and it would be another ten years before plane bombing was tried against captured German warships, even then without fully conclusive results.

Back in California that winter the Curtiss group continued its "trials and errors," Curtiss himself designing a heavier flying boat that might be serviceable in rough water. With Constructor Richardson and the naval personnel, as well as with his own men, he worked out new ideas for hulls, boats, and pontoons, finally satisfying himself and others that the single pontoon would ultimately prove better than the double one. Hulls were more troublesome because, when one had been built big enough and heavy enough to afford the pilot something better in the way of a seat than an exposed spot on the leading edge of a lower wing, the problem was how to lift it off the sea, even with such improvements as a pump to free its hull of water.

During that same winter of 1911–12 Lincoln Beachey, one of the outstanding early aviators, giving exhibitions off Los Angeles, raised more "ship-or-plane" arguments when he invited the destroyers at San Pedro to spot him by searchlight during his sham night attack on a fort. No one should have been astonished when the small destroyer searchlights failed to find Beachey in the darkness from a distance of seven miles, but the press, adroitly miscalling the destroyers "battleships," played up the incident as incontestable proof of the plane's superiority.

Chambers made good use of these developments to argue for more money. He was so far successful that Congress, in its second appropriation for aviation, gave the Bureau of Navigation $10,000 and also authorized the Bureau of Construction and Repair and of Steam Engineering to spend on aviation, respectively, $35,000 and $20,000 originally appropriated for other purposes. This was all in addition to $100,000 appropriated for the Army, but the grand total was still in very striking contrast to what was then being spent in Europe. France was prepared to spend $6,400,000, Russia $5,000,000, Britain $2,100,000, Italy $2,000,000 and Germany $1,500,000. Responsibility for this United States "go slow" policy of allowing so little for experiments and of buying nothing but tested improvements, thus keeping the nation an almost hopeless last in the race, was laid by Captain Chambers at the door of Congress, perhaps because he was not called to the hearings. The written record, however, shows that the Navy Department was actually not spending what money had been allotted, either for planes or for the flying instruments in which Chambers had become most deeply interested.

"Manufacturers and aviators," the captain wrote, "are beginning to realize that progress . . . is greatly dependent upon the perfection of instruments for safe guidance and automatic control; that there is something more than acrobatic skill required; . . . that the elimination of man as a factor of chief importance by . . . mechanism which will perform . . . the things he is prone to do indifferently, especially under the strain of fatigue, is a practical necessity." He wanted a robot pilot, a speed indicator, an electric stabilizer, and other instruments that would make navigation at night or in a fog as accurate in the air as on the surface. Optimistic over advances in planes and in motors, he insisted that only the best accessories would permit taking full advantage of these advances. To help such matters along, he submitted some designs of his own for stabilizers and indicators, but he got so little support from the technical bureaus that he felt like the proverbial prophet in his own country when on March 13, 1913, the Aeronautical Society awarded him its gold medal for achievement.

Some consolation came from the further active support of the imaginative, dynamic Fiske, now a rear admiral. For that officer the greatest value of aircraft lay in their possibilities as weapons, and at this early moment he began talking of torpedo planes. Thinking of "far-sighted eyes for ships," he contemplated using planes with the radio-controlled torpedoes, then laboring under the disadvantage that such control was faulty because at a distance from the ship the torpedo could not be seen. Why not send a plane out over the torpedo, either to keep the ship informed of its course or to direct it with instruments in the plane itself? Both these ideas gave way to the thought that the plane might better carry the torpedo straight to the target. Using a squadron of planes, a dozen torpedoes might be launched simultaneously from as many angles. With the aid of Park Benjamin, fellow graduate of the Naval Academy who had gone into patent law, Fiske actually took out a patent for an aerial torpedo in the spring of 1912, well before the Navy Department's real interest was aroused by those tried in Britain and in Germany.

Fiske's interest did not slacken when he became a division commander in the Fleet. He was anchored off Salem, Massachusetts, when W. Starling Burgess, an early plane manufacturer, came alongside in a hydroaeroplane to take him up for a flight over the harbor and bring him down more than ever certain that torpedoes were practicable and that bombers could defend the Philippines. Admitting that the vibration had annoyed him, he still held that there was "less jerking and swaying than in any vehicle except a sleigh," and that while there probably was "great exaggeration in the claims as to dropping bombs," there was nevertheless "certainly something in it." What the little squad of airminded naval men most needed was 50 Fiskes!

Their own greatest progress, just then, was with the problem of launching. Chambers, Smith, and Richardson had been working for a year on their catapult and they now produced a device operated by compressed air. First using an old torpedo tube, for which part of the hoisting gear salvaged from the veteran battleship *Oregon* was later substituted, they extemporized a makeshift model assembled at Annapolis. No one knew what such rapid acceleration might do to the human body, but Ellyson was ready to risk it and on July 31, 1912, he was shot along a wharf. Halfway down, as he reached flying speed, the nose of his pontoon was air-borne, but the rear end dragged until a cross-wind tipped him neatly over into the Severn, to come up uninjured himself but with a badly damaged plane. By November Richardson was ready to test a modification of the device at the Washington Navy Yard and this time Ellyson's hydroaeroplane was air-borne in a matter of seconds and making 35 miles an hour. A month later he succeeded again with a flying boat. Curtiss, watching this success, called it the most important advance since wheels were first put on landplanes. Catapults would need little deck space and would not interfere with gunfire. Recovery of planes might still have its problems, but launching was solved.

In the next year, 1913, another important event marked progress. In May the Massachusetts Institute of Technology decided to establish a course in aerodynamics and the trustees asked the Navy Department to designate an officer qualified to prepare and conduct it. After some delay the department chose Jerome C. Hunsaker, Jr., and that brilliant young naval constructor proceeded to establish a course so thorough and effective that all future ones have closely followed it. Starting from that first moment Hunsaker went so far in design and in the science generally that his name is today known around the world. Among his other services rendered in those early days were his trips abroad which resulted in reports on foreign research that threw much light on hydroaeroplanes as well as on dirigibles, especially upon Germany's relatively great progress with the latter. It was Hunsaker, too, who was chiefly responsible for the erection, at Cambridge, of the long-awaited wind tunnel.

CHAPTER III

The Chambers Board

DURING 1912 more "makey-learn" aviators had reported, most of them bearing names that would be long remembered. Ens. William D. Billingsley made a good start, only to meet early death in a flying accident. Ens. Godfrey deC. Chevalier was to have ten years of great accomplishment before he too lost his life. Lieut. Patrick N. L. Bellinger began what became a distinguished career that eventually made him the vice admiral commanding the Air Force, Atlantic Fleet, in World War II. In this year, too, the marines were represented when 1st Lt. Alfred A. Cunningham was assigned to aviation, closely followed by 1st Lt. B. L. Smith. Both were destined to make fine records.

As these new men learned to fly and as the older ones gained more experience, they tested the possibility of detecting submarines from the air. In average weather they found it not difficult to spot a submarine running awash or at periscope depth, but to pick up the same craft only a few feet submerged was quite another matter, even at a height of a mere 850 feet. Towers, who made the most complete reports, held that the muddy waters of the Chesapeake were an abnormal handicap and that the bay's bottom made the poorest of backgrounds for a silhouette. He advocated more tests in clearer waters such as those to be expected in Guantánamo. In the midst of these tests and reports, however, Towers found time, on October 6, 1912, to set a new world's record for endurance—six hours, ten minutes, and 35 seconds of continuous flight. Such were the records 37 years ago.

Another young officer who proved very helpful, though not strictly as an aviator, was Ens. Charles H. Maddox, a keen radio enthusiast, who designed and built a new set for planes. Replacing the clumsy early arrangement of dangling wires, cut off when a message had been sent, the Maddox set enabled John Rodgers to lift the range of successful communication up to 12 miles! Captain

Chambers began to hope for 50 miles and to talk of "no more homing pigeons."

Many of these experiments were carried out because of the General Board's interest in possible air tactics. While the board still believed that these tactics were likely to be limited to coastal patrol and scouting from ships at sea, it had in June, 1912, asked some further questions. What was the present plan for carrying planes aboard battleships and cruisers? Could they be got away readily and easily recovered? Could they serve as pilots for friendly submarines and as protection against enemy ones? How far could they withstand unfavorable conditions of wind and sea? For up-to-the-minute answers to these and similar questions the board recommended that the flying arm join the Fleet in Guantánamo as soon as possible.

Most of the aviators heartily endorsed this proposal. Motors might be unreliable and inaccurate, air compasses might restrict flights to within sight of the ships. No matter, the best path to knowledge was along the wake of the Fleet. Even though men and machines were too few in number and would be kept too short of gasoline to provide the air screen just then suggested by Comdr. S. S. Robison, later to be an admiral and commander in chief, they could simulate that screen. Learning how to maneuver to provide screens would make the problem that much simpler when there were enough planes and pilots, when better stowage made it possible for ships to carry large amounts of dangerous plane fuel. Moreover, being with the Fleet in Guantánamo would provide chances to practice locating an "enemy's" bases, destroying his shore batteries, mine fields, and submarines, or bombing his shipyards and his arsenals. Much of this was accomplished after the aviation camp arrived in Guantánamo in January, 1913. The fliers proved that they could locate submarines moving under the surface and that they could detect "enemy" surface vessels without themselves being seen. They acquired some practice in dropping missiles and in taking aerial photographs from as high as 1,000 feet. They also seized their opportunity to stimulate general interest by taking more than 150 officers up as passengers and by actually teaching a few to handle the planes.

All this was closely followed by the General Board, which continued to be interested in air tactics and had proposed, in December, 1912, the building of a new weapon of offense, the "aeroplane destroyer," with a speed of 80 miles an hour, a machine gun, and small bombs. Such a craft, said the board, would protect powder plants, bases, other vital shore stations from attack and should be very effective against dirigibles whose hydrogen content made them particularly vulnerable. At this the plane builders pricked up their ears and began to press for specifications which Captain Chambers and Constructor Richardson, with the advice of all the aviators, presently prepared. A two-seater flying boat was called for, with an enclosed body that gave a wide field of vision not hampered by "tractor" propellers, with dual controls, and a climbing rate of 100 feet a minute. In addition to its crew of two, the load capacity must be sufficient to carry gas and oil for four hours at the average speed of 50 miles. Either air-cooled or water-cooled motors were admissible but the former were preferred because of their lighter weight and lower fuel consumption. Floats of such metals as duralumin were recommended and, to permit amphibious use, wheels should also be fitted. Strength and stiffness were to be measured by the ability to withstand being blown across open water, with the motor cut, by a 20-knot breeze. Maximum speed was to be 55 miles an hour.

In approving this design Captain Chambers was looking for practicability and for safety, both of which he still held to be essential requisites of all planes. Admitting that high speed might sometimes be necessary, and recognizing that "worth-while" risks must be run, he nevertheless sternly forbade the naval pilots to "stunt for headlines" or to do anything else to confirm public belief in the great hazards of flying. For this reason he would not allow participation in public meets which might turn into Roman holidays and perhaps decimate the small group of naval men and machines.

To emphasize these restrictions and to guard, as far as possible, against accidents in the proposed wider scope of test flights and experiments with the Fleet, the physical requirements for aviators came in for more strict regulation. Since eyes, ears, lungs, and hearts, fully able to endure any strains on the deck of a ship, might have hidden weaknesses that would mean failure when 1,000 feet in the air, only the very best men must be allowed to take that risk. Accordingly, a special examination and a series of exhaustive physical tests were put together by army and naval medical officers, not to discourage those whose imaginations leaped at the thought of flying but to make sure that their qualifications as men could match the almost daily advances in the machine, thus permitting them to push American flying to a place beside, if not above, the European standard.

On the technical side Chambers continued to emphasize to all who would listen a lack through which aviators were "seriously handicapped." He declared that a laboratory was indispensable and further delay might contribute to humiliation in war. To support this, he wrote in an article prepared for the December, 1912, issue of the magazine *Flying*:

The work done by Prof. Langley at the Smithsonian Institution, in a brief period, over sixteen years ago, with meager resources and little encouragement, by means of an appropriation under the Chief of Engineers, U. S. Army, was such a valuable contribution to the science of aeronautics that the U. S., even today, is credited abroad with possessing a real aerodynamic laboratory. I fancy there are people in this country who believe that the work inaugurated by Langley is still proceeding in a systematic way, but it is unfortunate that his work was not permitted to expand and to develop into one of the first national institutions of this kind.

As another step toward all-around progress he had already proposed to the President the appointment of an aeronautical commission. Accordingly, in that same month of December Mr. Taft invited to the White House a group of nine men, including army and naval officers, civilian physicists, doctors, and engineers. Subsequently the group met at the Carnegie Institution, formed a board with Dr. R. S. Woodward as chairman, and immediately recommended that an aerodynamical laboratory be established under the Smithsonian. When it was realized that such a commission, appointed by the President without the "advice and consent of the Senate," could not legally be allowed even the traveling expenses of its members, Senator J. A. Reed of Missouri and Representative Richmond P. Hobson of Alabama, the *Merrimac* celebrity, introduced the necessary legislation. Unfortunately, Representatives Mann and Foster, both from Illinois, would not consent to a unanimous vote; the bill was stillborn. Not even $581.66, the niggardly sum already spent by the commission, was ever appropriated.

In the following May the Smithsonian itself came forward with a vote of its executive committee to reopen the "Langley Laboratory." Secretary Walcott of the Smithsonian named the civilian members of a committee to undertake this and a few days later

President Wilson, now in office, approved the appointment of Chambers and Richardson as members. After several meetings of the group had been held the Comptroller of the Treasury decided that the two, as military men, could not legally hold official membership, but they continued to sit unofficially for the next two years.

By far the majority of the officers of the Navy thought of aviation as an element of sea power and this conviction was only strengthened by the first debate in Congress, during its winter session of 1912, over the question whether the administration of aviation should be separated from that of the Navy in general. Officers were against separation because the belief that "only a sailor can fly successfully with ships" was solidly established, but the debate did give Chambers a chance to draw the attention of Congress to other ideas of his. He proposed that appropriations provide for prizes for "better planes and better motors." Noting that Lawrence Sperry had already designed a gyroscopic stabilizer, he urged Congress to encourage competition in this field as in other developments, and requested a total of $150,000 for these purposes. Since he failed to get the money, such experiments as could be made were not very profitable. In the summer of 1913, for example, a few tests made with gyroscopes, usually with Bellinger at the plane controls and Sperry lying on his stomach on the cockpit floor, accomplished little more than the discovery that the invention had two major faults. The first of these was its weight and the second was the tendency of the gyro to "precess"; that is, to have its axis pushed out of the line in which it had started spinning, by frictional forces on its bearings. The practical effect of precession was the turning of the plane into positions in which a crash was likely to be fatal and this was not overcome by installing two gyroscopes, designed to balance one another's errors, a change which had the further disadvantage of adding still more weight. It would be many years after these early efforts before technicians were able to compensate the errors of the gyro well enough to provide the automatic pilot.

News of such instruments or, indeed, any news of aviation, always drew the interest of Rear Admiral Fiske, since February, 1913, the Secretary's Aid for Operations. His interest was more than merely scientific, it was strategic. Where Chambers was constantly searching the horizon for safer aircraft of improved performance, Fiske had his eye peeled for hostile aircraft bursting through war clouds. To him, the immediate vital need of the

United States was more planes and more pilots. If there were great risks in the air, then let the planes and pilots face those risks for what they might nevertheless accomplish in the interest of national security.

Recalling his earlier idea of defending the Philippines by aircraft, the admiral spoke openly of hostile planes as a menace to United States security. Moreover, he declared that the use of airships abroad had "reached a state of development that our Navy cannot ignore," and recommended that the General Board be asked to express an opinion upon the advisability of acquiring airships to carry on experiments in scouting and countermining. As a result of this request certain figures were laid before the board which offer a good idea of where United States Naval Aviation stood just a year before Great Britain and Germany went to war.

There were in commission eight planes: three Curtiss hydroaeroplanes, two Wright hydroaeroplanes, one Burgess and two Curtiss flying boats. There was the station at Annapolis and the reserve base at Greenbury Point. All told, there were 13 officers who held pilot's licenses, with a record of 2,118 flights on which 1,470 passengers had been carried—flights that represented just over 500 hours in the air and just under 28,000 miles covered. Across the years, that score would compare with, say 1946, when naval pilots flew 3,500,000 hours, or roughly 500,000,000 miles.

The figures for 1913 came from Captain Chambers' report to the General Board, in which he went on to say that while the United States still led other nations in "specific development" of some features of aviation, he believed "the best inventors in this country have about reached the limit of their designing ability due to lack of scientific information." Neither Curtiss nor Burgess, he said, had a really outstanding aeronautical engineer; it was too early to gauge the possibilities of a young man just hired by the Wrights, Grover C. Loening.

What the British had accomplished was noted in the same report, as was the fact that France, where geography directed efforts at defense more toward the Army than toward the Navy, was still in the lead in the air. Due note was taken of Germany's superiority in dirigibles, with her seven Zeppelins, each able to carry 14,000 pounds, two one-pounder guns and four Maxims, with fuel for 30 hours at the top speed of 45.7 miles per hour. To these would soon be added four more airships, all to be supported by 13 mine-laying scout planes and, as a most important adjunct, enough sheds and berths for all German aircraft. She was being closely watched and copied by Italy, which had just announced the creation of an air corps with 11,500,000 lire to spend on several dirigibles, ten squadrons of "water-planes," and five squadrons of landplanes, with seven sheds and a program for training many more than her present eight pilots.

The board must have found all these comparisons odious, because it was not optimistic in its report of August 31, 1913. The United States Army, the board found, had only eight training planes, nine scout planes scattered through Texas, California, Hawaii, and the Philippines, no dirigibles, and but five pilots with eight in training; yet the Navy was in "an even more embryonic and chaotic state." Its equipment was scant and its men were all too few. As for direction and supervision, the board especially commented upon an officer under the Bureau of Navigation, with *"undefined duties and responsibilities and no powers,"* with collateral relations with the Bureaus of Construction and Repair and Steam Engineering, in a kind of general charge. Such a situation gave the board great concern over the possibility of an attack with nonrigids and planes transportable across the ocean by an enemy whose seizure of a Caribbean base might give him easy access to substantial portions of a vulnerable United States Coast and leave this nation with the unhappy prospect of trying to carry an attack against an enemy in control of the air. Altogether, the board's picture was a sorry one, yet it was no sorrier than that often painted by Chambers and the handful of devoted associates who had been carrying the whole burden. To brighten the colors the board proposed removing one dark shadow, "the supineness with which we have viewed the progress of aerial war preparation," by immediately organizing "an efficient naval air service."

Congress, said the board, should forthwith be asked to furnish funds for shore stations, equipment, training schools, and an adequate air fleet, which should include hydroaeroplanes and flying boats for short scouting, dirigibles for distant scouting or mine laying and, eventually, "the largest class of rigid battle-airships, with sheds and harbors located at strategic points." All these plans should be "immediately taken in hand and pushed to fulfillment" under an officer with full authority and the rank of captain, at least.

The General Board's pronouncement met varying reactions.

The Bureau of Steam Engineering, noting that no exact limit had been placed by Congress upon how much of the bureau's money might be spent in that year on aviation, held that if the money could be spared from other purposes, the Navy was "in a position to accumulate considerable amounts of apparatus." It proposed that the cruiser *Columbia* be made available as an "aeroplane ship" for all training and experimental purposes.

The Bureau of Construction and Repair was less enthusiastic. Clinging to its empire, it was "in full sympathy with the objects" sought, but contended that progress would be faster if use were made of "the present machinery of the Department instead of attempting to establish a new office or virtual bureau"; the latter innovation would "probably meet strong opposition in the present Congress and fail to pass." The bureau was willing to buy planes but thought dirigibles too hazardous to buy without specific congressional approval. When the state of the nation and the state of the world called hourly for speed in the development of United States flying, Construction and Repair favored "slow ahead."

Chambers, regardless of his personal future prospects, insisted that enough experimenting had been done, enough data on dirigibles assembled, fully to warrant proceeding with the whole program, especially including the separate administrative office. He wanted planes put upon existing ships, with carriers to come "only when we are satisfied we cannot get along without them." As a step toward "first things first," he drafted an order creating an office of naval aeronautics, but he was never able to get that order promulgated. It would have meant a drastic modification of the Secretary of the Navy's General Order No. 41, issued on June 23, 1913, two months before the General Board brought out its report. This order laid down responsibilities for aviation along the lines of similar responsibilities for ships; that is, Construction and Repair had supervision of the building of aircraft, including such details as hulls, landing gear, mooring gear, launching gear, and all buildings for storage, including hangars; Steam Engineering had supervision over motors, generators, lighting, signal systems, and the radio equipment. The Bureau of Navigation controlled the procurement and supply of precision instruments, as well as all personnel problems. The order had many loose ends but, in spite of its leaving much to be desired, a rather better understanding and cooperation were slowly becoming possible.

There was some evidence of this greater cooperation when Constructors Richardson and McEntee, at about this time, brought out their new design for hulls of flying boats, incorporating the "V-bottom, with step," which would become, after some modification, the standard type for the Navy. There was also a readier agreement following investigation of the aviation group's first fatal accident, which had occurred on June 20, 1913.

On that day Ens. William D. Billingsley was in the air at the controls of a Navy-built Wright type hydroaeroplane carrying Towers as his passenger. A downdraft, a sudden squall, or some never-explained mechanical defect made the plane "nose down." Billingsley pitched forward, completely losing control and the plane capsized. Since there were, in those perilous days, not even the elementary safety belts, Billingsley fell instantly to his death. Towers, with an amazing coolness that may have been due, in part, to his being an expert gymnast, clung to the strut beside which he had been sitting. As the plane whirled and spun through its wild plunge, he held on, to fall some 1,600 feet into the water. He was picked up badly injured but undaunted, and after four months in the hospital back to the air he came.

At about this time it was decided that naval aviators should be qualified in the various available plane types. "Wright men" were given instruction in the Curtiss and vice versa. This requirement was emphasized in the plan made at this time for the issue of naval air pilot certificates, to be awarded only after thorough tests of mechanical knowledge, powers of observation, and the ability to execute maneuvers in the air. The relatively simpler tests prepared by the Fédération Aéronautique Internationale and administered in America by the Aero Club would no longer be sufficient to meet the stiffening naval standards. Through 1915 the title of naval aviator would be given to all who passed these tests but in the following year this term was restricted to those who had qualified in preliminary training. Those who had satisfactorily completed advanced training in the type of duty to be expected in flying at sea were designated naval air pilots to indicate that they were qualified to command aircraft.

More attention was also given to the enlisted personnel, who had been rather unfairly handicapped when assigned to aviation. Under existing regulations highly deserving men could not be advanced in the mechanical ratings unless they had been found duly qualified by service aboard ship and by passing sea-going examinations. By allowing for recognition of the special services involved in aviation, the new order offered encouragement to others. Although a complete list providing for many highly specialized ratings did not become part of the definite policy for some years, the move in that direction at least brought good results.

Since this year had brought out so many divergent opinions as to policy, Secretary of the Navy Daniels, on October 7, 1913, established a special board to consider all views and "prepare a comprehensive plan for the organization of a Naval Aeronautic Service." Headed by Captain Chambers and therefore known by his name, the board had six other members. Towers, Richardson, and Cunningham were the "flyer-members," Comdr. Carlo B. Brittain represented the Bureau of Navigation, Comdr. S. S. Robison was from Steam Engineering, and Lieut. Manley H. Simons from the Bureau of Ordnance, all officers of recognized substance and standing.

After some 12 days' deliberation, this board recommended 50 planes for the Fleet with as many spares, and six more planes, with tents, to establish an advanced base ashore. The objective should be a mobile force, prepared for operations well offshore and, therefore, one plane with its necessary spare parts should be placed aboard each fighting vessel. Auxiliary vessels should be assigned to the specific task of carrying aviation fuel, oil, spare parts, tents, and the like, and these auxiliaries should be fitted to carry planes as "special ships." Dirigibles, notwithstanding their recognized stability and cruising range, were regarded as not essential until more imperative needs had been met. As an aeronautic station, Pensacola was favored for the flying school, the repair shops, and general training program. For scientific research, it was suggested that a staff of specialists be formed and given the use of the facilities of the Washington Navy Yard laboratory in cooperation with the Model Basin and the proposed national laboratory.

In details of training the board, basing its recommendations upon a plan by Ellyson, was explicit. Such training must produce practical ability in assembly, overhaul, and repair, supplemented by the study of available books on theory. Flight training should follow existing lines, with pilots who passed for air certificates considered eligible for an advanced sea section and graduates of the latter given duty in charge of planes aboard ship. In addition, some pilots should be assigned to laboratory research and some should be sent abroad to study foreign methods. Officers thus assigned—and this was to them a point of great importance—should be allowed to serve in flying duties without prejudice to other duty performed or to "sea service in grade."

Upon the proposal to establish a separate bureau within the department, the board followed its chairman and said "No!" Since, however, coordination between the various bureaus concerned must inevitably become more difficult, there should be created, under the Secretary of the Navy, an office of naval aeronautics as the absolute "essential to harmonious, rapid progress." Composition of the office should include, as a beginning, a director and his assistant, with one representative each from Navigation, Construction and Repair, Steam Engineering, Ordnance, and the Marine Corps.

Finally, the board offered some estimate of costs:

	BuStEng	BuC&R	BuOrd	BuY&D	BuNav	Total
50 aeroplanes	$295,000	$190,000			$15,000	$500,000
Fleet dirigible	60,200	112,200			600	173,000
Hydrogen sets	9,000	8,000				17,000
Double floating shed		90,000				90,000
2 vedettes	24,000	60,000			1,000	85,000
Mooring mast		1,200				1,200
Balloon		800				800
Hangars				$18,000		18,000
3 motor boats	20,000	11,000				31,000
2 tractors				8,000		8,000
Gas, storage				4,000		4,000
Maintenance		100,000				100,000
Advance base material			$269,300			269,300
	$408,200	$573,200	$269,300	$30,000	$16,600	$1,297,300

Here, at last, was the detailed outline of a real program and to Captain Chambers it appeared to justify his long effort to lay the foundation upon which others might build. For what it may have been worth to him, he had the consolation of that conviction when, in this same year of 1913, he had to take the hard personal blow of involuntary retirement from active duty. Although his long assignment ashore had been by official order, it was ruled that he had not had sufficient sea service in his grade of captain and that he was therefore not eligible for promotion. In the sense that he was never allowed to "hoist his flag" as rear admiral, he may fairly be called a martyr to Naval Aviation, and his invaluable

services were but dimly recognized when Secretary Daniels directed
that he remain on active duty "until a suitable relief could be
found." Although this resulted in his staying in the department
for another six years, it would no longer be as Number One in
aviation.

The blow to his personal ambitions did not destroy the captain's
enthusiasm, particularly in the direction of scientific and technical
research. Very shortly he was absorbed in Hunsaker's highly il-
luminating reports of his visits to Europe during this year to study
foreign research and the practical application that was being made
of it. France and Italy, incidentally also using many Curtiss types,
were moving well to the fore in seaplanes. Germany, while keeping
up in these, was farther than ever ahead in lighter-than-air craft.
Britain, although she had not bought her first planes or started her
flying school until 1911, was coming out with innovations such as
the conversion of the old cruiser *Hermes* into the earliest of carriers, designed to transport ten planes and to join in fleet maneuvers. From all that Hunsaker had to tell, it was clear that the
United States, first nation to fly, was now far behind in the international race to develop aviation.

CHAPTER IV

Pensacola and Vera Cruz

WHO would head Naval Aeronautics? To the aviators and to the slowly increasing number of believers in aviation, that was the vital question. "At one moment," wrote Admiral Fiske in his memoirs, "I seriously entertained the idea of asking the Secretary to let me give up Aid for Operations and take it myself," an admission which should remove any lingering doubt of the importance which he attached to the air weapon. As it was, after studying many names, weighing many reputations and, in the end, finding it necessary to overcome his choice's reluctance, he picked Capt. Mark L. Bristol, an officer of recognized ability and strong character. The more distant future would further prove Bristol's worth when he served with distinction in flag rank and as High Commissioner of the United States to Turkey. Reporting on December 17, 1913, as relief for Captain Chambers, he brought to his new desk great energy and the name of a firm, decisive administrator. Almost at once his slogan became, "Take the Air Service to Sea!"

Before he could accomplish that there were the immediate administrative problems to be solved. Beyond his own rather general orders to the duty he had, as a guide, nothing more definite than some regulations from the Bureau of Navigation on tests for pilots and the still effective General Order No. 41, allocating "cognizance" among the various bureaus. In making his early decisions and recommendations, he was not greatly helped by contemporaries inclined to urge him not to become "an empire-builder with a top-heavy organization." On the other hand Admiral Fiske was very helpful, for he made it clear that Chambers, still on active duty, would concern himself with scientific research and experiment, leaving to Bristol the coordination of "the work of the various Bureaus" in supplying necessary material, equipment, and personnel. While there were the usual predictions that a newcomer like Bristol would never mesh with old-timers like Chambers and

Towers, and that civilian engineers would side with one "faction" or the other, what friction there was may fairly be attributed to honest differences of opinion among strong-minded human beings. Even after January 7, 1914, when Bristol's so-called "central office" was moved from the Bureau of Navigation to the Division of Operations, cooperation continued to be good. To a degree, it was helped because Fiske took the opportunity to press an earlier recommendation from the General Board and secure presidential approval of a change in the Navy Regulations which, on the following July 1, established the "Office of Aeronautics." Thus, although the authority of Bristol's office was still not clearly defined, and although he was not given the title of director until November, the existence of a new departmental activity was recognized.

By a most happy coincidence, at the moment when Bristol took over a new Chief of the Bureau of Construction and Repair was also appointed. His name, already recognized in the Navy, would thereafter never be forgotten by the Navy or by naval engineers and architects everywhere—Rear Adm. David W. Taylor. A firm believer in the importance of aviation, he was a strong supporter of the study of aerodynamics, notably by such experiments as could be made only in a wind tunnel. Among the earliest of his many helpful contributions to flying was his successful fight for that tunnel and for the aerodynamic laboratory; perhaps of even more immediate and vital significance was the fine spirit of cooperation in which, from the first hour, he approached all the problems that he and Bristol had in common.

Closely associated with them both was Lt. Comdr. Henry C. Mustin. A few passenger flights at Guantánamo in the winter of 1913 had kindled his enthusiasm and he was now a fully qualified and able pilot. As the man who had designed the gun sights that had made it possible for Admiral Sims to revolutionize United States naval gunnery, and as the man who talked intimately and wisely of 25,000-yard battle ranges while his shipmates were fully occupied with getting gun pointers to hit at 1,600 yards, it was natural that aviation should offer him exactly the scientific and strategic study and work that best suited his abilities and his vision. Chosen by Bristol as a key man in the new organization he was, from the first, a strong advocate of the plane carrier as absolutely indispensable to success in commanding the air above a fleet. In the years to come he would be a prominent, outspokenly militant figure in aviation.

By the middle of January, 1914, Bristol had secured the assignment of the battleship *Mississippi*, already regarded as obsolete, as experimental vessel under Mustin's command with a berth at Pensacola, Florida. In that same month a start was made in erecting an air station on the site of the abandoned navy yard for the Navy's nine planes, with six qualified commissioned pilots, 23 enlisted men, some spares, a few stores, and a canvas hangar or two. Pensacola was not a very impressive place in those days, but after the beach had been cleared of old pile stumps and wreckage and after some old buildings had been adapted, the aviators began to feel at home and ready for work. It was typical of the obstacles apparently surrounding aviation on all sides that in April the *Mississippi* should be ordered out to join the Fleet and that the cruiser *North Carolina*, selected to replace her, should before many months be sent to Europe. Operation of Pensacola, when the files, the pay records, a plane or two, and even the enlisted cooks were all on a so-called station ship thousands of miles away, was a task tough enough to baffle even the hard-bitten, aggressive Mustin.

Even so, there was progress. In the hope of getting more able planes Bristol, with the advice of Chambers, Mustin, and Towers, sent a circular letter out to all designers inviting their criticisms and suggestions for a competition to produce a successful type. The letter brought immediate response from many of those who received it and plans for such a competition were well underway when the "Vera Cruz Incident" necessarily diverted all naval attention and postponed anything of the sort until about three years later when the nation was to find itself in a world war.

On the experimental side, Towers and the other pilots carried on tests of various types of propellers, of the Wright 6-cylinder, 60-horsepower motor; of the new Wright Incidence Indicator and "3-in-1" control; of the Renault motor for the Burgess flying boat; and of the new designs for catapults. After some further experiences in attempting to detect mines from the air, Lt. S. W. Bogan of the Marines made the suggestion that planes might further mine laying by reconnaissance flights to determine the color of water over the proposed field. By signals to mine layers they could then suggest appropriate camouflage paint for the mines before they were laid. This idea stimulated Mustin to propose that the selected areas be artificially muddied in advance of mining. It also inspired plans for equipping dirigibles to grapple for mines, but as yet actual mine laying from the air was not contemplated.

Down off Culebra, Puerto Rico, Lieutenants Smith and McIlvain of the Marine Corps had been exercising as a unit, using the Navy's one other flying boat and an amphibian type developed by Curtiss, at Chambers' suggestion, and familiarly known as a "Bat Boat." Smith, keeping up out of rifle range and outside the limit of elevation for ships' guns, had gathered valuable data on spotting possibilities and on the ease with which a force attempting to land in small boats might be bombed from the air. The approaches to Vieques Island, its roads, trails, and contours were charted from the air, while planted mines, even under rough water, were detected and accurately plotted. In this work the flying boat proved much the better type because the amphibian would not lift two men easily and did not handle well on the water. Considerable practice led to the recommendation that a unit should consist of five pilots with two flying boats and one amphibian. If higher speeds were required one landplane should be added. Further recommendations proposed that a transport, then under construction at Philadelphia for the Marine Corps, be provided with a deckhouse in which one plane could be kept ready for instant use, and also provided with special cranes and a catapult.

Thus, although still without full recognition from their brother sailors, and still lacking the support of a Navy Department really committed to the new weapon, the handful of aviators worked tirelessly at anything that might add to their knowledge and experience. They studied everything that came along, including intelligence reports, now more and more filled with the situation in Mexico and with a Europe driving toward war. Some reports contained the wildest stories, such as that of the German Zeppelins which could "see through the clouds" to locate targets on the ground; a rumor eventually found to be based upon nothing more novel than the ancient device of putting a man in a basket and lowering him on a cable.

Curtiss, however, brought back from Europe some dependable information, skimmed from the boiling pot of rumor. As to motors, he reported that current interest was fixed on the Mercedes, with which the Germans had made two nonstop flights of over sixteen hours' duration; the new Gnome, which was much better than the old one; and the Salmson, a water-cooled type. In plane types the

monoplane was a general favorite although the leading powers of
Europe all differed slightly in their tastes as they did in the importance which they attached to aviation generally. Both Italy
and Russia had appeared to like Curtiss designs but this was not of
great significance because Italy was "making very little progress"
and Russia was not yet really "air-minded." In England an immediate problem was the replacement of her hydroaeroplanes,
most of which had been smashed to pieces in recent encounters with
the proverbially rough English Channel. It was obvious that hydroaeroplanes, especially with two pontoons rather than one, were a
chief British interest but other advances were not being neglected.
In the House of Commons Winston Churchill had declared that the
new Short plane with folding wings would solve the problem of
stowage aboard ship, while new British radio equipment had raised
the range of communication with planes to 120 miles. That airships were not being neglected was clear from recent contracts
made; one with Armstrong for a large rigid and two small nonrigids; another with Italy for three nonrigids; and a third with
France for an Astra-Torres. On the side of defense against aircraft, the British were putting deck armor on the great battleship
Iron Duke as bomb protection and equipping her with a new three-
inch antiaircraft gun. Britain was progressing, but in Curtiss'
opinion it was in Germany that aviation was "on a broad, substantial basis" from which that country would soon move far ahead
of all others in the science of flying.

International figures, assembled at this time by the Office of
Naval Intelligence, were anything but favorable to the United
States:

| | Planes | Dirigibles | |
		Built	Building
Germany	500	20	5
France	500	18	8
Great Britain	250	7	8
Russia	500	3	7
Italy	150	8	5
Austria-Hungary	31	3	3
Belgium	27	2	
Japan	10	1	
Spain	11	2	
U.S.	19	0	

Fiske, always alert and progressive, immediately proposed buying planes from Europe. This, he insisted, would not only improve our position in mere numbers but also stimulate American manufacturers to build better planes in order to hold the government market. His proposal, supported by both Construction and Repair and Steam Engineering, resulted in the department's obtaining bids from such firms as Paul Schmitt, Nieuport, and Sopwith, and the ultimate ordering of two Salmson and two Mercedes motors, a few British instruments, and a Scheimflug aerial camera. Delivery under these contracts was effectually blocked by the war in Europe but meanwhile the attention of all hands was to be diverted to Mexico, toward which most of the Navy was soon steaming full speed across the Gulf.

In the Fleet that came to anchor off Vera Cruz was the *Nebraska*, and aboard her was John Rodgers, no longer on aviation duty but forever a flier at heart. To him the increasing imminence of hostilities with Victoriano Huerta suggested obvious uses for aeroplanes. In an official recommendation he declared that if Vera Cruz were to be bombarded it would be important "to place the shell with the greatest effect against the Mexican forces, with the least damage to non-combatants and their property." To this end planes could locate enemy concentrations and spot the fall of broadsides. Moreover, planes "armed with bombs and machine guns, might force a retreat without the use of heavy artillery and consequent damage to the city." If the enemy finally took shelter in the hills from a bombardment, planes would be better than infantry scouts to locate him, and they might thereupon bomb him out. Another very important use of naval aircraft might be above the clear Gulf waters in detecting mines. That recent intelligence reports at Vera Cruz should cover all details of military interest except aviation appeared to Rodgers to be explainable because no one in the Navy could say what aeroplanes might accomplish in war, for the obvious reason that no naval pilot had ever been subjected to war conditions. Here and now, said Rodgers, was the great opportunity.

Apparently, he did not know how far the interest of Rear Admiral Badger, the Commander in Chief, had been drawn to aviation by the exercises at Guantánamo and by talks with Towers. This interest now supported Rodgers' letter and the result was most informative. When actual intervention came, in April of 1914, the Navy had a Curtiss hydroaeroplane and two Curtiss flying boats on the *Birmingham,* one hydroaeroplane and one flying boat aboard the *Mississippi.* The former, with Towers, Smith, Chevalier, and ten enlisted men went to Tampico; the latter, with Bellinger, Saufley, LaMont, Stolz, and a slightly larger enlisted group, went to Vera Cruz. Tampico was dull, with little to do except stand by to make a demonstration if German men-of-war off the port tried any unfriendly move. At Vera Cruz, however, reconnaissance flights were frequent, with good results in gathering information valuable to subsequent landing parties. After actual hostilities opened, photographing from the air drew rifle fire and Bellinger's plane flew home with the Navy's first enemy bullet holes. This incident served to prove a belief already long held, that rifles would not bring a plane down unless they hit either the pilot himself, the fuel tank, or the motor.

Rear Admiral Badger spoke highly of the pilots' contribution but seized the occasion to note the shortcomings of the flying boat, inadequacies promptly emphasized by the pilots themselves. For work at sea they now favored the hydroaeroplane, particularly because in rough water it took up two pilots where the flying boat would not lift even one. Moreover the boat, a slow climber, would not get high enough and would not make satisfactory speed. All this adverse comment resulted in at least temporary abandonment of the flying boat in favor of a hydromonoplane, preferably of "parasol" type, which was the pilots' favorite of the moment. While it could easily be stowed aboard ship, it sat high enough upon the water to lessen the danger of dipping a wing under. If its motor were "tractor" rather than "pusher" it would be safer for the pilot. On the whole, because of less weight and easier getaway, one pontoon was liked better than two.

There was little chance to progress along this more advanced line of thinking because no sooner were the aviators back from the all-too-short Mexican experience than the beginning of war in Europe sent most of them overseas. The *Mississippi* was promptly sold to Greece, while her assigned relief at Pensacola, the *North Carolina,* had hardly been equipped and manned as such when she, too, was rushed to Europe without waiting to disembark her aviation personnel, including Mustin and several other pilots.

Towers, however, was left behind when she sailed. At Curtiss' request, he had gone to Hammondsport to help test the new flying boat *America.* Her hull was 35 feet long with a 6-foot beam. Her upper wing had a 72-foot span and a 10-foot chord. Her cabin, with dual controls, instruments, and gas tanks, was fully enclosed, and it took two 200-horsepower motors to get her off the water. She was a "monster" built by Curtiss at the suggestion of Lt. Comdr. J. C. Porte, a noted British flier invalided out of the Royal Navy but ambitious to be the first to fly the Atlantic. He and Curtiss had persuaded Rodman Wanamaker to finance the attempt, and they hoped Towers would not only test the *America* but eventually fly with her. World War I, however, changed all that, Porte going home to volunteer for service and leaving the tests to Towers. Eventually the British Government bought the *America* and shipped her overseas, to become the forerunner of the H-12, H-16, and HS-1, all types that were to give good service as anti-submarine patrols to both the United States Navy and the Royal Navy.

Other fliers left on this side of the Atlantic were Lieutenants Herbster of the Navy and B. L. Smith of the Marines, both of whom got in some bombing practice, generally at about 1,000 feet and while headed upwind. In those days the bombardier's left arm was strapped to the plane, permitting him to lean over the side and guide the pilot toward the target but finally requiring him to release the bomb with his right hand. Until the bomb was released its "wind-wheel" must be held and consequently, as Herbster reported, this bombing might have been more accurate, "if I had been able to disengage from the wheel sooner."

Even so, they scored near-misses. The first of four small bombs, dropped in the presence of a board of observers headed by Capt. E. E. Capehart, landed within 50 yards of a 6′ x 4′ land target of white mosquito netting and blew out a hole 30 inches across and 10 inches deep, with fragments scattering to 200 yards. The second bomb hit within 40 yards and dispersed to 300. Of the two others dropped, one in deep water, the other in shallows, neither was seen to explode. All the bombs "tumbled," straightened, then landed flat or at only a small angle, suggesting the use of longer types fitted with fins. Fragmentation must be increased and, for attacks on ships, contact fuses must be devised. Above all there must be better sights, better tables of flight, and better trajectory data. From these reports Captain Bristol made his plans for a Pensacola course in bombing, also recommending new designs for use against submarines, "a much larger bomb then . . . for the decks of ships," and a delayed-action fuse. As another logical result of this summer's work Towers was sent to London, Herbster to Berlin, and Smith to Paris, all as assistant naval attachés to study foreign aviation.

On August 6, four days after Europe burst into flames, the *North Carolina* had sailed for Europe on what Secretary Daniels had predicted would be a brief trip but which was to last 13 months. Her first visit being to France, Mustin had a few days among French planes and French designers, during which he found the hydroaeroplane in disfavor but was otherwise much impressed by French designs and technical niceties. Compared with a Morane-Saulnier, a Bleriot, or a Nieuport, the Curtiss seemed to him hopelessly inadequate. He liked the armor under the pilot which was becoming standard because German antiaircraft fire was steadily improving. Altogether, he found much in France that ought to be closely studied.

The *North Carolina* then cruised in the Mediterranean, with Mustin, Bellinger, Saufley, and other fliers still aboard. Also officially attached to the ship but actually left behind at Pensacola were Chevalier, McIlvain, and Bronson, all unable to draw their pay because their pay accounts were in Turkey. It took Rear Admiral Fiske until November to get the wanderers abroad ordered back and the homeless at home properly established, with the whole group regularly attached to Pensacola. Here the new commanding officer was Lieut. Kenneth Whiting, a welcome addition because he was the same daredevil Whiting who had been shot from the tube of a submerged submarine and who had taken part in every other dangerous naval enterprise he could reach. Aviation was just his dish and the early aviators must have wondered why he was so long in coming to it. Fleet Admiral Halsey, in his recently published autobiography, supplied an explanation with an account of a dinner in 1910 at which Whiting and Ellyson were his guests. At the time the two young men were in rival submarines but Whiting announced that he had asked for aviation duty. Ellyson thought this such a good idea that he copied Whiting's letter and to the astonishment of both, and to Whiting's great chagrin, it was Ellyson who got the assignment. Whiting was left "holding the bag" in submarines.

CHAPTER V

Spending the First Million Dollars

ALTHOUGH seven months had been lost because of the sale of the *Mississippi* and the abrupt departure of the *North Carolina* and although more discouraging delays lay ahead, one bit of encouragement came with Bristol's new orders of November 23, 1914, the first in which he was designated in writing "Director of Naval Aeronautics." Using this shred of recognition as reason for raising his voice, he declared that the Navy had only 12 planes for training purposes, quoted the Chambers Board's year-old recommendation for 50 planes and three dirigibles, and requested two planes for each of the 16 battleships of the Fleet. When this request, strongly backed by Fiske, reached the General Board, that body made it the occasion for remarking that no attention had been paid by the Navy Department to its previous proposals. It added that the existing situation was "nothing less than deplorable" because "aircraft are the eyes both of armies and navies, and it is difficult to place any limit to their offensive possibilities." Moreover, in the present state of aerial unpreparedness, scouting "would be blind" and therefore the board "could not too strongly urge that the Department's most serious thought be given to this matter" and that "an appropriation of at least $5,000,000 be made available immediately."

It was unfortunate that the General Board should be merely an advisory body, assembled to give the Secretary of the Navy a professional opinion upon anything that interested him. That opinion always had the prestige afforded by the high rank of those who gave it, but it was not backed by any authority under the law. Thus it might be outweighed by the opinion of the chief of some bureau of the Navy Department because his authority was clearly defined by law and his views could be given to the Secretary at any moment.

Nevertheless, the strong sentiments expressed by the board at this time show how it had advanced in its view of aviation. The recommendation for $5,000,000 during the fiscal year 1916 was made, however, to the Secretary of the Navy and it appears that this figure was not presented to Congress at this time. For the same year Bristol's own recommendation was for $1,187,600, again presented to the Secretary. The record does not show how these requested amounts appeared in what was finally submitted to Congress because the requests of all bureaus were presented as a total and the various bureau chiefs were called to the hearings conducted by the House Naval Committee. When Bristol testified, he repeated his figures and expressed astonishment over what appeared to be a reduction in them. "From an examination of the draft of the Appropriation Bill," said he, "it would seem that either other estimates for work under the various bureaus have been reduced considerably or else my estimates for aeronautics have been considerably reduced." He drew attention to the fact that "the appropriations for 1916 are no larger, and in some cases are less than last year."

Some warm debate followed between members of the committee. Certain of them were indignant that more had not been done, especially when it came out that the Bureau of Navigation had spent upon aviation only about one third of the amount previously allowed it. In his own appearances before the committee the Secretary of the Navy stuck to his statement that it was "hard to get good planes"—which, in truth, it was. At this late date it cannot be definitely stated how far the Secretary was swayed by his well-known bent toward a placid, wishful-thinking pacifism, but it is of record that Representative Ernest W. Roberts of Massachusetts, after telling his fellow members that he did not want "to doubt the good faith" of the Secretary, went on to say that, "in view of the slowness of the Navy Department . . . in going into aeronautics," he saw no great hope that the department would push aviation "unless they are pushed from this end." He proposed that $1,000,000 be appropriated and, in justice to Mr. Daniels, it should be noted that he was agreeable to this "provided the Navy could decide what kind of planes" it wanted.

The irrepressible Fiske did not fail to tell the committee that the German Fleet was more than a match for the United States Fleet and that a disastrous action between the two would surely be followed by air bombing of American coastal towns. Moreover, he said, with European nations now beginning to pour orders for planes into the United States, there was danger that these orders would leave American plants too burdened to undertake American orders when they did come.

When it finally recommmended $1,000,000 for Naval Aviation, the House Committee proposed placing that amount in the hands of the Secretary of the Navy. It was the committee's expressed opinion that this segregation of funds would produce more definite advances than would a loose distribution through the bureaus, and there is good reason to believe that it meant to make the Secretary, whether enthusiastic or not, definitely responsible. After considerable demur, on the floor of the House, against "so large a sum," the amount was eventually included as recommended in the Naval Appropriations Act of March 3, 1915.

A major issue at the time was the question of plane building by the government. Representatives Roberts and Frank Buchanan of Illinois were strongly in favor of this, on the ground that manufacturers with large foreign orders were tempted to skimp small home orders. Curtiss, for example, having received a considerable British subsidy to enlarge his plants, would naturally have no great interest in what Bristol might order, unless the alternative meant losing the business to a government-owned plant.

On this point the Secretary of the Navy said that his department had no plans for building but "might have to do it," while Rear Admiral Griffin said that his Bureau of Steam Engineering could build motors at navy yards only if necessary equipment were furnished and especially skilled labor employed. Admiral Fiske was against government building on the ground of unreadiness by comparison with private firms and the inevitable loss of time that must result. With him stood the bureaus in general, most officers arguing that government competition with industry would mean losing the ideas of inventors and designers, wasting officers in plants when they were needed elsewhere, and getting, in the end, government establishments that were inadequate. The Naval Committee's final stand was against government in business.

Giving some attention to laboratories, the same committee recognized that the Smithsonian had been right, months earlier, in recommending that its own inadequate Langley Laboratory be supplemented or replaced by a better one for the study of aerodynamics. The only other existing laboratory was at the Massachusetts Institute of Technology; the wind tunnel at the Washington Navy Yard was not complete and, notwithstanding the helpfulness of Admiral Taylor, the Model Basin could not devote itself exclusively to aircraft. The experimental station at Annapolis could make block tests of motors but had no instruments to check their performance in flight nor any way fully to test propellers. Pensacola had some excellent instruments but facilities were inadequate, especially for testing new devices in "wireless." Only a thoroughly modern laboratory would permit true progress toward that "command of the air" which Fiske unceasingly urged as "just as important as command of the seas, both for land and sea wartime operations." For these reasons the committee urged action to build a national aerodynamic laboratory, but it was not then successful and the struggle for such an establishment continued until well into 1915. In January of that year the Smithsonian formed a committee including Chief Justice White, Alexander Graham Bell, Senator Stone of Missouri, Representative Roberts, John B. Henderson, and Charles D. Walcott to address Congress on the subject. It urged authorizing the President to appoint an advisory aeronautical committee to direct the research programs of both military men and civilians. Emphasizing the action of Britain in establishing a national laboratory and a formal advisory committee, it listed impressive comparative figures in aircraft, ranging from France's 1,400 to the United States' 23, and insisted that the path to more planes led through properly conducted research.

Eventually, the words of such outstanding men became effective. In the Naval Appropriations Act of March 3, 1915, Congress authorized the President to appoint just the type of committee that Mr. Taft had long before created, only to have it destroyed. The new body was known as the National Advisory Committee for Aeronautics, and its 12 members were to include two from the Navy Department, two from the War Department, one each from the Smithsonian, the Weather Bureau, and the Bureau of Standards, with five civilians who were either familiar with the needs of aeronautical science or skilled in aeronautical engineering.

This committee still exists and it has long since established the record of contributing more to research in aeronautics than any other body in the United States, if not, indeed, in the world. As outlined in the act that created it, its duties were "to supervise and direct the scientific study of the problems of flight, with a view to their practical solution; to determine the problems which should be experimentally attacked; and to discuss their solution and their application to practical questions." If a laboratory should be placed at its disposal, the committee would be expected to "direct and conduct research and experiments . . . in such a laboratory." Showing a childlike faith in Captain Chambers' much earlier prediction that private funds to support such a committee and such a laboratory would be forthcoming, Congress went no further in its appropriations for clerical services, incidental expenses of the unsalaried members, and experiments than the munificent sum of $5,000.

In a more liberal humor toward the fliers, Congress cleared up the question of extra pay. Its legislation of two years earlier had been interpreted as applying only to officers who were fully qualified aviators, a manifest injustice in view of the graver risks run by novices. The new law gave such students a 35 per cent increase, allowing 50 per cent for the qualified pilots and for such enlisted men as might be on duty involving actual flying. In addition, a full year's pay was provided for the survivors of any officer killed while flying, with double disability pension for all who were injured in a crash. The previous limit of 30 officers to eligibility for these extras was raised to 48 officers, with 96 enlisted men for the Navy; 12 officers and 24 enlisted men for the Marines.

While this legislation was naturally welcomed by the personnel generally, Bristol was not so well pleased. He had contended that extra pay should be used only "to provide . . . life insurance which they cannot get from ordinary . . . companies," and he did not believe that it was so used. "Though I am in favor of the extra pay at the present time," he wrote, "I should recommend . . . in another year . . . doing away with [it] and if then considered necessary, to increase the pension to beneficiaries of officers and men killed." It has been said that this strong difference of opinion bred an unfortunate coolness between Bristol and his flying subordinates. As to that, it is not difficult to understand that the extra pay must unquestionably have been a strong incentive to go into flying. Indeed, one newcomer at the time said quite bluntly: "I wouldn't be flying if I hadn't been broke!" Yet it could hardly have been the extra pay that inspired performances like Lieut. R. C. Saufley's when, in this year of 1915, he took a Curtiss seaplane up to 14,500 feet and set a new endurance record of eight hours and 20 minutes in the air.

In the matter of pilot certificates, brought up at this time, there

was no difference of opinion. If aviators were to be given these
certificates only after they had been passed upon by a qualified
board, it hardly needed Fiske's reminder to make it clear that
such a board could be made up only of men who were themselves
aviators. Accordingly, certificates were issued to the seven
pioneers, Ellyson, Towers, Mustin, Bellinger, Herbster, B. L.
Smith, and Chevalier. Since Rodgers had been on other duty for
two years, he got no certificate at the moment but later on his name
was inserted between those of Ellyson and Towers. Cunningham
of the Marine Corps was not named in this list of pioneers, possibly
because, on August 11, 1913, he had requested detachment from
aviation duties for the reason, so history relates, that the young
lady of his choice declined to risk marrying a flier. Evidently, he
was more persuasive later because on April 27, 1915, we find him
back in aviation and ultimately listed as No. 5 among naval
aviators. These later changes have always complicated the exact
"precedence" of the early fliers.

Nearly all of these men were against the dirigible as too slow
and too vulnerable, views in which future history was to support them. Bristol, however liked the "Big Bags" and wanted
specifications for them issued to manufacturers. Lt. Comdr.
F. R. McCrary, as well as Richardson and Herbster, accordingly
came out with plans embodying some new ideas, such as "a car
. . . to allow for resting on the water or for moving on the surface at slow speed"; twin screws of swivel type; and a "secure
means" for making fast to the mooring mast. Bristol likened the
proposed ships to "Dreadnaughts," declaring that just as battleships did not move in enemy waters without a destroyer escort,
so the airship bombers of the future would cross the sky only under
"fighter" protection. Wrong about the dirigible as a bomber,
he was certainly right enough about future air tactics.

Counting upon early delivery of at least one training dirigible,
Bristol, with Fiske's backing, ordered from Pittsburgh a hangar
shed to house it. Its arrival at Pensacola was much delayed by
winter weather too severe for its builders but, in the end, the
hangar was received and erected long before its first inmate put in
an appearance. Meantime McCrary had been told to devote himself exclusively to dirigibles, beginning on June 1, as inspector of
a nonrigid ordered from Connecticut Aircraft Company, to be
delivered in October and to cost $45,636.25. One reason for the
award of this contract was the report that the company had just

hired an Austrian Zeppelin expert; a poor reason because his knowledge proved to be but slight and his ability too small to cope with novel ideas or prevent exasperating delays in construction. Nevertheless, training of personnel began under McCrary and Lieut. Lewis H. Maxfield, both to be prominent "L-T-A" men during the war, and all hands went to Akron, where the Goodyear Company, as the result of Fleet interest in spotting, were building a 19,000-cubic-foot, free balloon. While the men were "growing up with that one," Goodyear began building a kite balloon, thus leaving only the rigid dirigible to await the results of these earlier experiments.

To test the theory that getting better heavier-than-air planes depended upon buying some that were already being manufactured, bids were called for and contracts were let. In case this theory might prove to have been over optimistic, the specifications for such items as motors were made flexible, allowing for changes to be incorporated after rather informal discussion with the builders.

After the circular sent to manufacturers in 1914 had produced little that was new in motors, much less anything better, Bristol suggested that Steam Engineering designate an officer to specialize in the field even if the bureau itself did not take up design and manufacture. In April, 1915, Lieut. Warren G. Child was detailed to this duty, in which he was to remain for a long time the Navy's expert. Finding a suitable building at the Washington Navy Yard, he converted it into a test plant with an engine laboratory, to do for motors what tunnels could do for air frames and to be the scene, eventually, of the first motor competition.

While awaiting delivery of all this new and better material, Pensacola was administratively reorganized to handle it. Mustin, now the officer in charge, was designated "Commandant," to conform to naval standards for stations, a change which did not affect his actual duties but did give him much firmer standing in relation to his command, especially its marine personnel, and in relation to visiting ships and officers.

From the standpoint of the aviators, contemporary changes in high-ranking administrative personnel of the Navy Department were not so helpful. No one was astonished when Rear Admiral Fiske was replaced because, during his tour of duty as Aid for Operations, he and the Secretary of the Navy had had so many sharp differences that he was distinctly persona non grata. With the creation of the new Office of Chief of Naval Operations, the Secretary found in Capt. (later Adm.) William S. Benson one who was much more ready to agree with him without debate. When Fiske left Washington on July 1, 1915, he went to other important posts such as that of president of the Naval War College at Newport, but his continuing great interest in aviation could no longer be expressed in positive action. He could do little more than write letters of recommendation.

To the aviators this change meant a loss of standing. They knew, as did everyone else in the Navy, that Benson was a first-rate seaman and ship handler but what they wanted was someone with the imagination to go ahead with them in the science of flying. Whereas Fiske had been ready to permit a separate office in order that great emphasis might be laid upon what he called "the new weapon . . . far superior to any that we have had before," Benson tended to regard aviation as little more than something to be absorbed into the bureau system in which he believed; something at the moment too small to deserve more than desk space for an assistant to himself, rather than an independent, expanding office. Perhaps it was in part his responsibility for the continual readiness of the whole Navy that influenced him to get what little there was of Naval Aviation made a part of the Fleet; if so, then of course he had to act upon his own judgment. Nevertheless, from the aviators' standpoint, he was holding them back rather than pushing them ahead.

To some extent this impression was inevitable because all the fliers of the day were young men of relatively low rank, with little authority to say what should and what should not be done, which policy should be adopted and which abandoned. As for that, the whole history of Naval Aviation in this early period shows that the machine developed much faster than the rank of those who used it. In the ordinary course, promotions could not keep pace and years would pass before officers who had already attained rank decided to qualify as fliers and thereafter began to fill high places in the air organization. In 1915, with the new Chief of Naval Operations by no means an enthusiast, it was all the more difficult for the younger, more forward looking to get suggestions looked upon with favor.

Among the proposals which Bristol nevertheless made in that year was one for the assignment of more officers to aviation duties. He proposed to establish a quota of one officer with six enlisted men for each plane; one officer with 12 men for each dirigible.

Another of his recommendations called for a total of 120 planes and two dirigibles for active duty in the Fleet, with 28 planes for the naval defense districts. These, he said, would meet the "very least requirement" which was 24 fleet divisions of four planes each, with three reserve divisions, and the rest distributed for coast defense, at Narragansett, the Chesapeake, Guantánamo, Panama, San Francisco, Hawaii, and Manila. Each of the two dirigibles should be carried, said Bristol, on a ship especially designed for the purpose.

Bristol's further proposals, for administration, included a rear admiral as director, with a captain as assistant; two other captains to command the Fleet aircraft, and the special ships; nine commanders, 37 lieutenant commanders, and 148 junior officers. To the Powers That Were, such changes and enlargements appeared preposterous. What was now asked would appear, almost in a matter of months, a pittance, but was quite outside "front office" imagining at the moment. The heads of administration being inclined to wait and see rather than to move forward to meet a possible emergency meant that Fabius Maximus was at the controls and the administrative machine must be sluggish in take-off and slow in flight.

Out in the field rather more progress was being made, an outstanding example being the entry of the Coast Guard into Naval Aviation. At the suggestion of Capt. B. M. Chiswell of the Coast Guard, that aircraft might prove valuable in locating ships in distress offshore, Lieut. Elmer F. Stone of the same service was sent to the school at Pensacola. Eventually, he became Naval Aviator No. 38 and he was a co-pilot on the Navy's historic NC flights to Europe in 1919. At the same time the Coast Guard sent Lieut. Norman B. Hall to the Curtiss plant at Hammondsport for technical instruction.

Meantime, at Pensacola, plans for organized classes, disrupted by the Vera Cruz incident, were taken up again. In July, 1915, the first new class assembled with eight naval and two marine officers, while 20 enlisted men, including four marines, reported for ground work. Exercises for training, as well as further experimental flying by students or by the aviators returned from Europe, were designed to bring out the strengths and the weaknesses of existing planes as a basis for practicable air tactics. They included antisubmarine patrols and bombing, as well as spotting flights for battleship target practice and for the Coast Artillery. Bellinger,

for example, took the Burgess-Dunne flying boat to Fortress
Monroe, to spot mortar fire from the shore batteries. He met bad
weather and he had much motor trouble, both of which led to his
reporting his own effort as "only a glimpse of the possibilities of
an aeroplane in this connection." He found that his plane could
not carry two men and also carry enough fuel for more than 90
minutes in the air. He proved that colored stars of the Very pistol,
which he used to signal the result of shots, were indistinct by
day unless lampblack were used to make a lot of smoke. He could,
however, readily distinguish "splashes" from altitudes up to 8,000
feet and from his observations he concluded that a ship should get
"on the target" after four ranging shots had been corrected by
spotting.

Bombing tests were made with the redesigned Mark I and Mark
II bombs. Up to an altitude of 90 feet the Army had greater
success than the Navy with these bombs, but later in the year the
naval planes dropped bombs from 3,500 feet which straightened
up after falling 600 feet and hit the water nose on. From heights
of 500 to 600 feet near-misses were becoming frequent, but the
effects of shrapnel dispersion were still not impressive. Much of
the ineffectiveness of bombing in general was attributed to the
lack of a really good sight, the only one available being the somewhat primitive Sprengstoff A. G. Carbonit type, not very accurate
against a target 40 feet square. The Sperry instrument, brought
out at this time, weighed 60 pounds, which was too much for the
plane of the day, and it would not be until after World War I
that a really accurate bomb sight was produced.

Such exercises, making obvious the need for more of them,
caused Bristol to recommend and get approval for six more planes,
a dozen additional student officers, and the assignment of qualified
pilots to postgraduate work including exercises with the Army.
He also got authority to install a catapult on the *North Carolina*
from which, in the fall, Mustin's plane was launched. The operation was not wholly successful because of mechanical defects in
design and this catapult was removed. Modified designs, later
erected aboard other vessels, were also unsatisfactory because their
cumbersome equipment interfered with firing the ships' guns.

To Bristol, as to Mustin, carriers were indicated. Learning that
the Royal Navy had five of these special vessels nearly completed,
he urged "purchasing a merchant-ship and converting her" to
handle planes, dirigibles, and kite balloons. Unfortunately, Ben-

son and the Secretary of the Navy, presumably because they were still convinced that a ship with turrets could find space for planes, remained unimpressed and disapproving. It would not be until some years after World War I that the conversion of the collier *Jupiter* would produce the first United States carrier, the *Langley*.

On October 12, 1915, the department issued an order which, though loosely drawn, was tight enough and strong enough to pull the heart out of Naval Aviation. It effectively reduced the "director" to mere officer-in-charge status, in which he would serve as an assistant in the Material Division of the Office of Naval Operations. He was to have no planning functions and no real authority, his duty being described in the order as limited to making recommendations "as required," covering such matters as "the type, numbers and general characteristics of aircraft desired." Obviously, any recommendations made without being "required" were not likely to have much weight with either the Secretary of the Navy or the Chief of Naval Operations, whose approval was necessary to make any recommendation effective. In any event, whatever they did approve would be handled under the old system, with funds distributed among bureaus, and without any supervision by the aviation assistant tucked away in a corner of the Office of Naval Operations.

This new order left unanswered many questions of real importance to aviation. It did not specify who should draw up a general program, nor did it state, for example, who should deal with the National Advisory Committee. In short, it was more than anything else a brake on Naval Aviation progress. Since it was not to go into effect until the detachment of Captain Bristol, it left him five months during which he could continue to function as director; months which he devoted to the study of national production facilities, to some reorganization of the training program for enlisted men, and to placing orders under the authorized $1,000,000 building program.

To get a proper estimate of existing production possibilities he sent Mustin on a tour of the factories, then rumored to be crowded with foreign orders. Mustin reported the Wright factories to be without any foreign orders and, at the moment, in process of reorganization after purchase by a New York syndicate. Curtiss had delivered to Europe 125 JN tractor planes with the OX motors, and 40 American-type flying boats. He had on hand 200 of the JN type with OX motors, 100 RT tractor planes with

V-2 motors, and 50 American-type boats. His capacity was five planes, five OX motors and five V-2 motors a day, all of excellent workmanship. His research department under Dr. A. F. Zahm was active and progressive. A third firm, Thomas Brothers, had completed 24 planes of their T-2 type but these were still disassembled and without motors; its ultimate capacity would be two planes a week and it had no foreign orders on hand. Fourth, the Burgess Company had supplied 36 of the Type Q pusher planes, equipped with Sturtevant motors, to Great Britain, and although it had no foreign orders in hand, it was negotiating for a large Russian order. Its capacity was five planes a week, of excellent quality. Finally, the Sturtevant Company, with a one-plane weekly capacity and good workmen, was also without foreign orders. Hence it was clear that there were ample facilities to begin production for the United States Navy. However, only 29 planes had been ordered by the end of 1915, and Bristol promptly insisted that more orders must follow because "it would be a grave error in preparedness" to neglect them.

Declaring that bigger planes must come, with 1,000 and even 2,000 horsepower, Bristol also announced that the Navy would soon begin its own program. Work on the type known as 82-A was started in November, 1915, the design being a modification, by Richardson and his associates, of one used by private manufacturers. After a year this type proved to be excessively heavy in the tail and otherwise already obsolete. The Washington Navy Yard put into manufacture a new flying boat, fitted with twin and sometimes with triple pontoons, and planned as an improvement upon the type found unsatisfactory at Vera Cruz.

Motors were still disappointing. Toward the end of 1915 the National Advisory Committee for Aeronautics said of them that "invention is more active than design, and the painstaking research necessary is almost entirely lacking." Of those that were tested at the navy yard only two designs passed their contract tests. About all that could be said of motors was that there was now a place where the Navy could test any that might be submitted.

Easy mechanical control remained a matter of prime importance to the men who had to fly the planes. Bellinger, Saufley, and Bronson did not agree with Bristol's decision to adopt, as the Navy's standard, the modified Deperdussin control with its wheel on a vertical stem locked to the ailerons and its foot bar attached to the rudder. For the most part the pilots favored the Wright "three-in-one" control. When, however, it was learned that the Army had adopted the "straight" Deperdussin—that is, without the modifications—Bristol changed his own order and made the Navy's standard agree with the Army's.

To stimulate the training of enlisted personnel, Bristol directed Mustin to select eight petty officers of the Navy and two sergeants of the Marine Corps for instruction. When these were soon found to be making "excellent progress," Bristol again asked that special ratings be created for aviation mechanics on a permanent basis, to give the men "definite status" and "an added incentive" to advance themselves and thus increase the efficiency of the whole force. The result was a compromise, in which the Bureau of Navigation authorized the rating of "machinist, aeronautics," to hold while men were actually serving in aviation but not to apply when they returned to other duties. This inevitably left many men still convinced that their chances for permanent advancement depended upon keeping their feet on a ship's deck.

For such men as did volunteer for aviation duty one bit of encouragement came when the National Automobile Chamber of Commerce offered them free courses in the theory, construction, operations, and repair of gasoline motors. The chamber made this offer through Mr. Howard Coffin, who would head the Aircraft Production Board during the coming war, and Captain Bristol promptly accepted for the Navy. Although his acceptance had the approval of the Bureau of Navigation and the Chief of Naval Operations, there is no record that any advantage was taken of the opportunity. It was not until the nation was actually at war that enlisted men were trained at such plants as those of the Packard Company in Detroit.

CHAPTER VI

The General Board Recommends

IN February, 1916, Bristol recognized that his "signal number was up"—in landman's language, the highest authorities had had enough of him in Washington. Accordingly, he asked for orders to command the *North Carolina*, with additional duty as supervisor of all aircraft and aircraft stations and the further development of aeronautics. His purpose was what it always had been—to "take aviation to sea"; to give the Fleet what he, Chambers, Fiske, and all the aviators had so long urged: a real air arm. To his pleased astonishment, his request for this assignment was approved without demur.

Before leaving Washington on March 4 he wrote a final report which he could not make optimistic in tone. Listing 24 officers at Pensacola, he noted that but ten of these were qualified pilots, three other pilots being then on duty abroad as attachés and two more being assigned to inspection of aircraft construction. As was inevitable because of the Navy's general shortage, additions and replacements were coming very slowly, the eight officers who composed the class of July, 1915, having been followed by seven in October and two in January, with only one more in immediate prospect. Yet, even for this small group, available material was inadequate.

One free balloon had been delivered at Pensacola but the dirigible expected in the preceding fall had not yet been received. The airship shed, coming from Pittsburgh, was long overdue and the manufacturers of seaplanes were "meeting with a great deal of difficulty." On a contract made two years earlier the Wrights had yet to deliver one satisfactory plane and, while two "tractor" hydroaeroplanes by Martin had arrived, the two others being built by Curtiss had not. A dozen more, six each due from Sturtevant and from Burgess, might be expected "within a few days," but an experimental plane, by Gallaudet, was "delayed on account of

. . . the motors." Not even the great and exceedingly helpful enthusiasm of Rear Adm. David W. Taylor had achieved the impossible in expediting deliveries or in cutting all the bureaucratic Gordian knots of tape. In comparison with Europe, the position of Naval Aviation was very low.

This also applied to administration, as Bristol saw it. He was about to be replaced in Washington by Clarence K. Bronson, a junior-grade lieutenant hardly likely to succeed in real coordination where captains had failed. Bronson would be subordinated in the Office of Naval Operations to Capt. Josiah S. McKean, long known as a frosty sailorman but not as one with the great interest in an air arm which would lead him to take up the cudgels for it. Indeed, it would not have astonished Bristol, could he then have read what McKean, some four years later, would give as his own view of aviation in 1916, when he took it over. "It did not," he would say, "belong legitimately to my part of the department, but Admiral Benson and the Secretary did not think we were getting the progress that was to be expected . . . in spite of my protest they said that I had to take that thing and dig it out to the foundations, and find out where we were going . . . and organize it; and as soon as I got it organized . . . and . . . people trained to take it over . . . they would take it off my hands."

These were hardly the words of an air enthusiast, but Bristol did not have to read them to foresee that Bronson would be little more than an office boy, not allowed even to touch "the handle of the big front door," much less polish it. As for himself, Bristol cannot have had much confidence that his own voice, raised from the bridge of a seagoing ship, would carry into the administrative offices in Washington. Still, he could try.

It was in this frame of mind that he left Washington to take over the *North Carolina*. Joining the Fleet off Guantánamo at the end of March, he had four planes aboard and for a week he drilled with them as he saw fit. Then began a series of the most important exercises yet attempted: exercises designed to "establish facts as a guide for future development of aeronautics in the Navy" without regard to "preconceived ideas." Planned to be well within the capabilities of the planes, these exercises included reconnaissance flights, sham attacks upon oil tanks, machine shops, and ships, shooting at kites, scouting, and tests of radio communications. Notwithstanding a disappointing amount of motor trouble, the planes flew nearly 4,000 miles, but the results obtained served chiefly to emphasize how much there was still to be known about preparation and cooperative planning for such drills.

Constructive lessons were learned from the "attack" upon the *Petrel* by Chevalier and A. C. Read. The ship's commander reported that the planes were "never within the arc of fire of the 3-pounder and 1-pounder guns of the ship, except at a distance far too great to fire these guns." He added that one plane had passed over his ship at an estimated height of 3,500 feet and he believed that "if this aeroplane had bombs, it could have destroyed the *Petrel*." Further, the exercises brought into strong relief the many inadequacies of plane equipment and the Fleet's general lack of proper understanding of what the planes were attempting to do. For example, successive launchings from a catapult could be planned, but since the first launching almost invariably damaged the "car" through the shock of stopping it, the other planes had to await repairs to the catapult. Planes could make flights that were called "reconnaissance," but since they carried no cameras to record what they observed the term was an exaggeration. Spotting flights could hardly be fully successful when the pilots had not been trained as spotters, much less if the ships failed to signal that they were about to begin shooting, and least of all when inadequate radio forced the planes to report on "splashes" with a cumbersome triple-mirror heliograph. Orders to shoot down kites could be issued but could hardly be carried out by planes that carried no machine guns.

As a commentary upon these exercises Bristol a few weeks later forwarded a long report from Bellinger, which he described as the work of "an officer who has had long experience in naval flying and . . . the most experience . . . over the open sea." Weight must be given, said Bristol, to Bellinger's declaration that "water-aeroplanes . . . have been more or less overrated . . . and there is [none] built at present which is . . . capable of operating . . . in a moderate sea." Similarly, importance must be attached to the contention that scouting, with the undependable instruments available, was a difficult task, especially when out of sight of the ships; an impossible task at anything approaching the proposed scouting distance of 200 miles. When Bellinger said that "planes now owned by the Navy are very poor excuses for whatever work may be assigned them," and added that catapults were no better, he was giving good reasons for his conviction that the Navy must know more exactly what types it wanted before it could expect manufacturers to spend time and money trying to build them. Although Bristol did remark that Bellinger had not laid enough stress upon the need for better motors, he might have found this need implied in Bellinger's insistence that the Navy should do its own experimental building, especially in the "tractor" type used for training. Altogether, there was much food for thought in that long and rather discouraging report from Bellinger, especially because he was a man generally inclined to be optimistic and unargumentative.

It appears that Bristol himself did not, at this time, favor Bellinger's plan for experimental building at Pensacola. He considered that station already overworked and his view was that all design should be by engineers rather than by aviators because "the general idea of any certain group in the Navy getting off in a corner," to carry on "without full cooperation from the rest of the service is bound to produce poorer results than if the talent of all hands is used." Following this line of reasoning, Bristol remarked that "no design, invention, or research work should . . . [take] up any time that ought to be devoted to training officers and men to handle aircraft." He held that elementary training would fully occupy Pensacola and that the *North Carolina* "should be devoted to training officers and men for the Fleet and the open-sea work." If Pensacola and the ship could form a team with "each pulling the load given," real progress would be possible and modifications of design could be left to the Navy Department.

It is a fact that cooperation between Bristol and Mustin was not, at this moment, very close. Both were strong characters and neither was inclined to concede much ground to the other. At the end of May, 1916, this was recognized by Benson and orders were issued relieving Bristol of "supervision over all aircraft and aircraft stations and the further development of aeronautics in the Navy," leaving him responsible only for planes with the Fleet. He was, however, directed to comment on designs as they performed and also comment upon the efficiency of personnel sent to him. These comments could take the form of recommendations but they must be made to the Chief of Naval Operations. At the date of these new orders Bristol and Benson exchanged private letters. Benson deplored what he described as a lack of progress because designs were changed so fast that only "delays and disappointments" followed. He added that it had "finally been decided to try the experiment of putting aircraft in exactly the same category as other ships," with Bristol in charge of the "development of tactics and use of aircraft afloat" and "work at the Station" under Mustin. This reduction of his authority quite possibly affected what Bristol had to say on Bellinger's report.

That report was still going the rounds of the Navy Department when the General Board on June 24, 1916, issued the result of its latest three months' study of "the possible naval uses of aircraft . . . to enable the Department to undertake the orderly and systematic development of aeronautics in the Navy," a study supplementing the one made in the autumn of 1915. After declaring that not enough attention had been given to the strategical and tactical possibilities of the air arm, the board set forth several conclusions.

"Aeronautics," said the report, "does not offer a prospect of becoming the principal means of exercising compelling force against the enemy." To support this broad statement it cited the relatively small motive power and striking force of aircraft, considered as a part of the enormous expenditure of power in the destructive effort of a war. It therefore viewed planes as limited to scouting, patrolling, spotting, and controlling the shooting from ships, but held that they should "have some fighting capacity," because "at times, some of them must . . . support . . . the reconnoitering force." If the enemy were not in full command of the air, "it will frequently be possible for aircraft to utilize their very moderate lifting and transporting capacity by dropping explosives without prohibitive danger of counterattack from the surface."

Even in scouting, declared the board, estimated maximum ranges would undoubtedly be cut down in practice by surface haze, glare, and general weather conditions. In spotting, while planes might detect an enemy's changes of course, his launching of torpedoes, or the presence of his submarines, the pilots' confusion in attempting to spot gunfire from all friendly ships would be very great. Moreover, having a spotter "outside the ship introduces . . . difficulties in the chain of command between the spotters and the gun, which . . . may . . . neutralize . . . the direct advantage of spotting from the aeroplane."

As to bombing, the board held that the Navy might well "omit the heavy weight carrying type . . . since inaccuracy in aiming forbids . . . valuable service against anything but large land-targets." When accurate bombing became possible, this would best be done "from dirigibles whose size will permit . . . a large supply of bombs." As to "combat hydroaeroplanes . . . using the Fleet as their base," these did not, in the board's opinion, "seem necessary at present." Then the board added a paragraph that makes strange reading thirty years after it was written: "It seems that the aviation service as attached to the Fleet will not be of as great importance to the Navy as . . . to the Army. There is no substantial reason apparent at the present time to yield to the clamor of the extremists who assert the supremacy of aeronautics as a naval arm. On the contrary the aviation service with the fleet seems likely to be confined to a subordinate role."

Nevertheless, the board by no means advocated neglect of aviation. It proposed that three small nonrigid dirigibles for coast patrol be bought at once, with one rigid and one semirigid, each of 11,000-cubic-foot capacity, for experimental work. It also suggested, as the make-up of a standard air division, two planes, four officers, four petty officers, and four seamen; one division to be assigned to each battleship, two divisions to each scouting ship. For patrol of coastal areas the standard hydroaeroplane division recommended was one composed of three 7,500-pound planes, with eight officers, eight petty officers, and such mechanics and helpers as proved necessary. One such division was proposed for each naval district, not including those on the Great Lakes but particularly including the Canal Zone. The board was opposed to any plan for a "separate Air Force," and insisted that all commissioned pilots should be officers of the regular Navy, fully trained in seagoing duties. No pilot should continue to fly after he became 30 years old.

The board had not reached these conclusions without hearing many witnesses, the most outspoken of whom was Commander Mustin. He did urge that the Navy be given a separate flying corps similar to the Marine Corps, although there are those who say that his vehemence on this point was designed less to carry the point than to promote discussion of the whole problem of Naval Aviation. He also—with clear farsightedness—urged the immediate building of carriers, another point that he did not carry with the board. Proposing that dirigibles be abandoned as not worth the time and money, he declared that the Navy was wrong in trying to find one type of plane that would do everything. Instead, he wanted at least three types built, each for its especial purpose and, in design, representing what ship design represented, the best practicable compromise between the fundamental requirements of speed, armor, and fire power. One type should be a fast, low-flying torpedo carrier; another should be for spotting and scouting; the third, also fast but very easily handled, should be fully armed to defend not only itself but also the other two while they were carrying out their missions. Certainly it was in part because of Mustin's recommendations in March that the board, without waiting to make its full report, advocated spending as much as $5,000,000 on aviation during the next three years, specifically for purposes which it summed up as follows: to encourage invention and scientific progress; to equip ships and bases with planes; to launch an experimental Zeppelin program.

The board also continued studying all available information on the bombing then being carried on in Europe. The weight of bombs carried, the speed of bombing planes or dirigibles, the visibility of targets and the hits or near-misses scored; all these had come under exhaustive review to produce further recommendations in August for what was described as "active" and "passive" defense of naval shore establishments. Active measures included the use of anti-aircraft guns, searchlights, devices for accurate fire control, and, particularly, planes to attack approaching bombers. Passive measures included isolation of facilities; underground shelters and storage with duplication of vital stores at a distance from main warehouses; camouflage of all kinds; and such other measures as the flooding of dry docks when they were not in use.

Essentially these recommendations, destined to be as sound in 1941 as they were when made in 1916, were based on three assumptions: the enemy would take attack risks commensurate with the possible resultant gains; local defense could not be perfection itself but must be related to naval defense as a whole; no system of defense should be more costly than the value of its effect.

Considering "active" defense, the new 3-inch, 50-caliber gun, designed to reach an altitude of 24,000 feet, and the 4-inch, 50-caliber, designed for 41,000 feet, in theory covered the limit of visibility for antiaircraft use. In practice against such small targets, moving so fast, it appeared essential that these guns be grouped in batteries but even then they would not be fully effective at night or in thick weather. Therefore enemy bombers at 6,000 to 10,000 feet would, in the opinion of the board, often be immune to anything except the one truly effective defense, fighter planes.

Fundamentally, declared the board, the defense of the Navy's 74 bases on shore was the Army's problem. It was merely reiter-

ating a fundamental division of duties between the Army and the
Navy when it recommended small naval defense units of two combat planes and two seaplanes for each naval district, trained to cooperate with presumably much larger Army defense units. While
the war that now appeared imminent might not bring air attacks
upon the Atlantic coast, the board was providing against these in a
way consistent with the defense obligations laid upon each Service,
including those at the Canal Zone, where in the board's opinion
two seaplanes with trained personnel should be ready to work with
the Army.

Some effort to carry the General Board's recommendations into
effect was very shortly made. The Secretary of the Navy's order
issued in August, 1916, if it did not please the aviators, at least
clarified the administration of aviation. It directed that the Office
of Naval Operations consider all recommendations by the General
Board and then distribute the measures to be taken among the
various bureaus. It held the repair work by aviators in the field
down to minor repairs, prohibiting them from making alterations
to planes without going through all the bureau channels. On the
whole, in thus decentralizing rather than centralizing, at a moment
when aviation needed strong pushing, it appears to have retarded
rather than expedited the accomplishment of the board's real purposes. The order did, however, recognize that aviation must be a
definite part of the Navy's program of preparing for war and
this could be taken as a sign that aviation was "coming of age" in
the Navy. This was the view of those who recognized a case of too
many cooks but were less outspoken about it than Rear Admiral
Fiske, who would insist, to the day of his death, that he "lost flesh
. . . in fruitless exasperation" because "if . . . the Division of
Aeronautics had not been actually abolished, we could have started
flotillas of bombing-machines and torpedo planes across the ocean
on April 7, 1917."

The admiral's view was, of course, exactly opposed to that of
Captain McKean, who had been busily "digging into the foundations" and who would later say of his own policy in the autumn of
1916 that the "aircraft was simply another type of naval craft.
If we needed them at all, we needed them to make up a part of
a team . . . as we needed . . . destroyers . . . scouts . . .
cruisers or battleships; or, if they were such a peculiar animal
that they could not take their place in the fleet as a ship, and be
associated with the rest of the unit and as a part of the team, they

did not belong in the Navy; they were foreign matter." While this could hardly be called enthusiasm, McKean's reorganization did have some valuable features, such as better regulation of the inspection of materials and of construction. It had been the practice to send inspectors, somewhat at random, to plants from which they made their reports directly to Bristol, thus confusing the question of cognizance. Under McKean's plan every inspector received formal orders to report for duty under the officer specifically designated by the Navy Department as inspector of machinery for the particular plant. This tended to keep correspondence in official channels and thus diminish, if not entirely eliminate, letters between manufacturers and individual aviators.

Methods of testing planes were similarly modified. Previously, these tests had been made by boards of three aviators, who flew the planes and then submitted reports upon design, construction, and performance to the Chief of Naval Operations. Final acceptance or refusal, while actually made in writing by bureaus to which these reports were referred, generally represented merely formal ratifications of board findings. With mass production of planes in prospect, qualified aviators obviously could not spare the time for such tests, and the new plan provided for agreements with contractors under which they hired civilian pilots to make all preliminary tests. After these had been completed a final flight would be made, with a naval pilot either at the controls or riding as an observer.

Under another department order issued at this time, Pensacola was reorganized to conform more nearly to the pattern of the navy yards. Mustin himself, as commandant, had proposed several changes, among them the assignment of "an experienced Naval Constructor," by which term he meant to imply that he wanted Hunsaker; a faint hope indeed because Rear Admiral Taylor had just had Hunsaker recalled from Cambridge to head the new "Aircraft Division" of the Bureau of Construction and Repair. Other things that Mustin wanted were better tools and equipment for making repairs, greater facilities for experimental construction, and a wind tunnel. The Secretary's order went part way with him, establishing at Pensacola a manufacturing department and an experimental department. It was specified that these should be headed by officers who were qualified pilots but it was not specified that the commandant to whom they were responsible should also be an aviator. In the order of importance, the tasks and missions of the station were outlined as follows: (1) training of personnel, commissioned and enlisted, for aeronautic service with the Fleet; (2) repair and maintenance of school aircraft; (3) testing of new aircraft, new instruments, guns, bombs, and other devices connected with aircraft; (4) experimental work, consisting primarily of remodeling the design of existing machines to adapt them better for naval use, and development of new types of aircraft, motors, instruments, devices, and the like; (5) construction of new types of aircraft and motors; (6) collection of data on design, purchases, etc., of aircraft which are based on actual experience and making suggestions and recommendations of lines of investigation for the bureaus concerned which might lead to improvements in types of aircraft motors, etc.

It was sound policy to put training of personnel at the head of the list because the importance of this factor needed recognition. Actually, it had come nearly to a stop at Pensacola except on the lighter-than-air side, where McCrary and Maxfield were making considerable progress in instructing with the free balloon. Their pupils came along well, even though they had not had what Hunsaker had recommended for them, the advantage of previous instruction under Von Parseval, the German balloon expert. The same progress could not be made with the station's kite balloon because only a few days after it had at last been received and moored above the station it was torn adrift in a sharp gale and so badly damaged that it needed many months of repairs.

Lack of training naturally delayed the carrying out of all Pensacola's other assigned tasks; indeed, it emphasized the many material lacks from which aviation was suffering. There must be planes to fly and there must be men who knew how to fly them. Moreover, beneath the swelling black shadow of approaching war could be discerned other grim facts that lent weight to demands for complete plans to standardize not only personnel but also design, production, inspection, and testing, chief among these facts being several fatal accidents during the years 1915 and 1916.

The investigation of Lt. (jg) M. L. Stolz's crash on May 8, 1915, had indicated that he had been killed through having his head thrown back upon the motor. When Lieutenants Saufley and Rockwell, on June 9, 1916, were killed in planes which, like that of Stolz, were of the "pusher" type, the circumstances of these three tragedies led to strong recommendations that "pushers" be abandoned for the safer "tractor" type. Captain Bristol supported this view although he did remark that such a decision would suggest to the world "that we are arranging our machines to provide for hitting the water" instead of for staying in the air. If he had added that the change of type would have the effect of leaving the United States, at this critical moment, with only four planes in commission, none of them suitable for training purposes, he would have presented the strongest possible reason for speeding up the whole program for aviation. By the following April one would have no need to be a flier to appreciate most of the reasons for haste, but even the pilots would hardly recognize the picture of Naval Aviation as it would then be. To all intents and purposes there would appear, on a fresh canvas, a new sketch, followed by a clearer drawing and a painting in brighter colors.

CHAPTER VII

Effects of the War in Europe

THROUGHOUT 1916 inventors were busily trying out new ideas in flying, the most significant of these being the Hewitt-Sperry Automatic Aeroplane. Equipped with the gyroscopic stabilizer, a new steering gear called a Servomotor to control rudders and ailerons, and another special device to cut off the motors after any desired run, this plane had startling possibilities. Launched from a catapult or sent up from the surface of the sea, it could climb to a predetermined height, level off, and take up a prescribed course. After covering the distance for which it had been set, it could drop bombs or, if adjusted to do so, dive back to earth. While it remained in the air, however, its course could not be changed, and for this reason any inaccuracy of its compass, combined with any miscalculation of the force or direction of the wind, make it liable to serious error. Nevertheless, this was another important step along the road leading toward the accurate robot pilot used today.

Lieut. Theodore S. Wilkinson, one of the Navy's most brilliant young mathematicians and destined to become one of its prominent flag officers, made several flights beside Lawrence Sperry, with the plane kept under its automatic control until it was ready to come down. Wilkinson reported the control to be "adequate and excellent" and suggested that the Hammond wireless, already tested with underwater torpedoes, might be adapted for use when the plane was sent up with no one aboard it. Outweighing the value of the plane, however, stood its cost, the complications of transporting it and of launching it, its lack of any "homing" device, and its lack of complete accuracy in flight. Without such accuracy it might serve against a large land target but not against anything relatively so small as a ship. Although it was the most spectacular of several efforts to break the trail toward today's guided missiles, it necessarily remained through the years immediately ahead not much more than an object for further study.

Meanwhile Curtiss was working on modifications to enable his planes to carry an additional 250 pounds, an increase to be represented by machine guns and ammunition; an effort aimed at producing what the General Board, on the recommendation of Towers and Mustin, was now advocating: the high-speed fighter. Other designers were trying to improve the catapult by eliminating those complicated rails and tackles, so necessary in getting planes into launching position but so obstructive to a ship's guns and turrets. Such efforts were getting rather less encouragement from the Navy Department than they had received when aviation was under Captain Chambers. The interest of both Bristol and McKean was more administrative than scientific.

Captain Chambers himself sought to keep in touch with the experimenters but the truth was that his position was becoming more and more anomalous. Still *in* the office of aviation, he was no longer really *of* it, and with the Navy Department paying so little attention to him it was only natural that designers and manufacturers both came to consider him less and less. Indeed, he became so obscure that the Navy Department wrote him a letter in November, 1916, asking what he was doing, and thus learned that he was at Cohoes, New York, studying a new design for a helicopter. This design proved to be novel in many respects and Captain McKean did express interest in it, but its weight was too great, its motors too complex, and its controls in flight too complicated. Moreover, said McKean, "none has succeeded in solving the problem of safe descent in case of engine failure." Captain Chambers might do better to return to Washington and work on the "aerial navigator" which had long occupied him. One advantage to be gained in Washington would be that of talking with the man whom Rear Admiral Taylor had just secured to head his bureau's research into planes, instruments, and especially, wind-tunnel experiments—the very civilian expert who had done so much with Curtiss, Dr. A. H. Zahm.

The lifting capacity of planes came up again for study by the Bureau of Ordnance during efforts to equal if not improve upon what was understood to be the practice abroad in carrying torpedoes. When Construction and Repair fixed the carrying limit at two torpedoes of 300 pounds each, this fell far short of the Ordnance plan for supplying torpedoes of 1,000 pounds; the smaller one, even if it scored a direct hit, could not be expected to damage a capital ship very seriously. It followed that although designs for the carrying and the releasing devices were made at this time, their completion meant little more than that the aviation mill had begun to grind steadily upon whatever grist might be destined to come out of it. This was at least slightly encouraging to Rear Admiral Fiske, who constantly urged that only an improved weapon would furnish the United States with the means to attack and defeat decisively the experienced, seasoned German Fleet.

Here he was again rather at odds with the General Board. The board held that masses of material and personnel must be assembled at a given point in order to exert maximum force—masses of which aircraft could form little part. Fiske, on the other hand, while readily admitting that the enemy must be hit hard, insisted that aircraft, with the prime requisites of power and mobility, could hit hard and do it in the spot where the blow was least expected. "Is there," he asked, "no device by means of which large units of power can be carried, which is not subject to the limitations of speed and size that restrict a land battleship"—by which he meant a tank— "to small dimensions? Yes . . . it is called the battleplane." Should not its possibilities, "not only as a scout and accessory, but also as a major instrument of warfare," be immediately investigated? So vociferous in public did the admiral become upon these points that the Secretary of the Navy twice thought it proper to "slip a gag into his mouth," but notwithstanding that action Fiske continued to insist that planes and pilots could be produced in six months, while an adequate battle fleet would need years, to build it, to train its men, and to bring it to fighting pitch.

Supporting much of what Fiske said was Towers, who had returned from Europe in October with information and opinions of importance to the General Board in shaping its further recommendations. He reported that the British looked upon aeronautics as an important branch: "they do not consider they could get along without it and they are extending the use of it more and more." They had, he said, taken very young lads who had never done anything, trained them, and made fairly good officers out of them. The result was astonishing. On the material side, he described the British as realistic in classifying their planes as expendable from the moment of issue, and in making appropriate provision for replacements.

In dirigibles, the British had finally adopted the Zeppelin type, having become converted when these German craft, navigated by radio bearings, made attacks through snowstorms and rode out heavy gales. "A zeppelin," commented Towers, "can do the work of a light cruiser." It had higher speed, better vision, was less apt to be caught and could do many things much better. He held that the Zeppelin, because of its longer cruising radius, would be for years to come the best type for scouting.

Continuing, he spoke of British progress in photographic reconnaissance as "the most wonderful thing." Photographs taken at 14,000 feet had clearly shown the turrets on battleships and even brought out the chipped edges of concrete docks and piers. In tracking enemy shipping and submarines such photographs had been amazingly helpful. Further, he described the British as having "very radical ideas," the latest school advocating a small land machine on each capital ship to be sent up in battle and make a landing alongside a destroyer in the rear. Service of this sort, in battle, was considered as of sufficient value to justify the possible loss of both the plane and its pilot, and to provide that service the British were building planes that could fly for four hours at a speed of 95 mph equipped with radio good for 50 miles. Among these was the new Sopwith, able to climb 10,000 feet in about 12 minutes and good for a speed of 125 mph—altogether a much better performer than any contemporary French, Italian or German model.

As for carriers, Towers had found these to be, for the moment at least, not in great favor. If the United States were not to build them, he would agree, under protest, with the board's proposal to put two seaplanes on each battleship, four seaplanes on each cruiser, but he tried to convince the board that small, fast landplanes would be better for both types of ships. In this he assumed that the United States would improve its designs, and he recommended building a motor as good as the British "rotary motors with very blunt noses" and the Rolls-Royce, which he described as "splendid" by contrast with the Curtiss types used on this side of the Atlantic. Only fast planes could escape antiaircraft guns because, while the Royal Navy had made the 3-inch gun standard aboard ship, better and heavier guns were coming. German guns of the moment were shooting both shrapnel and explosive shell up to 18,000 feet and yet the Royal Navy's planes were successfully patrolling over the western front and actually making bombing raids into Belgium. Surely, insisted Towers, there lay in these facts a clear lesson for a nation likely to be drawn into the war.

Confirming Towers, Mustin also urged the use of landplanes, especially because, since they were not hampered by pontoons, their performance in the air was so much better. He considered an allowance of two planes to a ship to be meager and held that every available space should be used to carry more. While he and Towers appear to have represented the minority opinion among the aviators, they stuck to their guns and their arguments had at least some effect when the board, in November, 1916, brought out another of its reports. It would not go so far as to propose the use of landplanes but it did call for one type of small seaplane, weighing only about 1,250 instead of 4,000 pounds, this type to be complemented by scouting planes and patrol planes reduced from 7,000 to 5,000 pounds. A marked increase in numbers was stipulated, the new total to be 564 service planes, supported by such training planes as might prove necessary, with 19 kite balloons, 20 nonrigid dirigibles, and one experimental Zeppelin. In tabular form the proposed allocation was as follows:

	SEA-PLANES	LAND-PLANES	KITES	RIGIDS	NON-RIGIDS
For the present fleet					
2 seaplanes for each of 12 BBs.	24				
4 seaplanes for each of 9 armored cruisers.	36				
4 seaplanes for each of 32 merchant "C" fleet scouts.	128				
For ships authorized or building					
2 seaplanes for each of 15 BBs.	30				
4 seaplanes for each of 6 battle cruisers.	24				
4 seaplanes for each of 10 scouts	40				
For land services					
For the Advance Base Force.	4	2	2		

For coastal patrol	SEA- PLANES	LAND- PLANES	KITES	NON- RIGIDS	RIGIDS
7 seaplanes, 1 nonrigid per naval district (ex. Great Lakes) and outlying possessions	112			16	
For defense of naval stations, 13 units	26	26	13		
Experimental					1
School machines			as required		
TOTALS	424	28	15	16	1
25% reserve	105 [*sic*]	7	4	4	0
GRAND TOTALS	529 *	35	19	20	1

* Divided between 352 small seaplanes, 177 large seaplanes.

This was a long-range program for building up a real air arm and its issue at this time served to prepare the department and the Navy generally, in some measure, for the relatively enormous expansion which was nearer than many then realized.

Since even the additional aircraft contemplated in the program would obviously have to be supported from shore bases, the selection and preparation of these assumed importance, and to make these choices of sites the Secretary of the Navy by authority of the Naval Appropriations Act of August 29, 1916, appointed a special board, headed by Rear Adm. James M. Helm. In laying down the policy to guide this board Captain McKean was careful to say that "there is not enough experience . . . in the world for me to recommend what should comprise an aviation base," but he did suggest there should be "at least one station on the Atlantic and one on the Pacific." Captain Bristol, going much further, asked for bases on both Chesapeake and Narragansett bays, as well as for fuel and supply stations at Jupiter Inlet, Key West, Guantánamo, Samana Bay, San Juan, the mouth of the Columbia River, San Francisco, San Diego, both ends of the Panama Canal, Hawaii, Guam, and Corregidor. To these, he said, might well be added others at Magdalena Bay, the Galápagos Islands, the Gulf of Guayaquil, and the Gulf of Fonseca. Out of this list the Helm Board did not, however, definitely select any one place. Instead, after declaring that aircraft and submarines might well be maintained and supported from common bases, the board held that choice of exact locations ought to be made jointly by the Army and the Navy, thus ensuring the satisfaction of both services. The only definite recommendation in the report submitted early in December, 1916, was for the spending of $100,000 to make Pensacola a really efficient base for submarines and destroyers.

While the Helm Board was still sitting another board had been brought together, as the result of a suggestion made on October 11 by the Acting Secretary of War. He had proposed that he and the Secretary of the Navy nominate officers to consider methods of organizing a lighter-than-air service, with a view to securing cooperation between the Army and Navy in the development of airships and fixing their respective responsibility. The suggestion was agreed to and the General Board, at the request of the Secretary of the Navy, named as members Capts. Hugh Rodman and Josiah S. McKean, with Lieutenant Towers as the one aviation expert among the three. They sat with Lt. Col. G. O. Squier of the Signal Corps, Maj. S. D. Embick of the Coast Artillery, and Maj. D. T. Moore of the Field Artillery; curiously enough sitting without formal precept and without any identifying designation. The Chief of Naval Operations spoke of them as the "Joint Board, Army and Navy, re Division of Aeronautic Cognizance," a cumbersome expression which eventually would be shortened to Joint Army and Navy Board on Aeronautic Cognizance. It should be understood that this group was a different one from the already existing Joint Army and Navy Board, which brought together high-ranking representatives of both Services to study questions of national strategy.

The new "Cognizance Board" disposed of the lighter-than-air question by recommending that it be handled by men who most thoroughly understood it. This was to be accomplished by the appointment of three officers from each Service, all technical experts, under the direction of the Chief Constructor of the Navy, to supervise the building of a Zeppelin. Experience gained from experiments would then lead to appropriate planning for the future, in which the board believed airships "would prove a valuable asset." This recommendation was made promptly but not before this same board found itself confronted with other aeronautics problems passed on to it largely because it existed and was in session.

The new questions involved all types of aircraft and their assignment to the Services. Which should be responsible for what, and where should lines of demarcation be drawn between areas of responsibility? It immediately became clear that in the event of war the two Services would be operating together, with precedence going sometimes to the Navy, sometimes to the Army. Lines of demarcation should therefore approximate the coastlines and the division of responsibility could be made only in general terms. As finally accepted, these divisions were:

Army:
(a) aircraft operating in conjunction with the mobile army;
(b) aircraft required for fire control for coast defenses;
(c) aircraft required for the defense of fortifications, navy yards, arsenals, cities, and shipbuilding plants, powder works, or other similar important utilities, whether public or private, that are located on shore.

Navy:
(a) aircraft operating in conjunction with the fleets;
(b) aircraft operating from shore bases for overseas scouting;
(c) aircraft operating under the commandants of naval districts and advanced bases.

These broad definitions differed little from the original view of the Chief of Naval Operations that the Navy should be responsible for aviation with the Fleet, for overseas scouting by dirigibles and patrol planes, and for antiaircraft defense of naval establishments ashore; the Army for all air operations with troops, for air spotting of coast defense gunfire, and for antiaircraft defense of fortifications.

The board also dwelt upon the vital need for coordinating the two air arms. "A war with a first class power," it wrote, "will find the two services constantly operating together"; adding that "the coastline and the water areas adjacent thereto will become a theater of joint operations." Because of these recommendations and others it made as time passed, the "Cognizance Board" lived on until the authorities realized that it should be properly authorized and constituted. On June 24, 1919, it was redesignated the Joint Army and Navy Board on Aeronautics and from December 29, 1919, until its demise in 1948 it was known as the Aeronautical Board.

The value of such a group was so obvious that without waiting for this study of inter-service policy, which did not appear until

March 12, 1917, Benson, through the Secretary of the Navy, in February referred to it the old question of selecting bases. Fearing long delay and perhaps an ultimate decision no more definite than that of the Helm Board, he proposed a list of bases which he considered should be immediately established, naming the vicinities of Massachusetts Bay, Newport, New York, Cape May, Hampton Roads, Key West, Galveston, and the Panama Canal. Asked by the Secretary of the Navy to expedite its comment on this list, the Cognizance Board was only two days in approving it, with the substitution of Frenchmen's Bay, Maine, for Galveston and the addition, for the Pacific, of San Francisco, Puget Sound, San Diego, and Hawaii. As to specific sites in these vicinities, however, the board held that because the bases should be for joint occupation by detachments and equipment from both Services, selection ought to be made for each seacoast, by groups made up of expert representatives of the Services.

Officers were quickly appointed to pick the actual sites. The Atlantic Coast Panel, headed by Colonel Haan, USA, included, as its naval members, Captain Cunningham, USMC, with Lieut. E. F. Johnson, USN, for the First and Second Naval Districts; Towers for the Third, Fourth, and Fifth Districts; Bellinger for the Seventh and the Eighth. From the Navy's standpoint elements of importance were the estimated cruising radius of a dirigible and a seaplane, and these elements naturally suggested bases close to the ocean that must be covered, whereas the Army, speaking generally, required bases near the large cities it was expected to defend. Otherwise, all bases must be good sized, for fields and buildings, and in reasonable proximity to public utilities.

As a result of the studies made by the East Coast Panel ten sites were selected. Squantum, Massachusetts, was named as an army base, with provision for some use by the Navy if necessary, while Provincetown was designated as the Navy's, with similar occasional use by the Army. Montauk, Cape May, Hampton Roads, Savannah, Key West, Galveston, and Coco Solo were to be solely for the Navy, while Rockaway Beach was the one site chosen as "joint" from the outset. Eventually Chatham replaced Provincetown and Savannah was abandoned as unsuitable for the purpose.

The West Coast Panel, on which Captain Cunningham again represented the Navy, chose Ediz Hook on Puget Sound and Tongue Point near Astoria, Oregon, as combined air and submarine bases, with San Diego as another major air base. For operating bases the panel selected Morro, Monterey, San Francisco, Humboldt Bay, Coos Bay, Grays Harbor, Port Townshend, Bellingham Bay, and Lake Ozette.

All these discussions were precipitated and stimulated by current events. The visits to the United States of the German submarines *Deutschland* and U-53, during which the latter was able to sink five Allied merchantmen, sharpened the points at issue. As diplomatic relations with Germany hourly became worse, the lack of properly prepared bases became more and more a matter of significance. Within two weeks of the receipt of reports from the coastal panels the Navy Department began drawing plans for 11 bases, the sites chosen being in conformity with the recommendations made. The plans called for an average expenditure of about $300,000 on each base but an additional $1,000,000 was proposed for an experimental air station on the disused grounds of the Jamestown Exposition, together with a further $750,000 for a training school at North Island, California, and the same amount for adding to the air facilities at Pearl Harbor. At the moment of making these plans and estimates a total of 11 new bases loomed large, but by comparison with what lay only a few months ahead the number seems very small. Actual construction brought into being by World War I included 11 training establishments, 12 patrol stations and 13 refueling stations on the Atlantic coast; an assembly and repair base in Pauillac and 14 operating bases in France; six bases in the British Isles, three in Italy, and one in the Azores; one special bomber base in England and six similar ones in France; a total of 68 in all. What it had first been planned to spend was a trifle when compared with the $30,000,000 soon to go into this construction—a prodigious sum when considered in terms of the number of officers and men who were on duty in Naval Aviation at the end of 1916.

At that time the commissioned personnel numbered 59, of whom 26 were naval aviators and 30 were students, the other three being Naval Constructors Richardson, Westervelt, and Hunsaker. Of enlisted men there were 93 with the rating of airman, 125 students, with 233 mechanics and nonfliers, bringing the total to 431. There were not enough instructors for those in training, but Commander McCrary's recommendation that civilians be hired for these posts was not followed, both because the Bureau of Navigation did not look favorably upon the plan and because such experts were extremely hard to find. Thus, although the schools at Pensacola were equipped to handle two classes a year, each with 64 officers and the same number of mechanics, such an enrollment was difficult to handle without sufficient instructors, and no appreciable increase in aviation personnel occurred before the outbreak of war.

In a group so shorthanded it could not be expected that morale would be very high. McCrary reported that "there is a great deal of discontent and uncertainty among officers and men and something will have to be done soon or wholesale applications for detachment may come in." He spoke of a number of men "who cannot draw pay for the reason that the 96-list is full," by which he referred to the number fixed by law as eligible for extra money. As a means of lifting morale he proposed a scouting trip of five planes from Pensacola to New Orleans; a flight eventually made, after some months' delay, through the help of Towers in Washington.

Efforts of this sort, added to natural desires to "get into it somewhere," brought in many of the newly authorized 200 enlistments. Enrolling as landsmen for training, the men went to Pensacola where they were immediately examined for rating as machinist mate, second class, or quartermaster, second class. Those who failed were given three months' training and a re-examination, the special incentive being the provision that the top men in each class would get flight pay after six months' service and, at the end of a year, be examined for first class ratings. This had the effect of expanding Pensacola to capacity and putting it on a double shift, but this difficult situation was slightly relieved when Towers arranged with the Goodyear Company for pilot training in balloons at the Akron plant. A morale-raising move made at this time by the Navy Department was the issue of proposals for distinctive uniforms for fliers, with special insignia.

So stood Naval Aviation when on December 12, 1916, Captain Bristol was finally detached from it, to continue a very distinguished career elsewhere in the Navy. His post, without his formal designation as Commander of the Air Service, went to Capt. (shortly Rear Adm.) Albert Gleaves, previously commanding the Atlantic Destroyer Force from the cruiser *Seattle*. Handing over the responsibilities, Bristol, realistic in the outline he gave his relief, was bluntly so in his conclusion:

Don't get any idea that I have any pessimistic view of airplanes for Naval use. I believe in them. They are essential to our fleet just as much as all other types of war vessels we have or are providing. It is only that I give you the clear unadulterated facts so that you can tackle the problem as it is with no fictitious or romantic version of the situation. There has been an erroneous campaign of education going on throughout the world regarding aircraft. This war has been a Godsend for this education. The facts brought out by the use of aircraft in this war are befogged by romance, newspaper known exaggerations, the advertising of airplane manufacturers for pecuniary benefit, and the one-sided reports of operators, also colored for military reasons. It has taken, and will take, close study and careful investigation to separate the facts from fiction.

Whatever Rear Admiral Gleaves might expect, it could certainly be no immediate centralization of authority in himself. The Chief of Naval Operations was determined to keep aviation inside the traditional bureau organization. Until he found he could not fight a war that way he did so.

CHAPTER VIII

Preparing to Fight

THE Naval Appropriations Bill signed by President Wilson on August 29, 1916, provided $3,500,000 for aviation. It authorized the establishment of a naval flying corps, which, although it is still so authorized, never did come into existence. Further, it provided for a reserve flying corps and for the purchase of aircraft, including ten planes to be lent to the naval militia. Altogether, this bill represented a long-overdue advance; the opening of a new era in naval flying at which pioneers like Towers, Bellinger, Read, and the rest must have rubbed their eyes and asked: "How can these things be?"

The eyes of all those in aviation had naturally been turned toward what had been going on in the air over Europe. Because of obvious difficulties in air operations from the sea, European landplanes had progressed more rapidly than seaplanes. The Royal Naval Air Service, however, had employed both types in antisubmarine reconnaissance, scouting, spotting of gunfire, bombing, and aerial defense of the Grand Fleet. None of these efforts had been entirely successful but there had been enough progress to justify the Admiralty in pushing aviation vigorously. Besides developing blimps, it had built aircraft tenders capable of accompanying the fleet and it was projecting its first carriers. British flying boats, known as F-boats, were modifications of the Curtiss *America* which, as has been said, had been taken to England by Commander Porte; and it is to be noted that it was a further modification of the F-boat which became, after American motors were adapted to it, the United States F-5-L.

Meanwhile the Royal Flying Corps had been active, and at the very moment when Congress was debating this Naval Appropriations Act of 1916 these British airmen were engaged in their greatest effort to date, the battle of the Somme. At the beginning of that battle the corps had 28 squadrons, a number increased, in the face of losses, to 35 by November, 1916. As Saunders remarks in his history of British air power, aviation had by the latter date become a vital part of the war machine, a fact by no means overlooked by those on this side of the Atlantic who had urged the passage by Congress of an adequate appropriation bill.

The bill had not been passed without a hard struggle. Bristol had begun it by asking for $13,000,000, a sum out of which he hoped $6,000,000 would be spent in building two carriers. The Secretary of the Navy and the Chief of Naval Operations had butchered this figure down to $2,000,000, after which the General Board, acting on the request of Representative Britten of the Naval Affairs Committee that it make a study, had patched the cripple up to $5,000,-000. Rear Admiral Fiske told the Naval Affairs Committee that this last amount was ridiculously inadequate, taking the occasion to express "dismay" over the failure of his successor in Naval Operations to push "the work . . . of establishing a Division of Aeronautics and of developing" that branch. He had urged the assembly of 1,000 planes "to meet an attacking force" and "drop large bombs and launch torpedoes." He had described the way in which these planes, properly used, could completely disrupt an enemy's attempt to land from small boats. He had spoken of aeronautics as "the thing on which we can get to work quicker, and by which we can accomplish more than by anything else."

Money would stimulate private firms, declared Fiske, citing Secretary Whitney's appeal to Congress in 1886 for a new steel, armored Navy, when Whitney had insisted that if the "manufacturers of the country" knew the Navy had money available they would "come after it." Just this encouragement was needed by the makers of aircraft, said Fiske, and no time must be lost because "we are weak in battle-cruisers and in air . . . but in a year we can do much in air and little . . . in cruisers."

It is not hard to imagine the admiral's feelings when, even against these strong pleas, the Secretary of the Navy won the vote of a majority of the House Committee for $2,000,000; when even conference with the Senate raised the figure only to $3,500,000. To the aviators, however, an amount relatively so much greater than any they had known must have appeared fabulous. Although all chance of getting carriers was gone, they could hope for a real program of plane building and training.

Among the manufacturers, Burgess was then struggling with problems of stability, Curtiss with problems of motors and pontoons; Martin and Sturtevant were concentrating on the design of floats. Nevertheless, within two months of the act's passage, contracts had been let for 47 planes and two kite balloons, and before the year 1916 was out the figure for planes had been increased to 60. Curtiss obtained the largest contract calling for 30 N-9 seaplanes. This type was an adaptation of the Army's JN training plane on which Curtiss, with Richardson's assistance, had substituted a float for the conventional landing gear and, to compensate for the added weight, had increased the wing span. With an OX motor, a good propeller, and a new type of automobile radiator, it was to become the Navy's basic training plane. "Generally speaking," said Hunsaker, "when an N-9 cracked up, the pilot survived because of the low landing-speed and the tractor design."

In motors, the immediate results of testing numerous designs at the Washington Navy Yard had been "disappointing." Up to the fall of 1916 only two types had developed the required horsepower and performed well. While the existence of a plant where motors could be scientifically tested was an incentive to manufacturers, because it meant that hit-and-miss methods had been abandoned, they were still so short of producing first-class motors that Bristol proposed buying foreign makes. As a result Wright-Martin ordered 450 Hispano-Suiza motors from France and, notwithstanding the demands of the French Army, managed to get 100 delivered within the next year. Less fortunate was the Sterling Company, which was not permitted by the Admiralty to have even the blueprints of the British Sunbeam motor. Similarly, although there was correspondence on such foreign motors as the Rhone, the Gnome, the Anzani, the Renault, and the Salmson, none of these was bought at this time. If any attention was paid to a suggestion from the naval attaché at Berlin that a sudden end to the war in Europe would make it possible to buy for, say, $10,000,000 all the planes and dirigibles the United States could need, no action on the suggestion was taken. One very important result of this talk of buying abroad, however, was the entry into plane building of American automobile builders. Eventually it would be their skilled technicians who would be instrumental in producing that very useful plane motor, the Liberty.

In lighter-than-air craft, the Navy Department's first design had called for a rigid dirigible with 20 hours' endurance at a top speed of 60 mph under a full load of fuel, a crew of 20, and four machine guns. With this full load it must be able to climb to 4,000 feet; with fuel reduced to five hours' supply it much reach 10,000 feet. Its radio range was to be 400 miles, and it must be "capable of landing on water." Very shortly, these specifications were modified to reduce the crew to 12, the endurance to six hours at a maximum speed of 50 mph, and the radio range to 200 miles. The full load ceiling was raised, however, to 5,000 feet.

The training dirigible design, after modification of the original one, prescribed 45 mph with 12 hours' endurance at 35, a crew of three, a 150-mile radio range, and the ability and strength both to land on the water and to be towed through it. The length was to be 160 feet, the diameter 31.5 feet, the gasoline capacity 100 gallons, and, because weight was considered more important than provision for emergency, there was to be but one motor.

In January, 1917, Hunsaker's plans made it clear that this "B" airship for training could more than meet the specifications. These plans were accordingly approved, and in February the Secretary of the Navy unexpectedly ordered 16 ships to be built immediately. Of five firms who wanted to undertake this work, only one, Connecticut Aircraft, had ever built a dirigible and even that firm had had many difficulties. No rubber manufacturer had ever made a hydrogen-resisting fabric. For these reasons a conference held in Rear Admiral Taylor's office, finally decided to pool materials, information, and experience in order to produce craft with speeds of 35 mph at $42,000 each. Under this arrangement Goodyear built an erecting and testing shed at Akron, Ohio, in two months. Goodrich hired an engineer from Lebaudy in Paris. Pigeon Frazer built the cars for the Connecticut Company, while the United States Rubber Company made the fabric. Hall-Scott of San Francisco built motors. Nevertheless, when the Secretary of the Navy proposed that another 24 nonrigids be built, Rear Admiral Taylor made strong recommendations against doing this until the value of the type had been demonstrated. Since the much better "C-type" was soon to follow, it was fortunate that the admiral's recommendations were approved.

The first A-class airship, which would finally be delivered at Pensacola in the spring of 1917, was a failure from the start. It could hardly get off the ground, its motor was poor, and its envelope leaked. Nevertheless, because its builders, the Connecticut Company, had lost so heavily upon it, the contract price was paid. Soon afterward, when its car was being towed over the water, it was so badly damaged as to be not worth repairing; it was deflated and eventually broken up for its parts. That it should have been a failure is understandable after reading what Commander Mc-Crary, who had watched its building, had to say of the builders: "It could hardly be called an aircraft company. It consisted of a New Haven R. R. Lawyer [*sic.*] as financial backer; an ex-Amusement Park Concession operator as manager; an Austrian who claimed to have piloted a dirigible and two German mechanics who claimed to have been members of the crew of a Zeppelin. The 'plant' was a six-by-eight office . . . and a rented boat-shed."

Inevitably the greatly expanded construction program involved problems of inspection not fully solved by the recent reorganization of that service. Some plants had an officer assigned under Construction and Repair, others had one under Steam Engineering, and still others had one inspector for both bureaus. Where these inspectors were aviators, they were certain to have the goodwill of the contractors, but they were also quite certain to be handicapped because they were familiar with aircraft as fliers rather than as technicians. Their reports to the bureaus could not be as clear on the mechanical details as was desirable, especially because their scarcity in numbers made them likely to be transferred from one plant to another before they had mastered these details in the first one. Richardson, of course, was fully qualified because he was a flier as well as an engineer and a naval architect. The others were not so useful as inspectors, although as fliers they could not but consider themselves experts. Inclined to expect miracles, they were sometimes impatient of the plodding research often necessary to solve some problem which they thought should be simple. They were inclined to blame the bureaus for any shortcoming in a plane, especially when the fault led, as it sometimes did, to an accident.

Hunsaker, examining the Army's methods, discovered that its inspectors included an officer—presumably a flier—two consulting engineers, and as many as 30 civilian experts. He immediately recommended that the Navy also employ civilians, dividing the details of their duties just as the work was divided between the bureaus and thus permitting the release of aviators to other duties. In general this plan of Hunsaker's was adopted with good results; at Buffalo and at Boston, for example, the employment of civilian engineers served to answer many technical questions more readily.

The release of these aviators did not, however, solve the personnel problem. Nowhere in the Navy was the shortage of officers more acute than in aviation, which had never had enough adequately to assist Captains Chambers and Bristol in building up trained staffs for the bureaus or even in filling the training quotas or the regular classes at Pensacola. When production meant more planes, and also meant the prospective duty of training reserve, militia, and coast guardsmen as well as naval students, the lack of proper instructors was more than ever apparent. If Pensacola was to be assigned the officers and men it needed, these could come only from a Fleet already undermanned. On the request that these transfers be nevertheless authorized, the Secretary of the Navy's note, "Do not take them out now!" naturally resulted in delaying the training program. This was very marked toward the end of 1916, when more planes were gradually becoming available.

Congressional hearings upon the provisions of the bill for a Naval Flying Corps had brought out many arguments. Admiral Benson had opposed taking in civilians, training them for six months, and then giving them commissions. He preferred to see enlisted men taught to "chauffeur" officers who, as observers or on combat missions, would be merely passengers. Captain Bristol, insisting that command of aircraft required officers of the same skill as the commanders of surface vessels, advocated taking the civilians into such branches as the submarines for coast defense and letting the regular officers become fliers. Rear Admiral Blue, Chief of the Bureau of Navigation and therefore the target for every branch of the Navy wanting more officers and men, came out strongly for the separate corps as the only means of "creating, within a reasonable time," a force adequate to the Navy's need. Such a force, he said, could have only a nucleus of regulars. Other officers who appeared at the hearings argued that a civilian could be trained to fly in about six months, whereas waiting for graduates of the Naval Academy would mean waiting for six years while they got their full seagoing training. Since the six months' man could not be expected to perform any but aviation duties, these officers thought it logical that he be assigned to a separate corps. They therefore advocated legislation that would follow, in general, a draft prepared by Saufley before he was killed, a draft already approved by both the Secretary of the Navy and the President.

It had finally been written into this act of 1916 that there should be a Naval Flying Corps consisting of 150 officers and 350 enlisted men of the Navy and Marine Corps; to be in addition to quotas already established by law for these Services, but specifically not including in these stipulated figures those who might be already on temporary duty in aviation. Further, these additional officers and men were to be considered for permanent appointments in the Flying Corps and were to be eligible under the law for flight pay if actually flying.

To form the new corps the Secretary of the Navy was authorized to appoint two new groups of officers, selecting them from either warrant officers, enlisted men, or civilians. The first group was to contain 30 "acting ensigns," 15 appointed in each of the next two years, while the second was to contain 120 "student-fliers," 30 appointed in each of the next four years, making a total of 150. After three years' aviation duty all were to be eligible for promotion to "acting lieutenant junior grade," when they were to be given the choice of continuing as fliers or going into the regular Navy for sea duty. If they continued in aviation for another four years they might then become lieutenants, dropping "acting" from their titles. Those who stuck to flying might rise as high as captain, regardless of "sea duty in grade." To make up the authorized 350 enlisted men, one half was to be taken from the various branches of the Navy, the other to consist of recruits enrolled for aviation only. These were the main provisions which, as passed, were liked by many, disliked by as many more, including aviators on both sides. Mustin supported the act, Towers led the opposition. When the act became law Bristol made new recommendations as to the qualifications for pilots and as to the enlisted personnel, including uniforms, training, duties, and promotions. Taking the opportunity to strike again for centralized control of aviation, he strongly urged "officers of high rank for developing the Air Service . . . with practical flyers and . . . designers." These officers, he declared, were "more needed at the present time than anything else if we desire to get a proper Air Service in the quickest time." He was willing to go along with the act as far as it went in producing aviators. He was not interested in emphasizing the "separate" feature of the new force.

Mustin, on the other hand, had his own plan to meet what he described as the "present deplorable situation" in aviation personnel. From Pensacola, in October, 1916, he sent his proposal that there be immediately established "an independent organization although always auxiliary to the Naval Force," and what he sought was a cross between the U. S. Marine Corps organization and the British group subsequently known as the Royal Air Force because among all the air forces in Europe he thought the British "the most efficient." To speak his full mind on this subject he took 33 pages of single-spaced typing.

Beginning with the assumption that Congress had definitely intended to create this separate Naval Flying Corps, he urged that it be done because the "major activities" of aircraft were "along highly specialized lines distinctly different from the activities of Naval surface craft," and because aviators with the Fleet were "practically inert" until called upon for their specialty. Accordingly, he contended that this corps should be formed to include the officers then qualified as fliers, together with the newly authorized acting ensigns and any regular officers later assigned as students. Tours of duty with the corps should be for three years, with "frequent flying"; all such tours to be equivalent to sea service in qualifying for promotion. Aboard ship, corps officers should be a separate division of the complement and even those who were qualified as deck officers should in no case be required to stand watches immediately before or after the day they were to fly. Unquestionably, said Mustin, the aviators must be trained naval officers, who knew all about ships. They should not be mere observers, taken into the air as passengers, but must themselves be pilots. These requirements bore especially upon such duties as scouting because a scout must fully understand what he saw, "incorrect information being worse than no information at all." In order properly to report an enemy's movements, a scout must recognize all types of ships, formations, and tactical maneuvers. All such abilities must be combined in one officer because aircraft did not have enough "reserve horsepower . . . for carrying several officers and men additional to the pilot."

Above all, the officers of the corps must be highly proficient aviators, with full knowledge of aerial tactics. Peering, as he so often did, into the future, Mustin said this was because, while "there has not been time in the history of the aeroplane to perfect a system of battle tactics in groups; the first who [does] will . . . have a tremendous advantage over equal numbers of an enemy unskilled in formation . . . aircraft operations except, perhaps, scouting, will eventually develop into group flying." In his opinion training for such work, on top of all else that was required, would need anywhere from three to five years, especially for those who had not had the Naval Academy schooling in subjects such as higher mathematics and electrical engineering. Three years, perhaps, would be needed to get newcomers through elementary courses and into advanced training for flight. Even those who came in as acting ensigns might well need two years for the schooling alone.

The necessity for spending so much time was, to Mustin, a convincing reason for the separate corps. To make it *feel* separate it should certainly be under its own commandant. That officer should himself be a part of a definite chain of command which administered Naval Aviation in all of its branches. There must be an end to uncertainties between bureaus, which were apt to look upon aviation and the peculiar problems of aircraft design and construction as "a strange and relatively unimportant piece of work." Being rather more certain of the support of everyone in aviation for this administrative feature of his plan, Mustin drove hard for independent control by a director under the Chief of Naval Operations, as the only way to get true coordination. Aviation problems were new and difficult; bureaus were widely separated; only where the "whole time" of officers was devoted to aviation could real progress be made. Therefore, wherever work for the air arm differed from mere bureau routine, bureaus should transfer their supervision of that work to a central division of aeronautics. Heading that division there should preferably be an officer of rank who was himself a qualified aviator; failing that, he must at least be known "to have a talent for coordination and administrative work, and be provided with the necessary number of expert advisors under his direct control." These should include aides for structural material, ordnance, motors and equipment, both in airplanes and in dirigibles; as well as special aides for Marine Corps, reserve, and militia personnel. With all these, through the commandant of the corps, the director should administer regular fleet and shore aircraft, the fliers with the Marine Expeditionary Forces, all the Reserve Flying Corps and any militia detachments. Given such an organization, declared Mustin, there could be advance in design, maintenance, supply and, above all, training, combined to give the Navy a really efficient, well-manned air arm.

At the moment, said Mustin, there were but 14 qualified air pilots, of whom only four were at Pensacola. The 13 aviators from the line of the Navy who were still under training would require four to six months' advanced work before qualifying as pilots. Thirteen others, then still students, might so qualify by July 1, 1917. Of the total of 56 officers of the Navy and Marine Corps who had had flying duty, five had been killed, two relieved for temperamental and two for physical disability, and one dismissed; a combined loss of close to 18 per cent which, allowing for greater safety in the future through the use of "tractor" planes, might be reduced to 5 per cent. By July, 1917, it might be expected that there would be 38 pilots, of whom perhaps 20 would be ready to fly with a fleet in battle. Citing those figures, Mustin called the prospect unpleasant because "Our little squadron . . . would be of only momentary value . . . [and] no one can be expected to accomplish much if the odds against him are certain to be at least ten to one!"

Even by July, 1918, he estimated, the present rate would produce only 67 pilots, of whom 16 would have to be on shore duty. What was worse, these estimates took no account of probable "rotation" which would force fliers to return to sea duty or miss their promotion as Chambers had missed his. Ellyson, for one, was already out of aviation. Towers had asked to be relieved as air attaché in London because he was "running terrible chances" of not being promoted. Such a policy, said Mustin, could have been established only "by those who have no practical experience in flying and, if it is adhered to, the Naval Flying Corps will never be effective." Development was so rapid that one out of touch for a year or more required considerable retraining. In other branches of the Service a "rusty" officer could be useful while "catching up," and in ordinary naval duties he would not be "liable to kill himself and others." A rusty pilot going into the air would have no expert at his shoulder to warn him before he made a mistake when flying in formation. Even when planes became large enough to carry many officers and men, the one at the controls would have to make instantaneous decisions. To Mustin, the uncertainty of the length of an officer's assignment to aviation was "a constant source of worry." As he saw it, it appeared obvious that no one would care to risk his life in learning to fly if he had in mind the constant thought that he might at any time be transferred to some entirely different duty. This would be particularly true if it also meant possible recall to aviation at a future date when lack of practice had left him quite unprepared for advances during his absence.

As far as these recommendations might be pertinent, Mustin wanted them applied to enlisted men as to officers. He strongly urged permanent duty for the men, with the establishment of definite ratings to which they might advance without worry about service aboard ship. Since the new law provided flight pay for the *permanent* enlisted corps, he suggested that only those in the ratings of airmen and machinist, aeronautics, be made "permanent" members. This would obviate the injustice of allowing extra pay to men of other ratings not required actually to go into the air.

Some of these views of Mustin's were eventually adopted. On the other hand, although the act of 1916 is still on the statute books, some of its provisions have never been put into full effect. The men who flew for the Navy in World War I were not a separate air force but a part of the Navy. In World War II they were again an integrated part of the Fleet and it seems safe to predict that they will be just that for years to come. Nevertheless, Mustin's proposals were of the greatest benefit in setting the new course for Naval Aviation and in speeding its advance.

As far as immediate action went, the Navy Department's opinion of a separate air corps force was embodied in Captain McKean's letter to the Chief of Naval Operations. He urged "that all legislation . . . relating to the Flying Corps be repealed," and that "all officers required in the air service be from the regular Navy and Marine Corps, trained in their naval duties before going into Aeronautics and returning . . . after their greatest usefulness" as aviators was over, which he estimated would be after five years of flying. To provide for more officers he recommended that "legislation be enacted increasing the appointments to the Naval Academy . . . which [will] provide . . . 30 graduates each year in excess of the present number and thus permit the detail of 30 commissioned officers [to] . . . Aeronautics." Noticeably, in these recommendations, the captain appears to have made no provision for immediately producing naval aviators nor, for that matter, to have considered that the need for these aviators was immeasurably greater because of the imminence of war. His views were fully supported by the Chief of Naval Operations, who commented that he found the legislation impossible to put into effective operation. The outcome was that Naval Aviation on April 6, 1917, mustered but 48 officers with only 230 enlisted men—hardly what would be called a "striking force" today.

It has already been remarked that the same act provided for a civilian reserve. As part of this the Naval Reserve Flying Corps was planned, to include all officers and men who might be authorized to transfer to it from the regular service, as well as all civilian

fliers, designers, builders, photographers, and all others who could
be of use, enrolled "in time of war or . . . national emergency
declared by the President." No limit was placed on the size of the
Reserve, but all members must serve three months on active duty
during each enrollment, the periods of duty to be at least three
weeks long. Enlisted men who had had 16 years' service with the
regular Flying Corps might transfer to the Reserve, where they
would receive an annual retainer of two months' pay in addition
to full pay for any active duty. It was this corps that would attract
many collegians and others and grow, in early 1917, so fast that
it eventually furnished most of the naval fliers in the war. A case
in point was the "Yale Unit" formed into Aerial Coast Patrol
Unit Number One, under F. Trubee Davison. After training at
its own expense at Port Washington this unit would take part in
the late summer maneuvers of the volunteer "Mosquito Fleet" in
Gravesend Bay, spotting mines and practicing other exercises.
Early in the winter its members would leave college to gather at
Rodman Wanamaker's Florida seaplane base. Eventually, through
Towers and Assistant Secretary F. D. Roosevelt, all hands would
enroll in the Reserve Flying Corps, to be followed by another unit
from Yale and several from Harvard, Princeton and other sources.

A third important feature of the act of 1916 was the provision
for buying 12 planes to lend to the naval militia. To Bristol and his
associates this appeared a great step forward, because they had
not been able to carry out the terms of the department's General
Order No. 133, issued in June, 1915, authorizing the loan of the
Navy's planes to the militia. Indeed, any legislation for this organization was welcome because its development had been a problem ever since authorization of its air component by Congress two
years earlier, in April, 1914.

Rear Admiral Fiske, as one of his last helpful acts before leaving the Office of Naval Operations, had come out strongly for
an air arm in the militia. Like Bristol, he had sought to take advantage of the offers of such men as those led by A. B. Lambert
of St. Louis, enthusiastic amateur pilots who had wanted to fly
with the Navy at Vera Cruz. They were men like Glenn Martin,
Chance Vought, Lincoln Beachey, and Roy Knabenshue; a score
and more who were flying their own hydroaeroplanes and who
would jump at joining an air militia. To get them in, Fiske proposed that each state naval militia establish an air station of two
officers and six men, with two planes. "This is suggested," he wrote,

"because the time is not far distant when aeronautic service in the
Navy will not be considered as only voluntary."

The Navy Department's Division of Militia Affairs had accordingly distributed a circular letter to the state organizations
announcing that the Navy would lend planes and also give "refresher courses" to militia aviators at Pensacola. It was estimated
that these courses might draw, from 23 state organizations, some
64 officers and perhaps 300 enlisted men; a helpful number which
might be increased if war came to stimulate enrollment. Ten states
already had units and Curtiss had repeated his offer to train one
aviator from each, without charge. The Aero Club had started a
fund to give $40 toward the expenses of each of these Curtiss
students, and, after Pancho Villa's raids into the United States
the club had raised this contribution to $150. Moreover the club
offered to let its members train civilian beginners and also offered
to raise funds to buy reserve planes for the Navy. Since the Secretary of the Navy could not legally accept private funds, he
suggested that the Aero Club concentrate on the militia. The
club in June, 1916, opened a general subscription fund, under
this strong statement:

The U. S. Army and Navy have, together, less than twenty aeroplanes
available. Only half a dozen of the licensed aviators of the United
States have made flights of more than fifty miles, and none know even
the rudiments of military aeronautical requirements. Our Army,
Navy, National Guard, and Naval Militia have had no experience in
handling aircraft or operating with them.

If England with 3,000 aeroplanes and aviators and the output of
eighteen thousand men cannot supply sufficient aeroplanes for its
forces—what could Uncle Sam—who has less than a score of aeroplanes—do in case of immediate need?

To provide an aeronautical reserve, the Governors of the Aero Club
of America have started a public aeronautical subscription, similar
to the French and German subscriptions of 1912–13. These netted
$1,222,969 and $1,806,626 respectively, and were used to train aviators and to procure aeroplanes. As the New York *Sun* says editorially,
"Surely we in America, with our greater resouces, can do even better."

Rear Admiral Peary of North Pole fame, the chairman of the
National Aerial Coast Patrol Commission, had been enthusiastically supporting the militia program, getting good backing from
numerous noted civilians like John Hays Hammond for a plan to

establish aerial picket scouts along the whole Atlantic coast. The
Aero Club was ready to give money for this plan and Curtiss offered planes at reduced prices, with the same free training as for
militia pilots. Stimulated by this interest, Bristol had recommended a board, either of regular officers only or with civilian
members added, to establish qualifications for the militia that
would let the candidates understand what was expected of each,
and also to pick the right men. He had referred to Europe "where
sentiment was unfavorable toward officers who did not strive to get
to the front"; where those given posts at home felt "out of it."
This, he said, must always be the case but "the fighting force of a
country now is not only those . . . in contact with the enemy
but [also] is the reserve, the supply trains, the factories . . . the
general staff, and the business men and financiers. . . . The best
organization . . . is the one that places each man in that place
which he is best able to fill."

The requirements actually adopted included the passing of
written examinations as well as practical demonstration of ability
to fly. Under the terms of General Order No. 198, issued in March,
1916, the new course for militia aviators covered the Navy Regulations and all general special orders; the care of clothing, bedding,
and equipment; knowledge of navigation and the principles of
scouting; familiarity with aircraft and their fittings. Naval administration and business methods were also included, for officers
of and above the rank of lieutenant commander. Special courses
were in preparation for enlisted mechanics who would receive instruction at Pensacola even without advance training in flying.

Authority to borrow the Navy's planes under the new 1916 act
was therefore a great help to the militia program. By November
eight planes had been borrowed: one by California, two by Massachusetts, two by New Jersey, two by New York, and one by Rhode
Island, all of them different types. The loans were made only
where at least one officer of the militia had completed the prescribed three months' course at Pensacola, in each of which courses
four officers and 16 enlisted men could be handled.

While members of the militia, like the members of the Coast
Guard, might not be considered fully up to accepted naval standards in navigation, gunnery, and seamanship, there was not enough
time available to train them completely in such subjects. Instead,
the main effort must be directed toward training them to fly, and
consequently these students never were designated naval aviators

or given acting commissions such as had been provided for the new
Flying Corps. But they did learn to fly and when they got into
World War I they flew with great credit to themselves, their
Service, and their country.

CHAPTER IX

Under Pressure of War

IT is not astonishing that the Navy, even as late as April, 1917, gave little space to the air arm in its plans for war. Why should those plans have given space to six flying boats, 45 seaplanes designed only for training, three landplanes, two kite balloons, and one very unsatisfactory dirigible? What value as a striking force could be attached to these, manned by only 43 officers and just over 200 enlisted men of the Navy, with five officers and 30 men of the Marine Corps? To be sure, the Helm Board had recommended the construction of some air stations in the United States but none of these had been completed and when they were built they would be merely defensive. Moreover, when the early plans were being laid, the Navy Department knew little or nothing of what might be expected of the United States in the Allied efforts to fight an air war. Finally, the latest program outlined by the General Board had not been a war program but a long-range, peacetime program, by no means adapted to the probable needs of an air force on active combat service.

As soon as it became plain that entry into World War I was inevitable, some attention was immediately focused upon United States aviation. The earliest attention was not, however, particularly helpful, because it took the form of a bill, introduced into Congress by the always air-minded Representative Hulbert of New York, to create a separate national department of the air under its own Cabinet member. When this bill was brought upon the floor of the House, it was strongly opposed by both Services as well as by many civilians, and it was ultimately "tabled for the duration." In one form or another, through the years, it would appear again, usually sponsored and supported by persons not too well informed of the essential differences between war upon the land and war upon the sea. For the moment it was dead.

Before April, 1917, was out, however, changes in all United States planning were precipitated by the visits to Washington of the Joffre and the Balfour missions. To listen to the blunt language used by these missions was to realize that the German Army had beaten France almost to her knees, while the U-boats had drawn England's belt close to the starvation hole. Seven million five hundred thousand tons of Allied shipping had been lost, and against this loss U-boats were being built faster than they were being sunk. Anything these missions left unsaid was told to Adm. William S. Sims, who went to London in that month as the prospective commander, United States Naval Forces in Europe.

Sims lost no time in echoing the urgent call of the Allies for ships and planes. He put ships first because no system of convoys could be effective unless small, fast vessels to serve as escorts were so plentiful that any U-boat must risk her own life to launch a torpedo. Aircraft as used by the British, French, and Italians were helpful in protecting convoys, but they could not do it all. No program of plane building, wrote Sims to the Navy Department, should be allowed to interfere with the building of small craft to fight submarines. He nevertheless urged building planes to reinforce the British patrols over the coastlines and over the English Channel; to pick up the flash of a periscope reflecting a sunbeam; to peer down, through fog that shrouded friend and foe alike, upon a surfaced U-boat comfortably charging her batteries. He declared that the United States must eventually send innumerable planes to cover the battlefields as well as the oceans, to spot, to photograph, to rain down bombs. The sooner these planes got overseas the sooner the U-boats could be stopped.

To push what Admiral Sims described as "aeronautic developments" on this side of the Atlantic, the Navy Department had one good man in exactly the right place. John Towers, veteran of six years' flying, including a tour in London as assistant naval attaché for air, was now a lieutenant commander and in the previous fall, after Bronson had been killed, it had been Towers who took over the aviation desk in the Office of Naval Operations. By the spring of 1917 he had established much better understanding and cooperation in all the bureaus and had gone far to bring about the very thing for which Chambers and Bristol had struggled so long against misunderstanding, inertia, and bureaucracy—the centralized supervision of all aviation activities. In May, 1917, when Capt. Noble E. Irwin, a two-fisted sailor with no great enthusiasm for aviation, was ordered into the office over Towers' head, it naturally followed that there were some divergences of opinion between the two. In the main, however, because Irwin had boundless enthusiasm for winning the war, as well as the experienced judgment to recognize a thoroughly capable subordinate, he supported Towers as the directing spirit. This linking of the expert with the officer of rank made it possible for Naval Aviation to do its share in the combined effort of all hands, an effort that before long pushed petty differences out of the office windows in order to let common sense enter the office door.

Immediately the need for considerable expansion of the aviation office became obvious. Accordingly, sections for administration were established, with a section for training under Lieut. E. F. Johnson, and these were soon followed by others. Capt. B. L. Smith of the Marines headed the section for information and planning, while the new lighter-than-air section was at first headed by Lieut. J. P. Norfleet, later by that noted expert in this branch, Lieut. Zachary Lansdowne. All this expansion had been begun even before the arrival of letters from the Navy in Europe telling Irwin and Towers it would be "absolutely necessary for you to build up a large organization, even larger than some of the Bureaus, well fortified with numbers of technical men in all branches of the aircraft business." Eventually, when not even the conservatism of the Chief of Naval Operations could remain proof against the imperative demand for a separate aviation office, the Secretary of the Navy's order of March 7, 1918, made Irwin Director of Naval Aviation, enabling him to "draw enough water" in the administrative ocean of the Navy Department. Thus it became possible to hold well-organized weekly conferences with all the bureaus, and, as a means of stimulating inter-Allied cooperation, Flight Comdr. H. B. Hobbs, representing the Royal Air Force, could be invited to appear at the conferences in his official capacity. All this, however, was not fully accomplished until the nation had been nearly a year at war.

Such conferences were essential because the aviation activities of the bureaus were expanding rapidly in all directions. In Construction and Repair Hunsaker was now head of a much larger aviation section concerned with design, specifications, material supply, construction, and service. In Steam Engineering Lt. Comdr. A. K. Atkins headed an aviation division with the three sections of engineering, production, and operations maintenance, a division which began with Atkins and one typist but soon grew to 40 officers, 60 clerks, and well over 100 inspectors. In the Bureau of Ordnance a new desk marked "Aviation" took over machine guns, bombs, and sights for aircraft, through three sections known as experimental, technical, and production distribution, besides a special storehouse in Philadelphia where materials were tested and inspected for distribution. Still another bureau, Yards and Docks, established its aviation section under Civil Engineer (later Rear Adm.) Kirby Smith, a section destined to experience its first real activity in the construction of air bases overseas, as groups of trained workmen became the forerunners of today's familiar Seabees. Even the Bureau of Navigation, because it was responsible for the Naval Observatory, found itself under pressure for all types of precision instruments for aircraft. Because the Office of Naval Aviation had to deal with so many broad activities, it was vital that it be given a new, fully recognized status as supervisor and coordinator of them all.

In addition, the office had to face the all-important matter of greatly increasing aviation personnel in the Navy. To attack this problem, Towers was promptly made supervisor of the Naval Reserve Flying Corps, which was to be the main source of aviators, volunteers to the last man, in keeping with the Navy's tradition of needing no conscription. Normally this assignment, technically under the Bureau of Navigation, would have meant great complications for Towers but fortunately the Chief of Navigation was the able and distinguished Rear Adm. Leigh C. Palmer. These two made a private agreement under which Towers, without leaving his desk in aviation, could handle his end of all the intricacies of deciding what officers and what enlisted men were needed, where they were to be sought, and how they were to be trained.

Enrollments began at once. Civilians already qualified as aviators were urged to report at headquarters in their respective naval districts where it could be determined whether they met the Navy's educational and physical requirements and where their general reputation as citizens could be learned. Others who met the same requirements except for the lack of training as aviators were also urged to present themselves, and these were to be inducted into training which had three phases: ground school, elementary flight instruction, and advanced work in both of these. Skilled mechanics, carpenters, and engineers were invited to join the Reserve Flying Corps for a term of four years. The unskilled could enlist in a group known as Class 5, but this class filled most slowly because everyone wanted to fly rather than be left on the ground.

Moreover, one rating provided in this class was that of quarter-master, most ambiguous because normally this rating was considered distinctly seagoing. Unlike the army connotation of a man connected with supplies and stores, a quartermaster in the Navy is a man whose regular duties are carried out on the bridge of his ship, as expert helmsman, as assistant to the navigator, or as supervisor of the signalmen. Many of those who enrolled in the confident expectation of being taught to fly found themselves rated as quartermasters and intended to stay on the ground. Mistakes of this kind were numerous in the early days and it took months to correct them.

Machinists, meaning by that term mechanics of all sorts, were naturally in great demand, and their recruiting was pressed from the start. Behind them came the long column of specialists, some as commissioned officers, others as enlisted men to be trained to become officers, administrators, and machinery inspectors; aerographers, balloonists, pigeon fanciers, and groups for instruction in aviation intelligence. Since they all insisted that they had "joined the Navy to fight in the air," the problem of classifying and distributing them to appropriate training stations was as difficult as it was pressing, but at the outset all steps taken to solve the problem were supervised by Naval Aviation. Early in 1918, however, the entire training program was taken over by the Bureau of Navigation.

Pensacola was the only training station in operation at the moment of entry into the war. Its capacity was 64 pilots and the same number of mechanics, but this was ridiculously inadequate for the emergency. The courses were hastily expanded to accommodate the many recruits sent there immediately, in order to give them elementary instruction in naval practice, navigation, seamanship, and gunnery, all subjects in which the regulars of prewar years had been instructed at the Naval Academy. Temporary stations were established as soon as possible at East Greenwich, Miami, Key West, and San Diego. The Curtiss Exhibition School at Newport News, Virginia, was taken over for a group to be trained under Bellinger, and the Curtiss plant at Buffalo was occupied by another group under Lieut. W. Capehart with Naval Constructor E. L. Gayhart supervising the course for those who would become inspectors of machinery. James Knapp, president of the American Lithograph Company gave his private seaplane base at Mastic, Long Island, to the Navy, and by the end of May a patrol unit was in training there. Meantime, New York's militia station at Bay Shore and Massachusetts' militia station at Squantum were commandeered. At the Goodyear plant in Akron, Ohio, a school was opened to train recruits in kite and free balloons.

Many of these stations would be occupied only for limited periods, lasting until the bases which had been permanently selected could be constructed. Work on these bases was started very shortly, notably at Montauk and at Rockaway, the former being pushed along so rapidly that it could be commissioned in August, 1917, its first head being a young man whose name would rise very high in the history of the Navy—Lieut. Marc A. Mitscher. Meanwhile, the First Yale Unit, which had begun training at Palm Beach under Lt. (jg) E. O. McDonnell at a flying school owned by Rodman Wanamaker, soon moved up to Huntington, Long Island. In addition to Trubee Davison, its original organizer, who would eventually be Assistant Secretary of War for Air, this unit included Artemus Gates, who would become Assistant Secretary of the Navy for Air and thereafter Undersecretary of the Navy; Robert Lovett, another future Assistant Secretary of War for Air; and David Ingalls, who would become not only the Navy's only ace in World War I but also, in his turn, Assistant Secretary of the Navy for Air. As another expedient, through an agreement made by Towers with the Royal Flying Corps, United States student officers and flying cadets began their training as pilots, observers, and gunners under qualified Canadian instructors. Under an agreement made with the Canadian Government, Toronto was used in the summer and certain army fields in Texas in the winter for this work, designed to train ten United States squadrons. Eventually the program produced 37 officers and 80 observers. Among groups taking that training was the Princeton Unit, with which James Forrestal, destined to be Secretary of the Navy in World War II and later Secretary of Defense, was enrolled.

At the Massachusetts Institute of Technology, under the general charge of Lieut. E. H. McKitterick, a ground school was started. Begun to handle only student pilots, the courses were rapidly expanded to include a large number of those enrolled for nonflying duties such as those of inspection, an expansion which was the means of relieving Pensacola of some of its heavy burden. This Massachusetts school would carry on a good deal of the training until the Navy's large station at Great Lakes, Illinois, could get into full operation, a period of about a year. Long before that, however, the Great Lakes station would be in partial operation, and by December of 1917 it would be handling large numbers of both officers and enlisted men, its program gradually absorbing a number of the small, temporary schools and stations. This absorption would involve the overhauling of courses of instruction to standardize the curriculum, a work in which the services of Dr. Charles E. Lucke of Columbia University, commissioned a lieutenant commander in the Reserve, and his staff have always been described as of the greatest possible assistance.

Other training activities established included a course for balloon winchmen, 20 of them at a time, at the Pelham Bay Training Camp; a gunnery school at Miami; and a special radio school at the same place. One small detachment of marines was sent to the Army balloon school at St. Louis and from there to another school at Omaha; a detachment, incidentally, which would have the bad luck never to get overseas. Still another, a radio unit, was organized at Harvard University, its students supplementing their classroom instruction with practical training by periods spent in radio rooms aboard ship.

By the end of 1917 some of the confusion in enlisted ratings was cleared. Men who had been originally enrolled in such ratings in the regular Navy as quartermaster were given their discharges, immediately re-enrolled in the Reserve Flying Corps, and reassigned to learn to be what they had always wanted to be—fliers. Similarly when the Secretary of the Navy at this time called for 8,000 more men in the technical ratings, it was clearly specified that they were wanted for work on assembly and repair, not as ultimate pilots or observers. They were enrolled either in the regular Navy for the duration of the war or in the Reserve Corps. To augment the numbers answering this call special examinations were conducted at six different training stations, to hunt out personnel in other assignments who might meet the aviation standards, and in these examinations requirements for aviation ratings were modified to apply specifically to such duties as radio, gunnery, photography, and the like. Some 400 men were picked up in this way.

In May, 1918, partly because the prospect of enemy submarine attacks upon the Atlantic coast laid heavier demands upon the general defense facilities of coastal stations, the training program was again revised. For this reason and also because a year of experiment suggested many improvements and the need of further expansion, greater use of the inland training stations was sought. While ground school training at the Massachusetts Institute of Technology was continued with enlarged classes, a second such school was established at Dunwoody Institute in Minneapolis and a third one at the University of Washington, Seattle. An expansion followed in the study of aerology, the importance of which became more fully recognized with each passing day. Notwithstanding the early urgings of Captain Chambers and others, aviators had been inclined to classify the weather either as "good," when they could fly, or as "bad," when they were grounded, quite overlooking the many degrees between these two extremes. When they found themselves in war service, flying in Europe with the Allies, they discovered that such duties as escorting a convoy forced the aviator himself to be a judge of weather able to interpret by signs around him the advice of weather experts miles away. Consequently, in February, 1918, Dr. A. G. McAdie, director of Harvard's Blue Hill Observatory, was enrolled as a lieutenant commander to establish appropriate courses. After he had done this at home he was sent abroad to reorganize the United States Aerology Service at foreign stations where Americans were serving, a forerunner of the very much larger service established in World War II.

There were advantages and disadvantages in the use of civilian instructors and of colleges and their campuses for the training of officers and men. While it was of great assistance to be able to use buildings and equipment that already existed, it was inevitable that the civilian student body should be inclined to regard these facilities as its own and to resent "intruders." Also there was a distinct difference between the points of view of civilian and military instructors, the latter regarding the former as too theoretical, the former holding the latter to be both too practical and too concerned with military forms and procedures. One experiment tried was that of using chief petty officers as instructors; it was only a partial success because while these men were usually well informed upon their subjects they inevitably had difficulty in controlling student officers. Ultimately differences with civilians were largely reconciled and better teaching was made possible by using as instructors officers who had been through flight training and who had also learned something of the art of teaching from academic boards like that of the Massachusetts Institute of Technology. On the other hand, a difficulty never fully overcome resulted from delays in the receipt of necessary equipment for instruction. Technical advance in aviation being relatively so rapid during these war months, instructors were almost always aware that they were without the latest devices, and students came to think they were being taught what was obsolescent if not already obsolete. This was particularly true in classes which included students coming from the Fleet with a little experience.

As more was learned of Allied needs for support along special lines and as strategic and tactical plans were amended, corresponding modifications had to be made in the training programs. Thus the project for using towed lighters as seaplane carriers and the later project for bombing enemy bases with landplanes manned by the Navy both affected the training courses in the United States and changed the requirements for pilots to be sent overseas. Almost month by month the importance of keeping the home training program flexible became more and more apparent, especially because criticism by officers on duty abroad was often very sharp. Some of these critics insisted that aviators should have been taught much more of the mechanics of their motors, instruments, and planes. Others said that a pilot's having a "signed card" in his pocket was no real proof of his qualifications because he had probably been *taught all the wrong things*. Still others declared that only one "bomber" in ten had any adequate idea of the principles and the technique of bombing.

In retrospect it appears clear that great urgency combined with a swiftly changing technical situation to make it practically impossible for the United States to deliver pilots, observers, bombardiers, and mechanics trained to the minute. Unquestionably there was confusion and some unfortunate fumbling, especially in the early days, but there was no more of both than was inevitable in a nation plunging into a war for which it was in every mental and physical, not to say moral, respect totally unprepared.

In practice much that was lacking in the training of those going overseas was supplied during a few crowded weeks or even days at foreign stations, partly by Americans who had landed a little earlier, largely by Allied instructors. Where and for how long this final training could be given was left entirely to the discretion of Admiral Sims and his senior aid for aviation, Capt. Hutch I. Cone. The number of those who received such training, in all more than one quarter of the United States Naval Forces in Europe, together with the number of those who enrolled to go abroad but did not get there, appears in the table below:

Officers sent overseas   1,237
Officers serving in the United States 5,479
                                                               ——————
                                                                6,716
Enlisted men sent overseas   16,287
Enlisted men in the United States   14,406
                                                              ——————
                                                               30,693
Total at home and abroad, all ranks and ratings   37,409

The record made by these men, eventually dressed in the forest green uniform and (when they had earned it) wearing the prized gold-wing badge, will stand comparison with the record they and their successors would build with the far more advanced weapons and the much wider opportunities of World War II.

CHAPTER X

Procurement in Wartime

IF the wartime increase in their personnel staggered those who had been the founders of Naval Aviation, the huge expansion of their material should have floored them. Where the Navy had not been ready with stations, schools, and training equipment to handle large additions of men, it was equally unprepared to embark upon what was nothing less than big business. Yet embark it did, with results which, all things considered, were to prove markedly effective.

The National Defense Act of June 3, 1916, had provided for a census of American industry, with the purpose of determining just what plants could be converted, either immediately or within a reasonable time, to the manufacture of arms and munitions in enormous quantities. This census had collected a great deal of valuable information, but much of this was worth more to other branches of the Armed Services than it was to Naval Aviation. What had been sought was priority for government orders at all existing plants, but the fact was that the plants then building aircraft were already working almost exclusively on government orders. As far as they were concerned, priority was fully established and therefore the gain to aviation from the survey lay chiefly in learning what other plants might be converted to build aircraft.

In September, 1916, under the Army Appropriation Act of August 29, a Council of National Defense was created. This council was established as the result of the work of the Civilian Industrial Preparedness Committee, made up of prominent citizens who had long recognized the certainty of entry into the war and who had realized that such dreams as that of Mr. Bryan, with his "million men springing to arms," would amount to no more than dreams if there were no arms to which these gallant patriots could spring. The Preparedness Committee, after making nationwide surveys and musters of its own, brought impressive statistics to the attention of Congress, which responded by establishing the council in this act. Under the law no directing authority was allowed the council but it was given a position from which it could strongly advise those who did have authority. Made up of highly qualified experts from all industries, its collective voice was well worth hearing and heeding when it declared that, as between the two Services, "priority should be given to such needs of the Navy as are intended to be completed within one year." G. B. Clarkson, in his book, *Industrial America in the World War*, attributed this decision to the "hypothesis that, as the Navy was on a near warfooting . . . it should be allowed to complete the comparatively small effort that would effect the transition and get into action at an early date." This was a sound enough hypothesis upon the assumption that the Navy would be required to fight a conventional war of fleet actions, because for this its already established supply system appeared adequate if given priority. Actually, however, what followed was a war of small craft, surface and air, against submarines, an unforeseen development which involved many changes in material requirements. In aviation especially, the priority plan did not solve all the problems because that branch had so little advance information as to its probable needs. Moreover, it had to overcome such obstacles in the path of rapid procurement as those which arose from the forehandedness of General Squier in pre-empting, for the Army, a very large proportion of the nation's existent aircraft-building facilities.

To carry out any procurement program proposed by the National Council or by any one else, money was the first essential and happily this was forthcoming. The Appropriations Act of April 17, 1917, added $3,000,000 for Naval Aviation to the $3,500,000 provided August 24, 1916; the Deficiency Act of June 15 added another $11,000,000, and this was further increased by $45,000,000 on October 6, 1917. The sum allotted in April was to be spent at the discretion of the President, the June sum at that of the Secretary of the Navy, but the purpose of both provisions was the same. The earlier amounts were appropriated shortly before President Wilson drew upon the Council of National Defense to form the War Industries Board, at the head of which he put the shrewd and forceful Bernard M. Baruch. This board would prove able to hold a reasonably even balance between industry and government, accomplishing its essential purpose of expediting the production of all the thousands of things needed

immediately to fight the war. Under circumstances which were
certain to make materials scarcer, to use up the limited supply of
machine tools, and to restrict the labor market, the delays that
actually slowed the war machine would have been far more serious
if the "Baruch Board," as it was soon familiarly known, had not
been on hand to shorten those delays by prompt decisions and
vigorous pronouncements.

The next forward step in aircraft procurement came in May,
1917, with the establishment of the Aircraft Production Board.
This was done at the instigation of Charles D. Walcott, secretary
of the Smithsonian Institution and chairman of the National
Advisory Committee for Aeronautics, a group whose great services
to the nation have already been suggested in these pages. Mr.
Walcott proposed that the board be formed to "consider the quantity production of aircraft . . . and to cooperate with the officers
of the Army and Navy and of other Departments," and also suggested that there be a "Joint Technical Board of the Army and
Navy . . . for determining specifications and methods of inspection for all aircraft . . . for the two services." In approving the
Aircraft Production Board, to be headed by Howard E. Coffin,
the Council of National Defense stipulated that it should have
no powers beyond those of conferring and advising. As time passed,
however, and as the Baruch Board absorbed the general functions
of the Council of National Defense, the Aircraft Production Board
was invested with more of the color of authority. Because it was
given strong backing by Baruch, it could stimulate progress in
the building program by clearing away such complications as
that which loomed up when a horde of agents descended upon
Washington to sell foreign planes and motors to the United States,
an effort which many considered deliberately designed to slow up
building in this country. In all matters of aircraft procurement
the Aircraft Production Board soon had what amounted to "the
last word."

On this board the Navy was most ably represented by Rear Adm.
David Taylor, whose profound knowledge, great personal charm,
and infinite tact were very potent factors in securing what the
Navy wanted. Even General Squier, certainly a highly efficient
representative of the Army on the board, never got "across the
hawse" of Admiral Taylor to monopolize the ears of the four
civilians who made up the balance of the board's original membership! An excellent example of the admiral's success was in the

very early matter of allocating plants to build aircraft and parts for the Services. Under his steering the board decided that the Navy should get a part of the Standard Aircraft plant at Elizabeth, New Jersey, and the full output of the following: Aeromarine Plane and Motor Co., Keyport, New Jersey; Boeing Airplane Co., Seattle, Washington; Burgess Co., Marblehead, Massachusetts; Canadian Aeroplanes, Ltd., Toronto, Canada; Curtiss Aeroplane and Motor, Ltd., Toronto, Canada; Curtiss Engineering Corp., Garden City, New York; Gallaudet Aircraft Corp., East Greenwich, Rhode Island; L.W.F. Engineering Corp., College Point, New York; Victor Talking Machine Co., Camden, New Jersey.

Beyond such recommendations as this, which had almost the force of an order, the board acted as mediator and conciliator rather than as an actual procurement agency; that is, it studied programs and policies and then gave almost "compulsory" advice, but it left the actual making of contracts to the Services themselves. In the Navy, negotiations for building were made almost wholly with experienced, well-equipped contractors, under the deliberate policy of not draining scarce material and skilled labor away from firms hard pressed to make deliveries. In this the Navy followed the advice of the Aircraft Production Board and worked closely with it.

By the end of the first summer of war the board's authoritative position was impaired by the creation, in the Army Signal Corps, of a special unit known as the Aircraft Equipment Division. Three civilians, already members of the Production Board, were commissioned as army colonels and were assigned additional duty in this new division, with the inevitable result that confusion as to their exact status resulted. Were they working with the Aircraft Production Board, for all Services, or were they working only in the interests of the Army?

When Congress, by the act of October 1, 1917, gave the Aircraft Production Board legislative standing, it nevertheless empowered it only "to supervise and direct . . . the purchase, production, and manufacture of aircraft, engines . . . ordnance and instruments used . . . including purchase, lease, acquisition or construction of plants . . . Provided, that the Board may make recommendations as to contracts and their distribution . . . but every contract shall be made by the already constituted authorities of the respective departments." Under this law, the board was redesignated the Aircraft Board and was reorganized by adding two more civilians as members, taking out one of the three new colonels and adding Captain Irwin and Lt. Comdr. A. K. Atkins to support Rear Admiral Taylor. Before long, moreover, under an interpretation of the new law by the Judge Advocate General of the Navy and through an order approved by both the Secretary of War and the Secretary of the Navy, the board officially reverted to the status of a "clearing house," acting in little more than its advisory capacity. As the chairman said in a letter to Senator Chamberlain, its functions were "entirely industrial, having no relation to [those] of military and naval authorities controlling . . . personnel, maintenance, service, and repair." The chairman added that "the officers of the War and Navy Departments . . . skilled in the service side . . . cannot be expected to have intimate knowledge of . . . manufacture . . . or of industrial organization . . ." Nevertheless, its recommendations still had very great weight.

The other body, created in May, 1917, by the two Secretaries at Walcott's suggestion, was the "Joint Technical Board on Aircraft, except Zeppelins." Its tasks were to advise upon types of planes and of motors, to "standardize, as far as possible, the designs and general specifications of aircraft except Zeppelins," and to decide other technical questions referred to it by either Service. This board, too, lacked the authority to enforce its views, but much attention was accorded the programs for the Army and Navy which it promptly issued and similar attention was given the recommendations on technical matters which it made frequently thereafter.

Pending definite understanding of exactly what was needed by the Allies in the way of planes, it was impossible to lay down a schedule of manufacture which would specify actual numbers. In the middle of May, 1917, there was talk of 5,000 planes for all purposes, but by the end of the month the Joint Technical Board had raised that figure to 7,775 of which 7,050 were to be service types. These figures had hardly been mentioned when France asked for a United States program which would put 4,500 planes at the French front by the spring of 1918, a request that brought from the Technical Board the comment that it would involve building a total of 10,000 training planes and 12,000 service planes. The making of such widely different estimates within one month is a clear indication of the generally confused state of planning for either United States Service, for the two together, or for the Allies.

A typical problem demanding quick solution was that of motors. Should the United States adopt its own motors for mass production or should the best of the European motors be built in American plants? If the latter course were taken, machinery in the United States would have to be adapted before it could turn out foreign models in quantity. Might it not therefore be better to rely upon American engineers to design something mechanically as good as anything built in Europe and, from the standpoint of those who must soon be rolling countless motors off the assembly lines, much better?

A British technical mission was in the United States, with blueprints and a few mechanics to build Rolls-Royce motors, the most powerful and generally most reliable of the foreign types. Much handwork was necessary in their construction and the mission's estimate of an 18-month output reached only 2,000, whereas the requirements of the United States were already being put at ten times that many. With this in mind the Aircraft Production Board at the end of May decided that a new American design was needed, and on the suggestion of a member, E. A. Deeds, called in J. G. Vinson of the Packard Company and E. J. Hall of Hall-Scott Motors, both of whom had had much experience but neither of whom had yet produced a wholly satisfactory motor. On a morning late in the month of May these two men, with a small group of other engineers and draftsmen, disappeared into the Willard Hotel in Washington, to emerge five days later carrying fresh blueprints. Specialists all over the country were given a hurried opportunity to criticize what was a new departure in 8-cylinder and 12-cylinder design, and when none condemned the drawings the Aircraft Production Board boldly decided to authorize mass production orally and by telegrams to various manufacturers. On July 3, just 35 days after the original rough sketches had been made, Packard delivered in Washington the first completed motor. This 8-cylinder, 225-horsepower design was christened by Rear Admiral Taylor the Liberty.

Early reports on performance were so enthusiastic that plans to build the Rolls-Royce at the Pierce Arrow plant in Buffalo could be dropped. A little later, when it was decided that 12-cylinder Liberties would do even better, there followed a reshuffling of the orders which had already been placed for 22,500 of the 8-cylinder models. Since mass production was really underway by that time, even the delays caused by this change were not so long that the deliveries hoped for by the beginning of 1918 could not very nearly be achieved—a great tribute to American manufacturers.

In June of 1917, before the success of the Liberty was assured, a joint Army and Navy commission had been sent abroad to study Allied progress in the design and building of aircraft and to recommend a complementary program for the United States. Headed by Maj. R. C. Bolling of the Army, the commission bore his name but it included Capts. V. E. Clark, E. S. Correll, and H. Marmon for the Army; Naval Constructor Westervelt and Lieut. W. G. Child for the Navy; and Mr. Herbert Hughes, of the Packard Motor Company, as civilian expert. It was hoped to perfect immediate plans under which factories in Europe could meet the requirements of United States forces in service planes, carrying this load until the American factories were adapted to take over. As it turned out, however, this commission's report was not made until September, by which date the plans drawn in the Bureau of Construction and Repair for flying boats had been completed and actual building had begun. Time was of such importance that the American program was launched as soon as assembly lines could be fitted to handle the Liberty motor.

When the commission's report was finally made, it recommended that the air power of the Navy might most quickly and effectively be applied through kite balloons on destroyers, with flying boats for patrol or for antisubmarine attacks. The commission also reported upon its efforts to secure examples of foreign planes and motors to serve as models from which mass production might be developed in the United States. Among these was a De Havilland light bomber which actually was put into production by the Army without, however, any provision for producing its motor, armament, or other accessory equipment. In the outcome, the winter of 1917 would be over before all the types thus obtained by the commission had been received, and this would be too late to make them of any great use. Much the same result applied to the commission's recommendations as to foreign motors, such as its comment that the Rolls-Royce, most powerful of those in use abroad, "required very skillful mechanics to keep it in commission at the front," and its suggestion that the United States begin production of the Hispano-Suiza, Gnome, and Rhone, while carrying on experiments with the new Bugatti and Lorraine-Dietrich, and waste no time on the Renault, Fiat, or Isotta-Fraschini because these were considered too heavy per horsepower generated. By the time these recommendations had been received it had already been decided that the Liberty should go into mass production. One thing the commission did effect was an arrangement for the concentration of European plants on the building of theoretically up-to-the-minute fighters, while the United States should build training planes, heavy bombers, and flying boats.

The commission described French manufacturers as confident that they could not only supply the needs of their own air service but also furnish the United States with 8,000 combat planes, 8,500 motors, and about 1,000 training planes; all these, however, contingent upon the delivery from the United States of the necessary raw materials. The theory was that manufacture in France in such quantities as these would make it possible for American naval aviators to get into action overseas before any substantial number of flying boats could be delivered by the United States. Bolling reported that he had placed orders, for delivery by June 1, 1918, of the following: 725 Nieuports for training; 150 Spads for training; 1,500 Breguets; 200 Spads for service; 1,500 Nieuports for service operation; 1,500 Renault motors; 4,000 Hispanos; 3,000 Gnomes; 500 S.I.A.-6B reconnaissance and day bombing planes; 200 to 300 Caproni biplanes. Eventually, the French proved that they had been far too optimistic in estimating their own building capacity. Of the total numbers called for by their contract with the United States, signed August 30, 1917, only one third, including those for both the Army and the Navy, had been delivered by May, 1918, whereas all were to have been delivered by June 1.

Technical members of the Bolling Commission, including representatives of both Services, made a supplementary report covering several recommendations. Because almost daily improvements in Allied designs were being made as the result of practical experience in combat, and also because of the long distance between United States factories and the front, great stress was laid upon rapid delivery of materials for plane building. Such materials occupied relatively less cargo space than was needed for finished planes, and they would be an important help to production overseas because, in the words of the report, it was certain that "it is not going to be possible to produce more battlefront airplanes than there will be use for."

If, however, the decision should be made to carry out an extensive program of manufacture in the United States, shipping the assembled planes abroad, then, said the report, very large stowage, repair, and assembly plants would be required, near Paris for the Army and on the seacoasts of France and Great Britain for the Navy. Since Allied facilities were already strained to the limit, the United States would have to build and man the additional stations, an undertaking which would involve the organization and training of "mechanical regiments."

The commission also recommended the establishment of a new joint Army and Navy technical board to provide a special technical intelligence organization with very broad authority over aircraft supply and operation. In England and in Italy, where such organizations existed, they had been very effective; in France, where there was nothing of the kind, conditions were described as "closely approximating unfriendliness between the air departments of the two services, which had resulted in marked differences in the developments of these two air departments." Further, if great numbers of planes were to be bought in Europe by the United States, the commission considered that there should be established, say in France, a special industrial organization in which was vested high authority to supervise the program. It was suggested that this organization might be made a branch of the existing Aircraft Production Board.

Westervelt and Child, representing the Navy among the technical members, noted that "Great Britain and France . . . have not realized until lately the importance of [aerial] measures [against submarines]. The time which will be required for them to establish sufficient stations . . . will be many months, and the United States can extend the availability of these stations by establishing and operating as many as possible." The two concurred in a recommendation made abroad that the United States expand its air patrols on the coast of Ireland, on the coast of France, and, if possible, on the coast of Portugal. They also expressed their "settled conviction that the importance of bombing operations with direct military ends in view cannot be exaggerated." Quite possibly it was what these two said that most influenced Rear Admiral Taylor and Rear Admiral Griffin to endorse the recommendation that air offensives against U-boats take precedence over all other aviation measures, a definite policy established by the Aircraft Board on November 8, 1917.

When it came to building under this policy, it was the Liberty motor which marked the great advance in the flying boat program.

The largest of the older boats, the H-12, of limited cruising radius and small bomb-carrying capacity, had been replaced by the HS-1, but the latter proved disappointing because the motor built for it lacked power. At the end of October, 1917, however, an HS-1 equipped with a Liberty rose so easily and quickly from the waters of Lake Erie that observers telegraphed the Navy Department: "*This* is our patrol ship!" From that moment, as far as motors were concerned, Whiting would be quite right when he said "our eggs are certainly in one basket." Fortunately the Liberty proved to be just the stout, strong basket that the hour demanded. Even when the still larger H-16 flying boat came to be built it could get all the necessary power from the Liberty.

Originally it was proposed that three of the H-16 boats, with ten of the HS-1 and seven of the small R-6 training planes, should be sent to each United States naval air base established overseas. Since the estimates called for full replacement every three months, and since other planes of all three types would be needed in the United States, this allocation implied the delivery during 1918 of 2,630 HS-1, 788 H-16, and 4,478 R-6, a building program which almost no one believed possible of achievement. These figures had hardly been worked out before they were modified by the discovery that the Liberty was "too much motor for the R-6," a plane already unpopular with aviators overseas. This led to replacing it, for the European program, by the flying boats, and also led to a general recalculation of requirements. After considerable slashing of the figures submitted, those finally adopted in October, 1917, constituted what was known as the "Seventeen Hundred Program": 235 H-16, 825 HS-1, and, for home training, 640 R-6. Motors, allowing for estimated replacements, included 2,289 Liberties and 200 of the Curtiss V-2 type. Kite balloons to the number of 600, mostly of the Cagnot-M type, were included on the recommendation of the Bolling Commission that, launched either from land or from ships, they would be useful in spotting submerged submarines.

For training purposes, in addition to the R-6, the Army's JN and the latter's half sister in the Navy, the N-9, were accepted, and plants already operating could produce these types fast enough to meet the needs of student pilots taking the six months' course. Contracts for most of this production could therefore be made with Curtiss, the balance being distributed between Burgess, Boeing, and the Aeromarine Company, always provided that a solution could be found for the problems arising from the patent laws and the royalties they prescribed. As early as February, 1917, the War and Navy Departments, alive to these problems, urged the National Advisory Committee for Aeronautics to appoint a special subcommittee to find a solution. By July that subcommittee, of which Towers was a member, had succeeded, with the assistance of various other boards, in getting the producers organized into a Manufacturers Aircraft Association, pooling the basic Curtiss patents and the basic Wright patents with enough others to make the rather astonishing total of 192. A "cross-license" agreement was drawn, under which all concerned could be satisfied with royalties and so general was the satisfaction that some 50 companies in all joined the association before the end of the war.

Notwithstanding that everything was being planned with civilian builders, it had for some time been evident that to provide a dependable source of flying boats and seaplanes there must be some form of government-owned factory. An agreement having been reached with Congress, the Secretary of the Navy, on July 27, 1917, authorized $1,000,000 to build a Naval Aircraft Factory. Ground was broken at Philadelphia in August, the first mechanic was hired on October 1, and the manufacture of the first flying boat began on October 17. On November 28, just 114 days after the award of the contract for the building, the entire plant had been completed at a cost of about $3,750,000 under the supervision of Comdr. F. G. Coburn of the Construction Corps. At the end of March, 1918, the first H-16 boat was finished and ready for testing. By June a production rate of one flying boat a day had been reached, while by comparison with the average cost of building the first ten boats the current average cost represented a reduction of one half, a figure comparing very favorably with costs at private plants. The main difficulty was the employment problem, a serious one because of the Navy's fixed policy of not attempting to lure good workmen away from private concerns. Certain exemptions were made in civil service requirements which had further complicated this problem, and ultimately about one quarter of the whole force employed was made up of women. Not only did the factory run at full speed in manufacturing but it also established a training course for enlisted mechanics to familiarize them with construction and with machinery which they would ultimately have to maintain in the field.

As combat operations by the naval air arm expanded and intensified, the building program was necessarily revised until at the end of 1917 it had grown to include 864 twin-motored H-16's the latest flying boat. By January 1, 1919, Curtiss and the Naval Aircraft Factory together could produce 384 of these boats, but to provide the rest it became necessary to evolve a plan for sub-contracts. Under this plan yacht builders, woodworking and metal-working plants of many kinds, and even piano makers, were called upon to produce various parts of the flying boats for assembly at the Naval Aircraft Factory. No sooner had this been effected than it became clear that the British F-5 flying boat, with its double bomb-carrying capacity and its greater cruising radius, might to a considerable extent properly replace the H-16; modified to permit using the Liberty motor, it could be produced in quantity in the United States. This change was made and, by April, 1918, the Naval Aircraft Factory was producing the type, renamed F-5-L, with numerous subcontracts similar to those just described. Within another few weeks the factory had become, to all intents and purposes, an assembly, rather than a manufacturing plant and for this reason had been considerably expanded in size.

Meantime, in lighter-than-air craft, some difficulty was experienced in producing a durable fabric, until information upon researches conducted in England became available and was so well applied that American fabric eventually became the best used by the Allies. In May of 1917 Goodyear completed the first of the B-class nonrigids ordered in February, and sent it upon a test flight from Akron to Chicago. Within ten miles of the latter city shortage of fuel forced the ship down into a meadow, but even so the flight was the longest on the nonrigid record up to that time, good evidence that Hunsaker had a sound design. At intervals during the succeeding months sister ships were delivered until by the end of the year six were operating from stations on the Atlantic coast. Each one showed a few improvements over its immediate predecessor, such as leaving off one vertical fin, simplifying car suspension to bring the car closer to the envelope, installing air pipes on the ballonets inside the envelope and, through better propellers, increasing speed from 40 to 48 mph. Before the war ended these ships trained about 170 lighter-than-air pilots, of whom many went overseas to operate Allied dirigibles.

This building program, with its many successive modifications, obviously required huge sums and presented many problems that involved "carrying" contractors for considerable periods. Prices,

too, were a continuous question of give and take. Although the War
Credits Board and the War Finance Corporation, both established
by President Wilson in April, 1918, eventually took over the whole
financial problem, it was the Aircraft Board that hit upon what
was known as the "bogey price" contract, under which any manufacturer was assured a 15 per cent profit on his work and might,
if he saved on costs without skimping specifications, add to this a
bonus representing one quarter of the sum he saved. Solutions
such as this were generally applied throughout the whole procurement program, as combined for both Services, but occasionally
there arose a special case in which the Navy had to find for itself
a particular procedure. One instance was the critical matter of the
supply of spruce, the Navy finally going into the market to buy
great quantities of the New England variety which, in the long
run, proved quite as good as the Sitka spruce that had been almost
wholly bought up by the Army.

When the results of the huge procurement program came to be
added to the results of the wide-spread training program, the
outstanding question was: given this material and these men, what
could Naval Aviation do to help win the war?

CHAPTER XI

Early Effort Overseas

O F the various United States armed forces sent immediately to Europe, one of the first to get there was a detachment from Naval Aviation. Seven pilots and 122 mechanics, divided between the colliers *Jupiter* and *Neptune*, landed at Bordeaux and St. Nazaire respectively in the first week of June, 1917. Appropriately enough, this advance guard of fighting men was headed by impulsive, fire-eating Lieut. Kenneth Whiting.

The group had no planes and was sent over primarily to show a war-weary France that United States forces were actually on their way and thus be an antidote to the epidemic of unrest, nearly amounting to mutiny, affecting the French forces. Almost by accident, however, the result was to be much more important and far reaching because of the enthusiastic initiative of the man in command. Whiting's written orders merely told him to proceed to Paris and to keep the United States naval attaché there informed of his movements. When he had asked, in Washington, for detailed instructions, he had been given nothing beyond the advice that if he wanted to go to the war zone—as anyone who knew Whiting could be certain he did—he had better get started before some change of policy should cancel his orders. Upon this he had moved at once, and as soon as he reached Paris he began to act very much at his own discretion and on his own judgment.

Immediately he went into conference with the French Naval Chief of Staff, Admiral De Bon, and the Chief of the French Naval Air Force, Captain Cazenau. Although technically quite without authority to make commitments, Whiting agreed, with these officers, that American pilots would be trained at the French Army School, Tours, while American mechanics went to the machine school at St. Raphael. Further, he agreed to a plan for manning certain French air stations with American personnel, beginning at the Dunkerque Seaplane Station with some of Whiting's own men and following this by assigning other detachments, as they might reach France, to such stations as Le Croisic, St. Trojan, and Moutchic. Although these agreements were duly cabled to the Navy Department, it is worthy of note that they were made without consulting Admiral Sims who through some unexplained administrative oversight had never been told that Whiting and his men were coming. It was from the ever-watchful British Admiralty that Sims got his first news, coupled with an inquiry as to this extensive planning for France while relatively little had been done about England. This naturally put Sims in the embarrassing position of having to admit that the whole matter was a mystery to him, and he sent immediately for Whiting. If history had not already established the admiral's qualities of leadership, his action in this instance would prove them. When he had studied what Whiting had done he approved the whole plan and commended Whiting for his initiative. Any question of action without authority was dropped into the files.

It is safe to say that had conferences been held at the level of the high command before Whiting acted, air bases in England and Ireland would have been chosen ahead of any bases in France, for supporting aerial operations against U-boats. Nevertheless the bases in France were to be of importance in forcing the enemy out into the open sea, where targets were more widely separated and danger to Allied shipping was therefore relatively less. If the concentration of so much American Naval Aviation in France could not be considered strategically justified by the state of the antisubmarine war at the time of Whiting's agreements, it did prove sound in the end.

Whiting's more detailed recommendations proposed that pilots, observers, gunners, and signalmen be sent to France as rapidly as possible, the basis of their suggested assignment being an estimated total of 200 officers and men for each station. In addition, he asked for prompt consideration of a much broader French plan, calling upon the United States to take over 12 seaplane stations and three dirigible stations, all of which were either to be completed by the French from an unfinished state or, in some instances, built by them from plans to paint. On this point he was supported by Capt. R. H. Jackson, the naval attaché at Paris, who went even further to recommend the manning of five more stations: Brest, Ile Tudy, and Arcachon on the Atlantic; Antibes and Cette on the Mediterranean. To explain the French plan in detail Whiting arranged for the return to Washington of Capt. B. L. Smith of the

Marine Corps, who made representations that were shortly supported by those of Naval Constructor Westervelt and Lieut. W. G. Child of the Bolling Commission. Eventually, in August, plans for the first four bases were approved by the Secretary of the Navy with the remark that, "when practicable, the further assistance in aviation that has been requested will be given." A month later the Navy Department approved the program for 15 bases, five of which were also to have facilities for handling kite balloons and dirigibles.

At the head of the list of bases established as the result of this approval stands Moutchic, commissioned on July 17, 1917. From there the earliest flights by American aviators were made within another ten days, or only six weeks after the first group had reached France. Not far behind followed Le Croisic, built largely by German prisoners whom Whiting called "the best workmen in Europe" and pushed through by Lieut. J. L. Callan, who has already been mentioned in these pages as one of Glenn Curtiss' early civilian pilots, flying with Ellyson and Towers. Callan had entered the Naval Reserve as a lieutenant of the line, but after brief service on the cruiser *Seattle* he had left her in a French port to return to his first love, the air. Later on, considerable further use would be made of his abilities.

At St. Trojan and Dunkerque skeleton American crews were soon active, each as an earnest of the many more that were to come; a total then expected to reach, within the next 12 months, 3,000 officers and men. Arcachon was begun in November and St. Trojan in the following January; L'Aber Vrach, Fromentine, Guipavas, and Gujan in February, 1918. At Tréguier and Paimboeuf French construction was so far along that United States forces, when they eventually arrived, could move in immediately. These were exceptions, because in most cases the French had been far too optimistic in their promises to build. Skilled labor in France other than the German variety was extremely scarce and daily becoming scarcer; materials were not locally available and their importation from the United States was made anything but easy by the demands from everywhere else in Europe. Captain Jackson and Whiting both urged that portable hangars and barracks be sent and that personnel allotments be revised to provide for taking over all existing French bases and completing them. Nevertheless, even after Adm. H. T. Mayo, Commander in Chief of the United States Fleet, on a visit to Europe, had expressed to the Navy Department his ap-

proval of these recommendations, it still remained a practical
impossibility to meet them all.

During the summer of 1917 studies of the whole air situation
had been progressing at headquarters in London. Originally this
study had been begun in response to a dispatch, very revealing
as to how little was known in the United States, which had been
sent to Admiral Sims in the spring: "Immediate and full information is desired by the Navy Department as to the present development by the British of their naval aeronautics. What style of
aircraft is most used and what is most successful over the water?
What is the method of launching at sea when carrier vessel is under
way? For coastal patrol and searching what are the types of aircraft used?"

After replying in detail to the specific question, the admiral had
made recommendations that the United States send carriers, tenders, kite balloons, and whole squadrons of seaplanes with high-
powered motors and adequate spares. All these, he had said, must
be manned and serviced by trained men in almost unlimited numbers. As he and his staff saw the situation, it should be possible
for American naval forces eventually to take over, from the hard-
driven British, not only wide areas of the sea but also the protection of those areas from the air. With his strong convictions
daily growing stronger, the admiral continued to move toward that
end.

By September his forces were getting fresh inspiration from the
new aid for aviation, Capt. Hutch I. Cone. Realizing that more
rank in aviation was imperative and seeking "an able administrator, not necessarily an aviator," the admiral had asked for the
transfer to his staff of this lean, sandy-haired former Engineer
in Chief of the Navy, who was then serving as Marine Superintendent of the Panama Canal. Sims always knew his man but here was
one man known to the whole Navy for his ability, progressiveness,
and trenchant, witty comment. A year earlier there had been many
among the pioneers in Naval Aviation who had urged that he be
chosen to succeed Captain Bristol because of the help he had been
giving aviation on the technical side and because he could be
counted on not to hesitate in making his own decisions or in pressing
for action by higher authority. As aid for aviation, he provided
both the rank and the ability which the admiral needed to represent
him in all inter-Allied conferences on the war in the air.

Fitting into the organization, Cone gathered about him Comdr.

F. R. McCrary as lighter-than-air expert; Civil Engineers Ernest
H. Brownell and David C. Copeland to handle problems of construction; Lieuts. N. R. Van der Veer and Harry F. Guggenheim
as aides. Later his deputy in France would be Capt. Thomas T.
Craven; in London Lt. Comdr. W. Atlee Edwards, who also served
as liaison officer with the British Air Ministry. It would have been
difficult to find a group better qualified for these assignments.

Cone's earliest move was a tour of Ireland with his experts, examining possible sites for American operating air bases. Presently he agreed with the British that there should be four of these:
Queenstown, Whiddy Island, Lough Foyle, and Wexford, all four
eventually to come under the command of McCrary, with headquarters at Queenstown, where the United States destroyers were
based. In the original British proposals two other Irish sites had
also been included as suitable for American balloon stations, Lough
Swilly and Berehaven. Cone objected to both of these on the
ground that because United States ships were not operating in
adjacent waters there would be no need for American aircraft.
When he discovered, however, that construction work at Berehaven was well along, he changed his mind as to this station and
some American balloons were finally established there. Before
long it was to become apparent that they would be more helpful in
France and they were accordingly transferred cross-Channel with
consequent temporary United States abandonment of Berehaven.

A similar tour of England ultimately resulted in the establishment of a United States assembly-and-repair base built by the
British at Eastleigh, near Southampton, and of an operating
base at Killingholme, on the east coast near the mouth of the
Humber. Because Killingholme lies almost directly opposite the
Heligoland Bight, the British considered it particularly important and had already begun the construction of a base. Eventually the United States made it one of the most powerful air stations
in Europe; some 2,000 men and about 50 seaplanes were based
there for patrol flights that covered a total of 100,000 miles.
Not long before the end of the war, when the enemy's offensive
threatened the bases in the Dunkerque area, numerous planes were
flown to Killingholme from American bases in France and held
there in preparation against a possible final sortie by the German
High Seas Fleet.

From England Cone went to France. After approving all that
Whiting had accomplished, he took command and proceeded to

choose, as the principal air station in that country, the small town
of Pauillac, in the heart of the Medoc wine country near Bordeaux.
Well situated as to security, reasonably accessible to merchant
ships because of good depth of water, and with space to expand
if necessary, the choice proved a good one, and it was to Pauillac
that United States planes eventually came in hundreds. True, there
would be considerable delay in their operation because, although
the base went into commission in December of 1917, it was not until
the following April that motors and planes began to arrive from
the United States. Even then, both planes and motors were often
delivered damaged in one way or another, while some planes arrived without the right motors and without spare parts. More
than once, although originally consigned to Pauillac, they were
landed at Brest or somewhere else. Eventually Pauillac would become a factory-town, with sawmills, sail-lofts, machine shops, warehouses, hospitals, barracks, garages, besides several long docks
which contrived to handle not only the merchantmen from overseas but also the so-called Suicide Fleet, that small group of converted yachts doing escort duty with French-bound convoys. The
base commander, at the peak, was Capt. Frank Taylor Evans,
son of Fighting Bob. His father's equal as a blue-water sailor,
he was much more generously supplied with the milk of human
kindness; an inspired leader of his own forces and particularly
successful with local authorities because he was perfectly at home
in the language of the Paris boulevards; altogether a most happy
selection for a difficult, exacting duty. Over 7,000 men would
finally make up the command, to assemble, overhaul, and test aircraft, as well as to form what would become the distribution center
for aviation personnel in Europe. From Pauillac men went to all
the 28 bases finally to be operated under the United States Navy
in Europe; some occupied after they were finished by the French,
British, and Italians; others taken over half finished and completed; still others built from the turning of the very first sod.
Since all of these except Eastleigh, Moutchic, and Pauillac itself
were "operating bases"—that is, used for combat activities—their
need for additional personnel and replacements was continuous.

An early question for Cone's further study was whether or not
he should establish an air base on Belle Ile, off the southern French
coast, famous as the site of Sarah Bernhardt's summer home but,
at this moment of war, of possibly greater importance for seaplanes. Ultimately, after Cone decided that a seaplane tender

operating offshore would be as much use as a base on the island, the French abandoned this particular proposal. Similarly, on a British suggestion that the United States take over the aircraft at Le Havre, Cone's decision was that the French were already so well established there that they should not be disturbed.

With these Channel and near-Channel bases chosen, attention turned to questions of future operations, and this brought to the fore the British idea of launching bomber-seaplanes from lighters or barges, towed as near the targets as possible by destroyers and then partially submerged to permit launching the planes. Under this plan the British proposed to build and furnish 50 units while the United States provided 30 lighters and 40 planes, all to be in readiness for a heavy offensive in March, 1918. Admiral Benson, on his November, 1917, visit to London, approved the plan and cabled the Navy Department to begin immediately upon a building program to produce 30 lighters, 40 H-16 planes, and 100 motors. He also directed that 100 pilots, with the same number of observers and half as many special mechanics, be put into training for this project, while 600 additional enlisted ratings were to be assembled and trained to man Killingholme and the other bases. Whiting, placed in direct charge of this operation as prospective commander at Killingholme, made a trip to Washington to expedite the building program, which was given priority over all others dealing with the war in the air, and to do what he could to further plans for training personnel. Meanwhile pilots, observers, and ground crews already in Europe were being given opportunities to serve with the British Air Force for bombing and combat experience.

At the European end work upon a bombing project was advanced when Admiral Sims obtained the Navy Department's approval of his proposal to establish a planning section at London headquarters. This section, which could take immediate advantage of intelligence information, made studies covering the general strategy of the war and collaborated closely with the Admiralty. Capt. N. C. Twining, as Chief of Staff, was ex officio head of the section but its chief working members were three other outstanding captains, F. H. Schofield, Dudley W. Knox, and H. C. Yarnell. They made most of the studies, with the occasional assistance of Capt. L. McNamee and of Col. R. H. Dunlap of the Marine Corps. None of these officers was an aviator, nor had any of them a technical knowledge of aircraft; all of them were exceptionally equipped, mentally and professionally, to grasp the strategic possibilities of the use of aircraft. Generally in full agreement with the views of Captain Cone, they reached a series of decisions in which the essential feature was the advocacy of a continuous bombing offensive as the only hope of defeating the U-boat. They held that such an offensive, directed especially at U-boat pens, should be carried out even at the expense of reducing the air escort given to convoys.

Putting any such plan into operation was delayed by one matter demanding attention both in Washington and in London. This was the enemy's effort to create a strong impression that U-boats were about to invade the United States coast in force, an effort based upon the correct conviction that Washington would not dare to let Americans believe themselves inadequately defended. The Helm Board, reconvened in October, 1917, recommended additional air stations at Morehead City and Wilmington, North Carolina; Georgetown, Charlestown, and Beaufort, South Carolina; Daufuskie Island and Brunswick, Georgia; Fernandina, Jacksonville, Tampa, and St. Andrews, Florida; Mobile, Alabama; Port Arthur and Galveston, Texas. At the same time Captain Irwin urged the enlargement of all the bases already built or building, while Whiting, back from Europe in January, 1918, suggested that the best defense against expected U-boat raids would be coastal stations at regular 120-mile intervals, each maintaining 24 H-16 boats, with small refueling posts between the larger stations. Later, in May, 1918, when the expected raids began to come, only a few older bases were really ready: Chatham, Montauk, Bay Shore, Rockaway, Cape May, Hampton Roads, Miami, Key West, and Coco Solo. Among these Bay Shore, Miami, and Key West were used chiefly for elementary training; Pensacola and Hampton Roads chiefly for advanced work. The pilots who finished at either of these stations were required to get their final training at Moutchic in France under Allied instructors or under Americans already experienced overseas.

In January, 1918, negotiations for some time in progress with Portugal terminated in the establishment of a base at Ponta Delgada in the Azores, and 90 qualified pilots of the Marine Corps were sent there. Unfortunately, their planes were already obsolescent because they had no radio equipment and because they were capable of only a bare two hours' flight, handicaps which made the base little more than a "token" air factor during the war.

Meanwhile Cone, acting always with the unqualified approval

and support of Sims, took up the question of how to help in the Mediterranean. Conferences with the Italian authorities, begun in November after the catastrophe at Caporetto in October, had brought about a lift in the Italian national morale. The man who had been so successful at the French bases, Lieut. J. L. Callan, was shortly sent to Rome to report upon the whole situation. His knowledge of the Italian language and his previous experience, gained while still a civilian, as flying instructor for the Italian Navy, enabled him to perform this duty with distinction. From Captain de Filippi, head of Italian naval aviation, he learned that the latter was expecting 50 American pilots, all trained and ready for duty on the Austrian front; an expectation not at all justified by the contemporary plan in Washington which called for sending 50 students for training in Italy but ultimate use in France. Thanks to Callan's tact, supplemented by the efforts of Comdr. Russell Train, naval attaché at Rome, under whose general direction Callan acted, the Italians were persuaded to accept the Washington plan, but they continued to press for another group of pilots, trained as they had at first proposed. The training school at Lake Bolsena was assigned for use by the American fliers, and it was further suggested by de Filippi that United States forces, preparatory to an offensive against Austrian submarine bases at Pola, take over three stations, arranged in a crescent around Pola: Porto Corsini, Pescara, and San Severo, all of which the Italians expected to have ready by March, 1918. "Taking over" was to mean manning the base with pilots and mechanics, the Italians to maintain the base itself and to supply the planes. For example, 80 Caproni bombers were to be supplied for San Severo.

This Italian proposal was not approved. Such a major operation as it was likely to involve appeared, at the moment, to be impossible of accomplishment while the bombing of German bases was being carried out. It was, however, agreed that the United States would man the seaplane stations at Porto Corsini and Pescara, where the forces would operate under the Italian vice-admiral commanding air patrols for the district. Administration, however, was to be by United States officers, under the general supervision of Cone in London. The Italians were to continue training American pilots, in groups of 50, at the Lake Bolsena school, and they were to keep groups of skilled mechanics at the seaplane stations as long as these might be needed. Further, they were to maintain the schools and the stations in equipment, including planes, motors, fuel, lubricants, hangars, barracks, and mess facilities. Under these circumstances, and because construction of the Italian bases was practically complete whereas the French bases were unfinished, Callan recommended that some personnel be diverted from the latter to the former, and Cone, believing that the morale of the United States fliers would be improved by such a course, agreed. A preliminary detachment reached Lake Bolsena in the middle of February under Ens. William B. Atwater, and this was soon joined by an additional 35 officers and 300 enlisted men.

It would not be long before the Italian program would flounder. The Caproni land bomber was regarded as much more effective than any seaplane, and for this reason agreement had been made with Italy that the Caproni firm would furnish such planes in exchange for raw materials from the United States. Then it was learned that the United States Army had previously ordered 200 Capronis which had not been delivered, the Italians offering the excuse that they had not received the raw materials. Upon this the Navy agreed to deliver its own materials, a promise which led the Army's representative to protest violently that the Navy, because it had its own ships to carry cargo, was taking an unfair advantage. This army officer told the Italian Minister of Aeronautics that the Navy, as represented by Commander Train and Lieutenant Callan, had no authority to make any agreements. Very promptly the two naval officers went to the Minister and told him they did have authority. With the approval of Cone and Sims it was then agreed that materials shipped to Italy should be enough to replace all that might be used in building planes for the Navy and the Italians promised 30 Capronis for June and July, 1918, 80 more in August, and 20 a month thereafter. By negotiations with the Army on high levels amicable arrangements were made for the delivery to the Army of certain material brought in by the Navy, the Army to pass this along to the Italians and in return to accept planes and turn them over to the Navy. This proved to be an excellent agreement in theory but in practice it was a failure.

Callan, in his testimony before a committee of Congress some years after the war, said the army officer at the Caproni factory appeared to be a determined obstructionist because he refused to allow naval men, sent to the factory for instruction, to enter the buildings, and also put other obstacles in the way of progress on the Navy's program. Certainly that progress was very slow and the delay had a definite effect upon plans for a naval air offensive.

This was particularly disappointing because, after the "towed-lighter" plan lost favor when some of the lighters were photographed by enemy Zeppelins over the Heligoland Bight, the demand for Capronis as the best type of long range bombers grew greater. Since the Italian factories could not meet the demand, naval bombing operations suffered accordingly.

CHAPTER XII

Plans, Projects, and Operations

BRITISH Admiralty Intelligence, inspired and driven by its grizzled, razor-minded director, Rear Adm. Sir Reginald Hall, was extraordinarily efficient. It furnished Admiral Sims with information that was almost chapter and verse on the distinguishing numbers of U-boats about to leave their home pens, on their speed, the stores and torpedoes they carried, and the various positions at sea for which they would head. This last was of immense value, for it meant that some in-bound United States convoy could be diverted, by radio, well away from what would have been a fatal rendezvous. Repeatedly, the accuracy of the information was proven by some lone merchant ship flashing her SOS from a spot on the ocean only a biscuit's toss from the designated position, at an hour very close to the U-boat's predicted time of arrival there. Sometimes the U-boat surfaced after the torpedo had struck home, permitting her number to be checked as further proof of accuracy.

There were never enough surface craft available to chase all these U-boats, or even to intercept them for an attack. Thus they were far too free, after they found themselves quite regularly cheated of offshore convoy targets, to change their practice and concentrate in bottleneck waters like the English Channel and the Irish Sea, through which so many convoys must eventually pass in close formation. Here the enemy had the further advantage that these waters were as cloudy and hard to see through from the air as were those Chesapeake Bay areas of which Towers had long ago complained. Even for use in the shallows, moreover, sound devices in 1917 were very far from what they would become in 1942. By the time the United States Navy became really active in Europe, a graveyard of sunken hulls had accumulated less than ten miles off the British coasts.

Notwithstanding these handicaps, had the British had enough planes in 1916 and themselves been able to man the many air stations which the Americans would eventually establish, they could have greatly reduced that graveyard. This was not so much because of the attacking power of aircraft, a power then still in its infancy, as because of the moral effect of such craft on the U-boats. A plane or a balloon in the air above a convoy might be an indication of the ships' positions but both were more useful than an escort on the surface at detecting a periscope or an oil slick. It was a simple matter for either to summon destroyers, with their dreaded depth charges, and to remain, like a gigantic buoy, in the vicinity of the enemy. In countless instances reports of attacks by depth charge, sent in with the welcome note "Enemy destroyed," were made possible by aircraft which did not drop even one bomb. Since the U-boats were very well aware of all this, "Keep 'em down" became more than a mere slogan. A sky crowded with aircraft would have meant a sea much less often broken by the swirl around a rising periscope. Sooner or later a U-boat must rise, because in those days underwater stays were limited and subs had to surface to recharge their batteries at far shorter intervals than now.

As it was, there were too many U-boats willing to take the chance. Such a fellow as the famous *Penmarch Pete*, lurking close inshore under the beam of the big French lighthouse, could bag as many as four or five ships a night from some south-bound coastal convoy. German Naval Intelligence must also have been good, because all too often the ships sunk would be the particularly valuable members of that convoy. Every day the war continued made it more evident that defensive measures like espionage, patrols, and coast watchers would never really stop the U-boats. Only a strong and continuous offensive could do that.

Quite early in 1917 the situation had been summed up at Admiral Sims' Headquarters in a few paragraphs describing the Channel and the Irish coast as the U-boats' "favorite localities in winter," with activities of the summer months extended "to seaward and to the . . . Bay of Biscay," while the waters off Scotland and the Mediterranean were listed as "operating areas throughout the entire year." Admitting that the enemy controlled the air over the North Sea, from Dunkerque northeastward, this estimate also recognized the high quality of enemy antiaircraft fire which forced Allied planes to great altitudes and made bombing difficult. The tasks properly to be assigned to the United States naval aircraft were therefore outlined as follows: (1) to make our primary air effort a continuous bombing offensive against enemy bases, avoiding sporadic offensives; (2) to make our secondary air effort a patrol in readiness for tactical offensive; (3) to depend upon kite balloons for patrol and escort work.

It was naturally the first task that had always had the greatest appeal for both British and American naval airmen. Whiting, in August, 1917, proposed getting at the offensive by building seaplane carriers to take the bombers to points from which their short cruising radius could permit them to go in over Kiel, Wilhelmshaven, Cuxhaven, and Heligoland as easily as they could already attack Ostend and Bruges. This was no new idea for Whiting. More than a year earlier he had recommended the purchase of the big railroad-ferryboat *Henry M. Flagler*, on the ground that her double-deck construction, providing both protection for planes and a launching platform, made her ideal for experimental purposes. The recommendation had been disapproved at the time but it is interesting to note that 25 years later, in World War II, two such ferryboats were converted into aircraft transports.

It was the lack of carriers that had drawn so much favorable attention to the British towed-lighter plan, only to have doubt cast on its feasibility partly because of the enemy's prowess in aerial photography already mentioned, partly because the Admiralty finally decided that not enough destroyers could be spared for such operations. Lieutenant Commander Edwards described that plan as "fantastic" but no more so than many another that was "given a trial and, if it failed, shrugged aside as part of the game." Although war was a time for trying anything, however fantastic and costly, other plans for assuming the initiative in the air were somewhat less visionary. Edwards himself proposed taking over the British stations in the vicinity of Land's End and handling the whole patrol of the west coast of Ireland. This, he said, "would complete the defensive organization west of the meridian of Greenwich and in the enemy submarine zone." With a supply base at Plymouth, there would then be a complete chain of United States stations from Lough Foyle to Arcachon which, with the base in the Azores, should permit controlling all the main approaches to Europe for troop and supply ships in convoys from overseas. Noting that existing plans were mainly defensive, Edwards urged that the plans for 1919 include offensive operations from the east coast of England to the east coast of Italy. To carry out the latter he recommended two landplane bases in Italy and the organization of a southern bombing group to eliminate Pola, Trieste, and any other Austrian bases; operations which would, he said, require a 50 per cent increase in the number of planes based at Porto Corsini and Pescara. The increase in Italy should be in landplanes as much the more effective there. Even if the use of such planes by the Navy necessitated some form of amalgamation with the Army Air Service, Edwards considered that the advantage of having the planes would offset the disadvantages of the amalgamation. For the heavy bombing operations he proposed building large, five-motored flying boats, mounting ten machine guns and capable of carrying 3,000 pounds of bombs in flights of not less than 15 hours, to be driven, if these should have become available in time, by steam turbine motors rather than by Liberties. The Caproni bombers, he said, should be replaced as rapidly as possible by the new Super Handley Pages. As far as seaplanes might continue to operate, he recommended that the H-16 be replaced by a new design, better equipped to fight the Germans for mastery of the air over the North Sea; a type for which, he said, specifications should be drawn in Europe and submitted to the Navy Department.

Contrasting with Edwards' views came Maxfield's, sent in from Paimboeuf where he commanded the lighter-than-air forces. Agreeing that control of the North Sea and destruction of enemy submarine bases were the two main objectives, he was confident that nonrigid dirigibles could operate with the Fleet, protect convoys, and patrol all harbor entrances against enemy mine layers, provided bases for them were established at Penmarch on the coast of Brittany and at some point on the south coast of England. He wanted a new nonrigid of 10,000-cubic-meters capacity, carrying a 75-mm gun, two machine guns, 800 pounds of bombs, and fuel for 25 hours at cruising speeds. Other features which he thought the new type should possess included two motors of 250 horsepower, pusher propellers, a covered nacelle, facilities for cooking or heating food, metal water ballast tanks, increased visibility from the bridge, bombing sights through the nacelle, hand starting gear, and space on either side of the motors for men working upon them. He considered the nonrigid superior to the kite balloon for convoy work and also compared the dirigible with the seaplane to the advantage of the former. Declaring that commanding officers of seaplane bases were coming to his view, he said that the dirigible could be more accurately navigated, could leave its base at night to meet a convoy at dawn, and could await the convoy at any given point; that it could use its listening devices from the air and keep in constant radio touch with shore bases; that it could follow an enemy submarine in any direction; that it had a greater range of speeds than the seaplane and would, in the course of a year, roll up just as many flying hours. His was a clear case of enthusiasm for the weapon for which he was responsible; over-enthusiasm, perhaps, but in retrospect an interesting commentary upon the general development of the plans up to that time.

McCrary also favored the offensive and he suggested that the towed lighters might still be used if they were protected by "a number of fighting planes assigned to the Squadrons which operate from the decks of ships." Rather than increase the number of stations in Ireland, he favored using mother ships in protected harbors to supply men and materials to two or three planes coming in for temporary mooring. Two kite balloons, he said, should be carried in each convoy, ready for inflation at sea. Even if such balloons, in the air, might betray the convoy's position, their value would offset this weakness.

Callan, in Italy, called the Adriatic the "most vulnerable front," where a little heavier pressure might cause the collapse of the Hapsburg Empire. He urged taking over one squadron of 80 Capronis at Poggia and perhaps another from the British, to make the offensive against Pola a continuous one. This would require occupying the station at Ancona and building another at Vallona, for both of which more personnel and more supplies would urgently be needed. He held that the towed-lighter plan might operate here for long-distance reconnaissance flights, but on the whole he preferred carriers to lighters for this service as well as to protect Allied convoys. He, too, recommended discontinuing sporadic raiding in favor of the offensive which, once started, should never stop until enemy vessels and bases had been destroyed in such numbers that enemy morale shared the same fate. The islands of Paveglia and Sacca Sessola, in the Gulf of Venice, should be taken over, and an assembly plant built at Venice itself, while a large bombing base at Ferrara could be used to spearhead the proposed drive. The so-called Briscoe mission, visiting Italy late in 1918, was won over to Callan's view, but Admiral Sims disapproved that part of it which contemplated taking over Ancona. Eventually, in conferences with the Italian air authorities, it was agreed to proceed immediately with the Paveglia-Venice plan, the United States Navy to furnish several hundred men for the necessary construction of runways and buildings. Doubt of the advisability of this was expressed by Edwards in London, the already evident weakness of Austria-Hungary leading him to consider the effort, which would mean four months' work, as not worth while. Since the Briscoe report was in such marked contrast to these views, another special board, headed by Whiting, started for Italy to re-examine the situation and was en route when the armistice was signed.

Still another plan, regarded by many as preposterous, originated on the western side of the Atlantic in the fertile mind of Commander Mustin. Calling the craft he proposed a "sea sled," he described it as "in effect, a double set of floats." One set, he explained, was for cruising and would be designed to stay on the water "when the aeroplane takes the air: the other set, permanently attached to the aeroplane . . . for landing and flotation only." In short, bombers were to be transported on motor-driven sleds and launched when sufficiently close to their targets by the combined thrusts of the plane motor and the sled motor. He admitted the obvious disadvantage that the seaplane, once launched, could not be picked up but must, after its bombing mission was completed, find its way back to a base. The sled, however, could be handled by a crew of one and could get back with its own power. The type, he said, would be "in a way, a freak, for it has no use other than in warfare."

He called for 1,200 sleds, each to carry one seaplane equipped with machine gun or camera; 2,000 sleds to handle planes able to carry 500-pound bombs; and 2,400 more sleds for planes big enough to carry one 2,000-pound bomb or one aerial torpedo each. Granting that his numbers were large, he held that construction was well within the capacity of the American automobile industry and that lesser numbers would not permit the essential mass attacks in "simultaneous operations by many large squadrons." He proposed the use of Texel Island as a base, since this would convert the Zuyder Zee, with the waters near Vlieland, Terschelling, and Ameland, into what would amount to a huge aerodrome from which these great squadrons could take off together.

On paper and in tests with models, Mustin's idea proved to have so much to recommend it that he was promptly ordered into the Bureau of Construction and Repair to supervise a building program and full-scale tests. These tests, made with a Caproni bomber, were successful even though this big, lumbering plane was no easy load to handle; but the sled program as a whole proved to be another project which could not be tried in battle before the war was over. The ultimate result was that Mustin's sleds were actually used only in offshore rescue work, a service in which they did prove to be very efficient.

Meanwhile, armed with these various recommendations, Cone, with Captains Craven and Schofield, had conferred with Admiral Salaun and other French authorities late in the summer of 1918. It was agreed that no more stations need be established in France and that Dunkerque should be changed from a seaplane base into a landplane base as the center of a number of such bases assigned to offensive bombing. Belle Ile again came up for consideration, only to be rejected even though it was admittedly better for landplanes than its lack of harbors made it for seaplanes. On the material side, it was agreed that France needed no further seaplane hulls from the United States but should be furnished with motors and with various material for the construction of Zeppelin hangars. Two French dirigibles were to be sold to the United States, one to remain in Europe, the other to be sent home for experiments and for the training of personnel.

A little later, at conferences with the British air authorities, the latter proposed that the United States forces expand their activities widely. In addition to the operations from Dunkerque and Killingholme, as well as over the Bay of Biscay, the British proposed to turn over antisubmarine and coastal patrol, long-distance reconnaissance, and bombing operations in the Adriatic and the Strait of Otranto and also on the Irish coast, keeping in their own hands all other operations from Great Britain, the Mediterranean, and the Aegean. The American position, however, was that the primary effort of American forces should be in a continuous bombing offensive, which would require the production of long-range, heavily armed planes and also involve the gradual break-up of "mixed" forces in order to bring American units under American command.

By the end of September, 1918, agreement was reached, chiefly in line with the views of the United States. It was tentatively proposed to put 18 squadrons in the Adriatic, 12 for day, six for night work. Except for the patrol of the North Sea Mine Barrage and for occasional operations under the British commander of the east coast of England, there was to be no expansion of the American effort in England. No operations were to be added on the west coast of Ireland. General advance toward American command of United States forces was to be made. Major emphasis was laid upon ceaseless bombing of enemy bases and it was considered "extremely desirable to increase the American Bombing Squadrons in the Dunkirk Area to six day and six night squadrons."

On the whole seaplanes were falling into disfavor for bombing operations, attention being concentrated upon landplanes as having far longer range and much greater capacity for bomb carrying. Admiral Sims' planning section advocated designing a special type, to be more wieldy than the current ones and to be equipped to defend itself against enemy aircraft. Pending definite action upon this recommendation, it would be necessary to obtain landplanes from the Army which, as has been noted, had cognizance over the principal producers of these. It was planned, when sufficient planes and personnel became available, to organize six squadrons for day bombing, six more for night bombing, and use them with similar British squadrons to deliver a ceaseless rain of bombs upon submarine pens and any other objectives that were properly naval. Some elements of the Army, led by Major General Foulois, head of the Army Air Service overseas, contended that landplanes were strictly army weapons and that the Navy had no business attacking land bases. Foulois' objections became stronger when the War Department, because of its expanding needs and lagging production, found itself unable to fill the Navy's requests for planes and therefore referred these to General Pershing. The latter, however, had the whole broad picture more clearly in mind and he agreed with Admiral Sims that the important thing was to win the war. If the Navy could gain that end by bombing submarine pens, by all means let the Navy do it—a view in line with that of Sims, who held that the use of landplanes by the Navy was not necessarily an indication that the Navy was encroaching upon the Army's territory.

Unfortunately Foulois remained obstructive, next raising the specter of the German summer offensive as a reason why no planes could be spared by the Army. There were some rather acrimonious exchanges between Foulois and Cone, and these were intensified by current rumors of a plan to consolidate all air forces under one head. Foulois wanted to be that head while Cone and Edwards, provided planes could be obtained and bombing begun, were willing to risk even subordination, if that must be the price.

Eventually the Navy's requests for army planes were for 75 of the bombers with 40 single-seat pursuit planes for escort purposes, wanted by July 1, 1918, followed by 75 fighters by October 1. The War Department agreed to supply the October needs in fighters but insisted that the question of bombers must be settled by General Pershing. It seemed to escape General Foulois that the German summer offensive would in any case be over before the planes wanted by the Navy could reach Europe and that adequate logistic support of the American Expeditionary Force would become impossible unless the U-boats were stopped.

There were many discussions, particularly after the first Handley Pages received from the Army proved unsatisfactory. Even though the Army offered to make good all defects, the attention of naval airmen turned to Capronis. As has already been noted, Capronis were another disappointment, and for a time it appeared that the whole bombing offensive, known as the Northern Bombing Project, was doomed to failure. The Navy was determined that this should not happen.

Capt. David Hanrahan, appointed by Admiral Sims to command the whole project, pushed it vigorously from headquarters at Autingues. Liberty motors began arriving at Eastleigh and at Pauillac, slowly followed by planes. Some planes came with warped wings or with other defects such as incomplete wiring, while even the motors were sometimes improperly assembled, all defects that caused heartbreaking delays and necessitated what were almost miracles of overhauling. Since it had been decided, however, that the Navy "must provide suitable aircraft for this purpose," no effort to provide them could be spared—and none was.

Personnel requirements had been estimated at about 530 officers and ten times as many enlisted men. Preliminary training in night flying for those pilots who already had at least 40 hours' solo to their credit was begun at Miami under Lieut. Richard E. Byrd. From that school the officers went overseas for further training in British planes such as the Sopwith, which they flew with the Royal Air Force, notably Squadrons 213 and 214. Meanwhile enlisted men, trained as far as might be, were assembled at Eastleigh and other stations for final instruction.

By September most of the American-manned stations in Europe were in operation. Although it was rare for more than two planes to be sent out at any one time from Lough Foyle, Wexford, Whiddy Island, Queenstown, and Berehaven, altogether they managed to fly over 45,000 miles in patrols and to make attacks on seven U-boats, seriously damaging at least two. Killingholme, which had begun operations in July, was better off, with 46 planes and 1,900 personnel. Regular patrols were flown from that station by day and by night, until they had covered 100,000 miles, with credit for one sinking and a number of "possibles." In September some planes were moved to Killingholme from the French bases, on the chance that the High Seas Fleet might attempt a final sortie, but this never materialized.

Toward the end of June Capt. Thomas T. Craven, at Cone's request, took command of the French bases and Cone himself went to London headquarters. By that time, Ile Tudy, Le Croisic, Dunkerque—all seaplane bases—were established, Paimboeuf was ready for dirigibles, and Pauillac and the Moutchic school were in operation. A few other French stations were completed and ready for American planes.

Flights from Dunkerque were begun September 1, 1918, but they continued only ten days before it was decided to abandon that base. Arcachon started its flights early in October and, as more planes arrived overseas, Tréguier was ready in November. At La Trinité the first kite balloon from the United States was delivered on October 18. The first formal patrol from Le Croisic had gone into the air on November 18, 1917; the last one would be flown on December 13, 1918, as an escort to President Wilson, arriving in France for the Versailles Conference. During those months 27 submarines were sighted, 25 attacked, 12 described as "damaged."

The first independent Northern Bombing Group operation was carried out on the night of August 15, 1918, when a single Caproni, flown up from Italy shortly before, went over Ostend and dropped 1,250 pounds of bombs on the U-boat pen there. Unfortunately this particular plane on each of its next two attempts was turned back by engine trouble, a circumstance which forced the decision that Capronis, even if they could make the hard flight over the Alps, would not do for northern bombing.

At about this time, three marine fighter squadrons reached Europe. Under Major Cunningham, they were based in France, at Oye and at Le Frêne, where the pilots were rotated in their assignments in order to permit each to fly on three missions as a member of one or another of the Royal Air Force squadrons. Since not enough American planes had been received to organize independent squadrons, such planes as had arrived were loaned to the British and it was not until October 13, 1918, that Marine Day Squadron 9 carried out the first raid in force by a unit of the Northern Bombing Group.

During that same month Captain Hanrahan had three Capronis, four DH-9, and seven DH-4 planes actually flying, with some 200 other planes of various types in process of assembly and test. At the outset the Northern Bombing Group had been placed under the operational direction of the British admiral at Dover, who selected the group's targets. Presently, however, as evidence that the enemy was weakening began to pile up, it was decided that the bombers might be used to greater advantage if they were attached to the 5th Group, Royal Air Force. When this had been agreed to by all the High Commands, the group found itself raiding over canals, railroads, supply dumps, and airfields, completing eight of these raids into Belgium during the month. Other American naval pilots flew with French and British land squadrons over Steenbrugge, Eecloo, Ghent, Deynze, and Lokeren, besides destroying the munition works at Bruges, blowing up a lock gate at Zeebrugge, and bombing several enemy destroyers away from their berths alongside various docks. Now and then, when they were operating independently, members of the group got a little combat experience in brushes with the enemy. Through a series of such brushes, in which he shot down at least five planes and balloons, Lieutenant Ingalls of the original Yale Unit qualified as the Navy's only ace in World War I.

As the German retreat continued the group moved forward until by November 1 one day squadron had reached the enemy's abandoned station at Knessalare in Belgium, while several other day squadrons were close behind it and the leading night squadron had reached Marin Alta. At that date the group had a force of 250 officers and 2,400 enlisted men in the field, backed by about the same numbers in reserve at British bases. All hands were just getting into fighting condition when Armistice Day halted operations and made it unnecessary to carry out the extensive plans for bombing in 1919, laid upon the foundation of the lessons learned. An idea of the number of missions actually flown may be had from the following table, based upon the Navy's using bombs weighing from 500 to 1,500 pounds while the Marine Corps' smaller ones weighed 50 to 100 pounds:

Pounds of Bombs Dropped

Naval pilots flying with Allied units	54,332	
Naval observers or gunners with Allied units	21,984	
Naval personnel, Northern Bombing Group (night)	22,670	
		98,986
Marine Corps pilots flying with Allied units	15,077	
Marine Corps observers or gunners with Allied units	625	
Marine Corps personnel, Northern Bombing Group (day)	11,614	
		27,316
TOTAL		126,302

Considering the short period of time covered, the figures are impressive, and a longer war would have made them much more so. The coming of peace brought a feeling of security which allowed dust to accumulate upon many of the lessons learned and this meant that they had to be learned anew, years later.

CHAPTER XIII

The Record of Accomplishment

TOWARD the autumn of 1918 it had become evident that planning in Naval Aviation was well ahead of existing operational needs. A month later the obvious weakening of the enemy made it clear that these plans must be slowed down. In personnel, whereas the Navy had just agreed with the Selective Service Board that 15,000 drafted men should be allotted each month for all branches, it now appeared that it would be possible to end the war with volunteers and without drafting even one man. Pilot training, notably in the night-flying groups, was cut down in order to graduate not more than 200 pilots a month from all stations, while the ground school output was reduced by half, and no more officer candidates were enrolled. At the same time the material production program was slowed, especially in the manufacture of the HS-2, the F-5, and the trainer planes. Even so, there would be a very considerable final surplus in these types and also in the foreign planes owned by the Navy when the armistice was signed.

This "breather" allowed time for looking into some criticisms of the program, including comments made by Assistant Secretary of the Navy Franklin D. Roosevelt after his visit to Europe in August, when he described as "scandalous" the lack of follow-up from Washington and the evidence of improper inspection before material was shipped abroad. At the Navy Department's order Sims convened a board to "make a thorough investigation of past and present conditions as to the supply and shipment of all naval aircraft material and if unsatisfactory [determine] who or what is responsible." Accordingly Commanders Westervelt and Smead, with Lt. Comdr. Nelson Pickering, Lieut. J. S. Jones of the Pay Corps and Ens. Ralph S. Barnaby, met under instructions to visit all the bases in England, Ireland, and France. These officers had been serving as inspectors since August, 1918, but Sims now expanded their duties.

As the board very soon discovered, difficulties in carrying out the program had been legion and mistakes had been all too numerous. What might have been done more thoroughly, at less cost, under a long-view plan of preparedness, had been accomplished, to a greater or less degree, under the heavy pressure of emergency. Personnel had been rushed through training, and officers without any practical understanding of the Navy had found themselves, a few short weeks after they had been in civilian business not even within sight of the sea, pushed into responsible naval positions abroad. As the board would particularly note, the performance by these officers of their unfamiliar duties and the success with which they rose to their responsibilities were a very high tribute to their spirit and their adaptability. That a few made mistakes or failed in what was asked of them was no occasion for astonishment.

Very much the same comment applied with equal force to the enlisted personnel, thousands of whom found themselves lifted out of wheatfields in the center of the United States and landed on the edge of European towns whose inhabitants could not speak English but would do almost anything for an American dollar, a situation often demanding delicate handling. Other thousands who had known only enough about automobiles to drain a crankcase found themselves overhauling Liberty motors on which the lives of their shipmates might depend. Short handed and half trained as it had been, the enlisted personnel, too, had built up a fine record.

On the material side there had been vexatious delays, misunderstandings, and errors of omission and commission. Base construction, for example, had lagged because not enough civil engineers had been available as supervisors and because far less than enough skilled labor could be sent across the Atlantic. Any such careful planning as that which in World War II produced the highly effective construction battalions was almost wholly lacking in 1917. The best that could be done was a hurried muster of whatever talent was in sight at any given moment and an equally hurried dispatch of it overseas. The material was disorganized through hasty assembly at United States ports and over-rapid loading into vessels of which many were destined to be sunk by U-boats and some to reach ports quite different from those to which their cargoes had been consigned. In the latter instances the material had then to be subjected to all the difficulties of European transportation systems disrupted by war.

This problem of delivering materials naturally applied particularly to all the spares required by Naval Aviation overseas. Crankshafts, propellers, starters, tachometers, and everything else went astray or, when delivered at their designed destination, proved to be unsuited to the planes and motors already there. Very often these planes and motors should have been on some other base at that moment. Even the bomb gear, finally delivered overseas in September, 1918, proved defective and had to be returned to the United States for rebuilding. Similar gears, on order in England, fell so far behind their delivery dates that American planes finally had to use French gear and French bombs.

Packaging, too, had been hurried and frequently marred by inexperience. Such an item, for example, as caustic soda, had been shipped in uncrated drums, causing frequent bursting with resulting loss of the soda and costly damage to other cargo. Storage facilities abroad had been inadequate, inventories had either been incomplete, or, because of the pressure of operations upon insufficient personnel, omitted altogether.

Viewed from a really critical angle the whole picture was not a pretty one, and the board did not hesitate to note all its dark shadows, easily discernible by hindsight when the pressure of a night raid or a dawn change of base had been removed. Nevertheless there stood out, at the center of the picture on which the eye must inevitably fall, the essential fact that Naval Aviation had made a very considerable contribution to the American effort to help win the war. Its 1,147 officers and 18,308 men in service overseas had taken part in and produced 22,000 flights. From its 20 patrol bases it had patrolled a total of 791,398 sea miles, not including the distances flown by United States pilots as part of Allied units. Finally, of the three men from his whole command recommended by Admiral Sims for the Congressional Medal of Honor two were naval aviators—Lt. Comdr. Artemus Gates, for a gallant rescue under fire of several British aviators shot down off Ostend; and Ens. C. H. Hammon for a similar rescue of a fellow pilot shot down off Pola.

When the board's report was submitted to Admiral Sims, he forwarded it with comments which so fairly summarize all these matters that they seem worth quoting in full:

The Force Commander is strongly of the opinion that the organization of the U. S. Naval Aviation Force in Europe for which no precedent existed, was accomplished in a most efficient, energetic and expeditious manner. Organization on entirely new lines from those which had hitherto existed was required and promptly created. At every stage of this work definite plans were drawn up, submitted and carried out to the Force Commander's entire satisfaction insofar as was possible with the inadequate material and personnel at hand.

The Force Commander feels it incumbent upon himself to call attention to certain difficulties encountered in the organization of Naval Aviation in Europe and the following points are, therefore, set down, not in the spirit of criticism, but in order that future undertakings of a similar nature may not suffer from like causes:—

(a) Lack of a definite, pre-arranged plan for the establishment of a Naval Aviation Force on Foreign Service.

(b) Lack of adequate personnel with special reference to commissioned officers in the early stages of organization. The number of regular officers in Europe was exceedingly small and, for this reason, but very few could be diverted from their regular stations and duties to assist those charged with the organization of the Naval Aviation Force. It was necessary to place inexperienced officers in positions of great responsibility. Many Reserve Officers were of inestimable value and brought to the work a zeal and intelligent interest which contributed largely to the results accomplished, and in many instances these officers were seriously handicapped by their exceedingly junior rank which made it difficult for them to negotiate successfully with Foreign Officers of high rank with whom they found themselves officially associated. Every effort was made to have these officers promoted, but in the majority of cases our recommendations were not acted upon.

(c) Shortage of officers with business experience in the Supply Department, which was of paramount importance, both in shipping the materials from the United States and in the execution of the work in Europe. Experienced, qualified officers of previous training in Supply Department work should have been detailed for duty in handling Aviation material or capable men should have been selected from export shipping and trading business, enrolled as Reserve Officers, and put in charge of the following: contracts, tracing and receipt of railroad shipments, loading of vessels in the United States and of the corresponding duties in Europe.

(d) Transportation difficulties abroad which were accentuated by the enemy drive in 1918 to an unexpected and unavoidable degree.

(e) Insufficient training of the flying personnel sent from the
United States, which imposed upon Naval Aviation, Foreign Service,
the additional duty of further training this personnel in order to make
them available for war flights.

In summation, the Force Commander desires to emphasize his ap-
preciation of the valuable duty performed by Captain H. I. Cone,
U. S. Navy, in having organized and operated the U. S. Naval Aviation Force, Foreign Service.

Completed by this endorsement of the admiral's, the report was
handed to the Assistant Secretary of the Navy in December, 1918.
Through some mishap this original was lost and the carbon copy
then sent from Europe did not reach the Secretary of the Navy
until March, 1919. It then bore the further forwarding endorsement of Captain McKean, still the Assistant Chief of Naval
Operations, who remarked that Admiral Sims' comment applied
equally well "to the work that had to be accomplished in the Department under the Director of Naval Aviation in the way of new
organization for which there was no precedent," adding that "it
was due in a great measure to the organization at home that the
Foreign Service was able to accomplish what it did." For the lack
of prewar planning for Naval Aviation the captain gave the
highly interesting explanation that "in view of the fact that the
Navy Department . . . had never expected to extend its activities to European territory in case of war and that Aviation was
such a new activity, it is hardly to be expected that the Department
would have pre-arranged plans for Naval Aviation Forces on
Foreign Service, prior to the present war." As to the shortages
of personnel and delivery, the captain explained that "the exigen-
cies" had required that much that had been intended for Naval
Aviation be diverted to other branches of the Navy and he thought
great credit was due the office for having sent overseas what could
be thus diverted! Altogether, Captain McKean's defense of the
whole establishment of Naval Aviation appears to have been de-
cidedly more spirited than his support of it at the time when he
joined the Office of Naval Operations.

There were some grounds for satisfaction over what had been
accomplished on this side of the Atlantic. On the Atlantic coast
12 patrol stations had been established with 13 rest and refueling
points at intervals. In August, 1918, work began on a base at
Halifax and on another at North Sydney, Nova Scotia. By Sep-

tember flights had been made from both places by planes escorting convoys. A base at Cape Broyle Harbor, Newfoundland, was contemplated but never built.

Schools in operation included three ground schools, five elementary flight schools, and two advanced flight schools, with numerous facilities for practice in aerial navigation, gunnery, and bombing. About 4,000 pilots had been trained by November, 1918, while 30,000 enlisted men had passed through technical training. On the material side, 24 manufacturers, employing 175,000 persons, were equipped to build 21,000 aircraft a year and the record of actual deliveries had reached 16,000 planes and 25,000 motors. The latter, in November, 1918, were coming off the assembly lines at the rate of 4,000 a month with the expectation that by March, 1919, this output figure could be raised to 10,000. Considering the very great difference between the position of aviation in general in 1917 and its position in 1941, the accomplishments of World War I compare very favorably with those of World War II. In the earlier war it required a year after the United States began hostilities to get the air program fully underway; in the later war, it was eight months after Pearl Harbor before Naval Aviation was ready for Guadalcanal and many more months before the air drive across the Pacific could be launched.

Demobilization after the armistice was rapid—as much too rapid as it always will be in democracies. Except for certain specialists needed for the roll up abroad, no further personnel was sent overseas, and while those already under flight training were temporarily permitted to continue in service, no further enrollments were made as the routine of discharging began. Construction on stations abroad was stopped; on stations in the United States it was suspended. No more material was shipped, contracts for plane building were canceled, and arrangements for the sale of surplus planes were made. Signatures upon the armistice were scarcely dry when the Secretary of the Navy issued his first order requiring rigid curtailment and economy. The official copy of the armistice had hardly reached Washington when the House Appropriations Committee began talking of hearings on a bill to turn all surplus funds back into the Treasury.

Naturally this precipitated something of a crisis. The Navy Department's plans provided for spending about $123,000,000 on aviation in the remainder of the fiscal year 1919, more than half of this sum being allotted to the settling of claims and contracts.

The balance was to have been used for completing and maintaining nine air patrol stations and 25 rest stations on the Pacific Coast, in Alaska, Hawaii, and the Philippines, to supplement the proposed 20 patrol and training stations and 34 rest stations on the Atlantic coast, as well as for the lighter-than-air experiments and the general training program. Inevitably all these plans would have to be changed to meet the idea expressed in the slogan, "The war is over. Let's get out of it and forget it!"

As to personnel, this would be especially true after such orders as that of the Secretary of the Navy dated November 15, 1919, opened the way for so many enlisted men to secure their discharges. Family problems, private business, or a desire to continue one's civilian education could be advanced as legitimate, acceptable reasons for getting out of uniform. Under one head or the other almost any man could leave the Navy and a great many did. By January 1 prospective cuts by Congress in the Navy's personnel made it necessary for the Navy Department to direct the substitution of as many civilians as possible for enlisted men in the administrative offices in order to increase the use that might be made of such enlisted men elsewhere. Meanwhile, liquidation of naval property left in Europe proceeded slowly, through the inevitable complications of determining what was and what was not worth bringing back, of finding shipping space, of protecting what was to be left overseas, and finally of disposing of what was salable at anything like fair prices. What with rent charges, claims for losses of every possible description, transportation of material from "somewhere in France" to a shipping port, and all the hundred details involved, the work was clumsy and costly. The French, making the most of their "buyers' market," drove such hard bargains that, in many instances, huge properties were practically given away. Portable buildings, construction materials, trucks, and the like, for which the Navy had expended a total of nearly $750,000,000, were sold much below cost to the Committee for the Relief of Belgium, to be used in that country and in the devasted regions of France. As late as October, 1919, French claims covering aviation material of various kinds delivered to the United States Navy at one time or another were still being received. Indemnities for "damage" to French property had not been paid in full and the stations at Arcachon and Moutchic were still unsold. Official French objection to the sale of buildings and materials to private individuals was a stumbling block in the path toward settlements and many months would elapse before the books could be closed. In England, on the other hand, because there was no objection to private sales, progress was more rapid. The air stations were all closed very rapidly and by the middle of August, 1919, more than half of the outstanding bills and claims were paid. The Canadian problem was readily solved by giving Canada all the equipment which the United States Navy had supplied to Halifax and North Sydney. In Italy a similar procedure was followed but at Ponta Delgada in the Azores all equipment was disassembled and brought home. Altogether, material demobilization was very costly but no one had ever imagined that it would be anything else. At least the loss could be measured in dollars to be written off the national ledger, whereas the effect of rapid demobilization upon the position of the United States as a world power is less easily determined.

CHAPTER XIV

Postwar Problems

NAVAL AVIATION had made a good record during the war. In spite of many difficulties and more than one failure, it had achieved with credit an expansion to relatively enormous size in material and personnel. At the date of the armistice it had stood ready to launch what would have been the one strictly American naval offensive. If its progress and performance had not converted all the skeptics, many of these had become convinced that aviation, as an arm of sea power, must thenceforth be reckoned with to the fullest extent. Unfortunately there remained too many others still adhering to the opposite conviction, still insisting that aviation should be completely subordinated.

To the well informed the major problem was that of integrating aviation with the Fleet, a step long ago urged by Captain Chambers. They recognized that Admiral Mayo, the Commander in Chief, had been right in pointing out that the effort of the Navy's air arm during the war had been spent in "conducting operations . . . in bombing and on escort duty," leaving little or no opportunity for work with the battleships. Accordingly, as soon after the armistice as January, 1919, a squadron of H-16 flying boats was sent to the Fleet, wintering at Guantánamo.

For the first time the planes had a makeshift tender in the mine layer *Shawmut*, commanded by Capt. George W. Steele, who had been an assistant to Captain Irwin during the closing period of the war. Steele had the impressive title of Commander, Air Detachment, Atlantic Fleet, in itself a great incentive to the flying boat men under Lt. Comdr. Bruce G. Leighton, to the two Sopwith Camel crews working under Lieutenant Commander McDonnell from the launching platform of the *Texas*, and to the six kite balloon crews already established ashore at Guantánamo. Intercepting exercises were held, in which the flying boats charted the position, course, and speed of an "enemy" fleet and on at least one occasion directed a submarine attack upon it. Shifting their base from Guantánamo to Port au Prince, then to Kingston, and then back to Guantánamo, the fliers demonstrated their mobility, the improvement in their radio communication, and the very considerable increase in their acccuracy in dropping bombs near improvised targets. Spotting practice, although it was marred by the wrecking of one H-16, was successful enough to be very encouraging, while McDonnell's flights from the turret top earned from the General Board the admission that the performance had given it "confidence in the adaptability of the airplane to the battleship" and the further comment that "your success . . . has taught us the necessity of having airplanes for spotting." Experience gained in these ways was supplemented by what the marines were getting through their fliers in Haiti and Santo Domingo, where they had established flying fields for operations with their battalions then intervening in these islands. Both landplanes and seaplanes, flown under service conditions and with none too many facilities, proved that they could stand such conditions. Later, in May, when the Fleet came north, further gratifying results were obtained by the air detachment, deprived of the services of the *Shawmut* but temporarily based upon Hampton Roads, in numerous flights made chiefly with the F-5-L boats.

To look ahead a little, the worth of the *Shawmut* was so evident that it led to the making of fuller plans for that necessary adjunct of Naval Aviation, the seaplane tender. Clearly, if such tenders were available, the large flying boats would be able to go wherever the Fleet went, meeting an obvious essential of any effective flying arm. Accordingly during the next two years there would be numerous experiments, beginning with the use of the converted yacht *Isabel* and some of the war-built Eagle boats, continuing through the partial conversion of the destroyers *Harding* and *Mugford,* and leading to the assignment of the mine layer *Aroostook* as seaplane tender for the Pacific Fleet. She was helpful but she could not do much more than "fill in" whatever service was not supplied by the air station at San Diego to the 18 seaplanes, six "left-over" balloons, and two airships making up the Pacific Fleet Air Force. If the personnel should be brought up to the allowed complement of 56 officers and 400 enlisted men, the *Aroostook* would be far too small to house it. Clearly something bigger and more appropriately equipped was required and conversion of the auxiliary cruisers *Charles* and *Yale* was given consideration, only to be abandoned because of the relatively great cost of this work. Similarly, tentative plans to use the two captured German ships, renamed *DeKalb* and *Von Steuben*, were abandoned when these vessels had to go to the Army as transports. Attention then centered upon "B-type" hulls, left over at Hog Island from the Shipping Board's war construction program.

Arrangements for the conversion of four of these hulls into destroyer and aircraft tenders were completed, only to be disrupted by a misunderstanding between the Army and the Navy which was never quite clearly explained. The Steele Board, organized for the purpose, went to Hog Island in November, 1919, ready to redesign the four ships to serve as tenders for both lighter-than-air and heavier-than-air craft. To their astonishment they discovered on arrival that work on three of the four had already gone too far under army plans to make them of use to the Navy at less than prohibitive cost. After considerable further discussion with the Shipping Board, the Emergency Fleet Corporation, and the Army, the Navy was in the end perforce content to take this fourth hull, eventually commissioned in December, 1921, as U.S.S. *Wright*, the first of her type and for many years the last. Notwithstanding strong appeals to Congress by Secretary Daniels and others, no further funds for building tenders were appropriated. Like so many important factors in the problem of keeping Naval Aviation in the air, this one had to be met by makeshift—the continued use of mine craft, Eagles, seagoing tugs, and almost anything else that could be pressed into the service. Quarters aboard such craft were cramped, living in general was hard, and stowage space was inadequate, but in one way or another the result was "make do" and, even as late as World War II nine converted mine sweepers were still servicing the Navy's aircraft.

Another effort toward consolidating Naval Aviation with the Fleet was expended upon studying the possible usefulness of the torpedo plane. Interest, aroused during the war through the sinking of a Turkish transport by a plane from a British cruiser, was stimulated in the period immediately after the armistice when a British destroyer, at full speed, was "sunk" in a sham battle by six torpedo planes scoring at least four "hits." This brought a comment from the captain of the battleship *Texas* that a carrier like the *Argus* or the *Furious*, "with twelve or fifteen torpedo planes, should be a match for a whole battleship division." All hands did not agree, however, that special planes were needed; Captain Steele, for example, insisted that since the Navy would always have torpedoes, it should be simple, if the need to use them from the air arose, to "hook them on" to any aircraft. Steele also held that the low altitude at which a torpedo-carrying plane must fly would entail the "inevitable destruction of the plane" by enemy guns; better, said he, to try to sink enemy ships by bombing. The Bureau of Ordnance, for its part, pointed out that the "dropping of a torpedo within sight of a vessel would immediately disclose the character of the attack," whereas a destroyer's underwater torpedo might not. The bureau considered that where torpedo planes were used, the best chance of success would attend an attack by a number of them upon a group of ships so restricted in course and speed that they could not readily maneuver to avoid the oncoming torpedoes. In any event, said the bureau, the use of torpedoes weighing less than the standard 3,000 pounds would probably not be worth while because even this standard size did not always damage a capital ship enough to sink her. Such torpedo plane practice as was begun in the Fleet in consequence of these various recommendations did not amount to very much. The chief obstacle to success lay in the planes used for the purpose—the R-6-L float plane brought out during the war and not nearly rugged enough to handle its fuel load, a crew of two, and a 1,000-pound torpedo. It would be another two years before much headway was made along this line.

Meanwhile consideration was given in the Navy Department to three reports made at the end of 1918 by Admiral Mayo. The first of these discussed the Royal Navy's advances in aviation, with new planes for carriers, both seaplane and landplane, and with new and improved types of aircraft; the second dealt with British progress in lighter-than-air flying; and the third presented the admiral's recommendations for the United States naval air service. It was in this last that he urged using planes with the Fleet, contrasting the 22 British battleships carrying turret platforms for handling planes with the one American battleship, the *Texas*, fitted with a platform but not regularly equipped with planes.

The admiral recognized that any program, even if it were presented to the Congress with the full approval of the General Board and the Secretary of the Navy, would be subject to drastic curtailment. Nevertheless, he called for a naval air service "sufficient in all respects for reconnaissance, spotting, carrying torpedoes, anti-submarine patrols and escort duty"; all these re-

quirements to be met, as might prove best, by lighter-than-air
or heavier-than-air machines. Aerodromes, hangars, and bases in
adequate numbers the admiral considered mandatory; stations
for kite balloons must be established, he held, in close proximity to
the Fleet base, and the equipment of appropriate stations for
properly training personnel was equally vital. Further, he ad-
vised the designing and building of carriers for all planes, with
the provision of not less than two of each type, each able to carry
25 planes at a speed equal to that of the swiftest battleship. Pending the completion of these carriers, two turrets on each battleship and battle cruiser should be fitted to handle two small
reconnaissance planes, while each scout cruiser should carry one
of these. In types of aircraft Mayo called for scouts, fighters,
torpedo carriers, and seaplanes, with rigid dirigibles for scouting
and nonrigids for patrol and escort. German Zeppelins being
admittedly by far the best of their type, he urged that the Navy
take over at least two of the Zeppelins allotted to the United
States under the terms of the armistice. As one means of maintaining such an air service, the admiral recommended the careful
disassembly of those two costly plants, Eastleigh and Pauillac,
their transportation, and their reassembly in the United States.

Among aviators there was general enthusiasm for most of Admiral Mayo's recommendations as representative of the informed
naval consensus. On the carrier question, however, room had to
be made for warm debate among those whose ideas varied between
the conversion of ships already afloat and the building of entirely
new designs. Whiting and Irwin, for example, were strongly opposed to the suggestion of Lt. Comdr. Albert C. Read and some
others that one of the battleships be converted into a carrier.
They objected to the small stowage space that would be available for planes, the smoke menace amidships, the low headroom
between decks, and the lack of adequate quarters for a large personnel. Cone, on the other hand, did not agree that special vessels should be designed, declaring that "development is going to
be so rapid that by the time you get your carriers built you will
find you have to make all your ships carriers." McDonnell held
that the "usefulness of the plane-carriers would be almost unlimited" because, in his opinion, "they might finally replace the
battleship fleet itself." Capt. Ernest J. King, later the Fleet Admiral, with characteristic bluntness insisted that there had "never
seemed to be any doubt" that carriers were essential. In his view,

planes carried by various other ships might all be lost before an action was finished, and reserve planes could come only from a carrier.

Comdr. William S. Pye, already regarded as having one of the Navy's best strategic minds, supported Whiting and the other carrier advocates with the comment that "the heavier-than-air craft, except the seaplanes and coast-defense torpedo planes, must be carried in ships which accompany the Fleet, or in ships of the Fleet." He had no doubt that, "in the future, the airplane-carrying ship will be as important a part of the Fleet as the destroyer or similar type." Even though the cost might be great, he insisted, "an efficient Navy cannot be maintained without such ships."

Captain Twining, lately with Admiral Sims as Chief of Staff, held that "the first phase of any future Naval engagement will be an Air battle," which might easily be the deciding factor in the engagement. Hence, he declared, every fleet "must carry a large number of fighting planes" or lose command of the air above it. It must be able to defend itself completely against every form of air attack and also be able to drive home such an attack of its own. Agreeing with him in principle but not in detail were those officers who remained convinced that the first step should be to convert a merchant ship and, from experiments with her, determine the best design. Running through the whole debate, making every argument a conditional one, was the still undetermined factor—how much money would Congress give Naval Aviation?

Estimates for the fiscal year 1920, made before hostilities ceased, had totaled $225,000,000 for aviation. Since all concerned agreed that this sum was certain to be considered excessive in peacetime, and reductions in the establishment were likely to begin almost immediately, it was brought down in Captain Irwin's office to $85,700,000. It was expected that this amount, after providing for the conversion of two ships into carriers for existing bases on the American continent as well as proposed bases in the Pacific possessions and for some experimental work, would cover the following new construction:

108 fighter planes
4 patrol planes of the large NC type
54 patrol planes of small size
108 fleet planes of a type to be determined

   300 trainer planes
   560 kite balloons
   114 twin-engined coastal nonrigid dirigibles
    12 nonrigid dirigibles of large size
     4 zeppelins
     3 free balloons

Compared with prewar figures, these sums seemed large. When it is understood that their basis was the prospect of a national policy designed to keep the United States in that position of world leadership which the war had provided, the figures were small. In the Navy's view the bitter experience of trying to meet an emergency with nothing was to be avoided in the future if that were possible. The years would prove that view correct.

So much for material. The problem of personnel was equally perplexing because until the weapons had been selected it was impossible to estimate the exact number of men needed to man them. One thing, however, was certain; the war-trained force of officers and men was rapidly disintegrating. Under all the demobilization orders being issued, it would become possible for almost any man to get his discharge from the Reserve or from the "duration" groups. Reduced to its "regulars," Naval Aviation would be lucky if it were left with 50 officer pilots and a few hundred enlisted men. Without special legislation by Congress, there was no method by which either officers or men of the Reserve could be transferred to the regular Service; no way to do with them, and obviously no way to do without them. With the entire Navy certain to be greatly reduced in personnel, aviation's hopes for recruits from that source were low indeed.

This was the situation which confronted Capt. Thomas T. Craven when he came to Washington in the spring of 1919 to be the relief for Captain Irwin. The prospect of a naval fight had no terrors for him because since the earliest days of the Navy there had been at least one Craven on the list of officers, and he himself bore the name of his ancestor, famous old Commodore Thomas Tingey of 1798. Captain Craven was a gunnery expert rather than an aviator, but he was not so bound to the ancient traditions of sail that he could not mentally bridge the gap between the surface of the sea and the clouds above it. His experience as Captain Cone's chief deputy in France, followed by his duties in disposing of surplus aircraft material in Europe, had taught him much

about aviation; his professional soundness gave him a good grasp
of the relation that should exist between a plane and a battleship.
When Admiral Benson had cabled him at Brest, suggesting the
new post for him, he had at first declined because he had not yet
had command of a battleship, but after being assured that both
Admiral Benson and the Secretary of the Navy were determined
to support Naval Aviation he had accepted. In after years, when
he was a vice admiral looking back at the past, he would say that
this acceptance had "preceded a stormy assignment."

Even before he took over his new office he could see storm clouds
gathering over questions of administration. Affairs in Naval
Aviation had been very complicated during the war and it was
inevitable that there should be many opinions as to the appropriate future procedure in handling those affairs. Recommendations
as to the method of fitting the office into the postwar structure of
the Navy Department would come from officers who were regular
aviators, from air-minded members of Congress, and from men
who had flown with the Navy and were now again becoming
civilians.

From one of these last, Lieut. Graham M. Brush, came a letter
to the Navy Department, written as he was about to get out of
uniform in March, 1919. In it Brush advocated the immediate
creation of a separate bureau of aeronautics as the only means of
"getting anywhere" in avoiding the long delays, misunderstandings, and frequent lack of final decision which he had noted during
the war months and which he attributed chiefly to the requirement
that all questions be submitted to the conflicting views of seven
bureaus. His letter was forceful and so clearly expressed that
Captain Irwin had circulated it for comment before Captain
Craven reached Washington. Most of the comments had been
unfavorable.

Steam Engineering, holding that most of the delays and difficulties had been caused by the inexperienced personnel in so
many places during the war, could "see no reason" for any new
bureau. Navigation regarded the administrative difficulties as
having been inevitable in a new and rapidly expanding organization. Ordnance was firmly against any new bureau. Since Rear
Admiral Taylor was temporarily absent from his desk, the acting
Chief of Construction and Repair proposed delay until the admiral's return. Meanwhile Hunsaker prepared a long memorandum describing the Brush plan as not unlike that proposed

by Mustin some time before, but admitting that there might be great advantage in having one engineer direct the work of those designing and those constructing aircraft. Brush's provision for such an officer would mean, said Hunsaker, distinct advances in technical directions. The many cases of "crossed wires," which Hunsaker freely admitted, were due, he declared, to the fact that most of the officers under the director of Naval Aviation during the war had been fliers who did not have enough technical knowledge. Replace these, he said, with officers of broader training, make the Chief Constructor of the Navy the consulting engineer for aviation, and it should prove unnecessary to organize a separate bureau.

Called before the General Board, Hunsaker elaborated on his memorandum, particularly as to engineering problems and the difficulty of getting decisions. He spoke of the "excessive conservatism" displayed by so many officers and regarded this as another reason for establishing single responsibility because "you can get one man to take a chance where you may not be able to get four or five." Moreover, "when vessels that cost $10,000,000 or $15,000,000 are [to be] built, you do not want to take a chance. When it comes to an airplane at $10,000 or $15,000 you must take a chance." He deplored a tendency which he saw in the bureau to say, in commenting upon designs proposed for aviation, "while we agree . . . that you [Aviation] ought to have that kind of apparatus, we will give you what we have. Someday, if we have something better, we will let you know."

Among others heard by the board, Captain King favored combining the existing Office of Aviation with the other branches of Naval Operations. Whiting, on the contrary, thought separation the only solution. Captain Cone, although he backed Whiting, feared that the establishment of a separate bureau might be impracticable at the moment. On the whole, he said a separate advisory council on aviation might serve the purpose. These were typical of the many different views to be expected when considering any great change in an administrative organization that has "worked pretty well for years."

As prospective director, Craven's statements to the board in May, 1919, were of great importance. Being a comparative newcomer, he cautiously said that it would be "undesirable to disrupt the Navy Department for the advancement of aviation alone." Nevertheless, he held it to be "necessary to do something . . .

to keep abreast of the time" and agreed that, under existing administrative organization, it was "very hard to pin definite responsibility on any one bureau or any one individual." Until that could be done, he did not see how to "accomplish very much" for aviation. If there were to be no separate bureau, he suggested there might be at least an advisory council such as Cone had proposed, composed of one officer from each of the existing bureaus concerned, all assigned to duty under the director of Aviation with the task of coordinating bureau activities to prevent overlapping and duplication. He agreed with Hunsaker on the present lack of cooperation between the engineers in various bureaus and the nontechnical fliers, a lack which was evident even though all hands "worked as hard as they could." What he then said to the board was later expanded in a formal letter written in July. In this he proposed that the advisory section be made large enough to include three aviators, one as head of the section, one to represent lighter-than-air, and one to represent heavier-than-air. The other members might be two representatives from Steam Engineering, two from Construction and Repair, one each from Ordnance, Navigation, Yards and Docks, and Supplies and Accounts. So broad a group, he believed, would "fill the most urgent need . . . of bringing about closer cooperation and mutual understanding" in a way very like the purpose originally proposed by Captain Chambers and so often repeated during the years between 1910 and 1913. Like Chambers, Craven believed that the proposed new section could keep informed upon the progress of aviation outside the Navy, using this as well as the Navy's advances to plan new designs, locate better materials, originate and supervise further experiments.

Quite as important to Craven as this unsettled administrative organization of Naval Aviation was the question of its future personnel. Discussing this before the General Board, he had stated that all hands must be given a definite status and that "officers of the Navy . . . connected with aviation for long periods should be recognized as specialists." He did not argue for a separate corps but for regulation that would permit officers to keep on flying without fear of being regarded as no longer sailors and therefore ineligible for promotion. To him, as to all the fair-minded, the thought that Towers, Mustin, Bellinger, and a dozen others who had led the way into the air instead of serving on shipboard should fail of promotion was simply unthinkable. It is of record that both Mustin and Towers were passed over at least once.

Mustin himself again brought forward his plan for a separate flying corps, with provisions for rotating officers between this corps and regular seagoing as well as for recognizing flying duty as the equivalent of sea duty, and for extra pay when flying. He did not, however, offer a solution of the very controversial problem of the assignment of officers who had grown too old to fly, or express any opinion whether such officers should be given the command of carriers even though they had no experience in commanding other types. His plan found many opponents, Admiral Badger for one remarking that "We in the Navy have always opposed, for good and sufficient reasons, the establishment of special corps of officers." Many held that temporary ranks would create injustice and ill feeling, while others asked how officers, classified "for aviation duty only," were to be listed with their contemporaries of the regular line? Studying the possibility for transfers from the Reserve to the regular Navy, others immediately raised the question of the status of those who were transferred compared with that of Naval Academy graduates. Were all to be required to pass the same examinations in all branches of the profession or were these specialists to be advanced in the rarefied atmosphere of "aviation only"? Much the same questions were asked in relation to the possibility of making pilots from among the enlisted men. All agreed that these questions must be answered if Naval Aviation were ever to have the 700 pilots who represented its minimum requirement.

Admiral Mayo, again describing the aviators as "an essential fighting arm of the Navy" which must be included in all strategic and tactical planning, proposed his own plan. Being strongly against any separate corps because it would lead to "jealousies, lack of cooperation and inefficiency," he suggested an immediate call upon the regular line for 50 volunteers for aviation duty, all to be under 25 years old. To these he proposed adding 100 young men to be obtained among volunteers from the next graduating class at the Naval Academy, and then adding 200 qualified pilots transferred from the Reserve. With the 25 pilots of the regular Navy whom the admiral counted as still "available," these recruits would bring the total on hand up to 375. Temporarily, the balance might be made up by recruiting into the Navy ex-Army pilots and untrained civilians, but this last group should be replaced, said

Mayo, as rapidly as possible, by newly graduated midshipmen. Since this plan would necessitate a great increase in the strength of the Naval Academy, the admiral proposed that such an increase be provided by giving each senator and representative an additional appointment, besides authorizing ten more "at large" appointments by the President. From each of these larger classes, as it graduated, a group of volunteers could be drawn to replace the temporary aviators, eventually building up a permanent personnel of 700. The youngsters would serve four years as fliers but two of these were to be spent aboard ship where the other duties of a naval officer could be learned. To avoid any possible injustice to those who might have come in from the Reserve, these men should be given opportunities to qualify by examination for retention as regulars. No fliers were to be given extra pay because, in the admiral's opinion, such pay led to jealousies among officers of the same rank but different duties. Instead, he proposed that legislation be enacted to permit the government to pay premiums on insurance policies which would protect the dependents of aviators.

After listening to these various views and many others, the General Board on June 23, 1919, issued its conclusions in the form of a report upon "Future Policy Governing Development of Air Service for the United States Navy." The basis of this policy was contained in the following paragraph:

To ensure air supremacy, to enable the United States Navy to meet on at least equal terms any possible enemy, and to put the United States in its proper place as a Naval power, fleet aviation must be developed to the fullest extent. Aircraft have become an essential arm of the fleet. A naval air service must be established, capable of accompanying and operating with the fleet in all waters of the globe.

This was definite enough. In its recommendations, the board was not quite as specific as Admiral Mayo had been, either on personnel or material, but it followed the general line of his views. For example, while it agreed that pilots should ultimately all be graduates of the Naval Academy, it stressed the importance of immediate legislation to hold the war-trained reserves and to offer them inducements to transfer to the regular Navy. It also advocated encouraging colleges and universities to establish courses in aeronautics, for which the Navy should provide summer training for students at its various stations. Pending increases from such sources, at least some of the shortage of pilots should be made up by qualifying enlisted men as pilots. Congressional action to make these efforts possible was strongly urged by the board.

On the material side, the board's recommendation represented about the average naval opinion. It favored the equipping of battleships with planes but insisted that carriers were an essential because individual ships could not carry planes in sufficient numbers. For temporary use and for experiments the conversion of one collier into a carrier was recommended, the *Jupiter* being named, even though Adm. Hugh Rodman, by this time Commander in Chief in the Pacific, had protested that her conversion would spoil a good collier to make an indifferent carrier. Ultimately, said the board, there should be one carrier for each squadron of capital ships. In order that there might be floating repair shops, with adequate quarters for flying personnel, the board further recommended the immediate conversion of two fast transports, one for heavier-than-air, one for lighter-than-air craft, with the further recommendation that there eventually be provided one seaplane tender for each battle squadron.

In shore establishments for aviation the board held to its recommendations made a year earlier. Two more stations should be added on the Atlantic coast, one on Narragansett Bay, the other on Chesapeake Bay, each with accommodations for at least 30 ship-type planes, 20 torpedo planes and bombers, and six balloons. Similar stations should be built at San Francisco and on Puget Sound, with a third, smaller in size, at the mouth of the Columbia River. The Marine Corps air stations at Quantico and at Parris Island should be pushed to completion and a third station should be built at Dutch Flats, San Diego. The schools at Pensacola, Akron, and San Diego were regarded by the board as highly important and their continued expansion was urged. All forms of elementary training should be strongly supported and advanced training should be instituted at the proposed new station on Chesapeake Bay. In all this training, as well as in actual operations, the need for the closest possible cooperation with the Army Air Service was emphasized as an essential of the general policy, and in order that close touch with foreign progress might be established and maintained the assignment of officers as naval attachés for air was strongly urged. In conclusion, the board said, in substance: "Aviation as an adjunct of the fleet is of such vital importance . . . that no inferiority must be accepted . . . Naval aircraft are as essential to the fleet as destroyers, submarines or fast cruisers."

The board was entirely sound and it had well expressed the progressive naval view. Since the Chief of Naval Operations, while not in full agreement, was generally so, the board's policy finally got the Secretary's approval, although this was given with a hint of the probably unhelpful attitude of the Congress.

On Capitol Hill the Navy's liaison officer with Congress was Lt. Comdr. Richard Byrd, well suited to the assignment by his knowledge, his record of achievement in the air, and his temperament. He was not long in notifying those in the department that "the Republican majority considers that the desire of the people of this country is that all Army and Navy appropriations be cut down to the minimum." Explaining this attitude in 1919—so like the attitude of 1945—Byrd added that "the majority of the Congressmen do not . . . desire to cut . . . but they must disregard their personal feelings to represent the wishes of their constituents." He ventured the further prediction that parsimony was "a passing fancy" and that greater liberality might be expected in future sessions. It would have been a better guess to predict that what Congress did in 1919 would set a precedent for the next 20 years, and that the valiant few would find themselves still struggling to obtain fully adequate support for Naval Aviation even when the outbreak of another war had become a matter of months, perhaps mere weeks. In 1919 Craven must have shared with all hands a feeling of relief over being able to concentrate upon something as encouraging and stimulating as the Navy's announced plan to fly the Atlantic in "one big hop."

CHAPTER XV

The Navy Flies the Atlantic

IN enthusiasm for aircraft and aviation generally, Rear Adm. David Taylor yielded to no man. During the first weeks of war, when he had to read the depressing reports of scores being rolled up against Allied shipping by the U-boats, he pondered the capabilities and disabilities of aircraft as a weapon against submarines. Such phrases as "maximum range of flight" and "greatest possible bomb load" were constantly in his mind, because he was well aware that a major factor in the current design of American aircraft was the recognized necessity of stowing such craft aboard ship for transportation overseas. As a result of his study of the situation he wrote, for circulation in his own Bureau of Construction and Repair, a highly significant memorandum. In this he suggested what was needed was a flying boat not only able to make the long flight to Europe but also stout enough, if it should be forced down, to *"keep the sea* in any weather." Discussing this with those three stars among his subordinates, Richardson, Westervelt, and Hunsaker, he said to them, in effect: "Gentlemen, give us something that will cross the Atlantic, nonstop, and be able to take on a U-boat on arrival!" So great was his confidence that he remained undisturbed when, later, the Bolling Commission reported it to be the "all but unanimous" belief of "practical and experienced men" that flying boats large enough to be effective against submarines could not be built. Being himself a practical and experienced man, his comment was something like "We shall see about *that!*"

When it came to design, those three constructors, working together, probably could have made Jules Verne appear a dull, unimaginative clod. If they had any doubt of being able to meet Admiral Taylor's requirement, they did not show it as their ideas took form on paper. By September, 1917, even before formal approval had been obtained from the Secretary of the Navy, they called in Glenn Curtiss. Within two days of that conference

Curtiss was back with alternative designs: one with four engines developing 1,700 horsepower, the other with three engines and 1,000 horsepower. Otherwise, the two designs were in general identical, new features being a hull considerably shorter than those then in use, and a method of supporting the tail by outriggers from the upper wings and from the after end of the hull. Curtiss claimed that the outriggers provided stronger tail support and also permitted giving the rear gunner a clear field of vision, without which the earlier flying boats were particularly vulnerable to fire from enemies they could not see. After long discussion the smaller of the two designs was chosen; Curtiss was told to go ahead, and, to compliment both the sponsor and the builder, Navy-Curtiss or NC was the identification assigned. Curtiss, undaunted by the unprecedented size of the new type, set to work at his Buffalo plant, continued at Garden City, and by January, 1918, had his detailed plans completed.

The earliest proposal had been to prepare for a nonstop crossing from Newfoundland to Ireland, but closer study of what might be expected in the way of wind led to fixing 1,300 miles as the maximum for one flight. On the question of wind resistance, Richardson was given the job of redesigning the hull to make this resistance as low as possible without sacrificing the ability to carry a crew of five, with equipment, spares, guns, ammunition, and five tons of gasoline. When his modifications had been approved Curtiss made one hull, contracts for two others being given to Lawley and Sons, yacht builders of Neponset, Massachusetts, while the fourth went to the famous Herreshoffs at Bristol, Rhode Island. Constructor McEntee was then called in to supervise, at the Navy's Model Basin, innumerable trials of the models for these hulls.

Considering the novel design and remembering what was then known about the building of aircraft, progress was rapid. By October, 1918, the first NC was ready at the Rockaway Naval Air Station, standing 68 feet three inches long, with what was then the largest known wing spread—126 feet. On the first tests it lifted nearly 25,000 pounds, its only fault being a tail heaviness which was readily corrected by relocating the horizontal stabilizer. Its three Liberty engines were efficient but the consensus was that the design ought to have four engines; a correct decision because NC-2, thus equipped, easily lifted 28,000 pounds or over 6,000 pounds more than its required load. Had not hostilities ended so suddenly, the type, with improvements suggested by war experience, would materially have hastened progress in aviation during the succeeding 20 years.

After successful tests, NC-1 was also equipped with four engines and then sent up in an effort to break the record established by the new British Handley Page—40 passengers carried in actual flight. On November 25 at Rockaway 50 men were loaded aboard and taken into the air without difficulty. After a short flight NC-1 came down with the new record and proceeded to unload 51. For an hour and a half Machinist's Mate, Second Class, Harry D. Moulton had been the Navy's first aerial stowaway.

A little later a disastrous fire and a bad gale combined to rip the tail of NC-4 and one wing of NC-1, with the result that these two were repaired by dismantling NC-2, leaving only three ready for that unprecedented ceremony, their commissioning on May 2, 1919, as Seaplane Division One. In selecting the pilots of the squadron first consideration was given to those who had been kept in important posts in the United States and so missed their chance to go overseas during the war. Towers was named division commander and with him in NC-3 was Richardson as copilot. Bellinger, with Mitscher, took NC-1, while Read, with Elmer Stone of the Coast Guard, got NC-4. By this time it had been decided that even though the war had ended the Navy should have its chance to be the first to cross the Atlantic by air, and the words of Read are a good expression of the general naval view of such an enterprise:

If the flight were successful, not only would an immense amount of valuable . . . information be obtained concerning long-distance oversea flying, but Naval Aviation, the Navy Department, and the whole country would receive the plaudits of the entire world for accomplishing a notable feat in the progress of the science; the mass of the people would be made to realize the importance of aviation as a valuable arm of the naval service and the way would be blazed for others to follow and thus act to promote a commercial transatlantic service.

Since good flying weather might be expected in May, all plans were pushed toward making May 6 the day to start the boats from Rockaway for Trepassey in Newfoundland, whence they would leave, as soon as might be, along the chosen route via the Azores and Lisbon to London. Another good reason for hurrying lay in the fact that three teams of British aviators were already up at St. John's, Newfoundland, getting ready to compete for the prize of $50,000 offered by the *London Daily Mail* to the first men to make the crossing. Finally, that intrepid pair, Captain Alcock and Lieutenant Brown, was reported en route for Newfoundland with their Vickers-Vimy bomber. Even the Navy's own lighter-than-air men were not to give up the Atlantic crown without a struggle, for the nonrigid C-3, under Lieutenant Commander Coil, later to be lost with the ZR-2, had sailed up from Montauk Point in the record flight of 1,050 miles in 25 hours and 10 minutes. No one could guess, then, that a gale would tear C-3 from her moorings and wreck her.

As soon as the three NC's had taken off, on May 8, for Trepassey, NC-4 began having trouble with her oil pressure and had to reduce speed. This was followed by the breaking of a connecting rod, which drove her down to the sea off Cape Cod and involved a long "taxi ride" to the air station at Chatham. There the work of replacing one engine, added to several days of bad weather, brought the delay up to six days during which the other two boats, already at Trepassey, were impatiently awaiting the signal to go and watching their British rivals, also weather bound. On the morning of the 14th the NC-4 was nearing Trepassey when her radio reported that NC-1 and NC-3 would start east that afternoon. The harbor proved too rough, however, driving the two back to their moorings and thus allowing NC-4 to get into port and to be, on the afternoon of the 16th, the first to take the air. With Read and Stone were Lt. Walter Hinton as relief pilot, Ens. H. C. Rodd, radio operator, Lt. James Breese, pilot engineer, and Ch. Mach. E. C. Rhoads, reserve engineer.

Sixty-eight destroyers had been strung across the ocean as "marker buoys," supported at 400-mile intervals by five battleships to act as weather stations. All these ships were to use smoke by day and searchlights by night, and as the planes passed overhead star shells were to be fired until a radio check-in from each plane had been received. Against the possibility of having to make forced landings on the sea, the flying boats were provided with bow flares to illuminate the surface. Among their special instruments they had not only a new type of bubble sextant designed by Byrd but also the drift and speed indicator which he and C. B. Truscott had developed, as well as a course and distance indicator. The flight would show that these aids to navigating in the air were more reliable than most of the pilots, at the outset, believed them to be. At the first nightfall, after a rough day, the running lights of the flagship, NC-3, failed, making it difficult for the other two to keep touch with her and introducing the danger of collision in the air. The NC-4, however, with a reversal of the bad luck that had at first followed her, gathered speed and left the others behind.

As the visibility had been good she had sighted the first 16 destroyers, but shortly after dawn on the 17th, fog banks loomed ahead. Sharing the plane's controls in half-hour hitches, Hinton and Stone managed to lift their big craft over one bank but only to plunge her into another. They could no longer see the ocean, and though they had the "needle and ball" instrument, installation had been too recent to allow for training in its use for flying. Once the plane got in a tight spin, threatening disaster, but it came into the clear just in time to permit the pilots to orient themselves and retain control. On they went, under an overcast and above a fog that "broke" just often enough to let them get an estimate of their drift and change course accordingly. They had been 15 hours in the air and were between two layers of fog when Read, peering down through a thin spot, saw a rugged coastline which he concluded must be Flores in the Azores. At once, he spiraled down close to the sea, where visibility proved to be excellent. He resumed course, and although he hit more fog even at a low level, it cleared enough for him to make a landing at Horta, the end of a 1,200-mile flight at an estimated speed of 78 knots.

If Read "got the breaks" he had earned them; for one reason because he had shown greater confidence in his navigational instruments. NC-1, after going through the same fog, was doubtful of her compass and decided to come down to the sea to take bearings. This was unfortunate, because when she landed in the 30-foot seas that met her she was so damaged as to be unable to get up again. She was about 100 miles from Flores as she began to "taxi" toward that island. Before long she met the Greek steamer *Ionia* to which she transferred her crew in the ship's boats. The attempt to take the plane in tow failed when the hawser parted, with the result that NC-1 capsized and presently sank.

NC-3, the flagship, lived through an epic of her own. Forty-five miles from Flores she came down to get her bearings because of doubt about the bubble sextant, landing in even rougher water with heavy damage all around. Through her receiving set she could hear the destroyers searching for her west of Flores but her efforts to report that she was south of the island did not get through. For two days and two nights her crew kept going under a jury-rigged sail, improvising sea anchors, pouring oil on the sea, and shifting their places from one wing to the other to keep from capsizing. Then, seven miles from Ponta Delgada, they sighted the destroyer *Harding*, promptly hauled down their distress signals and hoisted their colors to show that they were determined to make port under their own power. Sailing stern first, they had almost reached the breakwater when the right float let go, to drag by two wires and be cut loose just in time to keep the plane above water. With three men running from wing to wing to meet each ground swell, she reached the mooring buoy, finishing what Read of the NC-4 called "a triumphant demonstration of courage, expert seamanship and the seagoing qualities of the hulls." Since Read himself was still held at Horta by weather, he did not reach Ponta Delgada until a day later, when he flew in, to find the shipping dressed for the occasion, a hundred whistles blowing, the governor and the entire population on the waterfront, and a small mountain of congratulatory cables.

Since nothing was heard of the British planes after their start from Newfoundland, suspense in the Azores ran high. Even on May 27, when the NC-4 finally got away for Lisbon, she still did not know whether she was truly the pioneer. In the original plans it had been provided that Towers, if any boat were damaged, might shift his flag to another. Under the circumstances, however, it was decided that he would go on by ship, as was certainly fair to Read.

After leaving Lisbon, an unexplained oil leak necessitated a landing on the Mondega River, near Figueire in Portugal. In getting up again after repairs she had a brief grounding on a sand bar, fortunately without damage, and after getting into the air again she had to make an overnight stop at Ferrol, Spain. Thus it was not until May 31 that Read landed at Plymouth, England, to be received by the Lord Mayor at the slab commemorating the sailing of the Pilgrims 300 years earlier. He had beaten the British because Hawker and Grieve had made a forced landing 1,200 miles from Newfoundland and it was not until June 14 that Alcock and Brown flew nonstop from the same place to Ireland.

From this first transatlantic flight the Navy got valuable data on long-distance flying and on the possibility of wide reconnaissance through the air. Much, too, was learned about ship-to-plane radio communication, the radio direction finder, the sextant, the drift indicator, the new zenithal-projection chart and the need for far more exhaustive study of weather in the upper air. Altogether this proof of Admiral Taylor's clear vision of the quality of American designs marked a tremendous step forward in the art and science of flying.

Brought home with her crew by ship, the NC-4 was soon launched upon a recruiting flight. In the four months from September through December, 1919, she visited 43 cities along the Atlantic and Gulf coasts and flew up the Mississippi as far as Cairo, Illinois. Hundreds of thousands of American citizens saw and cheered her before she finally reached the Smithsonian Institution, but the record does not show that these citizens made any concerted effort to influence the deliberations of Congress upon the future of flying in the Navy.

It was the future that deeply concerned Craven, who had taken office as director on July 7, 1919, four days before the passage of the act for the fiscal year 1920. Not content with all the slashes that the Navy itself had made in its estimates for aviation, Congress cut the amount still further and hit upon a final figure of $25,000,000. As some few had foreseen, this would establish a long-lasting precedent, and through the next three administrations the cry of "economize" would drown out any other.

As though this alone were not discouraging enough for Craven, it was shortly followed by action of the Chief of Naval Operations on the various recommendations for reorganizing the internal administration of Naval Aviation. On August 1, 1919, Admiral Benson reduced the director to the level of head of a section in Naval Operations, leaving him what had now become a meaningless title. Next, many of the duties and functions which had been the director's during the war were returned to the various bureaus, while others were distributed among the other sections of the Office of Naval Operations.

Thus Craven, Whiting, Read, and a small staff became part of the Planning Division; Maxfield and Bellinger were transferred to the Material Division; Chevalier became a member of the Division of Operating Forces; aviation gunnery went to the Division of Gunnery Exercises and Engineering Performance; and radio went to the Communications Division. From half a dozen different divisions those essentially concerned with flying would be able to signal to one another across the corridors of the Navy Department or, if they had official business with flying schools, air stations, or depots, they would be permitted to write to the commandant of the naval district under whom that particular activity was placed by the new order. Captain Craven described his own position as that of "the so-called Director of Aviation, ever responsible for failures . . . with the directional authority of a weathercock on the roof of a New England farm." He was expected to be fully cognizant of every aviation activity in every bureau, whether or not he had even seen the plan before it was put into operation. On top of the other obstacles, he also found the files of Naval Aviation distributed in a dozen places because their contents bore upon something no longer under his direct supervision. He may have hoped that his position was likely to become less anomalous when, within a few weeks of this reorganization, Admiral Benson was relieved by Adm. R. E. Coontz. That hope, however, must have been dashed when Rear Admiral McKean, in presenting him to the new chief, remarked that "Craven has numerous assistants and too many office rooms. A single room is all that he requires." Craven was not the type to be consoled for lesser administrative powers by the thought that there would be less to administer.

That this would be true was easy to forecast from a study of the act of July 11, 1919, governing the fiscal year 1920. With the limited funds provided, it would soon become impossible to have on hand enough planes to train even the personnel that would be available; impossible to keep what planes there were in proper condition to fly. The act further limited the number of heavier-than-air stations to six, and the Navy chose Rockaway, Hampton Roads, Anacostia, Pensacola, Key West, and San Diego. Although lighter-than-air craft was not so specifically restricted, there were no funds for such important bases as Chatham and Cape May. The so-called Parks-McKean Board, appointed by Secretary Daniels for the purpose, was even then recommending new West coast stations at Ediz Point, Tongue Point, and Seattle, with Dutch Flats at San Diego for the Marines, but that board might as well never have met. Although Lakehurst, about to be evacuated by the Army, could be secured as a base for the Navy's lighter-than-air work through the years to come, the act in general took a view far too shortsighted to detect the 1940's, when naval air stations would sprout like dandelions in the meadows of the United States.

Some helpful provisions had been made by the act, and under these Craven had already started activity even before Coontz came into office. For one thing, the act authorized the conversion of a collier into a carrier, and since it had specifically named the *Jupiter* Craven had lost no time in getting the technical bureaus to start upon conversion. To be sure, they had barely gotten underway upon this when he found the orders countermanded by Admiral Benson, an embarrassing situation from which he extricated himself only by direct appeal to the Secretary of the Navy. On this occasion Mr. Daniels reversed his Chief of Naval Operations, directing that the conversion proceed and himself allocating to the bureaus the necessary funds. At the same time he authorized the equipping of eight battleships with turret platforms and the purchase of small planes, chiefly of the British Sopwith type, for use from the platforms. These were landplanes for which the original recommendation by the General Board had been that 75 scouts and the same number of fighters be obtained either from the Army or from foreign sources. The Chief of Naval Operations, however, was of the opinion that the use of landplanes from ships was not practicable, and the board's figure was accordingly reduced to a total of ten. These nevertheless proved enough to arouse considerable enthusiasm for "a plane on every ship," and led to numerous experiments with destroyers notwithstanding Captain King's caustic prophecy that "the first bad weather would settle that question."

Work went forward slowly on the *Jupiter* and nothing was done on two merchant ships whose conversion into tenders had also been authorized by the act of 1919. So slow would be the progress that it would be March, 1922, before the *Jupiter* emerged as the carrier *Langley*, soon familiarly called the "Old Covered Wagon," first of a long line of illustrious sisters and half-sisters. Much water would roll past all the Navy's bridges before, by the outbreak of World War II, the strength of that line would reach eight carriers of various types and sizes.

Some progress in lighter-than-air work was also authorized by the act of 1919, in that it provided for the purchase of one rigid dirigible abroad and the building of another at home. These provisions were timely because interest in dirigibles had received considerable impetus from the visit to the United States of the British R-34, first airship to make a successful crossing. She helped smooth the way to an agreement with the British under which their uncompleted R-38, representing the newest and supposedly best type, was to be finished and turned over to the United States at a cost of $2,000,000. At the same time arrangements were made for the training in England of American personnel for the new ship, which was given the American designation ZR-2. It took two more years to build her and then, on August 24, 1921, when she was making her fourth trial flight, she fell into the Humber River, burst into flames, and killed Comdr. Lewis H. Maxfield and all but five of her crew of 49.

In this same year 1919 the ZR-1, afterward known as the *Shenandoah*, was begun. It had at first been contemplated that her construction would be by automobile manufacturers, perhaps Ford or Packard, but this plan was abandoned in favor of the Navy's doing its own building, the parts to be made at the Philadelphia factory, their assembly to be at Lakehurst. The final structural design was a combination of the British and the German types, with modification of the fins, strengthening of the longitudinals, and a special nose to permit mooring by the bow. The Maybach motors built by the Germans proved best and the designers returned to them after trying both Liberties and Packards. Built of duralumin furnished by private aluminum firms, the airship would need the largest hangar in the world and this would not be completed at Lakehurst until 1922. It would then serve, after the *Shenandoah's* tragic end, to house the very successful *Los Angeles*, built by the Germans at Friedrichshafen under the terms of the Versailles Treaty and originally known simply as ZR-3. For all these ships helium would be unquestionably the best inflating gas, and work upon Texas plants to manufacture it, begun in 1917, was still being pushed in 1919. Within another year 200,000 cubic feet of helium were produced, at a cost indicating that a government plant for this purpose would be a good investment even at a building cost of $7,000,000.

Toward the end of 1919 and in early 1920 Captain Craven was hoping for some progress through using the six airships procured from various European countries under authority of the same Act of 1919. From France came an Astra-Torres, a Vedette-Zodiac, and a Chalais-Meudon, but on their arrival it was discovered that no hangar in the United States was big enough to handle them. This meant that they had to be put into storage, and before any use of them for training purpose could be made their fabrics became so rotten that they had to be destroyed. The "O" type nonrigid, bought from Italy at a cost of $84,000 plus the salaries of two special technicians imported with it, did not reach the United States until the early autumn of 1919, when it carried out a few interesting, instructive tests, especially of radio communication and target gliders, before it crashed and became a total loss. From England came one nonrigid of the "North Sea" type.

Three new classes were designed in the United States. The so-called "G" class, practically a counterpart of the "North Sea," was planned to have a capacity of 400,000 cubic feet, an enclosed car with sleeping quarters for the crew, a three-inch antisubmarine gun, and a heavy bomb load; but it never got beyond the plan stage. The "H" was a self-propelled kite balloon, which could be inflated aboard ship, and it was stout enough to be towed in a strong wind. Because it had an engine it could handle itself in weather much too strong for the ordinary balloon, but its effectiveness otherwise did not prove great enough to warrant building more than one of the type. Third was the "J," a twin-motored affair, not unlike its "C" and "G" predecessors, but fitted with only one ballonet and a simple gondola. With all of these an impressive series of training exercises was planned, but as might be expected from the scanty funds available not all of them could be carried out. Led by McCrary and Lansdowne the lighter-than-air men wanted to learn all there was to know about refueling dirigibles from surface craft or from one another; about the handling of airships by ground gear on trucks, winches, or tanks; about lifesaving possibilities and meteorological usefulness; about landing on roofs and ships as well as on the water; about mooring devices, instruments, and possible new fabrics; about mine laying and bombing; and particularly all about helium gas and the possibility of such static discharges as, in the future, would destroy the famous *Hindenburg*. Attempts at least were made at all these training experiments and exercises.

It was these exercises that brought the "H" kite balloon into disfavor. As Admiral Mayo had expressed it, the observer in such a balloon found it "an unhappy place" when a battleship's salvo was fired below his basket, while even without that a merely "fresh" breeze would give him so much to do to "stay put" that he could accomplish little else. Most of the ships could see no use for the balloons that would compensate for the time and labor spent in caring for and handling them, a view supported by Adm. Henry B. Wilson, the new Commander in Chief in the Atlantic, in his conclusion that "the results of trials condemn the balloon as neither practical nor useful . . . on board the fighting units." Hence although the Pacific Fleet continued for some time to make experiments it was inevitable that the "dishing in" of balloons from the *Florida* and *Nevada* in the winter of 1920—accidents in which losses of life were but narrowly averted—should virtually end their use aboard ships.

All these postwar efforts at integrating Naval Aviation with the Fleet were subject to the same drawback, lack of sufficient personnel. The act of July 11, 1919, took very little account of such naval recommendations as those of Admiral Mayo for building up the air arm. It called for immediately reducing the enlisted personnel and set the limit for the Navy at 170,000, which must be reached by July 1, 1920. The allowance of commissioned officers was 4 per cent of the enlisted strength and there was no clause which permitted the transfer of reserve officers to the regular Navy. It was plain that when all ships, navy yards, and stations had been manned, aviation must come off a bad last.

CHAPTER XVI

Agitation for an Independent Air Force

IT is often said that ordinary Americans, under the pressure of daily life, lack time to study problems that bear on large concerns of national policy and consequently tend to accept, ready-made, any strong opinion they see in print. Those who hold this belief might well cite, in support of it, the history of aviation in the United States in the years immediately following World War I. Certainly, during those years, average Americans were strongly influenced by what was spoken and written by Brig. Gen. William Mitchell of the Army Air Service.

By most of his contemporaries Mitchell was regarded as an able flier rather than as a profound student of war, especially war involving sea power. All knew that he had played a prominent part in the Army's air effort over France in 1918 and that he had been decorated for these services. His convictions as to the importance of air power to any plan for future national defense were unquestionably sound and they were shared by a nucleus of soldiers, sailors, and civilians among his contemporaries. Essentially, the difference between the general and a considerable number of these contemporaries lay in their views as to the best method of obtaining popular and congressional agreement with their fundamental conviction.

General Mitchell chose the first of the two alternatives suggested in his own pronouncement that "changes in military systems come through public opinion or disaster in war." Through dramatic headlines certain to catch the eye, he appealed to the average reader; through challenging statements from the platform, he appealed to any audience that would listen. In a race for which the prize was public opinion he was never overtaken.

After the armistice of 1918 but before General Mitchell returned from Europe, Representative Ernest Lundeen of Minnesota had introduced into Congress a bill to create a separate United States air force. At that time the Navy Department took no open notice of the bill beyond reissuing the conclusions reached in March of 1917, by the so-called "Cognizance Board" of that period, accompanied by a word drawing attention to that board's definition of "the line of demarcation between the aviation activities of the Army and of the Navy." It is impossible, at this date, to say whether or not this action had any effect upon Congress, but the Lundeen Bill, duly referred to the Committee on Interstate and Foreign Commerce, died there quietly before the end of that session. It was during the next session that much more significance came to be attached to the word of warning which the Navy, in March, 1919, received from Hunsaker.

As a fellow passenger of General Mitchell on the westbound *Aquitania*, Hunsaker's observations led him to write that the general was "fully prepared, with evidence, plans, data, propaganda posters and articles, to break things wide open" for air power as the sole requisite of national defense in the future. This warning very shortly proved well-timed when Generals Mitchell, Foulois, and Chandler, with others of the Army Air Service and with the strong backing of Representative La Guardia of New York and Assistant Secretary of War Benedict Crowell, announced their intention of bringing about the creation of an air force entirely independent of control by either the Army or the Navy. Insisting that air power alone had won the recent war and would win all future wars unassisted, they grouped "ground-minded" officers of the Infantry or the Artillery with the "battleship admirals," dismissing the lot as of no importance and as quite incompetent to assist in solving current problems of development in the science of flying in the United States. To carry their point they were prepared to shoot at any head that dared to raise itself in opposition, and since heads were raised from many directions the shooting continued for some seven years.

Many officers and men in all branches had learned from the war a great deal about aviation and the importance of aircraft. They could appreciate that both sea power and land power must each thereafter depend heavily upon the strength of its air arm. They strongly favored building up the air forces of the United States but they wanted these forces maintained as separate and distinct units: one part of the Army, the other part of the Navy. Except for the "Mitchell group," both Services clearly recognized a fundamental difference in missions and a correspondingly great difference in the required methods of organization, training, administration, and operation. From the Navy's viewpoint the air arm must be a real element of the Fleet, its personnel must be sailors trained to work with other sailormen in scouting, patrolling, and escorting; in clearing the air above the ships of enemy aircraft and in covering the landing of amphibious forces on beaches; in defending merchant ships from enemy attack by air and sea; and in all else that was essentially the Navy's job. This should have a familiar ring because in the intervening 28 years that have seen another world war and even the first use of an atomic bomb nothing occurred that altered the Navy's fundamental opinion. Even today the Navy still holds that the mere ability to control a plane in the air while firing a machine gun or dropping bombs is only the beginning of training for war on the sea. It still disagrees with the conclusion of General Mitchell in his articles and books that "airplane carriers are useless weapons against first class powers," or that "an attempt to transport large bodies of troops, munitions and supplies across a great stretch of ocean, as was done during World War I from the United States to Europe, would [in a new war] be an impossibility." Writing in retrospect, Craven said that Mitchell's ideas "would have revolutionized our entire system of defense." He agreed that some, indeed most, of Mitchell's theories were correct but thought him wrong in arguing for a huge new organization in aeronautics which would deprive "sailors of scientific development, just as they were beginning to accept it as essential."

In 1919 the Navy would have had no quarrel with Mitchell had he proposed a separate air force such as has recently been established. What dragged the Navy into a fight was such statements of the general's as that made in September, 1919, to the House Military Affairs Committee, when he insisted that if he and his associates were "allowed to develop essential air weapons," they could "carry the war to such an extent . . . as almost to make navies useless on the surface of the water." He made the tactical error of backing this broad statement with the comment that "the General Board, I might say, agrees with me on that," a comment at variance with the truth. The board had invited the general to appear before it but it had not been impressed by his praise of the Royal Air Force. Most members of the board believed that the Admiralty had never ceased to regret consolidation because this had weakened the naval air arm—a view incidentally sustained between 1939 and 1945. Holding this belief, the General Board had been very far from agreeing with General Mitchell, and it immediately originated a Navy Department letter asking the War Department where the general had found grounds for his public statement. In reply the Secretary of War said that "a careful perusal" of the general's hearing before the board showed that he was "not justified in the conclusion." As was inevitable, however, very few of those who read the general's published statement ever saw that letter from Secretary Baker, and similar instances of this sort were not rare. Again and again he made the front page, whereas if a modification or even a flat refutation of what he had said appeared in print, it formed a small item at the bottom of an inside column.

In June, 1919, the Navy Department and the War Department, broadly in agreement and opposed to General Mitchell, took the step of reorganizing the Joint Army and Navy Board on Aeronautic Cognizance, renamed the Joint Army and Navy Board on Aeronautics. The board was given a broader precept to provide the closer cooperation clearly demanded by the experiences of war. Specifically it was directed to make recommendations on production, training, location of bases, purchase of material abroad, and the solution of all problems on aviation found in other departments of the government and among civilians, emphasis being laid upon the importance of reducing duplication to a minimum. Accordingly, in August, 1919, the board announced its policy:

Aircraft operated in conjunction with either military or naval forces shall be military or naval aircraft and under the command of the respective military or naval commanders.

Both the Army and the Navy shall confine the use of their aircraft to activities clearly connected with strictly military or naval functions as such are defined by existing laws and agreements.

To prevent duplication, and secure coordination, plans of new projects for the construction of aircraft, for experimental stations, for coastal stations, or for extensive additions thereto shall be submitted to this Board for recommendation.

In the interest of economy, heavier-than-air craft shall be used instead of lighter-than-air craft whenever the former can perform satisfactorily the required work.

Wherever possible, training and other facilities of either service shall be made available for use by the other.

Each service, before entering the market shall attempt to secure aircraft of the type desired from or through the other service.

As soon as any experimentation is inaugurated, all information pertaining thereto shall be exchanged between the Army and Navy Air Services.

All estimates for the Army and the Navy programs shall be presented to the Board for review and recommendation before submission to Congress.

Functions of Aircraft:

Army

(a) For offensive and defensive work in the field in conjunction with the various arms of the Service.

(b) For the general purpose of fire control information in connection with the coast defense.

Navy

(a) For use from coastal stations for convoy, reconnaissance, and patrol.

(b) For use from war vessels, bases, and carriers for reconnaissance and spotting, and for offensive operations against enemy vessels and naval bases.

Since this policy did not give the Army the entire task of "independent air operations," unless this could be inferred from the phrase "for offensive and defensive work in the field," it was natural that Craven liked it much better than did General Mitchell. As it stood, it was approved by the Secretaries of War and the Navy, but the former sent it to The Joint Board for comment. That board took exception to what it considered "defective wording" and to a "confining" of the tasks and functions assigned to each Service. In 1920 the board issued its pamphlet on *Joint Army and Navy Action in Coast Defense* which embodied the principles of the earlier report just quoted. Much discussion and numerous investigations followed the publication of this pamphlet, resulting in compromises rather than in a final, definite resolving of differences of opinion.

Early in 1919 the Secretary of War had appointed a commission to study European aviation. Headed by Assistant Secretary Crowell, it included Howard Coffin, wartime chairman of the Aircraft Production Board, Col. Halsey Dunwoody of the Army Air Service, Lt. Col. J. G. Blair of the Army General Staff, G. H. Houston, president of the Wright-Martin Company, C. M. Keys, vice-president of Curtiss, S. S. Bradley, general manager of the

Manufacturers' Aircraft Association, and, as sole representative
of the Navy, Capt. Henry Mustin. Essentially the task assigned
the Crowell Commission was a search for the best means of keeping aircraft manufacture in the United States alive enough
through peacetime to be able to meet military needs in wartime.
After touring England, France, and Italy, however, the commission in its report plainly showed that its greater interest lay in
promoting a single national air force.

The report advocated "concentration of air activities . . .
military, naval and civilian, within the direction of a single Government agency . . . co-equal in importance with the Departments of War, Navy and Commerce." It proposed a secretary and
an assistant secretary of the new department, who would direct
all types of flying, supply, research, and finance. If war emergency
arose, this department would be expected to furnish the Army and
Navy with whatever either might happen to need in the way of
squadrons of aircraft. It was generally understood that the commission's "slate" put Mr. Crowell down for secretary, General
Mitchell for assistant secretary for the Army, with Captain Craven
a similar assistant for the Navy.

This proposal was inspired by the army members and acceptable
enough to industry, but it was to be expected that Mustin should
file a minority report showing why the proposed organization
must inevitably leave the Navy without any worthwhile air arm.
Secretary of War Baker was even more outspoken than Mustin in
condemning the whole plan; his comment upon the Crowell Commission's report dismissed the suggestion of a centralized air service
as "going much too far." He described the pilots of the Army and
Navy as "specialists . . . of a different type from those needed
in civilian undertakings." Their efficiency, he declared, depended
upon "the most intense and constant associated training," while
their effectiveness rested upon "the concentration and singleness
of authority, command, and purpose." He thus proved himself, in
this debate, a good ally of the Navy. Indeed, it was with the cooperation of the Secretary of War that the Joint Army and Navy
Board on Aeronautics, now renamed the Aeronautical Board, was
strengthened by placing it under The Joint Board for the formula-
tion of general policy.

During the autumn of 1919 several investigations of the state
of American aviation were in progress simultaneously. In Congress
proposals for a single national air force drew the support of those

whose enthusiasm for economy was not combined with a sound grasp of military affairs. Before long Senator H. S. New of Indiana and Congressman Charles F. Curry of California introduced bills creating an air department, to administer all aviation in the armed services as well as all civilian flying. At the hearings on these bills before a House Subcommittee on Military Affairs, of which Congressman William F. James of Michigan was chairman and Congressman Fiorella H. La Guardia alternate chairman, the testimony sharply outlined the difference of opinion between the two departments on one side and the Mitchell group on the other. At the very moment when the general and his friends were pouring their ideas into the sympathetic ear of Mr. La Guardia, a War Department board under Maj. Gen. C. T. Menoher, Chief of the Army Air Service, was reaching a very different conclusion. This board ultimately declared that "whatever may be the decision as to a separate Aeronautical Department, the military air force must remain under the direct control of the Army," thus following the views of Generals Pershing and Wood and paralleling the Navy's opinion as to its own air arm.

At times the testimony presented to the James subcommittee was not strictly in accord with the facts. For example, General Foulois stated that it was only by accident that he had learned of the proposal to use the Navy's Northern Bombing Group over Belgium in 1918, yet the official files were crowded with documents showing that Army headquarters in France had been kept fully informed of every step. Again, although Callan was at hand to tell the exact story of the Capronis, Foulois repeated the old complaint that the Navy had cheated the Army out of these planes. Similarly General Chandler, complaining of the lack of inter-Service cooperation in lighter-than-air flying, added the insinuation that the Navy had "only a very small dirigible." To make that statement he must either not have known, or have chosen to ignore, the fact that the Navy had supplied the Army with several dirigibles of various types and was even then engaged in training lighter-than-air personnel for both Services.

Chandler's representations, admirably fitted to those of General Mitchell, were perhaps part of a wider design to take over all lighter-than-air flying. It is of record that Mitchell on October 7, 1919, the day before the Menoher Board made its report, stated to the subcommittee that "one thing we have not done is to develop any . . . rigid dirigibles . . . and we have attempted very strenuously lately with the help of the War Department to get the L-72, which is in Germany." It seems probable that Mitchell and Chandler were hoping that the publicity given to what they said before the subcommittee would influence The Joint Board as well as the public. This was important to them because when the Army-Navy Airship Board established in 1917 was abolished after hostilities ceased, it was The Joint Board that had taken up the study of lighter-than-air developments. However, any such hopes were doomed to disappointment when The Joint Board, on February 16, 1920, flatly recommended: "that the development of rigid dirigibles, including the incidental acquisition of dirigibles in foreign countries, be assigned to and carried on exclusively by the Navy and that the Army lend to the Navy any personnel particularly qualified in this work."

Under this policy the Army would transfer to the Navy all sites, such as the base at Lakehurst, which might be useful for dirigible experiments or for training. Thus the development of lighter-than-air craft was made the clear responsibility of the Navy, with the Army in a position to profit by everything that was learned.

With such a multiplicity of boards and committees debating the many aspects of the aviation problem there were bound to be many opportunities for fishing in troubled waters, and of these opportunities General Mitchell and his supporters were quick to take advantage. They had failed in the matter of airships, but a line cast in some other direction might easily bring up a prize catch, in spite of frequently drawing sharp retorts from the Navy Department. Most of these retorts were based upon a long, carefully prepared memorandum from Rear Admiral Taylor, reviewing cooperation between the two Services since the founding of the National Advisory Committee for Aeronautics in 1915 and deploring existing dissensions. Summing up, the Navy Department wrote that "in plain words . . . a few subordinate officers in the Army Air Service are determined to make friction and cause duplication, and then represent this as the normal condition." Under all the circumstances it was inevitable that the good in General Mitchell's ideas about aviation should be buried under the opposition aroused by his methods of advancing those ideas and by his use of personalities in argument.

Senator New's bill for a separate air force reached the floor of Congress but it did not pass. Its failure, however, did not deter the "separationists" from slipping into the draft of the Army Appropriation Bill for 1922 a clause directing that "hereafter the Army Air Service shall control all aerial operations from land bases, and . . . Naval Aviation shall have control of all aerial operations attached to a fleet." When Senator Page brought this clause to the attention of the Navy, the Navy Department pointed out, among other things wrong with the clause, the "impropriety of including in an appropriation bill for one branch of the Government, anything involving the policies of other branches." Captain Craven described the clause as outlining "the policy for coast defense of the United States, not as recommended by the War Department but [by] the aviation section of the Army." With Senator Wadsworth of New York the captain worked out a substitute clause which would leave the Navy undisturbed in its air stations, and this amendment, since it had the approval of both Secretaries, was finally included in the act as passed. Even then the safeguards were not strong enough, because the failure of the Wadsworth-Craven clause to define defensive patrols as "operations with the Fleet" left the "Mitchell group" an opening through which to claim jurisdiction over these patrols. Accordingly General Mitchell's next proposal was that the Army take over some 13 naval air stations, and in support of that proposal he presented a great many figures which were quite inaccurate. Moreover, as the Secretary of the Navy commented, the general continued to ignore the facts and to belittle all the work that the Army, the Navy, and the Aeronautical Board had accomplished together.

In a letter to the Secretary of War written in May, 1920, the Secretary of the Navy said it was

most unfortunate that the efforts of the War and Navy Departments and of the great majority of officers of the Army and Navy to coordinate the work of our Departments and to continue the cooperation which has existed in the past should be interfered with by an individual or by individuals. It would seem particularly unhappy at this time when there is so much constructive work confronting both the Army and the Navy on aeronautical matters.

To this Mr. Baker replied that new instructions had been issued to restrain army officers appearing before committees. While these instructions recognized the need for freedom of speech, they did "not contemplate nor permit the making of statements, especially with reference to the other coordinate Executive Departments, which may reasonably serve to discredit or reflect upon these . . . departments." These corrective steps, said Mr. Baker, would "insure that the policy of the Department . . . will be conformed with hereafter by officers of the Army who may have occasion to testify before the Senate Committees relative to Aviation matters." While the new instructions were plainly intended to curb such remarks as those of General Mitchell, they did so only for the few remaining months of the Wilson administration. When President Harding, on April 12, 1921, told Congress that aviation was "inseparable from either the Army or the Navy," the controversy on a separate air department might have been supposed to be at an end. In fact, however, the attention which was presently concentrated on bombing tests would revive the whole discussion and make it more acrimonious than ever.

CHAPTER XVII

The Bureau of Aeronautics

THE activity of General Mitchell had one effect that had not been foreseen by the Navy and certainly had not been intended by the general himself. His attacks made the whole Navy realize that its internal differences of opinion were of trivial importance beside the necessity of saving Naval Aviation from extinction, and upon that necessity all hands could agree. This brought about a really concerted effort to establish the administration of aviation on a much sounder basis, and here again General Mitchell was an unwitting help.

The press had given wide publicity to the idea of a separate United States air force, but this had served to unite the thinking of all friends of the Navy with that of Representative Frederick Hicks of New York. Whereas that gentleman previously had found his long-held plan for establishing in the Navy Department a bureau of aeronautics on an equal footing with the other bureaus hampered by widely differing opinions, including those of the Navy itself, he now found these opinions all swinging into line with his own.

Captain Irwin, while still in office as director, had reminded the General Board that "now, when the move is for a united air service," the urgent thing was to go ahead with the development of aircraft with the Fleet. He held that the Navy's hand was strengthened "every time we can show that we are using them in that way." Implied in this statement was the captain's conviction that real integration of the air arm with the Fleet was impossible without greater authority and independence in the administration of aviation. General Mitchell gave wholly unintentional support to this conviction by violently criticizing the lack of proper organization in Naval Aviation.

Captain Craven had been coming to the same view, more and more rapidly since the "reorganization" of August, 1919, had left him without any real standing. Notwithstanding Admiral Mc-

Kean's belittling references, Craven was determined to go down fighting for real authority and definite responsibility. He called upon a number of officers for comment on the situation, and among these Capt. David Hanrahan, former commander of the Northern Bombing Group, was particularly outspoken. Hanrahan condemned the existing organization as making "the outlook for the future of naval aviation . . . more or less hopeless." He found the director restricted to planning yet held responsible for many other aviation activities too widely scattered to permit proper, efficient, and economical administration. He was "firmly convinced that Naval Aviation will enlarge and grow far beyond its present restrictions and has to grow to keep up with the first-class powers abroad." Under the existing organization it could never grow.

This type of comment was exactly what Representative Hicks wanted. He was, of course, involved in all the inquiries by a Republican House into the Democratic conduct of the war, and well aware that one result of these inquiries was a tendency toward the creation of a separate air force to include all Services—the Mitchell idea. He also knew that the Navy, specifically Rear Admiral Taylor through Hunsaker, as an expedient designed to head off the Mitchell faction had prepared the draft of a bill establishing both a bureau of aeronautics and a separate naval flying corps. This bill differed from earlier proposals, made in 1919 by the National Advisory Committee for Aeronautics, to the effect that the Army, the Navy, the Post Office, and the Department of Commerce should each have a separate bureau of aeronautics, all to be coordinated under a supreme aeronautical board of civilians. Admiral Taylor's objections to this were that federal control of civilian aviation should not be exercised through the military Services but through a civilian board with which these Services should cooperate; that greater cooperation between the Services themselves would be secured by legalizing and strengthening their joint aeronautical board; and that aviation in the Navy should be segregated under the control and direction of a corps formed by temporary detail from all branches of the Service. When the Secretary of the Navy's Council, a special group of advisers, proved to be in general agreement with Admiral Taylor, the Chief of Naval Operations called a conference for the purpose of deciding upon the draft of a bill to create a bureau of aeronautics.

In general, the points made in 1919 by Lieutenant Brush of the Reserve were revived for discussion. His remarks upon the good results which should be obtained from a compact organization, gradually combined under the chief of bureau, took on added significance from what had been happening since Brush's letter was written; and opposition from other bureaus was weakened by the threat from outside the Navy. Hence the original plan proposed at the conference provided for both a bureau and a flying corps of 500 officers and 5,000 enlisted men, the officers to be given temporary commissions for terms of not over three years. When this composite draft found immediate disfavor in many quarters, the result was the assembly of a new group which included Rear Admirals Taylor and Griffin as well as the Chief of Naval Operations, Admiral Coontz. Ultimately, though a minority was still opposed, the draft sent to Congress for hearings was little changed. Mr. Hicks was prompt in commenting upon the "change of heart," because what he had proposed 18 months earlier, only to encounter strong naval opposition, was now brought forward as the right procedure. He then drafted his own bill, omitting any provision for a separate corps, but no action was taken at that session. During the next one, however, there were more hearings in February, 1921, and Admiral Fiske had his opportunity to say of the proposal for the new bureau that "if you can get that established to-morrow it will be very much better than getting it established the next day; the quicker the better . . . You cannot do anything toward development of scientific naval aviation unless you have it."

Two months later President Harding called a special session of Congress and in his message to it recommended "enactment of legislation establishing a bureau of aeronautics in the Navy Department to centralize the control of naval activities in aeronautics and removing the restrictions on the personnel detailed to aviation in the Navy." To the aviators, this was encouraging, and of further great importance to them was the attitude of the new Secretary of the Navy, Mr. Edwin Denby, who, perhaps partly because he had himself served in the Marine Corps, came out strongly in his comments to the congressional committees. "You know probably quite as well as I," said he, "the importance of aviation, the new element that has been projected into warfare upon the sea. It has not received sufficient attention by the Congress, by the people, or by the Navy." He expressed the opinion that naval air activities must be "centralized under one chief, of the same rank as the other bureau chiefs," and added his earnest hopes that the bill might pass.

Admiral Coontz was heard to very much the same effect, his statement being unusual in that he said "this is one case where the Chief of Naval Operations is willing to give up something." He went on to point out that both economy and efficiency should result from a separate bureau able to act with authority and not merely as one among ten other divisions in the Office of Naval Operations. "Neither I," said he, "nor any other human can properly handle it as it stands now." He believed that the Navy had, in the officer who had succeeded Captain Craven as director in March of 1921, just the man to head the new bureau. This was a newcomer to Naval Aviation, Capt. William A. Moffett.

Here was the very last man in the Navy who would willingly accept a vague responsibility or any such "weathercock authority" as that which had so long irked Craven. Moreover, he was a suave and polished negotiator, with Benjamin Franklin's ability to plant his own ideas in the minds of other men so delicately that the seeds would presently come to bloom as luxuriantly as though they had been indigenous. During his distinguished career in the Navy his critics would sometimes call him a publicity seeker, but the fact is that whenever a paragraph on Moffett appeared in print it would be followed by at least a column favoring the Navy. Highly qualified professionally, he was something of a genius at public relations. A diplomat being required to present the Navy's position, there could have been no better choice.

Moffett expounded before Congress his conviction that no organization can ever accomplish anything if its authority is not commensurate with its responsibility. He emphasized the vital importance of the effect a separate bureau would have on the morale and enthusiasm of the flying personnel. Civilian employee or naval man, airman or groundman, everyone in aviation must be able to feel that he belonged to something really alive and progressive. It would be better not to create any separate naval flying corps, for this might bring in aviators who were not seamen, but even at that cost there must be a separate bureau on a par with all others in the department.

Lt. Comdr. Richard Byrd was still the link between Congress and the Navy Department on such questions, and there is no doubt that he, with such support as that of Mr. Hicks, was able to accomplish much in the way of enlightening those who were either not fully informed or else awed by what they had heard from General Mitchell. When Moffett swung into action behind all the other efforts, the result became certain and, on July 12, 1921, the bill to create the separate bureau was made law. A month later Moffett, as a Rear Admiral, found himself the first Chief of the Bureau of Aeronautics.

He was ready with his plan of organization, which he presented to the Secretary of the Navy. Although criticism of the plan came from the older bureaus when they realized that the sponsors of the new one did not intend that it be merely a material bureau, by August 10, the date of formal "inauguration," almost everything that Moffett wanted was approved by the Secretary. The Chief of Aeronautics was named adviser to the Chief of Naval Operations on aviation and required to keep that officer informed on "all aeronautic planning, operation, and administration." On personnel, the new bureau was authorized to recommend the detail of officers to flying duties and the distribution of aviation ratings, as well as to recommend methods of training. Other bureaus were specifically required by the Secretary's order to perform their work in connection with aviation in a manner satisfactory to the Bureau of Aeronautics and to accept that bureau's recommendations as to the priority to be given the development of various types of aviation equipment. Within the limitations imposed by Congress, policy on the upkeep and operation of aircraft factories, experimental plants, and helium plants was similarly to be established by the new bureau. Altogether, this plan represented another long step forward for Naval Aviation.

When Moffett sent a draft of the new bureau's first circular letter through the department for comment and suggestion, the most constructive criticism came from Hunsaker. He correctly predicted that difficulty would certainly result from the confusion of authority over procurement between the Plans Division and the Material Division, a confusion which was to continue for 20 years until a Deputy Chief of Naval Operations for Air was established in 1943. Since in his view the new bureau was to be primarily a material bureau, with no more than remote control over training and operations, Hunsaker held that the organization "should be such that these material activities can be handled direct and with strict accountability." He was driving at the old conflict between the flier and the engineer, at the conviction of the leading aviators that they should be both planners and developers, both manufacturers and operators. Whereas Captain Chambers and Bristol, as well as their successors, had always demanded a say in design of planes and accessories, the two technical bureaus, Construction and Repair, and Engineering, had been just as convinced that aviators could not tell them how to run their own business. Both sides being entirely sincere in these convictions, friction and delay were inevitable. As Hunsaker saw the matter, the Plans Division might properly lay down the military characteristics required of new aircraft, but it should then leave it to the constructors to produce what was wanted. To make actual designs, Plans would have to have better aeronautical engineers than those in the Material Division, and the latter would consequently be robbed of any incentive to keep abreast of the newest and best in the field. In this conception of the problem Hunsaker was sticking closely to the Navy's long-standing theory of command. The top officers should tell their subordinates "what, when and where," then hold these subordinates responsible for the "how." Most wars have been won on that theory.

As finally promulgated, Aviation Circular No. 1 established four divisions: Plans, Administration, Material, and Flight. Notwithstanding Hunsaker's protest, Plans continued to have split jurisdiction over aircraft production, as well as over the trials which were to determine the fighting value of the designs as completed. Administration, in addition to office routine, was to handle financial and legal details, as well as the bureau's relations with the public. Material, largest of the four, was divided into three sections: design, procurement, and maintenance; while Flight was to be concerned with training and operations in general.

Inevitably there were some flaws in the new plan; flaws, that is, when viewed in retrospect and from the standpoint of those who favored the fastest possible progress in aviation. Most of these, however, were caused by the retention in various older bureaus of certain work which must now meet the approval of the new one. Thus the factory at Philadelphia, now required to build whatever Aeronautics wanted, was still to be run by the Bureau of Construction and Repair. Vital items of equipment, rapidly becoming highly specialized, such as ordnance, radio, and flying instruments, while also requiring the approval of Aeronautics, were still to be produced or procured, respectively, by the Bureaus of Ordnance, Engineering, and Navigation, the last-named also continuing to handle the training of personnel. It is possible that progress might have been more rapid had the new bureau immediately assumed these various functions and also taken over the experts that administered them, but at the time this would probably have meant too much of an upheaval and as matters stood what had been accomplished was a very great gain. A solid foundation had been laid for the much more extensive structure which would eventually be erected in World War II. The wider recognition of aircraft as an element of sea power was an indication that, whatever might be the subsequent appropriations of Congress for aviation, progress in the art and science of flying in the Navy would be along proper lines. With this in mind the new bureau stood upon its collective toes, ready to combat any attempt, by anyone, to strip the Navy of its flying arm.

FIRST FLIGHT FROM ANY SHIP

Eugene Ely leaving the deck of the USS *Birmingham*, November 14, 1910, at Hampton Roads, Virginia

FIRST LANDING ON A SHIP

Ely on the platform of the USS *Pennsylvania*, January 18, 1911, in San Francisco Bay

LIEUT. T. G. ELLYSON
Naval Aviator No. 1

1ST LT. A. A. CUNNINGHAM
Naval Aviator No. 5

COMDR. JOHN RODGERS
Naval Aviator No. 2

LT. COMDR. J. C. HUNSAKER
Aeronautical Engineer

PIONEERS OF NAVAL AVIATION

CAPT. W. I. CHAMBERS
1910–1913

REAR ADM. M. L. BRISTOL
1913–1916

CAPT. N. E. IRWIN
1917–1919

CAPT. T. T. CRAVEN
1919–1921

DIRECTORS OF NAVAL AVIATION

NAVAL AND MARINE AVIATORS IN 1914

Lieuts. V. D. Herbster, W. M. McIlvain, USMC, P. N. L. Bellinger, R. C. Saufley, J. H. Towers, Lt. Comdr. H. C. Mustin, Lt. B. L. Smith, USMC, and Ensigns G. deC. Chevalier and M. L. Stolz

CREWS OF THE NC TRANSATLANTIC FLIGHT, 1919

First row: Lt. Comdr. Read, Secretary Daniels, Comdr. Towers, Assistant Secretary Roosevelt, Lt. Comdr. Bellinger; second row: Ens. Rodd, Lt. (jg) Sadenwater, Lieut. Barin, Comdr. Richardson, Lieut. McCulloch; third row: Lieut. Breese, Lt. Comdr. Lavender (hidden); fourth row: CMM Rhoads, CMM Christensen, Lieut. Stone, USCG, and Lt. (jg) Hinton

A-1, CURTISS TRIAD
First U. S. Navy plane aboard the first catapult at Annapolis, 1912

C-1, CURTISS FLYING BOAT
Making catapult take-off at Washington Navy Yard, 1912

EARLY CATAPULTS

USS *Lexington* (cv-2)
Commissioned December 14, 1927, sister ship of the USS *Saratoga* (CV-3)

USS *Ranger* (cv-4)
Commissioned June 4, 1934, first ship in the U. S. Navy designed as a carrier

uss *Langley* (cv-1)

Commissioned March 20, 1922, after conversion from the collier *Jupiter*

uss *Wright* (av-1)

Commissioned December 16, 1921, first seaplane tender of the U. S. Navy

AH-7, BURGESS-DUNNE HYDROAEROPLANE, 1913

N-9, CURTISS HYDROAEROPLANE, 1916

F-BOAT, CURTISS, 1917

EARLY NAVAL AIRCRAFT

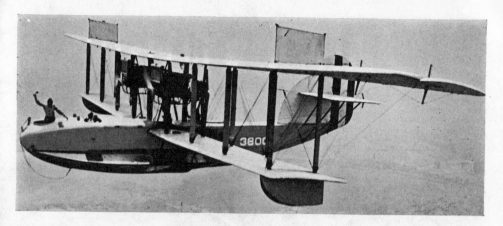

F5L, FLYING BOAT, 1918

NC, NAVY-CURTISS FLYING BOAT, 1918

UO-1, VOUGHT SCOUT-OBSERVATION PLANE, 1925

EARLY NAVAL AIRCRAFT

PN-9, NAVAL AIRCRAFT FACTORY, 1925

P2Y-3, CONSOLIDATED, 1933

PBY-1, CONSOLIDATED CATALINA, 1936

PATROL AIRCRAFT

O2U, VOUGHT, 1926

SOC, CURTISS SEAGULL, 1935

OS2U, VOUGHT KINGFISHER, 1940

SCOUT-OBSERVATION PLANES

DH-4B, MODEL OF THE ARMY DH-4, 1921

VE-7, VOUGHT, FIRST OF THIS TYPE PURCHASED 1920

DT-2, AN EARLY TORPEDO PLANE, 1923

FIRST PLANES TO OPERATE FROM A CARRIER

F6C-1, CURTISS, 1925

F4B-1, BOEING, 1929

F4F-3, GRUMMAN WILDCAT, 1940

CARRIER FIGHTERS

SC-1, MARTIN BOMBER AND TORPEDO PLANE, 1925

XT5M-1, MARTIN DIVE BOMBER, 1930

SBD-1, DOUGLAS DAUNTLESS, 1937

DIVE BOMBERS

T3M, MARTIN, 1926

TG-1, GREAT LAKES, 1929

TBD-1, DOUGLAS DEVASTATOR, 1937

TORPEDO PLANES

N2Y-1, CONSOLIDATED TRAINING PLANE, 1931, TAKING OFF FROM USS *Akron*

GOODYEAR OBSERVATION KITE BALLOON USED FOR PROTECTION OF CONVOYS IN WORLD WAR I

USS *Shenandoah* (ZR-1), 1923, FIRST NAVY RIGID AIRSHIP

Exercising primary responsibility in this field, the Navy investigated all military possibilities of rigid airships, blimps, and kite balloons.

LIGHTER-THAN-AIR CRAFT

CHAPTER XVIII

The Bombing Tests

I N the fall of 1919 Lt. Comdr. Bartlett had suggested that much information about bombing by aircraft might be gathered from a series of experiments using either captured German warships or vessels of the United States Navy which had been condemned to the scrap heap. His suggestion was well received but nothing definite was done until November, 1920, when the battleship *Indiana*, veteran of the Spanish War, was selected as the target for special tests. Bombs placed at calculated distances from her hull were detonated in an effort to learn the effect of "near-misses." After 14 of these, weighing from 200 to 600 pounds and placed at distances varying from 25 to 75 feet, had been exploded the ship began to settle. She was then towed into shallow water and run aground, after which heavier bombs were placed upon her deck. The explosion of one bomb of 1,800 pounds burst her superstructure and damaged her turrets to such an extent that only one conclusion was possible: a direct hit by such a bomb would put a ship of her class out of action. As far as they went these experiments were enlightening, but it was clear that many more tests must be made before exact conclusions could be drawn. Naval aviators were therefore eager to get more old ships and blow them to pieces in different ways under varying conditions.

A number of dilapidated German ships had been delivered to the United States. They included the battleship *Ostfriesland*, the cruiser *Frankfurt*, some destroyers, and a number of submarines. In February, 1920, a strong recommendation by the Bureau of Ordnance urged that some or all of these ships be used for tests. Originally it was suggested that the ships would make good targets for the Fleet's guns, which would destroy them in accordance with international agreement. Later it was decided that if the ships could "also be bombed from aircraft" there would be an excellent opportunity to gather information. This proposal led to months of discussion until, on January 1, 1921, the Secretary of the Navy gave orders to proceed with both types of tests and a few weeks later invited the Army to participate in them. The War Department referred this invitation to the Aeronautical Board, but before that board had acted the Chief of the Army Air Service submitted a proposal that obsolete ships be obtained from the Navy for bombing experiments.

Representative R. Anthony, Jr. and Senator New both introduced resolutions which directed the Navy Department to turn over to the Army one old battleship, two old destroyers, and two old supply ships, "to be used for the purpose of serving as targets for the development of aerial armament and methods of aerial attack against sea craft." Before these resolutions were passed, however, the Secretary of the Navy explained that they were unnecessary in view of the tests already proposed by the Navy.

During discussions between the Bureau of Ordnance and the Chief of the Army Technical Staff a debate on the possible effect of torpedoes made it apparent that the Army and the Navy saw eye to eye when examining the possibilities of aerial bombing and the claims of the army airmen. A significant feature of the agreement reached was the statement made after the conferences by the Army's representative, who said that he "would furnish no information to the Army Air Service" except through the Secretary of War.

At this stage of preparation for the bombing tests several misunderstandings arose. The joint Aeronautical Board came out with a formal suggestion that the Navy invite the Army to participate, but this was not until three weeks after the Navy's invitation had been sent. This same board stipulated that the Army's presence at the tests should not be construed as preventing the Army from "making at least two hits with the largest type of bombs that may be available," a clause which led to some further disagreements between General Mitchell and the Navy. The board also repeated the proposal that an old battleship be turned over to the Army with the Navy invited to assist in bombing her. This suggestion was taken up later.

Meantime the Navy's plans were announced as designed to determine three things: the ability of aircraft to locate ships in the coastal zone; the probability of scoring bomb hits on ships under way; and the damage which such hits might inflict upon ships of relatively modern design and construction. To begin with, the radio-controlled *Iowa* was to approach the coast somewhere within fixed limits on the Virginia coast while both the Army's and the Navy's planes searched for her. If found she was to be bombed only with dummies because the radio control had been very costly and the Navy could not afford to sink her. This was unfortunate because General Mitchell, while he agreed to participate in the search, declined to drop dummies on the ground that no useful information could be gathered without sinking her. He also held that the *Iowa* should be brought well inshore because to locate her 100 miles off would require a 400-mile flight by army planes from Langley Field. The mathematical basis for this calculation is not apparent at this late date.

In due course the Army Air Service asked for the old battleship *Kentucky* as a target, but she was in such bad condition that her repairs would cost more than could be spared from the Navy's scant funds. Because it was clear that the Army Air Service attacks, although described as "purely experimental," would make certain that the target was sunk, it was important that the target should be in the best watertight condition when the attacks began. Nevertheless, the Navy was entirely willing that some ship should be attacked, and further conferences led to the substitution of the *Alabama*, about as old as the *Kentucky* but much more shipshape.

Both Congress and the public displayed considerable interest in what was planned. In the House Mr. Hicks deprecated the tests as not likely to prove much if the target were immobile, undefended by its own guns, and unprotected by friendly aircraft. Mr. Anthony, an aisle or two away from Mr. Hicks, demanded to know "whether or not the Navy Department intends to furnish proper targets to the Air Service of the Army." As to the public, it was clear that what the public might think, after the tests, would have a considerable effect upon future expenditures for the Navy.

In a series of conferences on details of the tests, General Mitchell represented the Air Service while Capt. Alfred W. Johnson, then commanding the Atlantic Fleet Air Detachment, represented the Navy with Whiting as his special assistant. From the very first Johnson emphasized the point that the Navy was not seeking merely to sink ships but rather to determine, by careful procedure and frequent inspection of the targets, the effect of bombs of different weights, exploded at varying distances. It was with this in mind that the rules governing the tests were written, and General Mitchell, although he registered an objection against serving under Johnson, who was his junior in rank, agreed that he would abide by the rules. As to the *Alabama*, he recommended that the Navy use torpedoes against her because, as he put it, "neglect of . . . this weapon will permit foreign nations to obtain a lead which will be difficult to overcome"; a recommendation not clearly understood because the Navy had for years been devoting all available time and money to the development of torpedoes. Finally the general suggested that an attack upon the *Iowa* so far offshore would necessitate the use of seaplanes, which he considered too "sluggish" to be of any value against an enemy certain to be equipped with carriers and pursuit planes. The Navy's reply to this took the view that the purpose was not to test types of aircraft but to learn as much as possible about bomb dropping and its effect. This position on the point did not get much space in public print.

At this time Moffett wrote a long memorandum on the "Publicity Propaganda of General Mitchell Running Contrary to President's Policy." In this Moffett invited attention to what President Harding in his message to Congress had said of the need for close cooperation between Army and Navy in their flying efforts, and cited numerous instances in which he held that Mitchell had been uncooperative. He cited the crash of an army plane in which five officers had been killed—a disaster caused by the plane's lack of a radio over which he could have received the Weather Bureau's warnings but attributed by Mitchell, who had been "entirely and directly in charge of the operation," to the lack of a united air service. Mitchell's activities, said Moffett, "in advocating a policy opposed to that of the President and the Navy Department, and his false and misleading statements are delaying and hampering the efforts of those who are responsible for Naval Aviation . . . who are endeavoring to loyally carry out the orders and the policies of their superiors."

These exchanges were unpleasant, but meanwhile progress toward final plans continued and at the end of May, 1921, they were issued in detail. They covered attacks upon the German submarines, the *Iowa*, the German destroyers, the *Frankfurt* and the *Ostfriesland*, in that order. The U-117 was to be the first target, attacked by three waves of F-5-L planes with each wave dropping 12 165-pound bombs; then by five of the Navy's Martin bombers dropping 30 bombs; then by a division of six of the Marine Corps' De Havillands dropping 12 bombs. All these were to be followed by three waves of army Martins dropping 18 250-pound bombs, then by a wave of army De Havillands dropping 12 bombs, and finally by five more army De Havillands dropping ten bombs.

After three other U-boats had been sunk by destroyer gunfire, the games would continue with the *Iowa* test. Under radio control from the *Ohio*, five miles away, the *Iowa*, at the hour set, was to be somewhere between Cape Hatteras and Cape Henlopen, 50 to 100 miles offshore, headed west. When located she was to be attacked by navy planes of the F-5-L type, carrying 165-pound dummies of standard size and form dropped from 4,000 feet, then by NC flying boats with 500-pound dummies, and finally by army Martins carrying 1,000-pound dummies.

Continuing into July, the plan provided for an all-Army exercise in which one German destroyer would be bombed in any way the Army chose. Two others would then be sunk by destroyer gunfire. Ten days later the *Frankfurt* would be attacked from the air and two days after that there would follow the main effort against the *Ostfriesland*. If these larger ships survived bombing, they were to be turned over to the guns of the Fleet.

Few, if any, doubted that even a heavily armored battleship would sink if she were hit by enough big bombs. The uncertainty was chiefly over how big the bombs would have to be, how many small ones the ship could take without crippling damage, and similar unanswered questions. To get as many of these answers as possible, a special board of naval observers was appointed with orders to visit the target ship between the attacks by successive waves, inspect her decks, turrets, bridges, smoke pipes, engine room, and fireroom, and note the progressive disintegration. To cover the *Ostfriesland* completely on these points, it was specifically stated in the rules that not more than two of the 250-pound or 300-pound bombs should be dropped at a time, and where the 1,000-pound bomb was used, only one should be dropped between successive inspections.

The early exercises were carried through without untoward incident, the U-117 being sunk in 12 minutes by naval planes and the German destroyer G-102 readily sunk by army planes. While the *Iowa* was still far offshore the navy planes located her and carried out their dummy attack exactly as planned. In the *Frankfurt* test a 600-pound bomb landing in the water close to her bridge exploded with the effect of a mine, lifting her bow several feet and blowing out a hole big enough for the sea to fill two forward compartments, take her down by the head, and sink her. This brought the exercises up to July 20, the day set for the *Ostfriesland* tests.

The army planes were furnished with the Navy's compasses and bomb sights. To help them in their attack, destroyers, at seven-and-a-half-mile intervals, formed a line of "buoys" extending from Thimble Shoals in Chesapeake Bay seaward toward the target. Two of the Navy's planes flew with each army group, to give a hand to any landplane that might be forced down. Blimps from the Fleet were sent up to keep the Army informed, by radio telephone, of the wind's direction and velocity. Another blimp hovered over the *Ostfriesland* at 3,000 feet taking photographs, while three planes from each Service circled the ship at 2,500 feet for the same purpose. To make sure that each attack stopped when its prescribed number of bombs had been dropped, or whenever the board of observers wished to visit the ship, special signals were arranged by Captain Johnson, embarked in the *Shawmut* and in charge of the exercises. The procedure was laid down in these words:

No bombs will be dropped unless an *"All Clear"* signal, consisting of a large red cross and a ball, is displayed on white canvas on the *Shawmut's* forecastle. In case signal is rolled up, planes will cease bombing and await orders. This is particularly important as the target-ship will be inspected by a Board at certain times. In case of emergency, heavy smoke from the stacks of the *Shawmut* may be used as a signal to cease bombing in addition to withdrawing the *"All Clear"* signal.

To provide further against misunderstanding, General Mitchell was given written instructions that the *"All Clear"* must be recognized *immediately preceding each successive attack*. If the signal were withdrawn after an attack had begun but before an army group had dropped all its bombs, that group must at once cease fire. As still another emergency signal, a naval plane cutting the figure S in sharp curves ahead of the attacking unit was to be understood as an order to stop bombing. Finally, these special instructions emphasized once more the importance of dropping only the prescribed number of bombs, as well as the vital importance of stopping the fire if any 1,000-pound bomb made a direct hit, to allow time for inspection by the board. With these elaborate details in mind, it is easy to appreciate the significance of what followed during the attacks, which lasted two days.

On the first day the take-off of the first planes was delayed by weather too rough for the small boats that must transport the observers and by a low ceiling. Consequently the Army's request, repeatedly broadcast, for authority to make its attack had to be denied until about 2.15 P.M. Unhappily the army planes "jumped the gun" at 1.30, with the result that they reached the *Ostfriesland* before the Navy had completed its attack. Insisting that his planes had only enough fuel to stay in the area another forty minutes, General Mitchell pressed for permission to begin bombing and finally got it, even though this meant that the board of observers was deprived of any chance to visit the ship. Thus the "between attacks" data for that day were not obtained, from the Navy's standpoint a most unfortunate circumstance. This, however, was much less serious than the events of the second day, when both the Army and the Navy were scheduled to have their heavy bombers over the target at 8 A.M.

A few minutes before seven General Mitchell told Captain Johnson by radio that the Army's planes were already on their way out, adding the request that "they be not interfered with by Naval aircraft." The first army bomb having scored a direct hit, the rules required that attack be suspended until the board had made its inspection, and the *Shawmut* accordingly rolled up the all-clear signal. When the army planes paid no attention either to this notice or to the dense smoke immediately belched up from the *Shawmut*, Captain Johnson steamed toward the *Ostfriesland* until he was inside the 1,000-foot danger circle, at the same time telling the general by radio: "Cease firing. Observers going aboard. Acknowledge." The general's only answer was: "Martin bomber Number Twenty-three will let you know when it is safe to board the target," and this was followed by the dropping of five more 1,000-pound bombs, three of which scored direct hits. The army planes then went on to drop seven 2,000-pounders, some of which hit the ship and finally sank her.

The effect of these violations of carefully drawn rules was to destroy the value of these tests to the Navy. Much had been expected from the bombing of the *Ostfriesland* because, although the Germans had left her in poor condition, she was the largest, most modern vessel bombed up to that time. As matters stood, the Navy's board of experts, in its report upon the various bombings, recognized several important factors. All ships except the *Iowa* had been at anchor, waiting for planes which would be guided to their targets

by other ships and make their attack under ideal conditions of
visibility and low altitude. Not a man was aboard any ship bombed
to make repairs or, which might be much more vital, handle antiaircraft defense. Nevertheless, said the board, "the fact remains
that in every case of attack by airplanes by bombs, the ships so
attacked, whether submarine, destroyer, light cruiser, or battleship, were eventually sunk, and by airplanes with bombs alone."
In short, those hulls going down off the Virginia capes made a
realistic picture more convincing than any amount of abstract
speculation. Moreover, as noted by the board, aviation was as yet
by no means fully developed. To provide against that development
the board, before plunging into technical details, recommended
that the Navy immediately look to its defenses: passive in the
redesigning of hulls and the alteration of certain features, active
in the form of antiaircraft guns and especially in planes based
aboard the ships. Urging the adaptation of planes to battleships
and other combat craft, the board went much further to emphasize
the necessity of carriers, both to defend their own ships and to attack those of the enemy. Peering into the future, what the board
saw was not the extinction of the battle line, but instead a force
of battleships and cruisers proceeding under the cover of their own
air protection.

Not all officers were so deeply impressed. Adm. Hilary P. Jones,
then Commander in Chief of the Atlantic Fleet, in his endorsement
on the board's report, held that "the artificiality under which these
tests were carried out" had not been sufficiently emphasized.
Comdr. (later Rear Adm.) Alexander H. Van Keuren, a special
observer for the Bureau of Construction and Repair, made a report
freely admitting the power of aerial bombs but stressing what a
crew well trained in damage control might be able to do for a ship
attacked as the *Ostfriesland* had been. To these general conclusions should be added a great many technical recommendations
made by the board itself, covering everything from the need of
better instruments for aerial navigation to the importance of more
efficient types of ordnance.

In his own report to the Navy Department Captain Johnson
pointed out that the army planes, by their disregard of the prescribed rules, had made it impossible to gather the data sought
and thus had defeated the Navy's hope of discovering how existing
ships might be given better protection against bombing and how
future designs should be modified to the same end. He guessed

correctly that the publicity given to the sinkings would leave the public unaware that the tests had not been carried out according to plan. In a letter subsequently written in the Navy Department serious charges were made against Mitchell, but Theodore Roosevelt, Jr., then Acting Secretary of the Navy, decided that such a letter would stir up further political pother over the pros and cons of a single air force and also intensify ill-feeling between the Army Air Service and the Navy. As he did not send the letter the argument was left to the press, where it was carried on briskly. "Day of the Battleship Ended" was a ready-made headline. General Mitchell, for his part, made the public statement that he had himself originated the whole series of tests, and later, in his book *Winged Defense*, he asserted that the bombings had been carried out far at sea because it had been the Navy's intent to hazard the lives of army fliers.

In September the Army's planes bombed the *Alabama*. The night attack, with blazing flares, gas bombs, and machine-gun fire, was very spectacular but not markedly successful. No hit was scored with any 100-pound bomb, and of the seven 300-pounders dropped, two scored hits. In the first day attack, however, as many as 11 out of 36 small fragmentation bombs hit, as did two out of 14 300-pound demolition bombs. Of six 1,000-pound armor piercers dropped, none hit. Next day two hits were made with this weight bomb and one with a 2,000-pounder, while of several near-misses with both sizes, one or two were very close. Although no examination of progressive damage was made, the naval board agreed that this test confirmed the conclusion drawn from the earlier one that the cumulative effect of near-misses, rather than direct hits, had eventually sunk the ship.

General Mitchell during an address to Congress laid new stress upon his belief in a single air force and upon what he considered the Navy's relatively unimportant air effort. Once more he went astray in facts and figures, notably those bearing upon British naval air personnel, with the result that these figures were used in a speech on the floor of Congress attacking a statement by the Secretary of the Navy. At a moment when Congress was considering further reduction in the already inadequate personnel of the Navy, such an attack had its most unfortunate effect.

In January, 1923, General Mitchell, ostensibly as the representative of the President at a meeting of the National Aeronautic Association in Dayton once more, in strong language, eliminated the surface vessel and talked of a "true system" of national defense which would be to all practical purposes wholly in the air. Meantime he had his army planes darting around New York City laying smoke screens and pouring radio broadcasts over Washington, proceedings not halted by the War Department until they had continued for a month. In February a board headed by Maj. Gen. William Lassiter of the Army General Staff began hearings which led to recommendations for a feasible ten-year army air program, one, moreover, which would provide "great mobility and independence of action" without impairing unity of command. By April the essentials of these conclusions had become War Department policy. Although it appears to have been an objective of this policy to bring about a single appropriation by Congress for both Services, 60 per cent for the Army, 40 per cent for the Navy, that objective was not attained. Presumably this was because Secretary Denby of the Navy continued the fight to keep the naval air arm the Navy's own.

The sinking of the 20-year-old *Virginia* and *New Jersey* by army bombers in September, 1923, followed the general course of earlier bombings. Some direct hits and many near-misses were scored. On the army side, the chief result was a recommendation for airfields along the coast. It became clearer than ever to the Navy that ships unprotected by aircraft would henceforth be in grave danger of bombing attacks, the more so because as many as two direct hits or near-misses by 2,000-pound bombs would probably put any ship of the day out of action. For this reason the Navy, in the effort to build up immediately to the strength permitted by treaties, held that its air arm should be supported with funds, planes, and personnel to give the Fleet true air superiority.

In November, 1924, came the bombing of the unfinished *Washington*, doomed by the disarmament treaty of 1922. Alone among the ships bombed, she was modern in every respect, particularly in her compartment structure, and against her the Navy had its opportunity to try out armor-piercing air projectiles, mines, and torpedoes in attacks modeled upon those made against the *Indiana*. At varying distances from the hull 1,000-pound charges of TNT were detonated and 400-pound torpedo charges were fired against the side. Fourteen armor-piercing projectiles were dropped from 4,000 feet. After all that, it nevertheless required two-and-a-half hours of shelling from turret guns to sink the ship, a fact which led the battleship men to conclude that such ships still had a very

important future. The board of inspection supported this view
to the extent of deciding that a ship of the type could withstand
eight torpedo hits provided these were not bunched. Moreover the
Eberle Board, convened in 1924 to study recent developments in
aviation, including the record of all the bombings, came to much
the same conclusion. This board, after hearing the statements of
officers and civilian experts, held that a *Washington*-type battleship with personnel to man antiaircraft guns and repair damage
and with power on her pumps would be substantially secure against
sinking, even by better aircraft than those of the day. Although
General Mitchell suggested that the Navy "had not tried" and was
unwilling to admit that the battleship was done for, the facts indicated that such ships, provided with protection and aerial cover,
would for many years continue to be the Fleet's backbone. To
Johnson, Moffett, and others of the Navy, Mitchell's latest attacks
were "grave and baseless" as well as "without precedent in the
history of our military services." The general's articles, published
some months later in the *Saturday Evening Post*, were even more
irritating to them. They knew that the statement by the general,
that seaplanes forced to land upon the water would not stay up as
long as would landplanes, was simply not true. They knew that
the general's accusation that "the Board of Inspection was so slow
that they kept us flying around way out at sea about an hour" was
equally unfounded. In consequence, excerpts from these articles
and from other statements by the general were sent to the War
Department with another letter from the Navy Department describing them as "intentionally deceptive." As the Navy saw the
controversy, the general appeared to be trying to obscure the real
issue.

Notwithstanding such matters, the Navy did learn much from
the bombing tests. For example, even though many of the extrav-
agant claims of the Mitchell group were quite unsupported by the
facts of that hour and are not fully supported by the facts of this
hour, it was no longer possible for even the most hidebound to con-
tend that the battleship was unsinkable. The worst skeptic could
not longer dispute the importance of aircraft and the effect they
must have upon sea power of the future. The Joint Board, for one
body, immediately declared that the experiments "have proved
that it has become imperative . . . to provide the maximum possible development of Aviation in both the Army and the Navy."
Again, the tests indicated that seaplanes could not meet all of a

Fleet's air requirements because they lacked speed and could not maneuver freely. Forward-looking naval men were right in declaring that "operations on the high seas by aircraft are impossible without carriers. Until we get them, there will be no real Fleet Aviation." They were thinking well ahead of the still infant carrier, into the day when much larger aircraft bearing heavier bombs could be launched from and landed upon the broad decks of carriers.

CHAPTER XIX

Technical Developments

LOOKING back 25 years, it is easy to recognize certain effects, in the early twenties, of the vociferous arguments over the bombing tests or of the heated debates on whether or not the United States should have a separate department of the air. For one thing, it appears clear that the extremists of that moment were inclined to simplify the points at issue until the question became that of the airplane against the battleship. Ultra-conservatives, seeing only the limitations of contemporary planes in radius of action and in bomb-carrying capacity, would not admit that advances in aerial weapons could ever make them a decisive factor against great fleets. Ultraliberals believed just as firmly that the capital ship was already eliminated. Neither could see reason in the other's arguments.

This is not said in condemnation of the conservatives in the Navy, for these included many officers whose professional abilities are not to be questioned. Having lived through many periods of competition between the weapons of offense and the weapons of defense, during which first one and then the other had been in the ascendant, their view that the guns of the Fleet were still at the core of sea power was not unlike that of many army officers of equal rank and experience, who held that trench warfare as it was carried on in World War I had demonstrated that no future war could be won by weapons of offense. Similarly, the men who took the ultraliberal view are not to be condemned, especially since much of what they foresaw eventually came to be. In the long run, ways were found to combine the views of both factions and retain the best points of each.

Between those who held the extreme views stood a large group of the more moderate. Naval aviators were outspoken in their insistence that aircraft were still only in infancy and that every effort must be made to press the technical advances that would some day make them adult. Since this view was shared by many army fliers, it became possible for those in the lower grades to come together with less friction than was evident between the upper grades. This put Moffett "in the middle" because, while he was certainly a progressive as to aircraft, he had been raised a seaman, with 30 years in ships, and he was able to understand the language of brother flag officers. More than once it took all his suavity and tact to preserve peace between the two factions, but while he sometimes made concessions to each, these were never of the kind to delay real progress in the practice of flying. On the contrary, he seized every opportunity to promote, through inter-Service cooperation at lower levels, the all-important technical advances that resulted from every sort of experiment.

Although somewhat obscured by the publicity given the quarrels, there were many such advances during these years. For the Navy 1922 was notable because, on March 20 of that year, the *Langley* went into commission and began her very useful life as an aquatic guinea pig. Her flight deck, 534′ x 64′ was only about the size of the decks on the "baby flat tops" of World War II but it was big for the day and there were dozens anxious to test it. On October 17, 1922, Lt. Comdr. V. C. Griffin was the first to take off from that deck, in a VE-7-SF. Nine days later, with the *Langley* under way, Lieutenant Commander Chevalier, perhaps in recognition of the fact that no one had worked harder than he on perfecting the arresting gear, made the first landing in an Aeromarine. First to be catapulted from the deck, on November 18, was Commander Whiting, at the controls of a PT.

All these planes were types already in use because the Navy had not yet decided upon a design specifically for service aboard a carrier. Study of such designs had been started when the conversion of the collier *Jupiter* into the *Langley* was first authorized, but convincing experiments could not be carried on until the flight deck was actually available. In 1920, hoping to use Martin bombers on the *Langley*, the Navy had bought ten of these, but even when fitted with folding wings that made stowage aboard ship easier they proved to be too large. Moreover, since arresting gear was still in the experimental stage, the Bureau of Aeronautics concluded it would be wiser to perfect this gear and then design planes that met its requirements. Consequently, the first regular assignments to the *Langley* were conventional landplanes, built by Aeromarine and by Vought, modified only by strengthening their landing gear and by installing arresting hooks.

Before the *Langley* joined the Fleet, a landing platform was erected at Hampton Roads, simulating a flight deck and on a turntable in order that it might be trained into the wind. Upon this numerous tests, chiefly under the supervision of Lieut. A. M. Pride, a reserve officer of World War I who had joined the regular Navy and who is, at this writing, Chief of the Bureau of Aeronautics, were made with gear modeled upon the British type, using fore-and-aft wires about ten inches above the deck level. Pride soon learned that these wires served only as guides, and added thwartship wires in a modification of those used by Eugene Ely on the *Pennsylvania* in 1911. Many more experiments followed, both on the platform and aboard the *Langley*, the various ideas including converging wires, shuttle gears, and the so-called "slipper," which used a slot in the deck rather than a wire. A major difficulty was the tendency of this gear to make the plane, as it moved along the deck, exaggerate any angle of the landing wheels into a sharp turn toward the ship's side, and since heavier planes were constantly being produced, the problem appeared a never ending one. Bit by bit, however, there were advances, and by 1923 the captain of the *Langley* reported that he could handle with reasonable safety three heavy planes in seven minutes, a record offering an interesting comparison with the days of World War II, when three such landings in one minute were not uncommon. All through this decade the Navy called in many civilian consultants, including two much better known for their work on bomb sights, Norden and Barth, to assist in the evolution of such gear. Although the *Lexington* and *Saratoga* were fitted with both longitudinal and thwartship wires, the former were already falling into disrepute and by 1929 they were removed altogether. With hydraulic cylinders replacing the weights formerly hung on the ends of the thwartship wires, the type coming into use was the forebear of the efficient ones of World War II. To keep pace with this, there were numerous modifications of existing plane types, such as the DH-4, the DT, and the UO-1, until, in March, 1925, the Bureau of Aeronautics called upon four manufacturers for new models to fit carriers. Thereupon Martin produced an all-metal variety of the SC, Curtiss produced a number of F6C types, Vought the O2U, and Douglas the T2D. All these became the ancestors of carrier planes prominent years later in the Pacific.

During the same period there was considerable progress in catapults. Compressed air types, in use before World War I, were fitted to turntables, one of these being installed on the battleship *Maryland* in 1922, with a modified form on the cruisers of the *Omaha* class. Two years later powder replaced air as the propulsion charge, and a catapult of this type was erected on a turret of the battleship *Mississippi*, the turret acting as turntable. In 1927 a further modification in which the turntable was independent of the turret was tried on the battleship *Colorado* with such success that it was approved for her sister ships and for the 10,000-ton cruisers. As to carriers, the *Langley* had the old compressed-air catapult and, although not much used in actual aircraft operations, this tested the launching of various types of planes with good results in education. When the *Saratoga* and *Lexington* joined the Fleet they were equipped with a fly-wheel type but this was later removed and it would not be until the advent in 1934 of a flush-deck design powered by compressed air that the catapult became a dependable and much-used means of carrier launching.

Returning to 1922, it appears that the proposals made for that year by the Bureau of Aeronautics for aircraft in the Fleet followed the general outline prepared by Mustin a year earlier. Indeed these proposals were quite in line with what he had said as early as 1916 in an address to the Navy League, when he called for "high-speed fighting aeroplanes, the medium-sized torpedo-carrying aeroplane and the slow-speed scouting aeroplane." Thus, for 1922, it was planned that every battleship and cruiser should have two fighter planes and two observation planes, while each destroyer leader, each first-class destroyer, and each submarine of cruising size was to have one plane of each type. On aircraft tenders there were to be four observation planes and 12 patrol planes, and the complement for expected carriers was established at 30 fighters and as many observers, 15 scouts and 15 torpedo planes. This was the plan and, as a part of it, the Bureau of Aeronautics also urged pushing work on all shore stations for aircraft, including the installation of mooring masts for airships at San Diego, Pearl Harbor, Guam, and the Philippines. Originally this was offered as a four-year program, but when Moffett was unable to get approval, either from the General Board or in the Fleet, he modified the time to five years.

To all of this there were various objections, such as those of the Bureau of Ordnance to the effect that any planes on battleships must interfere with range finding and shooting. In a final recommendation to the Secretary of the Navy, made on November 19,

1922, the General Board came down to the figures of one observer and two fighters for each of 18 battleships, two observers for each of ten cruisers, one fighter for each of 18 destroyers, one observer for each of nine submarines, and a few of each type distributed through the ships of the supporting train. When the budget, as ultimately approved, did not provide for even this relatively modest program, Moffett concentrated upon urging that the battleships, at least, be equipped, but it would be some years before this was accomplished. The so-called five-year program did not come before Congress until 1926, after the Morrow Board as will be seen had made its exhaustive study of the whole state of aviation. In the meantime Fleet and shore stations continued to be handicapped, and such comprehensive plans as that for "Aeronautical Organization of the Naval Districts," drawn up during this period, had to be abandoned for the time being.

In addition to technical improvements, made in spite of the lack of enough money to carry out all the Bureau of Aeronautics' plans, this period produced evidence of advances in general thinking in the Navy. Shortly after aircraft had been introduced into the "games" played at the Naval War College that institution reported to the General Board that, while these games had not "proved . . . aircraft will entirely dominate . . . they have brought out the fact that, as much as any other auxiliary . . . perhaps more . . . aircraft can exert a decisive influence." Capt. (later Vice Adm.) Harris Laning of the college staff noted with satisfaction that officers coming in as students often showed very little or no enthusiasm for aircraft and then, as the games progressed, displayed great interest in the possibilities of air attack and defense. It appeared obvious to Laning that such officers, when they returned to the Fleet after their courses, would have convincing arguments to offer any remaining doubters, and this would mean progress.

Another very important step of that day was in the direction of large carriers. The Washington Disarmament Treaties, signed in February, 1922, set the limit for United States carrier tonnage at 135,000 and, under the capital ship limits, prohibited the completion of two great battle cruisers already laid down under the so-called 1916 program, ships whose engines and armament would have made them the most powerful units afloat. While these two hulls lay on the buildingways, the General Board first had under consideration two possible carriers: a 30-knotter for the Scouting

Force and a 24-knotter for the Battle Force; then moved to consideration of three alternatives: a 10,000-ton 15-knotter, a 20,000-ton ship of 29.5 knots, and, finally, a 35,000-ton class to reach 33 or 34 knots, depending upon whether or not their hulls were given "blister" protection against torpedoes. As was to be expected, the board's studies soon swung toward the possibility of converting the two unfinished battle cruisers.

Such a conversion was possible under the treaties because, while any new carrier was limited to 27,000 tons, there had been international agreement that any hull already under construction and otherwise due to be scrapped could be converted into a carrier of as much as 33,000 tons. Moreover, this agreement further provided for an additional 3,000 tons, if blister protection and certain specified deck armor were to be added. Since the *Langley*, defined as an "experimental" ship, was not counted against the allowance of the United States, it would be possible to complete the two proposed conversions, even at a total of 36,000 tons each, and still leave 63,000 tons of permissible construction in carriers. Moffett, foreseeing that Congress would scale down its appropriations made for classes of ships in which the United States was already at or above treaty strength, saw in this an opportunity to divert money to aviation and immediately came out for the proposed conversion. He drew fresh attention to the need for equaling Great Britain in carriers, in aircraft, and in flying personnel; a need all the greater because Japan was known to be planning to build up to her full "Three" of the Five-Five-Three treaty ratio if not, indeed, beyond it. For the United States to fail in this, he insisted, would be to invite ultimate disaster; a view in which he was naturally supported by Mustin, Johnson, Whiting, and others. They all emphasized the importance of size and speed in carriers, but because the tactical unit today connoted by the term "Fast Carrier Task Force" had not yet taken shape in naval minds, they laid chief stress upon aerial scouting and upon overhead protection of the battleline.

Thus the limitations of the treaties were turned to the advantage of aviation; an advantage all the more important when it became clear that the Japanese, by succeeding in their effort to get Article XIX into the treaty after their own island bases were nearly completed, had restricted United States bases in the Pacific to a most unsatisfactory status quo. The plan for converting the big hulls would provide, in the two tremendous carriers *Lexington* and

Saratoga, actually completed at 33,000 tons each, mobile bases with flight decks 800 feet long and more than 100 feet wide, almost unhampered because their "control islands" were set far over to starboard while their funnels were designed to keep as much smoke as possible away from their planes. When these two joined the Fleet, great possibilities would eventuate.

As one way of preparing for these possibilities, the Bureau of Aeronautics at Hunsaker's suggestion decided to put an entry in the 1923 Schneider Cup races. These had originated in 1913, when the French enthusiast Jacques Schneider, sponsored by the Fédération Aéronautique Internationale, offered his "artistic trophy and three prizes of $5,000 each" for international competition. Early American entries, Weymann in 1913, Weymann and Thaw in 1914, had bad luck and were unable to finish, and a postponement of the races until after World War I had followed. On their resumption in 1919 there were four races without American entries, but at Cowes, England, on September 27 and 28, 1923, three officers of the United States Navy competed, Lieuts. R. Irvine, D. Rittenhouse, and A. W. Gorton, with a fourth, F. W. Wead, in charge of the team. Rittenhouse and Irvine, each flying a CR-3, a Curtiss type built under contract with the Navy, finished well ahead of the field and brought the cup home on its first visit. Rittenhouse, the winner, reached an average speed of 177.38 miles an hour over the triangular course of 37.2 nautical miles with Irvine, at 173.46 miles an hour, not far behind. Gorton's plane, an NW-2, had been expected to do even better than these figures but it was damaged before the race and did not compete. In general, the lessons learned from the performance of the various entries in this race included practical demonstration that aircraft were becoming too complex and costly to permit private builders to compete with governments, and the further demonstration that flying boats were not capable of the high speed needed to win such races. Otherwise, the obvious effect was an increased interest in air races, and after a postponement in 1924 Lieut. James Doolittle of the Army, flying another Curtiss racer, the R3C-2, won the 1925 race at the hitherto unequaled speed of 232.57 miles an hour, while Lieutenants Oftsie and Cuddihy of the Navy, in similar planes, were unable to finish because of engine troubles. Thereafter the United States relaxed its effort to build racers and other nations beat Doolittle's record. Lieut. "Al" Williams of the Navy received official sanction in 1927 to fly a plane bought by private funds, but since that plane could not be tuned up in time for the race, it did not compete. In 1931 the British, with their third successive victory, retired the cup from competition. Proposals that a new one be offered were dropped when the British, agreeing with what Moffett had announced in 1930, declared that racing types consumed more money than could be spared from amounts available for the regular needs of aviation. Both nations, however, had learned more than they openly admitted, for the British winner in 1931 was the prototype of the famous Spitfires of 1941, and the Curtiss racer had a profound effect upon all later United States naval and military designs.

Other races, in which modified Curtiss types were flown by entrants from both the Army and the Navy, were those for the Pulitzer Trophy. Civilian pilots were frequent winners of this trophy but in 1923 the Navy's four entrants, headed by Williams in an improved Curtiss racer, the R2C-1, finished one, two, three, and four. That year was the Navy's big one in such competitions for it then held 23 of 78 world records and 21 of 34 world records for seaplanes.

Service types, with no special features for racing, were nevertheless used in races during the twenties, notably in those for the Marine Trophy given by Glenn Curtiss before World War I. Competition for this had been held from 1915 to 1919, then suspended for two years, and resumed in 1922 when the Navy entered ten planes, most of them just as they had been finished for regular service, and when Gorton emerged the winner in a TR-1. This was a modification of the TS-1, its most important feature being a Lawrance engine, developed by its designer with naval funds and the Navy's backing. It was a radial type, noted, in the *Aircraft Yearbook* for 1923, for "faultless performance" and "freedom (being air cooled) from radiation troubles." Hunsaker considered it a great advance and that he was right is indicated by its becoming the prototype of virtually all similar engines used by the Army and the Navy in World War II.

Lieut. H. A. Elliot, flying a Vought VE-7H, with a Wright liquid-cooled engine, was the only other entrant to finish in this race, but 1st Lt. (later Brig. Gen.) L. H. Sanderson of the Marine Corps was making by far the best time of the three until his Navy-Curtiss racer on the last lap was forced down by running out of fuel. In the seven subsequent years the race was flown five times, the winners being three lieutenants of the Navy, V. F. Grant, T. P. Jeter, and W. G. Tomlinson, and two marines, Maj. Charles Lutz and Capt. A. H. Page. Discontinued after 1930, the race left a lasting mark upon the design of service types because the speed required to win it had risen steadily from 112.6 to 164.08 miles an hour.

Besides what was learned from racing, these years saw an advance along the line of the torpedo plane. It will be recalled that Admiral Fiske had advocated such planes as early as 1912 but very little had been attempted until the first World War was well under way. In part this lack of progress had been due to the viewpoint of two groups, one favoring the development of a plane to handle the then accepted type of torpedo, the other holding that a special torpedo should be designed for the plane. During and after that war Fiske had kept the question alive and he was to a considerable extent responsible for the tests that had been carried out at the end of 1918 with an F-5 flying boat carrying a 400-pound dummy torpedo under its wing. These tests were held off the Naval Aircraft Factory at Philadelphia, where the narrowness of the Delaware River made it very difficult to handle the plane, and they were not as successful as those begun some months later at Hampton Roads. There, using an R-6 which had been slightly modified in design and equipment, Chevalier, with Lieuts. T. S. Murphy, D. B. Murphy, and L. H. Lovelace, successfully launched both dummy and live torpedoes, continuing to experiment with this plane until 1920, when the new Martin torpedo bomber, known as the MBT, became the first plane specifically designed for this work.

By May of that same year a torpedo squadron was established at Yorktown, where it spent considerable time practicing for the bombing tests against the German ships which have already been discussed. This squadron was the one to bomb the U-117 with light bombs, and in the offshore search for the *Iowa* it carried 1,000-pound dummies. What it might have succeeded in doing against the *Ostfriesland* was never learned because before its scheduled attack that ship had been sunk. By 1922 this and similar squadrons had the designation "torpedo," but they were more often used for duties such as searching, spotting, laying smoke screens, and towing targets for aerial gunnery practice. A year later they were furnished with the newer PT planes, built at the Naval Aircraft Factory, and these were followed, 12 months later, by the Douglas Company's DT, a type which, incidentally, would be the first naval aircraft to be based in the Philippines. In March, 1924, the same Griffin who had made the first take-off from the *Langley* was the first to land a torpedo bomber on her deck.

Less spectacular operations through which naval aviators gained experience during these years were photographic reconnaissances and surveys. These began with an air tour of the Palmyra Islands, about a thousand miles from Honolulu, while later extensive flights were made over the Florida Keys, the Navy's petroleum reserve fields in the western states, and numerous other areas. From these much was learned about two essential needs, better instruments and more training in their use for aerial navigation.

It was in the Fleet exercises of February, 1923, that aircraft were first included when, in that year's games, it was the task of the Black Fleet to attack the Panama Canal while the Blue Fleet and the Army defended it. As must so often happen in the history of the Navy in peacetime, lack of complete equipment made it necessary to designate the *New York* and the *Oklahoma* as "slow carriers" with the Black force, while single planes had to be rated as whole squadrons. Approaching the Canal, Black avoided interception and, more to the aviator's purpose, successfully launched its "squadron" over the Gatun spillway, to drop ten miniature bombs without being attacked either by defending planes or by antiaircraft guns. The value of even a slow carrier was shown when the *Oklahoma*, after very little maneuvering, catapulted her plane into the air without mechanical difficulty. Summing up these results, the commander in chief found solid ground for urging much stronger air defense of Panama and more catapults for his ships, two recommendations which were thus placed upon record although there were no funds with which to carry them into effect.

Similar lessons were to be learned from all the later exercises, such as those in which the *Langley* launched daily reconnaissance flights which proved how much more might be expected when more carriers were available. It became increasingly clear that continuous air protection would be vital to ships, that planes must be more durable and have a longer cruising radius, that both catapults and recovery gear needed further improvement and, tactically, that the officer commanding the Fleet's aircraft must be allowed considerable discretion in his operations. The conclusions drawn collectively proved how right Moffett had been in declaring, two weeks after the first landing on the *Langley*, that "the air fleet of an enemy will never get within striking distance of our coasts as long as our aircraft carriers are able to carry the preponderance of air power to sea."

CHAPTER XX

New Uses for Aircraft

WHEN Moffett made his prophetic declaration, one element
of air power destined to fill a brilliant page of history was
just beginning to attract the serious attention of the
Navy's fliers. As they carried on elementary experiments, none of
them suspected that he was helping to clear the air for a great
American victory years later. Who could have guessed, in the early
twenties, that the Japanese Fleet of 1942 would be stopped dead at
Midway by the United States Navy's dive bombers?

There are no documents to tell who first had the idea that a plane
could come hurtling down from a high altitude, apparently bent
upon destroying itself and its crew and then, in the last split second,
drop a bomb, nose up, and pull out. It seems certain that the pilots
of more than one nation in World War I, using the very inefficient
bomb sights of the day, simultaneously realized how much higher
would be the number of their hits if their bombs were dropped from
a point almost on top of their targets. During that war the British
began bombing at low altitudes, from level positions, but the bombs
they used were very light and they appear to have attached to the
practice only the nuisance value of its effect upon the Germans.
Only after the hostilities were over did aviators here and there,
needing no such special installations as were required by torpedo
planes, begin improvising gear and experimenting with bombs. By
1919 a small squadron of marine fliers in Haiti, under the direction of Maj. (later Brig. Gen.) L. H. Sanderson, using homemade
gear, was swooping down over guerrillas at the jungle edge, getting terrifying morale effects and causing a number of casualties
with light fragmentation bombs. These and other members of the
corps, notably a veteran warrant officer, Marine Gunner Elmo
Regan, continued similar experiments after they went back to
various posts in the United States.

In 1921 army pilots of the First Provisional Pursuit Squadron
when bombing the captured German ships went down to heights of

no more than 200 feet above their targets, and against a German
destroyer they scored enough hits to sink her, 21 in 44 drops. Some
time after that Maj. (later Maj. Gen.) R. E. Rowell of the Marines, sent to the Army's school at Kelly Field for advance flight
training, found diving to be a definite part of the experimental
work in progress there. Although still without a good bomb sight
the army men, using any convenient projection on their engines as
a front sight, lined up their targets as best they could and dove at
them on an angle of about 60 degrees. According to Rowell, most
of the pilots agreed that such attacks, against ships or shore stations armed with antiaircraft guns, would be possible only at the
risk of great loss in planes. This was also true at the Army's Selfridge Field, where Rowell next reported and where similar experiments were being made; but what he picked up at these two fields
led him in 1925, when he commanded a marine squadron at San
Diego, to put similar experiments into common practice. Before
many months, exhibition diving of the sort was being done by
marine fliers at various air meets along the California coast. It
was still generally believed that enemy personnel would be the best
targets for such attacks; and that much could be accomplished
against personnel was proved on July 17, 1927, when a marine detachment in Nicaragua, surrounded in a surprise attack by the
insurgent Sandino, was rescued by Rowell and his squadron, diving
with 50-pound fragmentation bombs. During succeeding years
there would be a good deal more exhibition flying and it is com-
monly believed that what Major Udet of the German Army saw at
the Cleveland air races inspired him to go home and organize the
Stukas that were so effective in World War II when he was a lieutenant general.

In all this it was not only the marines who began to take the
situation in hand, for the Navy's fliers were also very active. To
dive down, drop a bomb on a ship, and pull away before her guns
could be manned became an objective while a bomb sight accurate
enough to make such an attack really effective was still a sort of
will-o'-the-wisp. In 1925, when Capt. (later Adm.) Joseph M.
Reeves took command of the aircraft of the Battle Fleet, he was
given authority to assemble all the Pacific aircraft at San Diego,
to attempt the evolution of new tactics. With the help of Lieut.
(later Capt.) F. W. Wead, previously one of the Navy's racing
pilots, he issued a pamphlet familiarly known as "Reeves' Thousand and One Questions," one of which was "How repel a force en-

deavoring to land on a beach?" Among the aviators assembled to find the best answers were Lieuts. Frank D. Wagner, J. E. Ostrander, D. W. Tomlinson, T. B. Lee, S. H. Arthur, E. C. Ewen, and Robert F. Hickey, some of them among today's flying flag officers; all of them at that moment ready to try almost anything in their F6C planes, then regarded as rugged fighter types.

Machine guns, spraying their bullets over the landing party from planes flying low and level, seemed the obvious defense; but these pilots soon realized how quickly the target, at close range, would be lost to view, and also how exposed they and their planes were to antiaircraft fire. Before long they found themselves making their approaches to the target at altitudes of more than 10,000 feet, then diving at angles as steep as 70 degrees, to keep the targets in sight and also to substitute bomb dropping for machine-gun fire. Next, they realized that an attacking squadron must not come down bunched but from several different bearings and this led to making the approach in the familiar echelon pattern of wild geese or in what was called the ABC formation. To "see how the attack looked from the target," Tomlinson and Ewen, noted for their flying skill and sense of timing, were frequently stationed on the ground as observers who could offer helpful criticism of what their fellows did in the air.

This was Squadron VF-2, with Wagner as its commander, and by the autumn of 1926 it was making attacks on the battleships. On October 22 it made the first of these from 12,000 feet, after warning the ships just when it was going to do it. The approach at such a height was not detected, while the dives were so nearly vertical and the speed so great that the planes had pulled out, leveled off, and actually landed at Long Beach by the time the ships' crews could get to their battle stations. Thereafter, in order to give the Fleet more experience, such attacks were made in a series, rather than as a single dive from which the planes could roar away to safety.

Meanwhile, over in the Atlantic, much the same effort was being made by other aviators, led principally by Lt. Comdr. (now Rear Adm.) O. B. Hardison. In their attacks, gun cameras had been planted on the target ships but even these recorded almost no hits on the incoming planes. Lt. Comdr. (now Rear Adm.) A. C. Davis, then in the Bureau of Aeronautics, was in a position to contribute greatly to the advance of dive bombing, by rewriting the rules for gunnery practice and by arranging for the purchase of better bombracks and improved equipment for the planes. Others in the bureau had mental reservations about the suitability of existing planes for dive bombing, while the Fleet was dubious over diverting fighters and observation planes from their primary purposes, and it was not long before the Navy followed its classic method of conducting special tests. These were run off in the winter of 1926–27, with results clearly showing the effectiveness of dive bombing against personnel but also suggesting what it might accomplish against light craft and, indeed, against the crowded flight decks of carriers. After the usual board had been convened to make recommendations, the Bureau of Aeronautics, with the aid of the Glenn L. Martin Company, was ready in 1930 to test a type that could dive with a 1,000-pound bomb. During the next year the Fleet began getting the types from which were developed the planes so often and so convincingly heard from in the Pacific at Midway and in the years that followed.

While these powerful weapons of war were in the making, Moffett was not unmindful of what aviators might learn in the arts of peace, nor was he neglecting his great interest in airships. At the time of the creation of the Bureau of Aeronautics, lighter-than-air flying was under suspicion because of the tragic loss, in England, of the ZR-2 and so many of her American crew. This had left the C-7 the only United States airship actually in service, but Moffett was pushing what remained of the postwar program for dirigibles. At Friedrichshafen, Germany, the nonmilitary ZR-3 was under construction, while at Lakehurst, New Jersey, the more important ZR-1 had been laid down.

Following inquiry into the loss of the ZR-2 new studies of stresses and strains were begun, and to carry these further the National Advisory Committee for Aeronautics, at the request of the Navy Department, assembled a group of engineers under Dr. Henry Goldmark. These experts examined all available data and made the most exhaustive aerodynamical studies. In the end, they concluded that the Navy Department design provided sufficient strength for normal cruising at not less than 6,000 feet and at speeds of not more than 50 knots. All this was of added importance because it was clear that the fate of airships in the United States must depend chiefly upon the success or failure of the two then building. Further, because any such success must in turn depend upon having personnel able to handle the ships, and because only five men had survived the ZR-2, it was also important that a new start at training crews be made and this was done at Hampton Roads on July 1, 1922. By March of the next year the group was moved to Lakehurst where special instruction in ground school began under Capt. Anton Heinan, formerly of the German Navy and already employed by the United States to supervise tests.

On May 4, 1923, the big ship, soon to be famous as the *Shenandoah*, was launched. She was 680 feet long, with a diameter of about 79 feet, a gas capacity of 2,150,000 cubic feet, and a total lift of 65 tons. Each of her five gondolas mounted a 300-horsepower engine. Her first flight, under the command of Capt. F. R. McCrary, with Commander Weyerbacher and Captain Heinan aboard, was made on September 4, and like those immediately following, it was highly successful. Moffett's report to the General Board summarized her military value as due to a radius of scouting equal, in a given time, to that of three cruisers together; to her ability to make high speed, gain great altitude quickly, hover as desired, and receive or transmit information by radio. In any weather, said the admiral, she could travel 9,000 miles without a load or 5,000 miles with a load of 25 tons. Admitting her vulnerability, he claimed that this was relatively not as great as that of destroyers or cruisers, for they could be attacked in many more ways. Moreover, in his opinion, the dirigible of the future would be itself a plane carrier and therefore capable of defense against its chief threat, attack by aircraft.

In the very week when the *Shenandoah* was launched, Moffett had discussed with Stefansson, the noted explorer, the possibility of her making a flight to the Arctic. As the admiral saw it, such a flight would not only determine requirements for cold-weather operation but also gather valuable meteorological data and incidentally get favorable publicity for the Navy. It was proposed that the *Ramapo* and the *Patoka* should both be converted into tenders and equipped with mooring masts; the former to be sent to Nome, the latter to Spitzbergen. Each would carry three long-range scouting planes to assist in the operation, especially in the event of an accident. Three CS-2 planes and three SDW-1 were to be used, all under the command of Lieut. Charles P. Mason, who had been a test pilot at Pauillac during the war. When President Coolidge approved the plan in December of 1923, he noted that the Navy, through Rear Admiral Peary, had discovered the Pole and therefore the Navy should complete the exploration of the area. Less than a month later, however, a severe January gale tore the

Shenandoah from her mooring mast at Lakehurst. Her nose was damaged and several cells badly torn, but she rode out the blow and returned to her base under the direction of Lt. Comdr. Maurice Pierce who, with Captain Heinan, had fortunately been on board with a skeleton crew when the gale struck. At once the Arctic flight by airship was postponed.

During 1924, however, there were many other flights, productive of both experience for personnel and improvement in material equipment. Among the latter was an apparatus to recover water ballast and thus prevent hampering the ship by increasing her buoyancy as fuel was consumed, a difficulty that must otherwise be met by "valving" precious helium. The process was so efficient that "on one flight it condensed about 1,150 pounds of water from 967 pounds of fuel burned," thus giving the ship's commander "perfect control of the weight" and making it "unnecessary to valve gas except under the most exceptional circumstances"; these advances were regarded as more than offsetting the 10 per cent increase in the drag upon the ship due to the use of the apparatus and also as sufficient compensation for a substantial reduction in cruising radius.

This progress with the *Shenandoah*, and the expected early delivery of the ZR-3, led Moffett again to seek an expansion of the program. At the end of June, 1924, he drew the Secretary's attention to the British plan to build two superdirigibles and to Japanese intentions of duplicating that effort. Parity in naval building, he said, demanded that the United States not be left behind; but when the Chief of Naval Operations, Admiral Eberle, disapproved, the Secretary directed a delay in final decision until after the *Shenandoah* had taken part in the Fleet exercises that summer. Unfortunately, her showing at these exercises was not good because, although she did discover the "enemy," she subsequently lost contact because of bad weather. When heavy rain added nearly a ton to her weight, she had to release water ballast, with the result that when she dried out she was too buoyant. This could not be corrected because only three of her five engines were fitted with water recovery apparatus and she could not spare helium. It followed that in order to land safely she had to leave the exercises ahead of time and return to Lakehurst. This made it evident that such a ship, to be useful to a fleet, must be able to depend upon mooring masts distributed around the world, a considerable problem though not a very expensive one. Temporary masts were estab-

lished at Fort Worth, Guantánamo, San Diego, and Tacoma,
while plans were made for other masts at Boston, the Canal Zone,
and Hawaii. In October the *Shenandoah's* cross-country flights,
during which she tested the mooring masts on the West coast, indicated that such masts, installed aboard ships, would give her much
more mobility and far greater usefulness to the Fleet.

Meanwhile in August, 1924, the ZR-3 had been completed at
Friedrichshafen, where Lt. Comdr. Garland Fulton had been chief
inspector for about two years. Of nonmilitary character, she was
658 feet long, just under 91 feet in diameter and just over 104 feet
in height, with a gas capacity of 2,740,000 cubic feet. Her five
Maybach motors, of 400 horsepower each, gave her a cruising
radius of 3,500 miles and a top speed of 63.5 knots, with a useful
load of 30 tons. She was by far the strongest airship yet built, a
quality which would have far-reaching influence from the day she
made her first test flight on August 27. On October 12, under the
direction of Hugo Eckener, later well known as commander of the
Graf Zeppelin and the *Hindenburg*, she crossed the Atlantic, making the 4,229 miles to Lakehurst in 81 hours and 2 minutes. There
the hydrogen that brought her over was replaced by helium, a
water-recovery apparatus was installed, and on November 25 Mrs.
Calvin Coolidge formally christened her *Los Angeles*.

During the next year the two ships made many flights which
served to edify the public and, more important, to familiarize the
personnel with their operation. The *Los Angeles*, in addition to
her crew of 29, could accommodate 30 passengers by day and 20
by night, and this was especially useful for training purposes after
the United States secured international permission to use her in
exercises with the Fleet. More extended flights became possible
with an increase in the production of helium, something regarded
as of great importance when it became evident that helium, although safe where hydrogen was dangerous, would give the ships
only about 60 per cent of the cruising radius they could get with
hydrogen. This was a considerable handicap and it may have been
one of the contributory reasons why the idea of an Arctic flight by
airship was not revived by the Navy Department even after the
Italian attempts.

For heavier-than-air craft however, such a flight again came to
the front. In 1924, when Amundsen was preparing for another
polar expedition, it was agreed that Lieut. R. E. Davison, one of
the Navy's well-qualified pilots, should go with him, and Davison

actually did get as far as Spitzbergen in March, only to stay there until July and then return because the expedition did not succeed in raising enough money. An American expedition appeared to be very much in order, and in 1925 a naval detachment under Lieutenant Commander Byrd accompanied Donald MacMillan, also a reserve officer, into the Etah region. With Byrd, who had three Loening amphibian planes, went Lt. (jg) M. A. Schur, Chief Boatswain B. E. Reber, Chief Machinist's Mates A. C. Nold and N. P. Sorensen, and Naval Aviation Pilot Floyd Bennett, who had flown a UO-1 from his ship, the cruiser *Richmond*, off Greenland during the preceding summer. With this group Byrd flew through the thick summer fog, to cover 30,000 square miles of the polar wastes, collecting a mass of scientific data and much knowledge of cold-weather work in the air. He came home so enthusiastic that he persuaded Edsel Ford to support an attempt to fly across the Pole during the following spring, before Amundsen, who had once been forced down only 150 miles from the Pole, could try again. Ford brought John D. Rockefeller, Jr., Vincent Astor, and others in as fellow sponsors, enabling Byrd to sail for Spitzbergen early in April, 1926. His chief assistant was again Bennett, and on May 9 the two took off from Kings Bay in a three-engine Fokker monoplane. With the luck of clear weather and the help of a Bumstead sun compass and Byrd's own bubble sextant, they flew for 15 consecutive hours, circling the Pole for the first time in history and returning safely. Both were awarded the Congressional Medal of Honor and promoted by act of Congress but, for Byrd, at least, this would be only the first of his long series of polar flights and expeditions.

In this same period came the Navy's first serious attempt at a long-distance flight over the Pacific. The Army, while making its noteworthy flight around the world in 1924, had circled the oceans; but the Navy proposed to cross the Pacific in its widest open area. Accordingly, in 1925, that veteran of the Navy's earliest days in the air, Comdr. John Rodgers, was selected to command a flight from the coast of California to Honolulu, to be made by three seaplanes especially designed with metal hulls. Two of these were built at the Philadelphia Naval Aircraft Factory and designated PN-9 while the third was built by Boeing in Seattle and designated PB-1. On May 2 Lieut. C. H. Schildhauer flew one PN-9 for 28 hours, 35 minutes and established a new world's record for seaplane endurance. This was the same Schildhauer who was recognized in

World War II as founder of the Naval Air Transport Service familiarly known as "NATS."

In a general way, plans for the flight followed those used for the NC crossing of the Atlantic. At specified positions along the proposed course lay station ships, ready to use smoke and search-lights as "buoys" and also ready to lend a hand in any emergency. Since this was before the day of the modern radio compass, it was also the duty of these ships to give the planes their radio bearings as shore stations would do and thus help them to fix their positions as they proceeded. In addition, tenders and submarine groups were assigned special stations off the Hawaiian Islands, while one ten-der, with a squadron of planes aboard, stood by to furnish escorts or, if necessary, to start an aerial search.

Two of the new planes, fitted with all the instruments then in use, including earth-inductor compasses borrowed from the Army, wind-drift sights, and special towing sleeves for the radio antennae, were ready for a take-off on schedule but the Boeing plane was not finished until a few days later and, in its final tests, it performed too doubtfully to justify its starting. With Rodgers were Lieut. B. J. Connell, Chief Radioman N. H. Stantz, and Naval Aviation Pilots S. R. Pope and W. M. Bowlin. Under Lieut. A. P. Snody in the other plane were Lieut. A. Gavin, Radioman C. W. Allen, Aviation Pilot N. H. Craven, and Machinist's Mate C. Suttey. At two o'clock in the afternoon of August 31, with Moffett on hand to see them do it, they took the air. Four hours later Snody was forced down to a safe landing on the water, luckily so near the marker ship *William Jones* that she could promptly take him in tow. That left Rodgers in a position like Read's in the NC-4, alone over the Pa-cific.

In the early hours all went well, with nothing disturbing except that the fuel consumption appeared to be running about six gal-lons an hour over what had been estimated. This took on some significance when the tail wind with which Rodgers had started began dying down, and it became serious when the exhaust from the port engine changed color from blue to yellow, a definite sign of im-proper firing. When he was 1,200 miles out, Rodgers decided that before long he would have to come down near a station ship to re-fuel and to adjust the engines. Another 200 miles brought him within sight of the *Reno* where he calculated that he could reach the *Aroostook*, 400 miles ahead, with enough fuel to spend about 40 minutes in making a landing. Until that moment, keeping only near enough to the prescribed course to sight the station ships, he had not attempted to pass directly over them and therefore he had not been greatly concerned to note that the radio bearings they gave him, from distances over 50 miles, often proved, as he drew nearer, to have been a good deal in error. Now, with the weather thickening in rain squalls, and with a specific ship to find, exactness in these bearings suddenly became of vital importance.

According to the bearings he was getting, he was well south of the Aroostook, whereas his own navigation figures put him north of his proper course. At about three o'clock in the afternoon he decided to trust the bearings and make a search to the northward. At a quarter past four, 25 hours and 23 minutes after his take-off, his last drop of fuel was gone, and he was left with no choice but to land on the sea. The distance he had covered was not absolutely certain but the Fédération Aéronautique Internationale officially accepted it as 1,841 statute miles, a world's record for airline by seaplane.

Good airmanship having landed the plane safely, good seamanship took command. Fabric from the lower wing was fashioned into a sail, floor boards became leeboards and a course 15 degrees off the wind was laid for Hawaii. A rudimentary radio sending set was extemporized but this, again like those of the NC-3, served only to tantalize all hands. Since they could not get their position through to ships that were combing the ether with inquiries for it, there remained nothing to do but sail on.

The Aroostook was already looking for Rodgers. The Langley sent up her planes on daily search. Submarines steamed out from Hawaii and patrol planes left Pearl Harbor. A squadron of destroyers from the Fleet, then on its way back from Australia, ran search curves to the southward. But it was not until four o'clock in the afternoon of September 10 that the submarine R-4 sighted Rodgers, "under all plain sail" on his course, about ten miles off Kaui Island, with some 450 miles made good on the surface. To many here was proof that the Navy's aviators remained, fundamentally, sailormen.

Unfortunately the full worth of all these various experiences and achievements was not translated into an expansion of Naval Aviation. To some extent this was because the aviators had been gagged by the act of 1921, which created a Bureau of the Budget to review the recommendations of all departments of the government and to keep them in line with administration policies. In the act it was specifically stated that "no estimate or request for an appropriation and no request for an increase . . . shall be submitted to Congress or any committee thereof by any officer . . . of any department . . . [except] at the request of either House . . ." This meant that once an appropriation recommended by the Bureau of Aeronautics had been reduced by the Navy's budget officer or by the Bureau of the Budget, Moffett and his assistants could not protest unless Congress called them in, and not then unless committee members asked exactly the right questions.

During the years that followed, numerous cuts in the amounts recommended by the Bureau of Aeronautics were made by Rear Adm. Joseph Strauss, the Navy's first budget officer. One reason for these cuts lay in Strauss' realization that Congress was economy-minded; another lay in his own belief that although aviation had a place in the Fleet, it was not of paramount importance. His conviction was quite as honest as Moffett's, but the result was that their relations were sometimes rather strained.

Under his feet the budget officer had the sure ground of congressional determination that all the surplus in Naval Aviation, resulting from deliveries under the contracts of World War I, must be exhausted before any new material was bought. It was idle for Moffett to point out that only a part of this material could be used with any profit to the Navy, and that much of it was not worth its costly upkeep—two facts, incidentally, which would be recalled in 1946 when both the Army and the Navy made haste to scrap much of what was left over from World War II. It was even useless to answer the complaint of the manufacturers that neither Army nor Navy had any definite plan for aircraft by pointing out that both had programs which were being torn up by the economizers. Since the gagged aviators could say little or nothing to the contrary, Congress appears to have believed that it was giving them what they wanted and that any lack of success was due to fumbling by the military and naval authorities. In 1923, for example, the Bureau of Aeronautics asked for $21,500,000, but after the cuts a Congress that hardly can have been fully informed allowed it only $14,663,000. Indeed, it was not until 1925 that Congress appears to have realized that its own act prevented it from learning all the facts, and even then the condition would not be corrected fully. In 1926, of the $33,000,000 requested, Aeronautics got only about $19,000,000. Moffett could plead with the Navy's budget officer or with the Secretary of the Navy. Later, when an Assistant

Secretary of the Navy for Air had been appointed, he could plead even more eloquently with him; but unless personally summoned by Congress he could go no higher. General Mitchell had tried that expedient—and landed in a court martial. Others must have felt justified in playing safe, especially when it became evident that President Coolidge was determined to follow President Harding in economies, even if he were not quite so specific as the latter had been in declaring that he did not "hesitate to say that the repetition or advocacy of an estimate . . . in excess of the Executive recommendation will be looked upon as a sufficient reason to give instructions for severance of employment with the Government." As a gag, this was effective.

The Bureau of Aeronautics' four-year program proposed in 1921, and its five-year program discussed in 1922, were doomed. The latter called for 870 new planes in addition to those that might be required by any carriers built, but although fully approved by the General Board as the basis for the bureau's estimates and recommendations during the years immediately succeeding, it was cut before it ever reached Congress. Consequently, since the money was not appropriated, the program fell farther and farther behind the schedule, leaving the bureau more and more dependent upon the obsolescent if not already obsolete material on hand. This had its bad effect upon the aircraft industry and, even more unfortunate, a disastrous influence upon the morale of aviation personnel. Officers and men training with untrustworthy equipment became nervous and less efficient. As shortages in numbers became more severe, the load upon those remaining became greater and this could not but result in occasional grumblings about overwork and lack of recognition. Dissatisfaction produced more resignations and more discharges, more shortages and more complaints, thus drawing the vicious circle. The Fleet, attempting to use planes that were continually in need of repairs, found it impossible to keep adequate squadrons in the air, a handicap which gave the commander of the squadrons "great anxiety" and made it impossible for the commander in chief to carry out anything like the exercises that had been planned. Nowhere was Naval Aviation up to the standard which it had set for itself and which an uninformed public fully expected it to maintain.

CHAPTER XXI

Personnel and Training in the Twenties

THIS state of affairs persisted, notwithstanding such declarations as that by the General Board in May, 1922, which bluntly asserted that "the rapidly growing importance of aircraft" made imperative "the keenest possible effort" in their strategical and technical development. Instead of progress in new designs and experimental types, there continued to be a dwindling of World War I material without adequate replacement, and the inevitable result was inability to maintain anything approaching "treaty strength." As Moffett did not hesitate to insist, these deficiencies left openings for critics who declared that "aviation is not appreciated but actually neglected by both the Army and the Navy," claims furnishing ready ammunition to those still agitating for a separate air force. Nothing, said the admiral, could at once give the nation a proper defense and stop these agitators except adequate appropriations for Naval Aviation. As matters stood, he declared, what little money became available was being wasted in a hopeless struggle to keep the aircraft, the tenders, the supporting shore stations, and the personnel anywhere nearly up to date, without hope of getting ahead of other nations.

In personnel a real crisis came very soon. None of the means proposed for augmenting numbers, such as holding reserve fliers in service, increasing the size of the Naval Academy, transferring men from other branches of the Navy, or training more enlisted men as pilots, was in really effective operation. Indeed, none had been supported with sufficient funds for a thorough trial, even after the failure of a group of reserve officers to pass examination for transfer to the regular Navy had aroused Congress to an investigation of this failure. It still being the policy of the Navy Department that aviators must also be qualified seamen, the examination had been too broad in scope for men really trained only in flying. Although this was duly brought out by such senators as David Walsh of Massachusetts who condemned the loss of valuable men, neither the Navy Department nor Congress did anything to effect a change in policy or to provide money for adequate training of reserves.

Another harmful factor was rotation in duties. Among 100 officers trained at Pensacola during 1923, so many were presently ordered back to seagoing assignments, while others resigned and a few died, that the net gain was only 12 pilots. From those trained during the next year similar losses left but two additional pilots. At the same time the shortage throughout the whole Navy had been growing more acute since 1921, the year in which over 1,000 officers resigned or, as enlisted men temporarily commissioned during the war, reverted to their permanent ratings. This meant that it was impossible to get enough officers as fliers without crippling the Fleet and it also meant that junior officers hesitated to ask for aviation duty. Even the addition of flight training to the curriculum at the Naval Academy, while it was a good move and destined to become better, could offer no immediate relief in added pilots. By the spring of 1924, among 567 officers assigned to aviation only 308 were naval aviators, a figure representing a marked decrease since July, 1922. Since the tentative complement for the carriers included 175 officers for the various billets, with 3,000 enlisted men, and since the means for filling such a complement were nowhere in sight, the prospect of manning the *Lexington* and *Saratoga* was anything but good. Even if Moffett had been willing to lower the standard at Pensacola—something he flatly refused to do—existing law would not permit getting all the pilots and other aviation officers needed, while the training of enough enlisted men was impossible at a moment when the Bureau of Navigation was insisting that the demands for economy in the Navy must force the contraction, rather than the expansion, of the 21 training schools then in commission for all branches.

Nevertheless, as a means of stimulating interest among the enlisted men, the Bureau of Navigation had established some helpful changes in classification. In 1921 it had announced four of these, three to be known, respectively, as naval aviation pilot for seaplanes, for ship planes, and for airships, while the fourth was balloons. Men found qualified in any of the first three were allowed to wear the full wings of a naval aviator, but the balloon men were given only the left wing. In March, 1924, enlisted men were further encouraged by abolishing the four classifications and establishing in their stead the basic rating of aviation pilot. Even so, at the date of this change a total of only about 130 men qualified in the two types of planes or in airships were on duty, while at least double that many were needed. Moreover, even the best of those available left something to be desired because it could not be denied that their educational and general background was weaker than that of the men who had so promptly enlisted for the war. With a few notable exceptions, those who joined the Navy during this discouraging period of the twenties were not of a type to be completely dependable for an emergency in the air. It would have been quite unfair to require them to serve as more than second pilots and it was not to be expected that first pilots should have full confidence in such subordinates.

In addition to these shortages, there were serious ones in the air stations ashore. At one of these, work ordinarily expected of the enlisted personnel was accomplished only by taking on 1,000 civilians, at best an unsatisfactory expedient. On the other hand, in the Bureau of Aeronautics, where civilian experts of so many kinds were needed, severely limited funds prevented hiring enough and also prohibited advancing those that were employed to higher-paid positions for which they were fully qualified. To meet the continuing executive and congressional demands for curtailment of the civilian pay roll, it became necessary to let some of the best men take advantage of opportunities outside the Navy.

Under these discouraging conditions, Moffett nevertheless succeeded in maintaining some semblance of an aviation training program for the Naval Reserve. Even when the funds made available in 1920 to cover 15-day training periods for officers of the Naval Reserve Flying Corps were not provided thereafter, with the result that hundreds of aviation officers, thus deprived of flying, failed to re-enroll when their first four years in the corps had been completed, he refused to give up. Well aware that this corps was an essential to proper preparedness, he insisted that it would be better to drop something else, and in this view he persuaded the Bureau of Navigation to join. In July, 1922, that bureau announced that inactive officers of the corps would be permitted to return to 15 days of active duty which they would spend at the San Diego station, aboard the tender *Wright* in the Atlantic, or aboard the *Aroostook* in the Pacific; a good beginning but, to Moffett, no more than that. In seeking a firm foundation for this training, his next step, taken in November of that year, was to ask the Secretary of the Navy to make a public statement expressing the intention of the department to encourage aviators of the Reserve to maintain their proficiency as fliers and to keep abreast of technical advances. As tangible evidence of this interest, he urged that all commandants of naval districts be asked to foster the organization of units of the Reserve and to provide the necessary planes and equipment. In this way, he declared, those already qualified as pilots would keep their hands in, other officers and men would gain experience in maintenance, and new recruits would be attracted. He asked that $500,000, for the specific purpose of supplying what was required for ten localities, be added to the estimates for 1924.

He did not succeed in getting this sum but after the appearance of the new statement on naval policy, issued in 1922 and outlined in an earlier chapter, he made another effort to convince the Chief of Naval Operations that there must be a well-defined program for reserves. He proposed 13 separate units, to each of which there should be allotted two planes, under one officer and four enlisted men of the Reserve, all on active duty. Each of these units should provide preliminary flight training, each year, for ten students, rated seamen, second class, in the Volunteer Reserve and allowed a course of 45 days, to be followed by 45 days on active duty at a regular naval air station. He expressed the opinion that this program would permit enrolling 1,000 wartime pilots and, through the training given, add about 125 new pilots each year. Mincing no words, he told the Chief of Naval Operations that his plan would require, for aviation alone, about a quarter of the total sum appropriated for all training of naval reserves.

He did not get approval for some time but with the help of the Reserve itself he made a beginning. Hundreds of young men who had learned to fly during World War I wanted to keep on flying, and many others wanted a chance to learn to fly. Many wrote to the Bureau of Aeronautics declaring that if the Navy would make planes and instructors available they would contribute their time, their labor, and even their money. In response to letters of this sort Moffett, in May, 1923, lent the aerial police of New York City four N-9 training planes, his only condition being that the men who flew them must agree to join the Naval Reserve. Other localities or organizations, such as Chicago, Cleveland, Indianapolis, the District of Columbia, and Culver Military Academy indicated their interest in such programs, but none was as enthusiastic as Boston, where the old seaplane base at Squantum, built by public subscription in 1917, offered a convenient site. Lieutenant Commander Byrd, at his own suggestion, was ordered there and, since he had neither men nor money to get the base into operation, he "borrowed" material from a near-by destroyer base, recently decommissioned. The local Reserve turned to with pick and shovel, helped now and then by working parties from the First Naval District where the Commandant, Rear Adm. Louis De Steigeur, was sympathetic; and the result was that Squantum, although not the first to receive a unit for training, became the first real reserve air base. When it needed a landplane for training, the reserves secured this, parked it for a while on a neighboring civilian flying field, and built their own runway with cinders they also got from the naval district. This set the style for similar enthusiasm in other places where the love of flying and real patriotism combined to inspire the reserves throughout these lean years. In the very first summer, with scarcely any official recognition, Squantum and the aerial police unit at Fort Hamilton, New York, gave primary training to 33 students.

In November of that same year the Chief of Naval Operations approved the program, essentially along the lines suggested by Moffett. Next month a double unit, raising the total number to six, was established at Great Lakes, and within one more year a similar unit was organized at Sand Point. By the end of 1925 elementary training of reserves was in full swing at seven places, while advanced training was under way at four naval air stations; but the possibilities suggested by the enthusiasm of the reserves themselves had not yet been realized and adequate funds were still lacking. Further expansion had to wait until, as will be seen, the strong recommendations of the Morrow Board were followed by suitable legislation.

Meanwhile, Captain Mustin appears to have been the officer among Moffett's subordinates who was most closely associated with all the flight training programs for both officers and men; but with him, among others, were Capts. H. V. Butler and A. W. Johnson, Commander McCrary, and Lieutenant Commanders Bartlett, Chevalier, and C. P. Mason. All of these had a part in supervising instruction and practice in scouting with the Fleet, in spotting, torpedo handling, navigation, radio, gunnery, and combat exercises. Into one year's work they crowded both elementary and advanced training, after which the officers found qualified became naval aviators while the enlisted men of the same relative ability became naval aviation pilots.

This was seaplane work, but it had not been forgotten that seaplane pilots must also be able to handle the landplanes aboard carriers, and in 1923 this special instruction had been begun at San Diego and at Pensacola. To be sure, there had been a period, from October, 1919, to January, 1921, during which a number of naval fliers had been trained in landplanes by the Army at Carlstrom Field in Florida, March Field in California, and a little later at Kelly Field, Texas. Marine Corps fliers, after finishing at Pensacola, continued for some years to get additional landplane training at various army fields, but the Army had not had enough money to keep up the broader program. Moreover, after a board convened for the purpose had studied the question of cooperative training, it had been decided that more could be accomplished "along . . . strictly naval lines," and it was this that prompted establishing the courses at the two naval stations. To get as much realism as was possible ashore, landing platforms to simulate flight decks were built on the fields, thus beginning a practice still followed today. Before long Moffett could report that these new courses were less costly and more efficient.

Increased efficiency of the officers in aviation became general through these various modifications in training and it received an added impetus during this period from the success of the aviation courses added to the curriculum at the Naval Academy. These were proving so instructive that Rear Adm. David Taylor made them a sine qua non for all midshipmen whose academic standing warranted their applying for transfer to the Construction Corps. Since at least four hours' flight training was required at the academy, this meant that young men would take with them to their postgraduate work at the Massachusetts Institute of Technology in naval construction some practical knowledge of the problems they would meet in their study of aircraft structure and of aeronautical engineering.

As to the older aviation officers, there continued to be some controversy over a provision in the act of July 12, 1921, which required that at least 30 per cent of those of higher rank must qualify as observers within one year of their assignment. Moffett, however, welcomed this requirement, although it included himself. Having lost no time in taking and passing the necessary tests, he insisted that all his subordinates be prompt in following his example.

So much for the officers. For the enlisted men, one perplexing question continued to be the selection of clearly defined ratings and the fixing of the number of men allotted to each. As early as July, 1921, the Bureau of Navigation had established new ratings of aviation machinist's mate, aviation metalsmith mate, aviation carpenter's mate, and aviation rigger, undoubtedly an improvement over the former ones. Only a year later, however, Moffett had pronounced these unsatisfactory, because the names did not fit the work expected of the various specialists and because, as the numbers were divided, the distribution was resulting in too many chief petty officers, not enough of the lower ratings. Unfortunately no satisfactory solution was immediately found, leaving the question unanswered from year to year.

For training in the various ratings, Great Lakes continued to be the most important center for all forms of aircraft handling, overhaul, and repair, but Pensacola did conduct a few classes for mechanics of all kinds. These were in addition to its regular courses and it presently added another one for instruction in the folding and packing of parachutes which, after 1922, included all the types adopted even earlier by the Army. By 1924, although all hands in aviation had been furnished with parachutes, many did not know how to handle them because Pensacola had been too busy to teach them all, and to meet this emergency a special parachute course had to be established at Lakehurst.

In aerial photography contemporary progress was not satisfactory. Years before, when the functions of the director of Naval Aviation had been distributed throughout the Office of the Chief of Naval Operations, the photographic school organized by the director during World War I had been handed over to the Bureau of Navigation. Since it had thus become concerned with all the photographic activities of the Navy, the Bureau of Aeronautics had been unable to obtain particular concentration upon its personnel, and even after Moffett succeeded in getting the school transferred from Anacostia to Pensacola in 1923 the improvement was only temporary; within a year the school had to be closed for lack of funds. This was very discouraging to Lieut. L. A. Pope, a naval graduate of the Army Photographic School at Chanute Field, Illinois, but after some months he got authority to open a new course at Pensacola and this he contrived to keep running for another year. Incidentally, it was Pope, as a captain, who headed the Navy's organization for aerial photography in World War II and accomplished a stupendous task.

In gunnery training cooperation with the Army continued to be so close that the Navy was able to send some of its men to the Army's specialist schools at Raritan, at the Springfield Armory, and at the Colt Company's plants. While no rating as specialist had yet been established for the Navy's aviation gunners, it was not long before the value of this help from the Army made itself apparent in the number of naval men who had the fame if not the name, a number that remained not fully adequate but did represent a definite gain.

Meanwhile, other efforts included the training of men as well as officers in the handling of catapults at the Naval Aircraft Factory in Philadelphia, where a manual covering the Mark I type provided for a course of about six weeks' duration. By 1924 a catapult of the same type was erected at the San Diego Station and there some personnel selected from the Fleet was able to get at least a small amount of practical training. At the same time other small classes were studying the care and adjustment of aeronautical instruments and still others were established, whenever and wherever possible, to learn all they might of the advances in the design of aircraft engines. All these were kept running on a ropeyarn, the seagoing equivalent of the landsman's shoestring.

Every attempt to expand training was hampered by the continuing lack of enough adequately equipped shore stations. Original plans had called for proper air bases in the Philippines, in Samoa, and at Guam but, as has been noted, work on these was stopped by the stipulations of the Washington Treaty. Of the three, only Guam was far enough along to permit the eventual establishment of a small Marine Corps air detachment, the other two getting nobody. At the same time bases in the areas not affected by the treaty, such as those at Pearl Harbor and Coco Solo, suffered so sharp a pinch of economy that even the Chief of Naval Operations, in support of Moffett, could secure authority for only a very small expansion. Moreover, the additional personnel thus provided for at these two stations could be found only by slicing it away from the complements of the *Lexington* and *Saratoga*, an example of Peter's pockets being so nearly empty that even turning them inside out could produce little help for Paul.

Similarly, the plans of the Bureau of Aeronautics for continental stations remained in the paper stage. It was proposed to establish

18 of these at intervals of 300 miles, and to include chiefly those previously recommended either by the Helm Board or by the General Board. Some had been partially completed when the war ended, some not even started, while a few would have been new additions, such as those planned for maintaining aircraft tenders at Jacksonville, Miami, Tampa, San Luis Obispo, and Humboldt Bay. This modest program had the approval of the War Plans Division of the Navy Department, but not that of Congress which in every appropriations act after 1919 had continued to limit the Navy's air stations to six. Even the expenditure of a mere $825,000, recommended in 1923 by a board headed by Rear Adm. (later Adm.) Hugh Rodman as the minimum requirement over a period of 20 years, was never fully authorized. Comparatively little was accomplished until, years later, it became imperative to prepare in great haste for another war and then, as was unavoidable, the money spent was in far greater ratio to value received than it would have been under the plans of the twenties.

In other ways the Bureau of Aeronautics was getting good value for the money it was allowed to spend. While progress was slower than had been hoped, it was nevertheless progress, and it was made along many lines. One of these led toward standardization of such flight instruments as the compass and the sextant, marked advances resulting from studies made in cooperation with the Army, the Bureau of Standards, the Weather Bureau, and the commercial manufacturers, carried on with the strong backing of that invaluable body, the National Advisory Committee for Aeronautics. Another line led through experiments with substitutes for parachute silk, a material certain to be even scarcer and more costly than various other materials for which proposed substitutes were also tested. A third line of progress, this one on the lighter-than-air side, was marked by the production of better girders and simpler controls for airships and also by the compounding of a new antifreeze solution that did not eat into duralumin.

Duralumin itself was improved upon by new alloys found to be less susceptible to corrosion and to "combat fatigue." New metal tubing, replacing the wooden frames of aircraft, eliminated the waterlogging of these frames with the consequent addition of weight. When the PN-9, with its metal hull, proved satisfactory, it was not long before the use of metal spread to wings and tails, and by 1925 metal propellers, at first built in parts but later forged in one piece, were replacing wooden propellers as fast as these wore out. Still another discovery was a preparation which could be sprayed on these metal surfaces and become a good protection against corrosion.

No advance, however, was of greater importance than that toward better engines, which was made while Naval Aviation perforce continued to use up the overstock of Liberties on hand after the war. By this time liquid-cooled engines were developing as much as 800 horsepower, but the Bureau of Aeronautics had become increasingly interested in air-cooled types, agreeing with the view of the National Advisory Committee for Aeronautics, expressed as early as 1920, that air cooling would give ship-based planes that highly desirable quality, less weight per horsepower. In his annual report for 1922 Moffett drew attention to an air-cooled engine developed with the Navy's money and flown in the Navy's planes, a reference to the Lawrance-1, a radial type first built for racing. Four years later, as the aircraft industry was reorganized by combining various interests, two companies were building similar but much improved types; one was Pratt and Whitney's Wasp, the other was the Wright Aeronautical Company's Cyclone. These fairly settled the long argument between air and water in favor of the former, with the ultimate result that a long series of air-cooled engines, in planes varying from trainers through carrier types to the Army's giant B-29, was used throughout World War II.

All these gains did not mean that Moffett was reconciled to economy and, in retrospect, there appears only this of good to be said for it: it did enforce a search for equipment that would be less expensive yet more efficient. That search led to a new design of tank car which reduced the freight rate on helium from Texas to Lakehurst; to an improvement in wind tunnels which gave 25 per cent greater efficiency at no increase in operating costs; and, on what was perhaps a somewhat lower level, to a decrease in the price of winter suits for aviators from $315 to $125 each.

CHAPTER XXII

The Lampert Committee and
the Eberle Board

NOTWITHSTANDING their great enthusiasm for flying,
the leaders in Naval Aviation still had one foot on a deck,
to keep them in touch with their fundamental training as
seamen. Thus Mustin, a foremost expert in gunnery long before
he took to the air, never lost his vision of 16-inch turrets thunder-
ing at an enemy far beyond the skyline visible from the bridge
above them. Planes had their place in that vision and he meant
exactly what he said when he told the General Board in 1922 that
"our whole aviation program is laid out on the basis that the battleship is the dominant factor in Naval warfare, provided that it is
properly supported by aircraft." Similarly, Ellyson and King no
more forgot that they had once been "submariners" than did Whiting, whose name is still a tradition in the "Pig Boats." McCrary
and Lansdowne, destroyer men long before they thought of climbing into an airship, could never look down on a "Black Can" making its 30 knots on blue water without a pang. This is to mention
only a few at random, for there were dozens of others from small
craft, cruisers, or battleships, who would always cherish the particular type in which they had gained their experience and very
often earned their reputations for leadership.

As a group, these younger officers found substantial support
among forward-looking older ones like Fiske, Taylor, Craven,
Badger, Fullam, and Sims. Essentially, these and others had always thought of the Navy Department, the navy yards, the ships,
and the personnel as existing for the sole purpose of maintaining
at sea a fleet second to none afloat. They could think of any new
weapon in terms of its relation to old ones, in terms of the contribution it might make toward the paramount objective, United States
sea power. On the question of how to create and man an air arm
they might differ quite widely, but they were fully agreed that this

arm must be a part of the whole naval body and that every blow that it might strike must be under the direct control of the Navy itself. For example, it would not occur to them that concentrated bombing by any naval aircraft should be carried out independently of the supporting ships, and their viewpoint was the same on all matters of operation or administration. Thus, under the shrewd leadership of Moffett, there could be a strong effort to gain recognition for aviation, but no hope for any attempt to "take it out of the Navy."

On the other hand, it was not altogether easy to "get it into the Navy" in the sense that it should be a component part of the Fleet. This was because, to many seagoing officers aboard ships, aircraft were still experimental; indeed, they were regarded in some instances as rather a hindrance than a help. This is very clear in a memorandum addressed to Admiral Moffett, early in 1924, by Lieut. Arthur W. Radford, and of particular interest here because Radford has since been the Deputy Chief of Naval Operations (Air) as well as Vice Chief of Naval Operations, and is today, as an admiral, Commander in Chief of the Pacific Fleet. He wrote that the Bureau of Aeronautics was then "in the peculiar position of having sold Naval Aviation to the Public but not to the Navy as a whole." Proceeding, he spoke of flag officers, ship's captains, and gunnery officers who must have "tangible evidence" of flying and were therefore not interested in experimental planes. He held, for example, that certain of the new designs were sent to the Fleet before their defects had been removed, with the result that they broke down on occasion and tended to destroy confidence. Further, he suggested that the many battleships equipped with planes should be made to use them by awarding credits, for example, to ships that used their own planes for spotting gun fire, thus making the aircraft and the aviators part of the ship's company to which they were assigned. He held that commanding officers of the day were apt to feel that their pilots went into the air merely to collect extra pay and these must be persuaded that the aviators, their planes, and the catapults that launched them must be kept in first-class trim at all times in order to count for the ship in competition with others.

Suggestions of this sort were to bear fruit during the twenties, and as differences of opinion were composed there could be more and more progress toward the real integration of aviation with the Fleet. Nevertheless, conservatives and radicals, both within the

Navy and outside it, continued to press their views. Public interest grew greater as the Mitchell brew boiled over, leaving a residuum of ugly rumors of corruption inside the Army and the Navy, of excess profits made by the aircraft industry through what were reported to be monopolistic combinations. All these led the House, in March, 1924, to establish a special committee under Representative Florian Lampert of Wisconsin to make "Inquiry into Operations of the United States Air Service." This committee conducted months of hearings and investigations which included visits to New York, Pasadena, and San Diego by the group and numerous visits by individual members to plants and stations.

Early hearings covered the grievances of the aircraft industry, chief among which were: (1) the existing system of bidding for contracts; (2) the lack of continuity in governmental procurement programs; (3) the competition with private firms by the Naval Aircraft Factory; (4) the withdrawal of private capital; and, as a result of the others, (5) the low morale of the aircraft industry. The first on the list was of great importance because, both for the Navy and for industry, the making of contracts had long been a difficult problem. To an extent, this was due to the contracts being affected by laws, in some instances enacted as far back as 1809, which provided for competitive bidding and bound the government to accept the lowest bid irrespective of any previous demonstration that the low bidder could make good. To meet this situation, frequent use had been made of the "negotiated" contract, an agreement with some particular firm because it was the only one capable of making the item wanted. Similarly, there were numerous instances of the preliminary "development" contract, under which a qualified firm undertook, at an estimated cost to be met by the Navy, the making of a model embodying a naval design. Under such a contract it not infrequently happened that the firm in question either hit upon a new modification or made use of an element already patented by itself, either or both of which resulted in an improvement upon the original design furnished by the Navy. Such events immediately raised these questions. Who owned the finished article? Should the firm patent its new device and collect royalties or must the device be given gratis to the Navy? Should the firm that used a device previously patented by itself be paid the usual royalties by the Navy or not? Finally there were instances in which firms that had gone to considerable effort under development contracts found themselves confronted with competitive bids for mass production, only to lose the production contract to a lower bidder who had spent nothing upon development.

Typical of this was the building of the SC plane, an all-metal scout. The Curtiss Company spent time, labor, and material upon developing this type to meet the Navy Department's design and then submitted its bid of $32,000 each, for mass production. When the Judge Advocate General of the Navy ruled that the completed design was the Navy's property and therefore subject to open bidding, the Martin Company proposed a figure of $20,000 each. The Curtiss Company considered itself injured by this ruling and Moffett himself objected to it as likely to bring about congressional action eliminating "negotiated" and "development" contracts. In the admiral's view such a step would force the Navy, regardless of the standing of a bidder or the quality of his product, to accept the lowest bid, and also have the probable effect of retarding the building program. The National Advisory Committee for Aeronautics favored the negotiated contract but many smaller builders, lacking both capital and personnel to make such contracts, insisted that the Navy was playing favorites and thus preventing the smaller firms from growing larger through government business. It is not to be wondered at that such sharp differences of opinion upon matters already sufficiently complicated made it difficult for the Lampert Committee to find a solution that would satisfy all concerned. Indeed, this controversy has continued through the years, intensified by the War Powers Act of World War II which necessarily gave the government agencies wide discretion in the making of contracts. It is only in the act of 1947 that a workable solution of the Navy's procurement problem appears to have been found.

As to competition by the Naval Aircraft Factory, the department had always regarded the factory as a plant for testing manufacturing costs even though "overhead" never was given the importance it must have in estimates made by private manufacturers. The factory, however, usually built only a few of any particular model, leaving the rest to industry, and this, in the bureau's view, appeared to be a fair procedure. Industry thought it should build all the planes but Capt. (now Vice Adm.) Emory Land, head of the Material Division of Aeronautics, insisted that industry had practically done just that, except in the two years immediately following World War I, before the Bureau of Aeronautics existed. This difference might have been composed but industry made the further complaint that the Army and Navy, by disposing of surplus equipment after the war, at ridiculous figures, had still further injured the private firms and, by keeping other old aircraft and engines too long in use, deprived those firms of more orders. Curtiss, for example, declared that he was running at a heavy loss and would have to liquidate unless a definite procurement program, preferably one covering the Army and Navy together, could be established. This naturally led to further argument, reviving such questions as that of a separate United States air force and of the true significance of the bombing tests, with spirited exchanges pro and con. Since it was just after testifying before the Lampert Committee that General Mitchell was relieved as Assistant Chief of the Army Air Service, a "routine rotation" according to the War Department, this event also meant that another bone of contention was thrown upon the committee's table.

Meanwhile the manufacturers, through a special committee of their own, declared that "a primary requisite for a useful and successful aircraft industry is confidence and cooperation among the members thereof," and proceeded to offer "a code of proper conduct" to which 17 major producers presently subscribed. In addition to proposing rules for industry, this code held that the government could get satisfactory equipment only from companies capable of producing that equipment within their own organization; that the companies should have design staffs capable of handling peacetime problems yet easily expandable in time of war. Design rights must be mutually respected between the companies, each of whom should specialize in its own product in order to avoid duplication and to help the government achieve economies. All this meant that the government, in its turn, should do many things. It should adopt a "standard procurement policy," recognize proprietary rights, stop competing, improve its research and testing, give as much repair work as possible to private firms, and "assist the industry in the procurement of non-commercial supplies."

A conference, hastily called in the office of the Assistant Secretary of the Navy, appears to have concluded that the "code" was to be the basis of the findings of the Lampert Committee. Rear Admiral Moffett had some mental reservations that industry was using the investigation to "stampede" the government but he made no strong objections to the suggestions submitted. Unfortunately this resulted in congratulatory letters, addressed to him and to the Secretary of the Navy by industry and then made public, with the effect of making the Lampert Committee believe that the Navy fully agreed with industry. Mitigating this conclusion, however, was the committee's decision that there were no grounds for charges of corruption in the Army or Navy and that on the whole lack of progress really was due to paucity of funds, and this in turn was the result of too much attention by Congress to what the Bureau of the Budget said, rather than to the views of military and naval experts. The Budget Act was not amended to remove the gag rule but Congressmen became somewhat more thorough in their search for the facts.

The committee made numerous recommendations, including one for a separate air force and one central procurement agency. It wanted old equipment and material surveyed and condemned, and called for a five-year program from the Army and Navy under which not less than $10,000,000 each should be spent annually. It urged more training of aviators, specifically including reserves, higher pay all along the line, and special legislation defining the operations assigned to the Army and those assigned to the Navy. Insisting that aviators should be represented on the General Staff of the Army and on the General Board of the Navy, it recommended the further establishment of a single department of national defense under one civilian Cabinet member.

While the Lampert Committee was slowly reaching its conclusions, several other discussions of the national aviation problems were held and about a dozen bills, some similar in many respects, others diametrically opposed, were introduced in both the House and the Senate. As these went their way to appropriate committees, Secretary of the Navy Wilbur directed the General Board to "consider the recent developments in aviation," listen to "experienced officers of both the Army and the Navy," and then recommend "a policy with reference to the development and upkeep of the Navy in its various branches; i.e., submarines, surface ships and aircraft." This order resulted in the formation of a special group, headed by the Chief of Naval Operations and therefore known as the Eberle Board, which sat during the end of 1924 and the early days of 1925.

The members of the board all had high standing in the Navy. Next to Admiral Eberle in rank was Maj. Gen. John A. Lejeune, outstanding marine and at the time commandant of his corps. The six rear admirals included Charles S. Williams, president of the Naval War College, Joseph Strauss, the budget officer, Henry Hough, the Chief of Naval Intelligence, Hilary Jones, chairman of the General Board's Executive Committee, Andrew T. Long, and William W. Phelps, both members of the General Board. Comdr. W. W. Smyth, also outstanding among his contemporaries, was secretary. As a group these officers were conservative, and Moffett, for one, doubted whether without an airman among them they could give aviation a full and fair hearing. The record, however, indicates that the board, in its hearings, actually was fairer and more open-minded than many who appeared before it. To be sure, they were a little reluctant to admit the threat of aircraft against those battleships to which they had devoted their best years; but it should not be forgotten that the results of bombing tests against the *Washington*, carried on while the board was sitting, served to confirm rather than to upset its inner beliefs.

Those heard included numerous officers of all ranks from all Services and all branches, many already named in these pages, many others called because their expert knowledge or their experience might make some contribution. Civilian engineers, physicists, and manufacturers were similarly represented in numbers. In accordance with the convening order, the hearings covered the mission of the Navy under the national policy, its manifold tasks in supporting that policy, and the ways in which these tasks might most efficiently be performed. The board examined the position of the United States in relation to other great powers, naturally with particular reference to the international treaties recently ratified. Covering so broad a field, the record could not but be a long one and to read it is to realize that there were sharp brushes, both on and off the record, between those of opposite view; for example, Capt. A. W. Johnson, the progressive airman, and Rear Admiral Strauss, the budget officer who had already cut deeply into proposed appropriations for Naval Aviation. An idea of the extent of the hearings may be had from the fact that it required 80 sheets typed in single space merely to report the conclusions, many of which were compromises that raised almost as many questions as they answered.

Aviation, said the board, "has introduced a new and highly important factor in warfare both on the land and on the sea . . . Its influence on naval warfare undoubtedly will increase in the future, but the prediction that it will assume paramount importance in sea warfare will not be realized." Because the airplane was "inherently limited in performance by physical laws" and because the airship was too vulnerable, neither could be wholly effective without support and supply from surface ships. Nevertheless, aircraft have "made possible the accurate control of fire at long ranges and . . . vastly increased its effectiveness" while demonstrating "their great value to the fleet in scouting . . . and bombing." What more might be accomplished when the recommended carriers had been built, as they must be, remained to be determined, and the same could be said of the use of planes with torpedoes or gas and for the laying of smoke screens to protect ships. Certainly aviation had "taken its place as an element of the fleet and cannot be separated from it." Moreover, to take its aviators away from the Navy "would be most injurious to the continued efficiency of the fleet in the performance of its mission."

In the board's further recommendations were included governmental encouragement of all forms of civilian flying through the establishment of airways, of methods of inspecting aircraft, the training of fliers, and the licensing of both pilots and the planes they were to fly. No reasonable and proper effort to encourage the aircraft industry should be spared, and the creation and maintenance of a trained Reserve including pilots, observers, and ground forces should not be neglected. Most important of all, the Fleet should promptly be brought to full treaty strength, especially in carriers, while the appropriate personnel for these and for all other branches of flying should be increased in number, better trained, and placed upon a secure footing in relation to their other naval duties. Finally, the board found all these conclusions quite in line with the United States naval policy laid down in December, 1922, which was "sound and should be adhered to," especially because it had been approved by every witness heard.

The board had concluded its hearings and was about to issue its report when Moffett, presumably aware of the board's forthcoming recommendations on personnel, made his Assistant Chief of Bureau, Captain Johnson, the head of a board of aviators, with instructions to report upon "the status of the personnel assigned to aviation duty as relating to the whole Navy." Since the Eberle report would come out while this new board was sitting, it appears that the admiral wanted the latter to be in a position to examine some of the former's findings. In effect, that is what followed.

Beginning at the usual point, the rapid technical expansion of aviation without adequate personnel, the Johnson Board in its report on April 30, 1925, asked for a gradual increase to meet the aviation needs of a treaty navy, described as four admirals, 22

captains, 51 commanders, 123 lieutenant commanders, and 1,574
lieutenants of both grades, to be reached by 1935 and to represent
an increase of about 500 per cent over the figures of the moment.
Since such an expansion was impossible until the Navy as a whole
and the Naval Academy in particular had been increased in size,
the temporary expedient proposed was the assignment of ensigns
to flight training at Pensacola without the two years of sea duty
recommended by the Eberle Board. To cut attrition at Pensacola,
stiff physical examinations should precede assignment and some
training should be given at the academy.

On the question of allowable rank in aviation, the Johnson Board
held that promotion should follow its regular naval course. To get
commanding officers for the stations and for the carriers that
might be built, a number of captains should be quickly qualified as
naval aviators and then assigned to these commands, to be duly
succeeded by younger men advancing in rank during their years
of flying duty. On the other moot question, rotation or specializa-
tion, the board saw merit in both ideas but leaned toward the aviators by drawing attention to a report made by still another board
previously appointed by Rear Admiral Shoemaker, Chief of the
Bureau of Navigation. The pertinent quotation made it "apparent
that no officer can be really expert in all branches of the Naval
profession," and found it "necessary that each officer specialize
in at least one branch." To meet this, the Johnson Board presented a list of changes which should be made in postgraduate
courses having to do with aviation, including the assignment of
some officers to army flying schools. This last suggestion was evidence of the conviction that the Army, in certain respects, had
taken the lead and that the Navy could benefit by catching up with
army progress and then establishing similar schools and experimental stations of its own.

As to enlisted men, this board emphasized the lack of full success, thus far, in training them as pilots to make up the shortage.
Instead, it proposed more clearly defined ratings and the making
of more room for advancement through training at better schools
covering the many branches of aviation other than actual piloting.
Another important recommendation covered the training of the
Reserve to such a high point that it could, after a short "refresher
course," furnish 1,500 naval aviators within one year of the beginning of a war. The board had heard Whiting's "rotation" plan,
under which graduates of the academy, during 36 years' service,

could do 19 years of aviation duty at sea, 17 years ashore. It had also heard Bartlett's plan which was, in effect, an argument for a separate naval air corps, based chiefly upon the Bureau of Aeronautics' lack of authority to control its personnel without interference by the Bureau of Navigation, but also upon the idea that young officers would not under existing conditions volunteer as fliers. Both plans were sent in with the Johnson report made, as has been said, at the end of April, 1925. After studying that report Moffett, knowing that the Eberle Board had called for the determination of departmental policy on aviation personnel, and wishing to make sure that there would be no separate flying corps in the Navy, yet believing that other details of the Bartlett plan should be considered, prepared a request for still another board to draw up a final policy.

Meanwhile Rear Admiral Shoemaker, Chief of the Bureau of Navigation, had been asked by the Secretary of the Navy to make recommendations along the lines suggested by the Eberle Board and, in doing this, he helped bring to white heat the conflict between Navigation and Aeronautics. Not only did he suggest that the number of commissioned pilots be limited to 750, but he also proposed that extra pay for flying be reduced to ten per cent of base pay, with a sop to aviators of additional life insurance provided by the government. In addition, he most unfortunately sent his report to the Secretary of the Navy through the Chief of Naval Operations, with no reference to Moffett, a procedure within his legal rights but certainly not in the spirit of the Secretary's order of 1921, suggesting that Aeronautics have its say on all matters concerning aviation personnel. Moffett, on the other hand, was careful to forward the Johnson Board report to Operations through Shoemaker and, if this was designed to smoke the latter out, it certainly succeeded. The comment by Navigation filled 48 pages, also typed in single space, in which Shoemaker repeated everything he had already said and added considerably more. Declaring that the Johnson Board's report was "built about a predetermined opinion as to the position and specialized status of the naval aviator in the Navy, as distinct from an attempt to solve the aviation personnel problem of the Navy for the best interests of the service," he also revealed his position on other points. This was by stating his view that aviation had received "as much funds as could profitably be spent considering the stage of advancement of the art and its unproved value at sea." Such funds, he did admit, might be increased in the future but this should be only when, in the "reasoned opinion of naval officers . . . aviation supports its claims, and as the art of design and building progressed to the point where a dollar is obtained in worth of equipment purchased for each dollar appropriated."

The reading of the Johnson report, with Shoemaker's lengthy endorsement, presented the Chief of Naval Operations with a problem. He did act to the extent of disapproving any separate naval air corps and the assignment of officers to aviation duty only, but for the rest he resorted to the old expedient of suggesting still another board to settle the ratio of enlisted to commissioned pilots and the question of appropriate tours of sea duty for aviators. Moffett, hearing of this proposal, hastened to agree and on September 17 he suggested that Commanders Whiting and H. C. Richardson, with Lt. Comdr. R. R. Paunack, who were all aviators, be included in the new board's membership. This suggestion was of course referred to Navigation, where Shoemaker disagreed and made the counter proposal that the General Board conduct any further investigation found necessary.

Studying this mass of papers, the Secretary of the Navy began by disapproving any separate flying corps. He then asked the General Board to express its views and this group, perhaps because it had had enough of aviation for the time being, recommended that a wholly new board be appointed. This was on September 26, and very shortly the Secretary of the Navy made Rear Adm. Montgomery Taylor head of that new board, including four captains and two commanders in addition to Whiting and Paunack as proposed by Moffett, and one other aviator, Lt. Comdr. Marc Mitscher, who acted as recorder. Before this Taylor Board had been fully constituted, however, and while the Johnson report with its weighty endorsements was still a departmental shuttlecock, tragedy again struck Naval Aviation.

CHAPTER XXIII

The Morrow Board

O N September 2, 1925, Lt. Comdr. Zachary Lansdowne, veteran of numerous airship flights, took the *Shenandoah*, "Daughter of the Stars," out of Lakehurst. This flight, like others, was designed to afford training and experience but it had the particular purpose of complying with a request that the Navy test the new mooring mast for dirigibles, erected during that summer at the Ford field in Dearborn, Michigan.

The flight was uneventful until about four o'clock the next morning, when the ship was over Byesville, Ohio. At that time, her crew saw heavy clouds accompanied by severe lightning looming in the northwestward sky. Almost at once the head winds became so strong that even her five motors hardly gave the ship headway and presently her drift to leeward became faster. Her navigator, Lieut. (now Vice Adm.) C. E. Rosendahl, afterward spoke of a thin, dark, streaky cloud as just visible in the pale moonlight, and he had barely noticed this when the vicious squall struck. Caught in violently whirling upcurrents, the ship began to rise so fast that all efforts to check her were unavailing. At 4,000 feet she paused, then rushed higher. In the thinner atmosphere of the upper levels the expanding helium created so much pressure on the gas cells that they were in danger of bursting and the crew, already sent by Lansdowne to emergency stations, began opening hand valves to relieve the gas cells more rapidly than the automatic valves could do it.

The upward rush continued until, at about 6,000 feet, the ship met the down-currents of the storm. She was "heavy" now because valving so much helium had cost her buoyancy and, to check her as she began to fall swiftly, tons of ballast water were run overboard. In perhaps two minutes she fell about 3,000 feet, where she was struck again by upcurrents and flung up once more. In the hope that the next downthrust of the higher levels might be checked, Lansdowne gave orders to cut adrift the middle gas tank, designed so it could be "slipped" in such an emergency, and sent Rosendahl forward to supervise this effort.

It was just as he stepped up on the ladder leading from the control car to the keel that Rosendahl felt the ship incline to what he knew was a dangerous angle. In the next instant he heard the struts cracking and the metallic crash that meant structural members were parting and suspension wires snapping. From almost under his feet the control car tore itself loose, carrying Lansdowne, three other officers, and four men. Then, looking down through the grey dawn, he could see the whole after end of the ship falling, splitting into sections as it went. Both engine cars broke away, taking with them all the engineers. Not until long after would he know that the stern section, with Lieutenant Rauch and a few of the crew, by some unexplained miracle would reach the ground unhurt. For the moment he had all he could do to clamber into the forward section, now to all intents and purposes a 200-foot free balloon.

Up it shot to 10,000 feet, to be drenched in rain squalls, pounded this way and that, driven down to earth into the top of a tall tree, extricated, and at last, by the most expert "valving," brought to the ground and secured. Rosendahl and his small group of six were 12 miles from the crushed control car when they began searching for their shipmates. Three of those in the midship section and 17 in the afterbody were unhurt while two others were injured but recovered, leaving a total of 14 dead. Most of the survivors continue to be as enthusiastic as Rosendahl in advocating the use of airships.

The court of inquiry, such as always follows a disaster, found no grounds for such opinions as the one expressed by General Mitchell, that the tragedy was what was to be expected from the "incompetent, criminally negligent, and almost treasonable administration" of the air services by both the Army and the Navy; an expression, by the way, which led directly to the general's trial by court martial and his ultimate resignation from the Army. On the contrary, the court decided that the ship had been adequately prepared for a duly authorized flight; that there had been no warning of the storm; and that the ship had had no apparent structural weakness. It cited the numerous instances of individual heroism and the gallant efforts of groups to save ship and shipmates. It recognized the important fact that the use of noninflammable helium instead of hydrogen had resulted in saving many lives. As far as possible it established the facts; but it could not soften the heavy blow to aviation or halt the wave of adverse publicity that swept the country.

One great good did follow when the Secretaries of War and of the Navy together urged President Coolidge, as Commander in Chief, to call upon a group of highly qualified citizens to study the whole problem of "aircraft in national defense and to supplement the studies already made" by both departments. Hardly more than a week after the *Shenandoah* tragedy the President complied on September 12, and the distinguished Dwight W. Morrow was shortly named chairman of a board including representatives of the Army, the Navy, the aircraft industry, Congress, the judiciary, and the foremost experts in aeronautical engineering. The members were Maj. Gen. J. G. Harbord, Adm. F. F. Fletcher, Howard E. Coffin, Senator Hiram Bingham of Connecticut, Representatives Carl Vinson of Georgia and J. S. Parker of New York, Judge A. C. Denison, and Dr. W. F. Durand of the engineering faculty of Stanford University. Throughout the nation the opinions of such a group were certain to be respected.

The Morrow Board thoroughly examined every aspect of aviation in the United States. With hardly an omission, the views of every American qualified to express views were sought, and the four printed volumes reporting the board's hearings and its conclusions therefore constitute an exhaustive, indeed a monumental study of all aviation problems up to the time of sitting. In these pages it is possible only to outline the recommendations of some of the more prominent men among the hundreds called before the board.

The destruction of the *Shenandoah* and the emphasis laid by the Eberle Board upon the vulnerability of airships in general had put Moffett on the defensive but with characteristic vigor he refused to stay in that uncomfortable position. Instead he gave the board a vivid account of all that had been learned from the lost ship's many successful flights, and followed this by urging the continued study and development of the rigid airship by building at least one successor. As part of the "steady, farsighted, progressive" program, he asked for the establishment of a new base, on the West coast, for lighter-than-air elements. All this was very much what he had previously said to the General Board when he asked that body, in addition, to approve the immediate building of an airship of 1,125,000-cubic-foot capacity, for training purposes, with two giants of 6,000,000 cubic feet to follow.

As to industry, the admiral emphasized the friendly relations which existed between his bureau and the makers of aircraft, bringing out the efforts made by the Navy to improve those relations through its frequent invitations to industry to join in conference or to inspect the Naval Aircraft Factory; through its sharing of technical information gained from the racing planes; and through its consistent policy of encouraging at least two manufacturers for each design of plane. He was blunt as ever in asserting that the smallness of appropriations was at the bottom of the Navy's inability to give industry enough to do, to standardize types and thus permit mass production, or to arrange negotiated contracts with approved builders.

Turning to personnel, Moffett did not fail to make the point that the Bureau of Aeronautics should have complete control of whatever officers and men might constitute its quota. As one means of making that quota greater, he urged the revival of Admiral Mayo's plan for augmenting the number of midshipmen at the Naval Academy and strongly recommended a general increase in the enlisted personnel allowed the Navy. To provide adequate facilities for this personnel and for material he asked that the limitation to six stations in the United States, imposed by a clause in every appropriation bill in recent years, be eliminated from future bills. For much the same reason, he also asked that a part of the Army Appropriations Bill of 1922, in which areas of operation for the air arms of the Army and of the Navy were defined, be repealed because "while presumably this should be satisfactory it appears that in some quarters it has been, and in the future is likely to be, invoked to restrict and hamper the development of naval aviation." He recommended that extra pay for flying be authorized as long as flying continued to be hazardous. He urged the importance of carriers and, in general, he besought the board to recommend that the five-year program be definitely established with due assurance that it would be carried to completion.

Other officers of standing gave their views on these points as well as on others. In their essence, these views have already been noted in these pages. Whiting reiterated the "plan for personnel" which he had previously advocated, insisting that to follow this plan would do away with existing inefficiencies, such as jeopardizing promotion by long service in aviation, and the "rotation" system under which aviators, during periods of duty as ship's officers, must become rusty in their specialty. In all this Whiting was supported by Mitscher. Bellinger and Bartlett brought up the separate flying corps idea, the latter, in particular, giving details of the plan, including a plea for special schools in strategy and tactics for the corps. Of such schools high-ranking officers like Adm. C. F. Hughes, Commander in Chief, would have none because to their minds the Fleet was the proper school for these matters. Lieutenant Carpenter, another among those disagreeing with Bellinger and Bartlett, put his objections on the novel ground that "aviation is far too important a subject to be limited to the minor position implied by a corps," and he declared that all naval officers should be trained, at least to some extent, in flying and its problems. That outspoken Mississippian, Comdr. John McCain, years later to be vice admiral and Mitscher's alternate as a leader of carrier task forces, was bitter in assailing the separation of aviators as "a protective promotion device pure and simple." A corps of the kind would accomplish no good for the Navy, he insisted, because the specialists would neglect the sailors and the sailors would neglect the specialists. Lieutenant Commander Paunack, in his turn, supported the separate corps with an analysis of all the grievances of the aviators ranging from uniforms to promotions.

A similar clash of opinions was evident among the others on the long roll of experts, especially when they came before the board to discuss the bombing experiments. Here the range extended from the view of General Mitchell that it was "all over but flying" to the view of the former Chief of Naval Operations, Admiral Coontz, who called the experiments "absolutely inconclusive" because true battle conditions had not been simulated and because the target ships had been wholly without personnel to repair damage and fight back. He did not "think it possible to get anything out of . . . [such] a one-sided affair," and while he admitted to a belief in "stunts, so-called, that are of distinct advantage," except for these he "would put the money into legitimate lines of endeavor."

All the naval officers were opposed to anything like a separate department of the air for the nation and, except for the followers of Mitchell, so were most of the army officers. Major General Hines, Chief of Staff, insisted that the "training of all air units is based on the fundamental doctrine that their mission is to aid the ground forces." His Assistant Chief, Brig. Gen. Hugh Drum, held the Mitchell proposals "unsound from a national defense viewpoint, as well as from purely Army considerations." As he put it, "so far as the future of aviation can be foreseen, air power has no function independent of the Army and the Navy." Other army officers recalled the letter that General Pershing had written General Menoher in 1920 when the latter's board was in session; a letter in which Pershing, among a dozen other reasons against a distinct and separate air force, cited the inability of such a force to gain a final decision against a ground force, the necessity for close cooperation between the two types, and the impossibility of bringing about that cooperation except under the supreme command of the ground force. Admitting the wisdom of a "separate branch within the Army," General Pershing had insisted that he meant "separate" in the sense that the Infantry and the Field Artillery were separate, an argument repeated by the army men who brought forward the letter. In this stand they found themselves supporting not only the ranking generals like Hines, Drum, Summerall, and Ely but also such admirals as Eberle, Robinson, Coontz, Hughes, Sims, and others. They maintained that training and operation in the Army and the Navy continued to differ and that independent air missions should remain under the control of the high command in the particular operation. Great Britain was cited as an instance of the failure of amalgamation, the Admiralty being reported as finding it intolerable to be responsible for the success of the Grand Fleet without controlling that Fleet's air cover. While consolidation might, in the opinion of these officers, eliminate some overlapping and permit some peacetime economies, this must count for nothing against what might happen in attempting to fight a war under such a handicap.

Admiral Sims, while he stood with those opposed to taking the Navy's air arm away from it, did not hesitate to criticize the Navy's current handling of that vital weapon. Attacking a continuing tendency toward conservatism, he said that taking refuge in the familiar phrase, "a well-balanced fleet," was dangerous because it involved no proper definition of "balanced" and meant a defensive rather than an offensive policy. He insisted that the plane, already "a major force," was "becoming daily more efficient" with more and more deadly weapons. No battleship could hope longer to protect itself against planes except by its own planes, and a small carrier might, from far out of gun range, disable if not destroy a battleship. This must mean that in future the fleet that commanded the air would be the winner, and in this sense he saw the fast carrier as the "capital ship" of the future. Thus the admiral, conservative in the fundamentals of the chain of command, was in step with the progressives in aviation itself.

These are mere sentences from paragraphs, half pages from chapters, a dozen names from the legion paraded before the patient Morrow Board. All the prominent men in civilian flying had their day in court, and all of industry had an opportunity to present its grievances, its hopes, and its suggestions. Taken together, they enabled the board, in its report dated November 30, 1925, to reach many conclusions of great importance and make many recommendations. The board was strongly opposed to a consolidation of military, naval, and civilian flying into a single organization because it believed that even partial control of the civilian effort by the military would be a reversal of the policy that had made the United States a great nation. In effect, a supervision of civilian flying by the Armed Services would be a long step toward a Prussianism that would make all foreign nations suspect American motives. Instead, said the board, civil aviation should be given assistance analogous to that being afforded the maritime service, which was furnished with good lighthouses, a buoyage system, improved rivers and harbors, and invaluable up-to-date hydrographic information. Service to airmen should be rendered by the Department of Commerce, in which a special section covering the navigation of the air should be established.

As to the question of a merger, the board admitted that there might be some overlap in procurement which could be reduced by consolidation, but held that the saving thus effected would be far less valuable than the worth of competition between the soldiers and the sailors in aviation. Moreover, in addition to believing that the army and the navy fliers should be controlled by their own central military or naval authority, the board held that each branch was entitled to a top-level civilian representative and that the whole organization would be strengthened by creating posts for Assistant Secretaries of Aeronautics, not only in the War and the Navy Departments but in Commerce as well.

In commenting specifically on the Navy, the board praised its personnel and material but made numerous recommendations. It held that the Aircraft Factory should continue to do experimental and repair work but should not compete with industry in manufacturing planes and parts. Officers who had specialized in aviation long enough to bring their promotion into jeopardy should be promoted and, to avoid delaying the promotion of nonaviators in the

same grade, carried as "extra numbers" in the order of their rank.
To provide for command posts temporary promotions should be
made, but junior officers should be required to perform adequate
duty at sea before being advanced. The command of carriers, tenders, and shore establishments for the air arm should be given only to
men fully qualified as commissioned pilots of aircraft. There should
be careful search for means of attracting qualified technical experts, among officers and enlisted men, to the aviation branch.

In its consideration of the aircraft industry the board fully
recognized its vital importance in any program of national defense. After a study of existing aircraft builders and their resources, they were considered capable of expanding, within 12
months after the declaration of a national emergency, to a production of 15,000 planes a year; within six months more, to figures far
outstripping those of any foreign country. Nevertheless, because
no peacetime formula could provide for the enormous needs of
war, especially if designs were so frequently changed that it became impossible to lay up any reserve planes, it appeared advisable
to standardize design for periods of three years, with appropriate
provision for replacements and for the turnover of equipment at
stated intervals. Production orders should be awarded only to competent, well-staffed concerns, with due regard for their proprietary
rights and with every effort to further their work in research. The
National Advisory Committee for Aeronautics should expand its
assistance to inventors and to the advancement of commercial flying, an element of such importance that it should have every possible governmental support.

The prestige of Mr. Morrow and his associates aroused wide-
spread interest in their findings, completely overshadowing the con-
current sessions of the Taylor Board. This would have been true
even if the latter group had dealt conclusively with the problems
laid before it, which it did not do. It failed to establish a ratio between enlisted and commissioned pilots, and it begged the question
of high commands in aviation by suggesting that these be left to
the nominations of the commander in chief of the Fleet. As to the
promotion of officers who were pilots, after remarking that while
an officer's ability to fly might decrease with the years, his ability
to command might increase, it merely recommended that no aviator
be advanced to the rank of commander until he had served one year
as at least second in command on a cruising vessel. Otherwise, in
what amounted to a general review of the Johnson Board's findings,

it disagreed as to the wisdom of ordering midshipmen who volunteered for aviation to Pensacola immediately upon their graduation, and also as to proposed new ratings for enlisted men. Altogether, it was not a constructive report and when it was referred to Rear Admiral Shoemaker of the Bureau of Navigation, he said that "the good of the Navy" could be served only by a board of senior officers with "nothing to gain or lose . . . and no future that could be adversely affected." Oddly enough, the Secretary of the Navy in his turn confirmed the report "as modified by the first endorsement," which was Shoemaker's, thus straddling the whole matter without any explanation. Comdr. Dewitt Ramsey, later to be an admiral and Commander in Chief in the Pacific, but then at his desk in the Bureau of Aeronautics, correctly described this procedure as "queer," because Moffett was given no opportunity to comment; but in view of the inconclusiveness of the Taylor report there is nothing queer in the fact that no great importance appears to have been attached to it. At that moment what counted was the Morrow Board.

In particular, when that far-seeing board put an end to numerous long-standing dissensions and pointed the way to the solution of other vexing problems, it laid the foundation for a general belief that a truly constructive plan for aviation in the United States could at last be made. In this belief Congress very shortly began debating new legislation and within six months enacted three laws. The act of May 21, 1926, provided for certain aids to civilian flying and, as was very important, created the post of Assistant Secretary of Commerce for Air. The act of July 2 covered numerous other recommendations of the Morrow Board relating largely to the Army, but from the Navy's standpoint the most vital act was that of June 24. This authorized a five-year program for building 1,000 planes, with definite numbers of these to be procured each year until the total was reached, and with replacements which would serve to maintain that round figure. It provided for two dirigibles of 6,000,000 cubic feet each, to cost not over $8,000,000 in all, and for one metal-clad airship to be used for experiments. It laid down rules for procurement that would safeguard the rights of industry in making contracts without loss of protection for the government. It directed that the awarding of contracts, after competitive bidding, should be made to the lowest responsible bidder, with such awards subject to review only by the President of the United States or by the federal courts. At the top administrative levels it authorized the appointment of an Assistant Secretary of the Navy specifically "to . . . assist in furthering naval aeronautics." Considered as a whole, this was very progressive legislation.

CHAPTER XXIV

Five-Year Program of 1926

MOFFETT and his close associates welcomed the Morrow Board and the legislation that followed it as the right impetus toward that "steady, far-sighted, progressive development" they had so long been urging. They were pleased when the new post of Assistant Secretary of the Navy for Air was given to Dr. Edward P. Warner of the Massachusetts Institute of Technology, a recognized expert in aeronautical engineering with a wide acquaintance among aviators and others who believed in aviation. Hoping Congress would appreciate that better information on the Navy's needs could be obtained from this representative or from the Navy itself, all hands prepared to press forward.

Since the act of June 24 had been one of authorization only, it remained to be seen whether the next congressional appropriations would provide the necessary money. For the fiscal year 1927 Moffett made a supplementary estimate to cover the additional planes and the two rigid airships which would be required under the five-year program, only to have this estimate thrown out by the Bureau of the Budget on the ground that this program would not be begun until the fiscal year of 1928. For that year the first estimates, submitted as early as May, 1926, had already suffered a reduction by the Budget Bureau, and this was followed by several others which finally brought the original figure of a little over $40,000,-000 down to a little under $20,000,000, where it stood when hearings in the House began.

During these hearings an encouraging moment for Aeronautics came when the committee began looking into these drastic cuts made by the Bureau of the Budget. Representative Thomas Butler of Pennsylvania was led to declare that what that bureau had done to the original estimate would have the effect of changing the five-year program, already approved by Congress, into a ten-year program. Representative Britten of Illinois was even more emphatic, crying out that officers of the Navy, expected by Congress to execute the policies of Congress, were being stultified by a Budget Bureau with "more power here than Mussolini has in Italy!" In the end the House added $5,000,000 for new construction to the estimate given it and sent the question to the Senate. That body, also concerned about aviation, recommended still more money for new construction, with the final result that the total reached $29,500,000 of which $9,500,000 was for the building program over the next two years. This was a substantial increase but Moffett would still have to make full use of his diplomacy to persuade each succeeding Congress of the need for reasonable liberality. He did just that.

Any plan to procure more planes must embody decisions as to their type, their proper maintenance, and their employment, because the act of June 24 directed that two thirds of the ultimate total of 1,000 should be kept in commission while one third was held in reserve. To facilitate arriving at these decisions the Secretary of the Navy established a second Taylor Board in April, 1927, this time to examine the naval policy of 1922 and recommend any changes found to be desirable. The resulting report had several features, an outstanding one being the unanimity with which those heard by the board insisted upon the vital need for carriers, both to protect the Fleet and to carry on "scouting and offensive operations at a distance from the battle line." Another was the general condemnation of the so-called "multiple-purpose" designs, which made a torpedo plane, required to have very high speed and superior maneuvering qualities, also a scouting plane which had no great need for either of these qualities. Such an expert as Comdr. Newton White, for one, deplored this combination as producing nothing but an inefficient hybrid in which both types were ruined. A third feature was the emphasis laid upon fighter planes, upon dive bombers, and, in general, upon a closer study of high-altitude and low-altitude bombing. Finally, this report urged the building of the two big rigid airships for use, "primarily with the Fleet," to determine their true value to the Navy, leaving patrol work to nonrigids, the building of which was also recommended. This was the report of progressives because those sitting with Admiral Taylor included Moffett himself, Rear Adm. Frank H. Schofield, Capts. A. W. Marshall, J. M. Reeves, Henry V. Butler, J. J. Raby, and H. E. Yarnell, Commander Ellyson, and Lieutenant Commander Mitscher. Most of these, as they advanced in rank, would have high aviation commands and be enthusiastic supporters of the Navy's

air arm, especially the brilliant Yarnell and Schofield, the latter
a Naval Academy classmate and close friend of Moffett.

Reviewing the Taylor report, the General Board approved the
substance of its recommendations although conservatives among
these elder statesmen were inclined to hold back a bit on airships
and were not fully convinced that multiple-purpose planes would
not do. Out of these deliberations came the naval policy of 1927,
appreciably broader than that of 1922, making it the task of
Aeronautics "to direct the development and employment of Naval
Aviation primarily to the fulfilment of the principal mission,
namely operations at sea with the Fleet." Except for a protest that
classifications of plane types should have been more elastic, Aeronautics was satisfied with this statement of policy, but Assistant
Secretary Warner did suggest that the General Board, by dealing
more closely with him, might keep itself better informed. Accepting this suggestion, the board duly advocated a freer hand for the
experts, headed by Warner and Moffett, in developing planes for
special work.

As part of its building program, presented in late 1927, the
board recommended more than the original 1,000 planes and urged
the building of one 13,800-ton carrier in each of the next five years.
This inevitably met opposition from pacifist organizations and
from penny pinchers, with the result that Congress, even after the
failure of the Geneva Disarmament Conference, allowed only one
such carrier, eventually commissioned as the *Ranger*. She would
be a help but she alone could not meet the requirements of the
commander in chief and his higher-ranking subordinates, all of
whom supported Moffett's contention that the British *Hermes* and
the Japanese *Hosho* had clearly proven the value of the small carrier. With enough of that type the Fleet could keep many planes in
the air without the risk of losing one large carrier.

When it came to repair ships, only enough money was made available to install some aircraft-repair equipment on ships whose ordinary service was not restricted to the support of aircraft. Money
for tenders, too, was lacking, although Moffett had repeatedly
recommended their construction. He now urged the conversion "of
at least one, preferably two vessels" for this purpose, giving as a
particular reason the already obsolescent equipment of the tender
Wright, and the lack of ships to help her other than a motley group
including an ex-collier, a former mine layer, and several former
mine sweepers. No replacements were made possible, however, and

even as much later as 1931, when the redesignation of the air stations at Coco Solo and Pearl Harbor as Fleet air bases meant that
planes would be operating farther and farther afield, the only improvement in the condition of the tenders was some new gear for
handling seaplanes.

It is a little difficult to understand congressional reluctance to
appropriate money during this period, for it was marked by numerous events which created favorable public opinion of the Navy's
flying. In 1926 Lieut. (later Commodore) Ben Wyatt took off
from Seattle with two Loening amphibians, accompanied by the
tender *Gannet*, to conduct the successful Alaska expedition. A few
months later other groups made a broad aerial photographic survey of the Gulf of Mexico, Venezuela, Cuba, Panama, and Nicaragua. Then, early in 1927, Byrd began preparing to try crossing
the Atlantic in a Fokker with Balchen, Acosta, and Noville. To be
sure, the drama of this flight was reduced when Lindbergh, a few
days before Byrd was ready, startled the world with his gallant,
lonely crossing, but the Byrd flight was productive of very valuable scientific data on ocean flying.

In July, close behind Lieutenants Maitland and Hegenberger
of the Army, Lieut. Emory Bronte, USNR, flew from San Francisco to Honolulu, and a month later Lieut. W. V. Davis was at the
controls of the plane that won the Dole transpacific flight. As if
to crown these achievements, the long-awaited *Saratoga* was commissioned on November 16, to be followed by the *Lexington* on
December 14. The latter drew a little ahead of the former when
Lieut. A. M. Pride, the expert on landing gear, justifiably had
the honor of putting the first plane down aboard the *Lexington* on
January 5, 1928; but Mitscher was only six days behind him with
the first landing on the *Saratoga*, and on January 27 that great
ship was again in the news when the *Los Angeles* came safely to
rest on her deck.

As the Navy's one working dirigible, the *Los Angeles* was kept
very much in the public eye. In the fall of 1928 she flew down to
Texas, mooring to the new mast at the helium plant, Fort Worth.
Soon afterward she made a week's flight basing on the tender
Patoka, and followed this by dozens of flights across country and
along both coasts. When Goodyear's trapeze was completed as a
means of landing planes aboard the airship to defend her, the first
mid-air hook on and pickup was made on July 3, 1929, with Lieut.
A. W. Gorton at the controls of a tiny UO-1; but it was not until

September 29, 1931, that Lieuts. D. W. Harrigan and H. L. Young, were picked up at night in planes of the N2Y-1 type. Still another event in *Los Angeles* history was the successful launching from her, on January 31, 1930, of a glider carrying Lieut. (later Capt.) R. S. Barnaby. Taken together, these accomplishments served to feed the lively interest in dirigibles reawakened when the two giant ones had been authorized, and stimulated in March, 1928, when funds for the first of these, the *Akron*, had been appropriated.

To get a good design for the *Akron* a competition among possible builders had been held and this had been won by Goodyear with plans for a ship of 6,000,000-cubic-foot capacity, 780 feet long with a maximum diameter of 135 feet. Equipped to carry five planes for her defense, she was expected to make 80 miles an hour, and with a structure twice as strong as that of the *Shenandoah*, it was calculated that she would be able to withstand squalls of 30-knot velocity. All this was approved by Aeronautics, but before any contract could be written one of Goodyear's rivals, the Brown-Bovari Corporation, protested the decision and a new competition was arranged, only to have Goodyear again declared the winner. As finally signed in October, 1928, the contract required that firm to build two airships at a combined cost of $7,835,000, with the proviso that the second must embody any modifications found desirable after tests of the first. As this cost was greater than the amount originally appropriated, Congress added another $1,800,-000 and construction began in November, 1929, with completion expected by the autumn of 1931 and a plan to follow with the sister ship, the *Macon*, about two years later.

Because the German Maybach motor gave a better performance than any American motor yet developed for dirigibles, it was chosen for the *Akron*. Installed inside the hull, these Maybachs were fitted to a special type of shafting, with which it would be possible to get a vertical as well as a horizontal thrust, a feature which was expected to simplify both the ship's take-off and her landing. Moreover, once she was up, that arrangement would permit her to rise rapidly in case she were threatened by an air attack before she could launch her defending planes. As to these, they were to be of the Curtiss F9C type, weighing about 3,000 pounds each and especially designed for easy hooking on and for stowage inside the ship.

Such immediate and prospective technical progress in aviation was not accompanied by the improvement in the personnel situation sought by Aeronautics. For example, as one way to attract enlisted men from sea duty to flying duty, the rating of aviation pilot was broken into two grades, chief and first class. This was to make it possible for a man to qualify in the lower grade with a good chance to rise to the upper one. Actually, when the lack of enough money made it necessary to keep the men in the lower pay grade, men aboard ship thought they would lose rather than gain by the change of duty and many preferred to stay where they thought themselves more certain of promotion.

Economy being the slogan of the time, numerous strictures had to be placed upon aviation training. The courses at the Massachusetts Institute of Technology, for instance, had to be transferred to universities where support by state funds made it possible to keep tuition rates lower. Similarly, schools at important centers like the Great Lakes and Newport had to be closed, while training at Hampton Roads and a dozen other stations was skeletonized. Nevertheless, Aeronautics did manage to continue the Photographers' School at Pensacola, reopened in 1926 after being closed for two years, and here under Chief Photographer W. L. Richardson a fine record was made. The students presently included not merely aerial but all naval photographers except those working in the Hydrographic Office or under the Office of Gunnery Exercises and Engineering Performance, and it was the graduates of this school who eventually formed the nucleus of Captain Pope's organization in World War II.

The school for instruction in the repair of aerial instruments was also kept open and a school for aviation ordnancemen was organized somewhat later. A course in aerology, supplementing the one at Anacostia, was squeezed in at Lakehurst, but Moffett was not so successful with a plan to establish a parachute school where training could be more thorough than was possible by using a handful of parachute experts scattered throughout the Fleet. Indeed, this lack of proper instructors for all the schools continued to be a major difficulty because the Navy's reduced personnel had not enough qualified men nor could it find inexperienced ones with backgrounds making them capable of being quickly converted into "experts" and then used to train others.

Since the act of 1926 had made no provision for additional personnel to meet the 1,000-plane program, and since the whole Navy was short of officers, it is remarkable that Moffett succeeded in getting as many as he did, lending good color to the claim of the Bureau of Navigation that Naval Aviation, on a percentage basis, was doing very well indeed. This claim was emphasized by a comment in the 1928 report of the Secretary of the Navy drawing attention to the loss of general efficiency resulting from shortage of personnel and ascribing this shortage "in large part to the growing demands of the air Navy." It was a fact that the number of officers in aviation, representing less than 2 per cent of the whole in 1916, had grown by 1928 to 11 per cent. At the later date enlisted personnel numbered 11,000, indicating that it had doubled during the preceding five years while the Navy as a whole was losing 2,000 men. Nevertheless, although this might make Naval Aviation appear a sort of leech upon the whole body, figures based upon plane building indicated that it would need, within the next five years, 950 more pilots. It was in the effort to approach such figures that the Secretary of the Navy again urged an increase in the allowance of midshipmen, and this time he did secure legislation raising the number of appointments to the Naval Academy allowed each senator and each representative from three to four. His recommendation that the Navy's complement of officers, then 4 per cent of its enlisted strength, be raised to 6 per cent was not, however, equally successful and this meant that it would be illegal, by 1932, to give commissions to more than one half the graduating midshipmen. Many able young men would have to be discharged and so lost to the Navy.

Meantime, Moffett urged Congress to lower the percentage of enlisted pilots, fixed at 30 by the act of 1926, to 20. The higher percentage, he declared, had the effect of putting enlisted men in charge of air operations which should be carried on by officers whose background and experience made them better able to cope with an emergency. This was true, even though the course for enlisted men had been broadened to cover subjects in which, as a rule, they were not well grounded; and when the effort to reduce the percentage of pilots failed Moffett seized upon a suggestion made by Rear Adm. Richard Leigh, by this time Chief of the Bureau of Navigation. This was a proposal that the quality of enlisted men reporting for instruction at Pensacola would be improved if they had already passed through a screening at the Hampton Roads or San Diego station. Leigh, like Moffett, believed that any lowering of standards would mean more pilots but not better ones, and the result of their agreement was a ten-hour elimination course at the two stations named. Those who passed this course went to Pensacola, while those who failed took ten weeks of training at Great Lakes followed by six months of aviation training afloat and, if finally found qualified, went to Pensacola in their turn. This was helpful, but before long a board headed by Capt. (later Commodore) Byron McCandless would again recommend, instead, the acceptance of special enlistments for aviation duty only. To this Moffett demurred because he was convinced that to establish these would bring into the regular Navy a number of men who would not otherwise wish to enlist but whose interest in flying might well make them enroll in the Aviation Reserve.

This Reserve was always in the forefront of Moffett's mind, and to promote its efficiency he had arranged that 50 ensigns should be ordered to active duty beginning in July, 1927. As these young men had been flying the old N-9, their discovery of the great difference in the newer planes was a strong indication of the need for bringing the training of reserves more up to date. Accordingly a "refresher course" was established at Pensacola, for reserve officers who could qualify, after taking it, as instructors of their fellows. In addition, more advanced courses lasting 60 days and including 100 hours of flying were established with the understanding that reserves who did well in these would become eligible for one year's active service with the Fleet. Still looking ahead, Moffett then got approval of a five-year program, to begin in 1930, which would eventually provide 12 reserve air bases and five additional training units. With these he hoped to produce 450 naval aviators and 1,100 enlisted men for the Navy, with about 200 officer pilots and 1,000 men for the Marine Corps. After review in ground school and other practical instruction at Squantum, Far Rockaway, Great Lakes, or Sand Point, the student fliers were given 18 hours of flight training, followed by eight months at Pensacola, during which they must spend 215 hours in the air and after which they were commissioned and sent to the Fleet. To administer this program and to serve as his adviser on problems of the Reserve, Moffett arranged for the recall to active duty of Lieut. (later Rear Adm.) I. M. McQuiston, a World War I pilot who had been a moving spirit in the establishment of the base at Squantum. Before reporting to Moffett on May 31, 1930, McQuiston, without pay and wholly at his own expense, spent six months with the Fleet to catch up with the latest developments. Encouraged by Moffett and his successors as Chief of the Bureau of Aeronautics, this patriotic reserve officer, through the following years, made an invaluable contribution toward building that reserve organization which was to play so mighty a part in the victories of the next war.

At Pensacola it became very difficult to meet the demands of an expanding program for both the regular Navy and the Reserve. Plans for handling two classes a year were changed to provide for four classes, but this resulted in the complication that two student groups might both be ready for flight training when only one squadron of planes was available for both. Moreover, the four classes laid an uneven burden upon instructors, who were over-worked in one period, almost idle in the next; and this was over-come only by adopting a system under which 50 new students re-ported each month. Another improvement was an increase in the number of training squadrons from three to five, permitting two of these to handle elementary training while the other three gave instruction in large seaplanes, gunnery, and bombing; in spotting ships' gunfire; and in air combat tactics. As rapidly as possible commissioned pilots of the regular Navy were detailed as instruc-tors to replace enlisted men or officers of the Reserve, and this had a good effect. Relations between instructors and students were im-proved, and training proceeded more smoothly.

By this time relatively little weight was placed upon training "observers." Originally it had been expected that this duty would be generally confined to older officers who might in other respects be eligible for administrative aviation commands, but Moffett con-sidered it better for such officers to have had pilot training. Seeking older officers with "sufficient . . . experience to . . . administer commands, including aircraft carriers," he held that these should have had actual flying but only enough to enable them to see and understand what was being accomplished; and this, in his opinion, they should get from the 100 hours in the air required of them by existing law during their six months' course.

During this same period several efforts were made to provide technical training that would keep aviators up to date in that re-spect. The Chief of the Bureau of Navigation did not support Moffett in the view that new schools were necessary in design and maintenance, or in such elements of airship flying as fuel gases, refrigeration and water-ballast recovery, and the special care re-quired in storing or transporting helium. Instead, it was Leigh's view that the courses in aeronautical engineering already being given at the Navy's postgraduate schools were sufficient to round out the Naval Academy curriculum; but in the fall of 1927 Moffett did get authority to establish a three months' review course in motors and maintenance to which officers who had finished the ordinary postgraduate course could be sent. In operation for about a year, this school produced a few officers whose practical knowledge became of great assistance to Fleet air squadrons.

As it was daily becoming evident that aerology demanded more than the little time that could be given to it by the ordinary student with many other duties, a new plan was made for this. A few officers received special instruction in the science at Harvard or at the Massachusetts Institute of Technology, supplementing this by one summer at the postgraduate school in Annapolis and a second summer in Washington at the Weather Bureau, the Hydrographic Office, the Naval Observatory, and the air station in Anacostia. Altogether some 24 officers completed these courses to become expert aerologists.

Since 1925 the various departments at the Naval Academy concerned with subjects in any way related to aviation had introduced one phase of it or another into their courses, with the assistance of five aviators of the regular Navy specifically assigned to that duty. Ground-school subjects were supplemented by flight instruction and one half of the academy class of 1926 got 11 hours of flying in World War I types, the H-16 and the F-5-L, before graduation, while the other half got the same amount in the summer after graduation. Because this new training cut into the summer cruise or into time otherwise available for leave, many midshipmen thought that aviation was being thrust upon them and this created a poor general impression of that type of duty. At the same time, it was costing the Fleet half a squadron of fliers, sent to Annapolis in the season best suited to Fleet maneuvers; but this objection was overcome in 1929 by creating a special squadron permanently based at the academy to give instruction in spring and fall. The Bureau of Navigation, however, continued to look with a disapproving eye upon flight training for midshipmen, contending that they would get this training at the San Diego or Hampton Roads stations where they all had to go during their first year of sea duty. Their instruction at these stations was designed to give them all a general idea of what Naval Aviation was doing in the Fleet, but it was also planned to give experienced aviators a chance to detect and eliminate those unfitted for flying. On the whole, the tour appears to have had the effect of inspiring a good many to request assignment to Pensacola, but Moffett contended that their enthusiasm would fade if they were required to finish two years at sea before being given that assignment. Either send them to Pensacola as soon as they graduated, said he, or else let them get through the two years before taking to the air at all. After considerable effort he secured a brief trial of immediate assignment upon graduation, with the astonishing result that 238 members of the class graduating in 1930 volunteered for Pensacola and, among these, 186 were found qualified, a number doubling that drawn from the class graduating in 1926.

CHAPTER XXV

Aviation in the Fleet Exercises

QUITE apart from the growing enthusiasm among the midshipmen, many of the Navy's best older minds were becoming more occupied by aircraft and carriers. In the Fleet exercises of 1927 and 1928 the good use made of the *Langley* and her planes again demonstrated the vulnerability of the Panama Canal to air attack and also showed the vital importance of providing air cover for all convoys as well as for the battle line. Little by little the progress of the 1,000-plane building program was making it possible to supply, to ships of the various types, up-to-date aircraft with which war conditions could be more closely simulated. Finally, in January, 1929, came the moment when the *Lexington* and *Saratoga*, after "shakedown" cruises in which each had given an excellent performance, were ready to join the Fleet, to replace "constructive" carriers and make it possible to prove or disprove what had so long been mere hypothesis.

As the war games of 1929 began, it was assumed that hostilities had been in progress for some months. Adm. William V. Pratt was in the Pacific in command of the Black, or attacking force, which consisted of the Battle Fleet, a group of submarines, a supply train and, as originally planned, the *Saratoga* and the *Langley*. When it appeared that the latter ship would not complete her overhaul in time, the *Aroostook* was substituted, her one plane representing the *Langley's* squadron of 24. This force was about to attack the Canal, defended by the Blue Fleet under Vice Adm. Montgomery Taylor. Blue, concentrated in the Atlantic, was the Scouting Force, its submarines and supply train, and the *Lexington*, with the support of the army forces at the Canal, including 37 planes, and the naval defense force of the 15th Naval District with 12 more planes. Some of Blue's force was beginning the westward transit of the Canal at the instant when the game began.

Admiral Pratt had 116 aircraft, while Admiral Taylor had 145, the total representing by far the largest assembly of aircraft in any exercise up to that time. As the inferior in planes, Pratt based his plan upon avoiding air attack on his carriers and upon the probability that the Canal's defense against air attack would not be very effective. Accordingly he ordered the *Aroostook's* "squadron" to attack the Atlantic end of the Canal while the *Saratoga*, sweeping south of the main body, was to launch her planes against the Pacific end in time to make the two attacks simultaneous. He was of course aware that the *Aroostook's* squadron would be so far from its mother ship that it would not have enough fuel to return to her, but he counted upon that very fact as a reason for the attack being a surprise one and gave orders that the "squadron" should push home its bombing, then land on the beach and surrender.

On the morning of January 24 the main force of Blue, made up of a battleship division, the *Lexington*, and a squadron of destroyers, was 280 miles out from Panama when its scouts located Black. As the *Lexington* began launching her planes, the clearing weather revealed a Black battleship division within 30,000 yards, which meant that the carrier was under fire until the range closed to 16,000, when a squall obscured her. Very probably actual shooting would have sunk her but the umpires ruled her authorized to proceed at the reduced speed of 18 knots and permitted her to launch two air attacks against Black.

Meanwhile the *Saratoga*, with the cruiser *Omaha*, had continued south to reach position for her planned attack next day. On her way she disposed of a Blue destroyer but the Blue cruiser *Detroit* tracked her through the night and reported her position. The *Lexington*, dispatched by Admiral Taylor to the attack, found her prescribed slow speed such a handicap that she could not make contact. By next morning the *Saratoga* was in position to send in flights of 17 dive bombers, 17 torpedo bombers, 32 fighters, and three planes especially equipped for communications, all of which arrived over their target without interference. The lone Sikorsky launched from the *Aroostook*, perhaps because it was one plane and not the squadron Blue might be hunting, reached the Atlantic end of the Canal and carried out its orders exactly. Theoretically, the simultaneous bombings blew up the Miraflores and Pedro Miguel locks and damaged the air fields at Fort Clayton and Albright. Nine defending army fighters came up from these fields but they were hopelessly outnumbered and the *Saratoga's* planes returned to her with only one technical loss. As they were landing on her deck, however, Blue bombers from the *Lexington* came in, and the returning planes were unable to make adequate counterattack. Later the *Saratoga* and *Omaha*, while attempting to join their main body, instead met Blue's battleship division and came under heavy fire. The record indicates that the *Saratoga* was not sunk, however, for the next day saw her planes covering those of the main body, which were spotting a bombardment of the Canal. Her fighters went inland and had a brush with land-based Blue bombers just as the latter took off for what they thought was a bombing run over the *Saratoga* but which turned out to be over their own ship, the *Lexington*. Meanwhile the *Saratoga*, by that time defended only by her own guns, came under heavy attack by army bombers but was saved by the official ending of the exercises.

Although there were some unfortunate breaks in radio communication between planes, and several instances in which friend and foe had been mistaken for one another, the essential lesson was plain enough. Admiral Pratt's bold gamble had given carrier aircraft their first real opportunity and good advantage of this had been taken. The fast carrier for which Mustin, Whiting, and others had pleaded now occupied so definite a place that all existing plans for future war at sea must be revised to provide for it. Even those who still regarded the battleship as the chief factor of Fleet actions could not but admit the striking power of a properly handled air force, both offensively and defensively; and the report of Adm. Henry Wiley, Commander in Chief, emphasized the impossibility of beating off air attacks, either upon ships or upon the coastlines, with anything but stronger aircraft. The admiral also stressed the Fleet's need for numerous small carriers to replace the cruisers as scouts, a need made apparent by the difficulty with which the cruisers, during the exercises, recovered their returning planes. If any further argument was necessary, this was furnished by the exercises of 1930 in which the *Lexington's* planes, this time numbered with the "attackers," scored heavily against the defending battleships to show how suddenly command of the air might be seized and how much this command must affect the outcome of an action.

These 1930 exercises brought up for particular study the "carrier group," then for the first time defined as a complete tactical unit consisting, for example, of one carrier, four cruisers, and two destroyer squadrons. Vice Adm. Carey Cole, commanding the defending ships in the game, raised several questions. Even with its

great mobility, he asked, could such a group avoid attack by surface ships? Could it, especially at night, escape its enemy's torpedoes? What were its full possibilities as a means of reducing
enemy strength before a major engagement, or as a means of holding control of the air long enough for its support to arrive and
make that control complete? To all these questions Rear Adm.
Frank Brumby, commander of the attacking aircraft, gave answers wholly in favor of the air arm, and he urged the formation
of numerous carrier groups, to be trained for independent but
simultaneous attacks ahead of their supporting Battle Fleet.

In 1931 the games began with the assumption that "a Pacific
power" was attacking both the Panama Canal and a hypothetical
Nicaragua Canal at a moment when the United States was doubtful about the neutrality of "a European power." This made it necessary to keep part of the United States Fleet off New England but
it left the two big carriers with the defenders in the south. The conditions and the course of the game were such that both carriers
almost exhausted their fuel and thus became only 50 per cent effective against attackers who were able to land in two places and
establish air fields. Rear Admiral Reeves, commanding the striking
force, was moved to comment that "the air force cannot stop the
advance of battleships and prevent them from . . . landing," but
he did add that ships and planes were "mutually dependent," and
he admitted that the planes would "directly affect battleship design in the matter of maximum gun-range . . . by means of airplane spotting." Admiral Pratt, by this time ashore as Chief of
Naval Operations, found it "the consensus . . . that air attack
as a means of defense against approaching fleets is of less value
than had been expected," while Adm. F. H. Schofield, commenting
strongly upon the lack of effective methods of refueling carriers
at sea, was also inclined to doubt the effectiveness of planes. The
latter, however, when assignment as chief umpire of a later exercise gave him the opportunity to witness what he described as a
"beautifully coordinated attack" upon the *Saratoga* by planes
from the *Lexington*, modified his earlier views and called air operations "a demonstration of efficient training and of excellent material."

An important feature of this efficient training had been demonstrated by the dive bombers in attacks against the radio-controlled
Stoddert and the destroyers *Marcus* and *Sloat*. The vulnerability
of such small craft became particularly plain when they were

raked from close overhead with 50-caliber machine guns, whose shots penetrated decks and bulkheads; when 30-pound demolition bombs smashed searchlights, boats, and torpedo tubes. The conclusion was that bomber attacks, delivered with the viciousness of which the Navy's pilots were now capable, could be stopped only by much better shooting from many more antiaircraft guns than were then mounted by small or even by larger ships. Along similar lines, the effect of aircraft upon the operations of submarines was also made apparent when the subs, necessarily surfacing when they had scouting information to report by radio, found themselves promptly set upon by planes diving as falcons stoop to sparrows. Here were more problems on the relation of planes to ships.

Rear Admiral Yarnell, whose opinion gained weight as advancing rank broadened his responsibilities and emphasized his professional standing, took an active part in the study of the use of aircraft. After he had commanded the Blue aircraft in the 1932 games, he urged the importance to the Fleet of more carriers. He estimated that any plan to operate across the Pacific would necessitate the Fleet's having at least six, if not eight carriers of the large type, in order to launch, from far out at sea, air attacks upon an enemy's shore bases of such severity as would force his ships out into a decisive action. Against his view was that of others who favored building many small carriers because the loss of one or two would have less effect upon command of the air, and these differing opinions led to further discussions of the best way to protect carriers, large or small.

The cruisers built at this time under the Washington Treaty requirements were certainly stronger guards than any destroyers could be but they were not at all satisfactory in their means for handling their own planes. In 1930, when Moffett had arrived in London as one of the delegates to the conference called at the end of the first ten years of "disarmament," he had found great interest displayed in the flight-deck cruiser, and the agreement finally reached had permitted the United States to build eight of these, at 10,000 tons each, provided none was adapted "exclusively as an aircraft carrier." It was the consensus that carriers were fully provided for in the 135,000 tons which the United States, after some argument no doubt based largely upon the ground that it had utterly failed to build up to the old treaty strength, was permitted to keep as its allowance. This restriction on cruiser-carriers was particularly disappointing to the Bureau of Aeronautics because Moffett at that very moment had in his desk the plans for a 30-knot cruiser, armed with half a dozen six-inch guns and eight five-inch antiaircraft guns, and fitted to carry from 30 to 50 planes. Even if there were some delicacy about describing such ships as "cruisers" rather than as "carriers," Moffett wanted seven of them included in the building program; but the General Board would agree to no more than one flight-deck cruiser, recommending that the rest be as originally designed under the treaty of 1922 and demanding, instead, the building of another small carrier. Since even this recommendation came to nothing, the *Ranger*, as finally laid down in 1931 and commissioned three years later, remained the only carrier of her size in the Fleet.

Few though they were, the carriers afforded the pilots considerable experience, some of it of the most practical kind. For example, in 1931 the *Lexington* had been on hand for the Nicaragua earthquake, to fly doctors, nurses, medical supplies, and food into the devastated areas. This was very necessary support for the effort of the Marine Corps, whose experience during four years of operations, from a dozen fields in Nicaragua built by themselves, ranged from the battle of Ocotal, July 17, 1927, said to be the first occasion when dive bombers were used against troops, to the carrying of mails, money, and wounded. This cooperation between the marines and the carriers led, within the year, to the regular assignment of Marine Squadrons VS-14M and VS-15M to the *Lexington* and *Saratoga*, flying the O2U-1 plane, first of the Corsair series.

Progress of this kind was the cause of favorable comment like Schofield's, and the advent of the P2Y, forerunner of the famous "Catalina" flying boat, was similarly hailed. So, too, was the improvement of the turntable catapult which made it possible to launch different types of planes in succession, without changing gear for each type. On the other hand, too many planes, such as the patrol types that could make only 75 knots, were fast becoming obsolete without any provision for replacing them by newer types in sufficient numbers. This, however, was not a sudden development; in fact the Bureau of Aeronautics had become acutely aware of it as early as the period immediately following the business crash of 1929.

When President Hoover, on November 12 of that disastrous year, proposed that government funds might relieve some of the nationwide unemployment if applied to building for the Navy, Moffett had been extremely optimistic. He had immediately submitted a plan calling for $54,000,000 for Aeronautics, not to be used for carriers but for helium tanks and cars, radio equipment, navigational instruments, general supplies, and, particularly, for an airship base on the West coast. At the same time he had urged larger appropriations for planes for the *Ranger* and for a sister ship then not even authorized. As plans, these were good, but they ran bow on into the difficulties of securing sufficient funds during those first three years of depression. An estimate submitted by the Bureau of Aeronautics in May, 1930, was promptly cut by the Navy's budget officer from $53,000,000 to $35,000,000 and it was only after the most vigorous protest from Moffet that $3,000,000 was finally added to this reduced figure. Much the same fate met numerous requests from Aeronautics that the new aircraft, which would be needed when the *Ranger* and eight new cruisers joined the Fleet but which had not been covered in the original five-year program, be separately provided. In the end these planes were found only by reducing the patrol plane quotas assigned to the Fleet air bases at Coco Solo and Pearl Harbor, as well as those assigned the Asiatic Fleet. The smaller size of the planes consequently purchased had the effect of making a very considerable saving in the cost of the five-year program, but this, too, tended to underline the question as to what Congress had originally intended by the 1,000-plane figure. Was it to be the upper limit of the naval air arm or was it merely a figure from which the size of that arm could be determined as more ships went into commission and as new uses for planes appeared? This was a question not to be fully answered for years.

Appropriations for the next fiscal year offered proof of the want of a real answer. Under a change in the procedure for making preliminary estimates, providing that the Navy's budget officer allocate specific sums to each of the several bureaus, Aeronautics was asked to keep its figures inside $32,000,000. Moffett was quick to point out that this would give him, for 1932, less than had been appropriated for 1931, even though more planes were expected to be in commission. It would also mean further cuts in experimental work, already so seriously restricted by reducing funds that once represented 15 per cent of Aeronautics' total to a mere 6 per cent. Describing the way in which such a reduction was causing the United States to lose ground internationally, David Ingalls, Assistant Secretary of the Navy for Air since March, 1929, compared the progress of a few years earlier, when American planes capable of 265 miles an hour were the fastest in the world, with the current

moment when British and Italian planes, reaching speeds as high
as 330 miles, were making United States fighters obsolete. To the
previous adequacy of funds for invention, experiment, and improvement he properly attributed the advances made in a long list
of devices and types of equipment, such as air-cooled motors, super-
chargers, reduction gears, magnetos, and spark plugs; telephones,
radio and steering compasses, direction indicators, and drift
computers; safety belts, life jackets, and parachutes; machine-gun
sights, bomb racks, and gear for smoke screens; and, most important, arresting gear for flight decks. Without proper appropriations, he insisted, there could be no real advances in these or
in a dozen other elements of aviation in the Navy.

Notwithstanding such protests, appropriations continued to be
too small to cover all that Moffett had hoped to accomplish. For
example, the air stations, none too generously treated in the best
of times, now lagged far behind in what was needed if they were to
handle technical advances and to provide landing fields, hangars,
and barracks in proper ratio to the total number of planes. Under
the Employment Stabilization Act of February 10, 1931, the
Navy's Board for Development of Navy Yard Plans had prepared
a new schedule for improving these stations, but the humble beginnings made were blocked by reductions in regular appropriations
during the Hoover administration and the first months of the
Roosevelt administration. The two bases, at St. Louis and at Opa-
locka, Florida, added during this period were financed principally
by their local municipalities and not by federal funds. Only the
work at the new West coast airship base at Sunnyvale, California,
selected long before by a board headed by Moffett himself, made
real progress.

Current plans for future plane building were further complicated by a revival of the old questions dealing with the legality of
various methods of procurement, and the whole matter of competitive bidding as opposed to negotiated contracts was again discussed
from every viewpoint. In an effort to end the arguments, Moffett
made a statement deliberately designed to be a little ambiguous,
in which he suggested that the act of 1926, upon the whole satisfactory to all concerned, should not be amended while economic
conditions continued to be unsatisfactory, particularly because relations between Aeronautics and the aircraft industry were too
good to risk upsetting them by new legislation. Thus the status quo
was preserved for several years, permitting the completion of the

1,000-plane program ahead of the scheduled date. The final cost was less, by about $26,000,000, than had been estimated but, as was suggested earlier in this chapter, much of this saving should be attributed to the substitution of smaller, less costly, carrier-type planes for the patrol planes originally planned. No doubt industry could have used those additional millions because, as Moffett pointed out in his report for 1931, the building program for the Army and the Navy had been designed, in part, to keep industry on its feet until civilian demand for aircraft increased, and this increase had not come.

In addition to all the problems of building aircraft during this period, there remained the problem of how they were to be used; that is, how the Army and the Navy were to divide air responsibilities in national defense. The Joint Board, already described in these pages as composed of high-ranking officers of both Army and Navy assembled as policy makers, and considered of such importance that it was referred to in official documents as The Joint Board, had reviewed this distribution of responsibility during its study of the recommendations of the Morrow Board. In 1927 this board had issued a publication entitled *Joint Action of the Army and the Navy,* which made it the first task of the Army's air arm to operate with mobile ground forces while the Navy's air arm operated with the Fleet. In the coastal area, this paper left it to the Navy's aircraft to "support . . . local naval defense forces operating for the protection of lines of sea communication and coastal zones against attacks by hostile submarines or surface raiders," and left it to the Army's aircraft to defend cities, harbors, and munition plants in United States territory. It was also specified that in emergency either air arm was required to act "in support of or in lieu of" the other. This appeared a reasonable division but there was still contention between the Army and the Navy as to the latter's use of land-based torpedo planes, the Army claiming that such use was not in strict accordance with the "Joint Action" paper, the Navy holding that it was. This naturally led to arguments over the type of planes being built and The Joint Board took more than a year, from May, 1927, to October, 1928, to decide that there was no duplication of building in the two five-year programs.

This decision did not satisfy either Army or Navy and further arguments followed on the legality of earlier legislation. Specifically, there was long discussion of the Army Appropriation Act of 1920 which had given the Army control of land-based planes while the Navy, operating its planes with the Fleet, was to limit its shore bases to those needed for experimentation, construction, training, maintenance and repair, or support of Fleet operations. The Attorney General, asked to rule upon the legality of this act, spent six months in correspondence with the Secretary of War and the Secretary of the Navy and finally, in January, 1930, concluded that he had no jurisdiction. This was unfortunate, especially because the Navy's announcement in November, 1929, that it would base torpedo planes ashore at Coco Solo and Pearl Harbor had sent the Secretary of War hurrying to the White House. He wanted the President to issue an executive order limiting the Navy's land-based aircraft so severely that it would have made it impossible for the Navy to get any additional land-based types, and also to stop further expansion of the Marine Corps air arm. Strong language appeared in the resulting letters from both sides, with neither proposing anything agreeable to the other. The Navy wanted to follow the assignment of missions first proposed in 1917, amended in 1920, and again amended in the "Joint Action" just cited, while the Army still wanted an order changing these assignments to something in closer accord with what it believed were the traditional missions of the Army in coast defense. Neither side would give way, but in the autumn of 1930 the normal course of rotation brought to the high commands other officers who had new points of view.

Admiral Pratt, relieved as Commander in Chief of the United States Fleet, succeeded Adm. Charles F. Hughes as Chief of Naval Operations. In addition to the coastal defense controversy, he was immediately confronted with the problem of reducing the Navy, in accord with the recent London Treaty, without sacrificing national security. Concluding that reduced strength made mobility vital, he began reorganizing the Fleet to put all its components, including aircraft wherever based, under the direct control of its commander in chief. In reorganization he saw a possibility of solving the coastal defense question and, with this in view, issued the Naval Air Operating Policy, to become effective on April 1, 1931. While he admitted that many of the Navy's aviators might disagree, he used the military man's belief that "if you can take the offensive and keep it, it is far wiser than to assume the defensive at once," and declared it to be undesirable to keep any part of the Fleet waiting for the enemy to approach; that is, in defending the coast. Seeking a fleet "able to move quickly . . . with all its forces intact," he

considered that the air arm, as part of these forces, must be organized with the Fleet.

Admitting that situations developing in war might require special assignments of the air arm, the admiral said his was a peacetime measure, making it the primary task of Naval Aviation to develop the offensive power of the Fleet and of advanced base forces,
with the secondary task of providing for the defense of important
areas "if and when required." Mobility for aircraft was to be
achieved through carriers and tenders, such craft as might be assigned to Pearl Harbor and Coco Solo to be patrol types with
long range, attached to the Fleet and respectively under the commanders of Minecraft, Battle Force and Aircraft, Scouting Force.
Continental air stations were to be operated under the limitations
just noted as provided by the Army Appropriations Act of 1920.
Permanent overseas bases were to be for these purposes and for any
required cooperation with the Army in local defense, while overseas stations of "advance" type would be built only to meet actual
war requirements. Procurement of heavier-than-air types would
be limited to the needs of Fleet operations and of Marine Expeditionary Forces; of lighter-than-air types to what might be required to determine military value to the Fleet and for training.

All this appeared to make many concessions to the War Department's views, but Pratt considered this of little importance when
compared with what the new plan provided in the way of a fleet that
would meet its responsibilities. In January, 1931, he met Gen.
Douglas MacArthur, Chief of Staff since October, and reached an
agreement under which the Navy's air arm no longer had any burden of coast defense but operated only on its own side of a line
dividing it from the activities of the Army's air arm by respective
mission rather than by geography. The General Board, while it
supported Pratt's plan to make the air arm a part of the Fleet's
offensive strength, strongly disapproved leaving any feature of
coast defense open to further decision after actual war began. It
also held that to relinquish the Navy's claim to coastal defense
might have the effect of losing congressional support of the Navy's
shore stations and that Pratt's announced policy should be revised
to claim the coastal areas for the Navy. As far as the Army Air
Corps' continued aggression was concerned, the General Board was
right; the corps continued to seek control of all air stations ashore
even though the Navy stubbornly insisted that many of these, per-
forming naval functions, should remain under the Navy. This con-

tinuing controversy led to the introduction into Congress of numerous new bills designed either to merge the two air arms or to create a wholly separate department of the air under its own Cabinet officer. During 1932, an effort to add a rider to the appropriation bill, creating a central department of defense to include all military and naval branches, was very nearly passed.

Moffett had naturally played an active part in all these controversies but he had still found time to devote to airships, a field in which most of the contemporary progress had been made by the *Los Angeles*. During her comparatively long life she did well, making more than 300 flights and "keeping the air" for well over 5,000 hours in all. In 1931 she established a record for endurance by staying away from Lakehurst for 625 consecutive hours, maintaining herself at mooring masts scattered throughout the country. Almost everywhere in the United States she was a familiar sight in the sky, but when she went to the Caribbean for Fleet maneuvers she was not so successful. Although, as a part of the defending forces, she made numerous scouting flights and succeeded in picking up the enemy, she was herself discovered and almost immediately "destroyed by enemy planes." Vice Adm. A. L. Willard, under whom she served as a scout, commended her work and reported that rigid airships, when further improved, should be the source of much valuable information at the risk of relatively few lives, but his view was not generally supported. Schofield, for one, was strongly in "opposition to the proposed development of rigid dirigibles," finding their cost "out of proportion" and their "appeal to the imagination . . . not sustained by their military usefulness"; in substance, the more general opinion. After eight years of service, at least four more than had been expected, the *Los Angeles* was decommissioned at Lakehurst in 1932. Even then—although this was not suspected at the time—her retirement was to be only temporary.

She had been responsible for numerous advances, among them the important discovery that cellophane would serve to make gasbags quite as reliable as the far more expensive ones of goldbeater's skin. Handling her at her hangar had greatly improved the methods used by ground crews, and she had furnished many opportunities for experimenting with aerodynamic loads. Much that had been learned from her had been used in the development of the ZMC-2, the only metal-clad blimp built for the Navy and actually a rigid but, because she operated on the "pressure principle," classified as nonrigid; a 200,000-cubic-foot craft of aluminum-alloy sheets riveted together. Moffett described her as "purely . . . experimental . . . intended to test the practicability of the novel type of construction," and she did show unusual durability. She lost no more gas than did the average fabric-covered ship but her directional control, especially in rough weather or at low speeds, was not all that had been hoped of it. As the result of these studies and conclusions, contracts for the design and engineering analysis of similar craft were subsequently made, but no other was ever actually built.

The other nonrigid of the period was the K-class blimp, built as a training ship and important because she represented the first United States airship built to use gaseous instead of liquid fuel, an improvement adopted from experiments with the *Graf Zeppelin*. Gas was more efficient as a fuel and had the advantage of a density equal to that of air; hence gas consumption did not alter the ship's buoyancy, and the need to "valve" gas or to condense water from the exhaust was eliminated. Since the gas was carried in fuel cells inserted in the helium cells, there was no danger of fire. At the time of her first use she was considered to be too large for a nonrigid but she was actually smaller by a quarter than the K-2 type which saw so much service during World War II. Like the *Los Angeles*, the K-1 had about eight years of life.

These were matters of the greatest interest to Moffett; but a still more important event was just ahead. With the possible exception of Comdr. C. E. Rosendahl, survivor of the *Shenandoah* tragedy, passenger in the *Graf Zeppelin* on a world-tour, and destined to be the vice admiral commanding all lighter-than-air services in World War II, no one was as impatient as Moffett for the arrival of October 27, 1931. This date marked not only the annual Navy Day but also the commissioning of the *Akron*, the very latest in huge airships. When completed she was some ten tons over her designed weight, but her early trials and the routine flights that followed were highly successful. Because of a few relatively small injuries she was not able to take her expected part in the Fleet exercises of her first year, but she did make a flight across the continent to moor at the new Sunnyvale base. By the end of March, 1933, she had made 73 flights totaling almost 1,700 air hours. The last 15 of these flights were under Comdr. Frank C. McCord, an experienced airship officer, with a seasoned crew. When she left Lakehurst, in the early evening of April 3, 1933, to assist in calibrating radio direction finders in the New England area, there was nothing to disturb her but a little fog.

Rising through the fog, in a very light breeze, she headed for Philadelphia and, nearing that city a little after eight o'clock, she turned down the Delaware River toward the sea. By ten o'clock, near Barnegat Light, she ran into heavy lightning, with flashes around and above her at an altitude of about 1,600 feet. Because of this storm she changed course a number of times but appeared to be acting normally until soon after midnight, when she began to fall rapidly. Prompt valving of ballast checked her and then she rose almost as fast, to level off again at 1,600 feet. A few minutes later a heavy gust struck her with stunning force, the lower rudder-control rope snapped, to be followed almost at once by the upper control rope. She could no longer be steered, but by speeding up her engines she was steadied for a moment, only to begin falling once more, this time entirely out of control and with her nose well up. Plunging into the sea tail first, she broke in half, sank, and took with her 18 officers and 55 men. Only one officer and two men lived to be rescued by the merchant steamer *Phoebus*.

The Navy could not afford to lose any of those lives, least of all that of the *Akron's* ranking passenger, Moffett himself. It was ironical that he who had done more than anyone else to bring about the continuation of the lighter-than-air program should die in an airship, but there were stronger reasons than that for deploring his loss. For 12 years, under four different administrations, he had been Chief of the Bureau of Aeronautics, studying its problems, fighting for its advances, and accepting each gain merely as a step toward higher standards and greater accomplishments. To every effort to improve flying in the Navy he had given all his shrewd diplomacy, his energy, his keen sense of humor, and his unwearying youthfulness of spirit. All these were not easily to be spared by the Navy, but those who remember him will agree that he must have met death, as he had always met life, with a high heart.

CHAPTER XXVI

The Beginning of Expansion

IN that spring of 1933 there can have been but few Americans who anticipated the entry of the United States into another world war. Even if such prophets existed, not one of them would have predicted that the war would see the Navy's two top posts—Chief of Naval Operations, who must supervise both the Navy's plans for battle and its assembly of vast munitions, and Commander in Chief of the Fleet, who must direct the Navy's whole fighting effort—combined in a single individual, Ernest J. King. The Navy itself was not that farsighted, but at least the Navy had long known King as a most able seaman and aviator, as an officer of hard-driving incisiveness who would hold forever the courage of his convictions. He was only a rear admiral, with his pre-eminence still far ahead on May 3, 1933, when he became Chief of the Bureau of Aeronautics; but all hands could be confident that he would maintain the high standards for Naval Aviation established by Moffett. In the next three years that confidence would be fully justified, and through a fortunate combination of circumstances expectations would be exceeded, because President Roosevelt added to his enthusiastic interest in the Navy a warm personal regard for King.

From the very outset King's efforts were materially helped by the President's seeing to it that liberal allocations from the huge sums appropriated from the National Recovery and the Public Works Administrations were made to the Navy. Thus the severe cuts in aviation's estimates inflicted by the Bureau of the Budget could be healed by money from these outside sources; a treatment so effective that the sum total for fiscal 1934 finally rose to about $30,000,000 or approximately what Moffett had at first recommended for that year. Moreover, this was in addition to other millions similarly allocated for the purpose of building carriers.

It was high time something was done about carriers. Of the five 23,000-ton ships recommended by the General Board in the middle twenties not one had been built, and of the five 13,800-tonners later called for only the *Ranger* had been authorized. Launched on February 25, 1933, she would be commissioned a year later on June 4, but good ship though she proved to be, she could hardly be sufficient support for the big *Saratoga* and *Lexington*. Even before she was finished the General Board had decided upon 20,000 tons as the most useful size carrier and two of these were recommended for the 1934 program. Thanks to money received from the Public Works Administration, it became possible to lay them both down—the *Yorktown* on May 21, 1934, the *Enterprise* a few weeks later, on July 16.

Meanwhile Congress had been considering the so-called Vinson-Trammell Bill, authorizing the building of a Navy truly commensurate with the provisions of the London Treaty of 1930. As originally written, the bill was not specific as to aircraft, but that staunch supporter of the Navy, Representative Carl Vinson of Georgia, at the last moment inserted a clause "to secure the necessary naval aircraft for vessels and for other purposes." The language was made general at the suggestion of Lewis D. Douglas, then Director of the Budget, who fortunately foresaw that to fix a definite figure, as had been done in the legislation establishing the 1,000-plane program, might make the new law difficult to modify later. As finally passed, on March 27, 1934, the act permitted the Bureau of Aeronautics to add about 650 planes to the 1,000-plane program without worry over an exact limit.

This was more helpful than a provision of the same act establishing 10 per cent as the top profit permitted manufacturers working under contract with the Navy, because it aroused in a few builders, such as Boeing, a tendency to prefer army contracts in which no such limit was fixed. Also, some difficulty resulted from another provision, that at least one tenth of all planes and all engines must be built at the Naval Air Factory, because the factory had neither adequate equipment nor trained personnel to build engines. Fortunately there was a clause giving the President discretion in this particular matter, and he shortly directed that the engine building be stopped. All these procedures being merely authorized by the Vinson-Trammell Act, the necessary funds were duly provided in the Emergency Appropriations Act of June 9, 1934.

When even this act did not cover the cost of all that the Bureau of Aeronautics needed, further allotments were made from NIRA, WPA, and PWA; the Aircraft Factory, for example, received an

additional $3,000,000 with which to broaden its researches and ex-
periments, as well as to accelerate building the N3N-1 plane, then
considered best for training purposes. Through the active help of
the National Advisory Committee for Aeronautics, and through a
steady exchange of ideas with the Army Air Corps, Army Ordnance, the Bureau of Standards, and all other departments concerned, it became possible to make considerable progress in the
study of aerodynamics and kindred subjects.

Consequently this was a period that saw the development of numerous planes destined to give valiant service after 1941. These
types were provided with new airfoils, new engines that produced
higher speeds, new high-lift devices, improved qualities for taking
off and landing and, in carrier planes, with a longer cruising radius.
The Bureau of Aeronautics, "considering that the striking power
of scouting airplanes . . . on carriers must be increased," developed the VSB class, having all the virtues of the scout and also
capable of carrying a 500-pound bomb and launching it in a diving
attack. Since flying boats were also given greater endurance and
higher load capacity, and since there was contemporary improvement in instruments for all planes, progress during the period was
distinct.

At the same time, for the very plausible reason that many naval
air stations lay in areas where the relief of local unemployment was
of particular importance, there began an expenditure upon these
long-neglected spots of various sums from the Public Works Administration. Over the years ahead, extending as far as 1939, a total
of about $36,000,000 from this source would go into longer run-
ways with improved floodlighting, larger hangars, better living
quarters, more adequate shops with newer machinery. Upward of
30 stations appear to have benefited, those at which expenditure
reached over a million dollars including Lakehurst, Pensacola,
Seattle, San Pedro, San Diego, and the Naval Aircraft Factory.

While these improvements were in progress some changes in air
stations resulted from a new study, made in 1933, of the old question of duplication in the Navy's fields and the Army's, often side
by side. Examples were Anacostia and Bolling, San Diego and
Rockwell, Pearl Harbor and Luke, Coco Solo and France, where
facilities on adjoining properties had never been sufficient for either
and where each was ready to encroach upon the other. Each of
these pairs was studied independently but the reports on all agreed
that the collaboration which already existed in certain operations

should be extended to all, without however *combining* the operations. Not satisfied that these reports constituted a solution of the duplication problem, the Secretary of War and the Secretary of the Navy submitted to the President a joint proposal which he approved in an executive order dated October 26, 1935. Under this order the Army gave the Navy Rockwell Field in exchange for Sunnyvale, where it agreed not to erect any buildings that might interfere with the Navy's airships. Further, the Army was directed to vacate the area it was occupying on Ford Island as soon as space could be found elsewhere. Finally, the order specified that the Bolling-Anacostia area should be given new "metes and bounds acceptable to the Army and the Navy," whereupon the premises should be occupied by the Navy. Such changes in allocation, coupled with the improvements carried on, gave the air stations what amounted to a new lease on life, especially as they began receiving impressive increases in their allowances of planes as the old, slow building program was replaced by one which would rise steadily to an annual figure of over 700 planes.

This extensive building was not accomplished without a revival of the debate over the various kinds of naval contracts, chiefly as to the legality of a "negotiated" contract made with some particular firm without competitive bidding, originally to cover experimental work but later to apply to mass production. An example was the Navy's contract with the Great Lakes Company, which called for experimenting with a new design and then building it in quantity, a provision which aroused the Comptroller General to issue a manifesto on May 21, 1934. When he declared that "no similar purchasing procedure" would thereafter be recognized by him as an obligation against the public funds, the Secretary of the Navy issued an order closely restricting future contracts to competitive bidding. This precipitated a series of dissenting statements, beginning with a strong protest from King to the effect that rapid changes in design, as well as the shortness of the average plane's life, made the negotiation of "proprietary" contracts necessary, and to the further effect that the Secretary's new order would create "administrative difficulties" out of proportion to the "intangible advantages" that might be gained. These dissents evidently continued as long as the order remained in force, because a year and a half later we find the Bureau of Supplies and Accounts, purchasing agent for the Navy, making a protest similar to King's, and as far along as 1941 we find Towers, then Chief of the Bureau of Aeronautics, describing that order as an "obstruction to the expeditious conduct of business." There the order stood, however, until the Japanese attack on Pearl Harbor altered the procurement problem in a day and resulted in the subsequent handling of contracts under the far more liberal War Powers Act.

Given funds to provide more stations with better equipment, the Bureau of Aeronautics was able to make sounder plans for the employment and training of personnel. For example, Byrd's expeditions to the Poles, from which much had been learned, could be supplemented by other cold weather operations, in a foretaste of what aircraft are doing in that way as this is written. As early as 1931 the *Langley* and her pilots had shown that carrier operations were entirely practicable during a New England winter, and in the succeeding three years naval aircraft cooperated with the Weather Bureau in studying the climate of the Aleutian Islands. Squadrons of planes from the *Ranger* had similar winter experience out of Buffalo, New York, and Hartford, Connecticut, in preparation for their work in Alaskan waters during January and February, 1936. Meanwhile, more information about the weather was drawn from studies of typhoons off Shanghai, from flights off an especially equipped weather ship at Guam, the *Gold Star*, from searches into the upper strata of the air by planes from San Diego, and by balloons based on battleships and cruisers. The information gleaned from all these efforts was combined profitably with what came of a study of wind-gust velocities conducted by the Massachusetts Institute of Technology under a contract with the Bureau of Aeronautics.

Naval aviators continued to supply the Navy's Hydrographic Office, the Geological Survey, the Treasury, and other governmental agencies with data drawn from photographic reconnaissances and from aerial mapping, even while they themselves were getting invaluable experience in the special techniques required and also in the proper methods of establishing and maintaining advanced bases for aircraft. Similarly good results followed from their studies, in collaboration with the Army Air Corps, the Bureau of Air Commerce, and the Massachusetts Institute of Technology of that perennial problem for the aviator, fog and its possible dispersion.

With knowledge gained in so many ways it became possible to take service models of the constantly improving planes on longer and longer flights. In 1934 two squadrons flew nonstop from San

Diego to Coco Solo, and from there made one hop of it to Guantánamo. VP-10F picked up new P2Y-1 planes in Norfolk and ferried them to Pearl Harbor by way of Coco Solo, San Diego, and San Francisco; a demonstration of mobility not lost on those in the Navy Department who were studying war plans. In these years the emphasis was laid upon distances flown on regular missions rather than on what might be accomplished by special types such as those that had been produced in the twenties.

Every bit of what was learned in these various ways found its application in that most important of the work of the pilots, flying with the Fleet during exercises and war games, when every day had its lesson for those who wore the wings, for those who bore a hand in maintaining and launching the planes, and for those who watched them from the bridges of ships. It was these exercises that brought out the inability of existing carrier aircraft, because their range was too short and their load capacity too small, to do all that would be expected of them in the near future as bombs grew heavier. Again, through demonstrations of the difficulties experienced by both battleships and cruisers in expeditiously handling their planes, these exercises emphasized the need for more small carriers. Particularly, as the use of patrol planes became wider, it was in the exercises that the lack of proper tenders became glaring, but even as late as 1936 this lack had been met only by converting the *Langley* into a tender and, a little later, converting a few destroyers of World War I type. What was needed and recommended by the General Board was a special type of 20-knot ship of about 5,000 tons but of relatively light draft, equipped with large gas tanks and ample magazines and supplied with boats able to leave the ship and repair planes as they lay upon the water.

Still another conclusion drawn from the Fleet exercises applied to airships and struck what amounted to their death blow. The *Macon*, sister of the *Akron* and commissioned on June 23, 1933, not long after the latter was lost, did a little scouting with the Fleet and some excellent reporting of weather conditions. In contact with the "enemy," however, she was invariably "destroyed" by air attacks which her defending planes were unable to repel, and this was duly noted by Adm. David F. Sellers, Commander in Chief during that year and the next. Summarizing her efforts, the admiral described himself as "unaware of any conditions based either upon the record . . . of the *Macon*," or upon any other experience with airships, justifying further expenditure for them, an opinion fully confirming that of Schofield and others. King, for the Bureau of Aeronautics, suggested that the metal-clad airships then in the design stage, if stepped up to a speed of 100 knots and equipped to use gas fuel, would prove more useful, and he recommended that six of these be built. The General Board, in its turn, amended earlier pronouncements upon naval policy on rigids by recommending their development with an eye to their value for commercial purposes, while nonrigids were employed to train personnel. A proposal that the *Macon*, in the meantime, be used for long-range patrol flights came to little because before she had been in service for two years altogether a structural failure brought her down off Point Sur, California, where she sank on February 12, 1935, and was lost. Fortunately all but two of her crew were saved.

After this disaster the Secretary of the Navy requested a new study of dirigibles, which was completed in January, 1936, by a group of distinguished scientists headed by Dr. W. F. Durand and including R. A. Millikan, Theodor von Karman, William Hovgaard, Stephen Timoshenko, Alfred V. de Forest, Frank B. Jewett, and Charles F. Kettering. These gentlemen did not pause to decide whether or not a rigid airship had military value; they assumed that value and then expressed "the unanimous opinion . . . that the best interest of the services . . . both commercial and naval, requires a continuing program of construction and use." This led to plans for all sizes up to 10,000,000-cubic-foot capacity, some prepared in the Bureau of Aeronautics, some under naval contracts with the Daniel Guggenheim Airship Institute at Akron. Notwithstanding the adverse reports of four successive commanders in chief, the General Board then presented its own report, noting all the possibilities of scouting by airships able to make far higher speed than carriers and able to carry and launch their own planes, but also admitting their vulnerability. For commercial use in peacetime and for conversion to war purposes, the board recommended building another rigid of 3,000,000 cubic feet, and for this Congress eventually appropriated $500,000. Her plans and specifications were duly prepared, but since she was never built it remained for the *Los Angeles*, recommissioned after the loss of the *Akron*, to play a lone hand in rigids. Other progress in lighter-than-air was limited to the nonrigids, one of these being the *Defender*, bought from Goodyear in 1935, redesignated the G-1, and used for training with such success that seven others like her were built for World War II. Similarly, the TC-13 and TC-14, non-

rigids taken over from the Army in 1937, became the nucleus of
a war squadron, while two other types, bought "as is" from Goodyear and modified, became the L-1 and the K-3. The latter is of particular interest because she included all the improvements since
World War I that had stood the test of time. Her car, suspended
internally, was a frame of welded steel, thinly covered with aluminum alloy and streamlined, as were the outriggers and the cells.
Her fuel tanks were built into the car above the control tanks and
her bombs, carried beneath the car floor, could be released through
bay doors like those on planes. With all these improvements, and a
retractable landing gear, she became the model for a whole fleet
of nonrigids that would see active war service.

From the moment when it became apparent that the Vinson-
Trammell Bill was likely to become law, it had been clear that the
material expansion to be authorized by the bill must greatly intensify the shortage of aviation personnel. Under existing law,
the limit on commissioned officers of the whole Navy was so low
that it did not permit the commissioning of more than one half of
the class graduating at the academy in 1933, leaving the other
half to be discharged and sent home. With all branches of the Navy
inadequately supplied with officers, it would be harder than ever
to get candidates for aviation training, as Moffett not long before
his death had taken pains to point out to the Bureau of Navigation.
A board, duly convened in that Bureau, had recommended legislation to permit commissioning an entire graduating class and at the
same time to make subsequent classes larger by increasing congressional appointments from four to five. Failing such legislation,
said the board, there should at least be such as would allow midshipmen due to be discharged on graduation to accept commissions in
the Reserve provided they volunteered for aviation. This was considered better than bringing other reserves back to active duty,
a step opposed by the board on the ground that it might result in a
whole corps of specialists in flying who were untrained in other
naval duties, and on the further ground that too many reserves
might exert political pressure to keep themselves on active duty
indefinitely. Finally, the board's recommendations included one
that many of the naval aviators then on duty as observers aboard
battleships and cruisers could be returned to pilot duties if more
officers, to the number of about 70, were trained to replace them as
observers.

In general agreement with this board, Moffett had added some recommendations of his own. Remarking that numerous graduates of the Naval Academy assigned to aviation had been found to be below the physical standards of the Bureau of Aeronautics, he had proposed that the academy's standards be raised. Next, he had suggested that all ensigns and lieutenants, junior grade, in the Navy, who could meet the physical requirements, be "urged, but not compelled" to take flight training. Finally, he had asked for the establishment of a training status for student aviators from the Naval Reserve which would put them on a par with the Army's flying cadets and would allow for three years' active duty with the Fleet instead of only one. He had proposed a three-year limit because he held that longer service might stimulate agitation for transfer to the regular Navy, new arguments for a naval air corps or fresh outcries for an entirely separate air force.

The Chief of the Bureau of Navigation, in his turn, had proposed modifying Moffett's three years of active duty for reserves to two years, but after consulting the superintendent of the Naval Academy he had disapproved any raising of the physical requirements for midshipmen. With these modifications the matter had been submitted to Congress, with the result that the Vinson-Trammell Act had authorized the recall as ensigns of any of the class of 1933 who wanted to come back after their discharge and who proved to be still physically qualified, and also authorized commissioning the entire class of 1934. Upon this the Bureau of Navigation requested appropriations to cover the training during the fiscal year of 1936, of 328 reserve pilots in addition to those already provided for by law.

A particular reason why remedial legislation was needed could be found in the depressing effect of a recent modification in the laws governing selection for promotion in the regular Navy. By this change selection was carried down into both grades of lieutenant, with the provision that officers not promoted in these grades might be involuntarily retired after their years of service, including those at the Naval Academy, totaled anything from eight to 14 years. This made young men who were thinking of going into aviation uneasy lest they find themselves, after winning their wings as pilots, regarded by selection boards as not fully qualified in seagoing duties, unfit for promotion, and therefore facing involuntary retirement. Even when these laws were amended to give those not selected an additional period of six years in each of the lieutenant grades, not enough lift in morale resulted among those who had the commendable ambition of one day reaching a high command. They looked upon the act of June 5, 1935, which established "Aeronautical Engineering Duty Only" to supplement the "Engineering Duty Only" provided by earlier laws, with suspicion and many preferred to cling to "the Line" rather than go into aviation and sacrifice all chance of becoming battleship captains or admirals. As added discouragement Naval Aviation, at the very moment when it needed more officers, was actually losing them through another action by the Bureau of Navigation, taken for reasons which are now not altogether clear. This was the transfer to other duties of a number of warrant officers who had been in aviation for years, many of them as naval aviators, many of them as aviation pilots, all of them of great value because of their solid background of practical, technical knowledge. This was just as upsetting to plans for proper administration as was the continuing problem of getting officers assigned to higher aviation posts; a complicated matter because those fully qualified by flying experience were frequently regarded by the Bureau of Navigation as of insufficient seniority in their grades to justify their assignment. Since the Bureau of Navigation issued all orders to officers, that bureau invariably had the last word.

Meanwhile the Federal Aviation Commission, created by the Air Mail Act of June 12, 1934, had been directed by Congress to survey the national situation in aviation, including the state of both the Army and the Navy. In its findings that commission did not recommend any merger of all air forces but proposed that reserves for the armed forces be increased in numbers and be ordered to active duty for periods of three years. Even had existing laws permitted this, however, there would have been no great enthusiasm for it among the reserves themselves. The Naval Reserve at that moment was nursing a grudge based upon the fact that, among all of its former members who had transferred to the regular Navy after World War I, only 19 had been advanced by the most recent Selection Board. This grudge was not removed when King pointed out that the percentage of former reserves advanced in Naval Aviation had been greater than the percentage in any other branch; instead, it merely added to the grumbling over the lack of recognition of reserves on inactive duty, as indicated by the lack of appropriations for their proper peacetime training.

At the end of 1934 King again brought forward the proposal that aviation cadets be authorized. This time he secured the support of President Roosevelt, and early in 1935 Congress passed the authorizing act. Under it, graduates of recognized universities and colleges between the ages of 18 and 28 became eligible for one year of training followed by three years of active duty, with a rank just above that of warrant officer, just below that of ensign in the Navy or second lieutenant in the Marine Corps. During training they were to be paid $75 a month, with a subsistence allowance of one dollar a day, insurance of $10,000 on which the Navy paid the premium, and free uniforms. On active duty their monthly pay was raised to $125, with one grant of $250 for uniforms; and upon discharge they were to receive a bonus of $1,500. In return, they must remain single during the four years, and although they were not required on discharge to accept commissions as ensigns in the Naval Reserve, it was expected that they would do so.

Under this law it became the established policy to seek out those who had been members of some unit of the Reserve Officers Training Corps, or those who had completed a recognized course in aeronautical engineering, but anyone who had attended an army or naval flying school and failed to qualify was not considered acceptable. As recruiting began, it was soon apparent that 18 years was too young and the minimum age was accordingly raised to 20 years. All those chosen were enrolled as seamen, second class, under the so-called V-5 program for the Reserve, and put through an elimination course in flight training, after which the successful men were appointed cadets and sent to Pensacola for about one year of intensive instruction before going out to the Fleet. When the commandant of each naval district was given his quota and began recruiting, it was soon discovered that the best material was to be found among men of about 25. By July, 1935, 55 had been enrolled and of these, within another year, 50 were at sea.

On the whole they were enthusiastically welcomed afloat. Some of the top commanders were inclined to deplore their lack of general training, especially because unfamiliarity with gunnery made them less able observers than the regulars who had grown up in the Navy; but it is difficult to see how anything else could be expected of such a high-pressure system, and they did meet the essential requirement that they be good pilots. To make up deficiencies in general seagoing knowledge, courses of study and training were carried on aboard ship in gunnery, engineering, and other branches; courses so successful that the commander in chief, well pleased with the performance of the cadets, recommended their assignment to battleships and cruisers as well as to all other aviation billets. Thus, although the V-5 program had originally been intended merely as a temporary step on the way to building up a flying arm of regular officers, within a year the Bureau of Aeronautics put itself on record as ready to "accept the Aviation Cadet as a permanent fixture . . . to compose about 45 per cent of the Naval Aviators," because there appeared to be "little prospect of meeting . . . requirements from regular service sources." The continued increase in the number of planes and the amount of equipment combined to make it more than ever necessary to spread the regulars very thinly through the squadrons attached to the Fleet.

In the fall of 1936 the Bureau of Navigation proposed that the tour of active duty for a cadet be reduced from four years to two, with the privilege of volunteering to serve the other two years. The Bureau of Aeronautics was at first in favor of this change on the ground that it would stimulate enthusiasm for the corps among young civilians, but as it became apparent that authority for expanding the annual enrollment was not likely to be obtained, the bureau reversed its stand and Navigation accordingly did not press for the change.

This was at about the time when King completed his tour as Chief of the Bureau of Aeronautics and went back to the Fleet as Commander Aircraft, Base Force. Once afloat, he could see at first hand what an important part the cadets were playing and feel satisfied that he had made no mistake in pushing their organization. Presently he would discover how much could be done both for the Navy and for the cadets themselves by modifications of the original plan, and he prepared to cooperate fully with those who followed him in Washington to bring about these changes.

CHAPTER XXVII

The Approach to War

WHEN King ended his tour in the Bureau of Aeronautics on June 12, 1936, his successor was a "destroyer man," energetic, fiery Rear Adm. Arthur B. Cook. Like Halsey and numerous others, Cook had waited until he was well along in his career before deciding to qualify as an aviator, but he carried into the air all the impulsive enthusiasm that had marked his years as a surface seaman. His service had included the command of various ships as well as staff and administrative posts before he became Moffett's Assistant Chief of Bureau in June, 1931. He was in that office when Moffett was lost and thus, for a month, he acted as chief and he remained with King until March, 1934. All this made him well fitted to head a bureau of daily increasing importance. This was fortunate because in his three-year administration he faced the continuation of many old problems and also the advent of many new ones; the latter resulting essentially from two causes, the development of the political and military situation throughout the world and the technical advances in aircraft which produced changes in plans for their tactical use.

It will be recalled that this period of the thirties was marked by events of great significance beginning with the Japanese occupation of Manchuria in 1931. In 1933 Hitler became Chancellor, and two years later Mussolini invaded Ethiopia. After Germany and Japan withdrew from the League of Nations, there was little use in continuing the league's permanent disarmament conference and this, although it was never officially dissolved, did not meet after 1934. In March, 1935, Hitler announced the resumption of conscription. In December of that year, when the powers signatory to the Washington Treaty of 1922 and the London Treaty of 1930 held a preliminary conference because both treaties were about to expire, Japan demanded full naval parity. When this was refused she indignantly withdrew. Ultimately the United States, Great Britain, and France reached agreements among themselves, but these were so full of "escape clauses" that they amounted to very little. In July, 1936, a month after Cook took office, the Spanish Revolution precipitated more international complications, and in 1937 the Japanese and Chinese were fighting over the incident at the Marco Polo Bridge. That autumn President Roosevelt made his "Quarantine" speech at Chicago, with its much debated implications of changes in United States foreign policy. Six months later Hitler seized Austria and six months more brought the Munich meeting. Not long after this all hope of peace in the world ended.

The threat of war discernible in these events had drawn the attention of many officers to the organization of the Navy. On January 1, 1923, the Atlantic and Pacific Fleets had been combined to form the United States Fleet, and this had then been divided, upon the basis of what would be expected of each of the several groups in war, into the Battle Fleet, the Scouting Fleet, and the Base Force, each with its own aviation component. As an organization primarily for fighting, this one did not take full account of the fact that each of the three divisions included ships of various types and that a ship of one type required equipment, supply, and training which often differed widely from those required by another type. By 1928 Admiral Pratt, then the Commander in Chief, suggested the introduction of a "type-command" system for administrative purposes, by which he intended that all ships of any one type should be grouped under a separate commander who would schedule their repair and overhaul periods, see that they were supplied with fuel, equipment, and all other requirements, and also supervise their training in type tactics and in the indoctrination of their crews. This would relieve the commander in chief of endless administrative detail and give him ships which, in their respective types, were as nearly alike in equipment and training as it was possible to make them. He would then be able to select from each type as many as he wanted, to form an operating group on any mission he might plan. Such a group would be styled a task force, and it would include the required kind and number of aircraft.

This plan was not immediately adopted but it came up again when Admiral Pratt became Chief of Naval Operations in 1930. The efforts he then made to compose the Navy's differences with the Army over land-based aircraft, as well as his efforts to give the Fleet greater flexibility and mobility, were mentioned in an earlier chapter; among them was a step toward the introduction of type commands. The Battle and Scouting Fleets were redesignated

Forces, with a type commander named for each kind of ship, while aircraft, although still divided among the several forces, were all placed under the Commander Aircraft, Battle Force for "type" administrative purposes. Some officers who believed in the old organization thought Admiral Pratt's innovation revolutionary, but those who favored the task-force-type-command combination thought the admiral had not gone far enough.

After the exercises of 1932 one effect of the deteriorating situation in the Far East was the transfer of the Scouting Force from the Atlantic to the Pacific, to join the Battle Force, a move which revived the argument in favor of type commands throughout. In 1934 the then Commander in Chief, Adm. David Sellers, brought aviation into this picture by suggesting the creation of an air force, United States Fleet, its commander to operate directly under the commander in chief in assigning carriers and other units wherever they might be required and also to carry out the "type" administrative duties. To this proposal the aviators were favorably disposed but there were others who interpreted it as a move toward the dreaded separate air force.

It is apparent that Adm. W. H. Standley, by this time Chief of Naval Operations, did not approve the type-command theory because, from the letter he wrote in this year 1934, he omitted all provision for such an organization. Instead, he stated that the commander in chief might direct that type duties be carried out by the senior officer present in each type. This immediately aroused opposition from the Commander Aircraft, Battle Force, who then controlled the carriers and the planes, and also from the Commander Aircraft, Base Force, who similarly controlled the patrol planes, the utility planes, and the tenders. By 1937, taking notice of this opposition, Admiral Standley asked the Secretary of the Navy to refer the whole question of Fleet organization to the General Board. Among 17 high-ranking officers heard by that board 12 favored the task-force-type-command organization, while five believed that the existing organization, with a few minor changes, would be satisfactory. In the end the board accepted Admiral Standley's compromise, which retained the force organization but assigned all ships of a given kind to the same force, whose commander exercised the administrative functions. For battleships, cruisers, or destroyers, this was simple enough, but as the admiral himself admitted, aircraft continued to "present a peculiar problem," because they all had certain things in common that must re-

quire "somewhere, unified administration—such matters as flying
(as distinguished from operations), safety precautions, upkeep,
routine overhaul." To fit them into his so-called "combination organization," the patrol planes, but not the utility planes, were
shifted from the Base Force to the Scouting Force and, for training
and administrative purposes, all planes of the same kind were concentrated in the same force. Thus all the force components of the
Fleet were left with a hand in administration but planes with the
battleships or with the cruisers, as well as the utility planes, were
left without any type commanders in the proper sense of the term.
At no point short of the Bureau of Aeronautics was there any really
unified administration of aircraft and time would show that this
was a mistake. Improvements did not come until too late to be a
help to the bureau and its chief, Rear Adm. Cook.

To be sure, in attacking most of his problems, old and new, Cook
had the advantage that the clouds of war, drawing ever closer, had
the silver lining formed by increases in available funds. There were
some efforts by the executive branch to force the various departments of the government to economize, but in an era so marked by
lavish spending in all directions these efforts were hardly more
than sporadic. It followed that the Navy in general and the Bureau
of Aeronautics in particular continued to escape serious suffering
from cuts in estimates, made by the Bureau of the Budget or by
Congress, by finding an opening into the bulging moneybags of
NIRA, WPA, PWA, and several other of the government agencies.
Through the years leading to war the amounts appropriated in
the regular way were greatly augmented by allocations from these
sources, and since the appropriations themselves increased, the
total received by Naval Aviation was very substantial. Who would
have dared to predict in 1928 that in 1938 the Navy would be
spending $21,000,000 on a single contract, the record established
when the Consolidated Corporation was selected to build the PBY
Catalina flying boats?

This did not mean that the Bureau of Aeronautics received all
that it wanted, at any given moment; it did not. For example, estimates made in 1936 set the number of planes needed for 1938 at
468, divided into groups of 113 of new design, 260 as replacements
for aging planes, 22 for the reserve program, and 73 to allow for
an expansion of the aviation cadet program. The Navy's own
budget officer, over Cook's vigorous protest, reduced these by 11 of
the new planes and by approximately one half of those wanted for

the cadets; the Bureau of the Budget went even further by eliminating all the cadet planes. Similarly, the airship men were regularly disappointed by the lukewarm attitude of Congress toward even the nonrigids. When Admiral Standley—whose position as Chief of Naval Operations often made him acting Secretary of the Navy because of the illness of Mr. Swanson—proposed to spend as much as $270,000 of the appropriation for new construction on nonrigids, this relatively small amount was so heatedly disapproved that it evaporated. Planning the weapons of the future and their possible use is never easy, but if there is doubt about the availability of means of paying for them planning becomes little more than guessing.

In January, 1938, all planning was greatly changed by President Roosevelt's call for a naval expansion act which would increase the whole naval building program by 20 per cent; a call answered by the introduction into Congress of a bill subjected in its early draft to hearings made noisy by the outcries of those who always oppose any increase in the Army or the Navy for adequate national defense. The bill also revived old disputes over the results of the bombing tests carried out against the captured German ships of World War I, arousing all those who insisted that capital ships were no longer worth the money it cost to build them, inciting all the inventors and manufacturers of the country to reiterate their charges that both *Army* and *Navy* were neglecting what private efforts had produced in new designs and technical operation. For the Bureau of Aeronautics chief interest centered upon a clause put into the bill just before it became law on May 17, 1938, authorizing the President "to acquire or construct additional naval airplanes including patrol planes, and spare parts and equipment, so as to bring the number of useful naval airplanes to a total not less than 3,000"—a clause which immediately presented very obvious new problems. It was one thing to estimate that 428 of those new aircraft should be patrol planes for the Pacific; it was quite another thing to determine how that number could be maintained without providing considerably greater facilities at shore air stations. Moreover, to keep so many more planes actually flying would obviously mean that many more pilots must be put under instruction; something that could not be accomplished without finding students who would make pilots, or without building and equipping more planes in which to train them.

Personnel procurement would be a long-standing problem; but

a step toward providing greater facilities ashore was taken the end of 1938 when a board was convened to make recommendations for air stations. This board, called the Hepburn Board because it was headed by Adm. A. J. Hepburn who had formerly been the Commander in Chief of the Fleet, recognized the sudden demands that would have to be met if the approach of war should precipitate a great expansion of personnel and prepared its conclusion accordingly. It recommended the enlargement of 11 existing stations and the erection of 16 new ones to include Quonset, Jacksonville, Banana River, Corpus Christi, San Juan, Kodiak, Dutch Harbor, Kaneohe, Midway, Wake, Guam, and five other Pacific islands. Although these, with the older stations, would comprise what the board said was the "indispensable necessity of peacetime operation," they were not all undertaken immediately. Some very helpful funds were appropriated, but not until months later, when no one could any longer pretend that war was not imminent, did it become possible to build a naval air station almost anywhere and almost overnight, regardless of cost.

Under the provisions for further ship building, the Expansion Act made it possible to establish a program for building tenders which would be much more stable than the already noted makeshift of using the *Langley* and converted destroyers. The plans made called for laying down one large tender and four small ones in 1938, to be followed the next year by another small one, and in the year after that by a large one and a small one. This was a much simpler question than that of carrier building, for which the act also provided by disregarding the old treaty limit of 135,000 tons and going up to 175,000, and by directing the immediate construction of one ship.

This last requirement was disconcerting to both the Bureau of Aeronautics and the General Board in their common plans for building carriers. Under these the *Saratoga* and *Lexington* were to undergo some immediate modernization and, when they became over age within the meaning of the Washington Treaty of 1922, to be replaced by new ships of the same size: one in 1941, two in 1945, and one more in 1946. Drawings for these new ships had already been begun, but because many changes in design might come before the dates set for keel laying, they were hardly more than sketches and in no sense final enough for immediate use. The General Board was not inclined to recommend building a smaller carrier because not enough had yet been learned from the *Yorktown* and the *Enterprise*, commissioned respectively on September 30, 1937, and May 12, 1938, and therefore not yet sufficiently "shaken down" to furnish suggestions for modifying their design for use that same year for a new ship. Eventually, therefore, the ship laid down under the Naval Expansion Act was built on the plans of the *Ranger* and commissioned as the *Wasp;* a good instance of the Navy's perforce taking what it could get rather than what it wanted. Notwithstanding her small size, however, the *Wasp* lived to give a fine account of herself before three Japanese torpedoes finally sank her off Guadalcanal.

In Cook's administration much was learned from a study of the Fleet exercises. The 1936 games had subjected aerial scouting to an exhaustive test which threw strong light upon current methods of training patrol squadrons for extended operations. For the first time the automatic pilot, so many years before an object of Captain Chambers' interested attention, was given a real trial in long-range planes, with very instructive results. Its use was found to afford the pilots great relief from mental and physical strain, leaving them at their best to meet an emergency even if this should come after long hours in the air. In consequence, the Bureau of Aeronautics recommended the installation of this device on all patrol planes beginning with the P2Y, which had again added to its reputation for sturdy efficiency. Given this mechanical advantage and enough tenders to maintain their mobility, the patrols could do vastly better scouting and reporting, although the war games had made it increasingly evident that their type was of doubtful value for bombing attacks. In searching for an enemy they were likely to become dispersed into such small groups that they would be ineffective against good antiaircraft fire and practically helpless against enemy fighters sent up to intercept them.

Subsequent exercises yielded further valuable experience in planning and executing fast-carrier strikes against shore defenses and, in opposition, the use of shore defense against such strikes. For protection by gunfire against air attack the carriers operated inside a screen of heavy cruisers, close aboard, with an outer screen of light cruisers for security against surface attack. Visual signals directed these particular movements, in order that radio silence might be maintained, but in other operations the successful use, at distances of more than 100 miles, of radio bearings to direct planes on the proper course for an attack demonstrated that ship and plane communications were steadily improving. Still other exercises indicated that the obvious need of more large carriers for major operations was no greater than the need of many small carriers to escort troop transports and support minor operations. A 10,000-ton vessel for such purposes had been under discussion during the last 20 years, and Capt. J. S. McCain, commanding the *Ranger* in the 1939 exercises, brought new life into that discussion from a different point of view. At that time it was expected that the large carriers would have to operate 35 or 40 miles from the battle line, whereas McCain suggested that small carriers could dart out from that line itself, launch planes in five or ten minutes, and return before the enemy could attack. If fitted with an armored deck, he contended, these small carriers would have considerable protection even if they were attacked while out of the battle line. However, it would be some years before this idea would come to fruition.

Other lessons were learned from two special types of exercises which were features of this period. One was the importance of training patrol pilots in detecting submarines soon enough to "keep 'em down" if not actually to destroy them. The other was the vital role of aircraft in landing operations, as simulated by the Fleet Marine Force, a separate entity established in 1933 to operate directly under the commander in chief and by 1939 highly efficient. Most of the planes it used were flown by pilots of the corps but the Navy's aviators very often took part. Performance of all air tasks in landings became measurably better, one well worthy of mention being the advance of aerial photography to a point where negatives were developed and prints made in the air, the latter to be dropped either aboard the flagship of a force supporting the landing or at the headquarters of a shore force opposing it. With the disciplined efficiency and the inspired morale that have always characterized it, the Marine Corps wrote into the reports of these sham battles the preface to the brilliant history it would compile a few years later on the islands of the Pacific. Throughout all these increasingly intricate air maneuvers it was apparent that the competitive spirit —carrier against carrier, squadron against squadron, almost plane against plane—was aroused to a higher pitch than ever before and the fact that even this enthusiasm did not result in more than a relatively unimportant number of casualties was good proof of general efficiency. Unquestionably the quality of the flying personnel was very good, but still there remained the problem of how to get the personnel in sufficient quantity.

This was as true of enlisted men as it was of officers. Among the former, the special squadron of aviation pilots assembled for service with the Fleet continued to give an excellent account of itself, but that was only one squadron. Otherwise, it remained true of the broad average that the planes did best when piloted by naval aviators, with aviation pilots in subordinate command, and as greater numbers of planes were built the shortage of commissioned pilots consequently became more and more marked. This led to continuous requests from the Fleet for the assignment to aviation of greater numbers of officers, until Adm. Claude C. Bloch, as Commander in Chief, was asking for 150 annually. Even that many would mean that five out of each six pilots required must come from the Reserve, a situation likely to be marked by a lowering in all-around efficiency through shortened training at a moment when war was drawing nearer every day.

Vice Admiral Andrews, Chief of the Bureau of Navigation, told Congress that plans for personnel called for a total of 700 aviation cadets, but by this time the enthusiasm of the cadets themselves was lessening. To begin with, they considered their title misleading, as indeed it was, in view of the advanced flying they were doing with the Fleet. Next, to the cadets, it seemed belittling that they should be outranked by younger men fresh from the Naval Academy, a situation that might exist even after they had been naval aviators on active duty for several years. Their pay, especially when it was compared with what they might earn by leaving the Navy to enter commercial flying or join some aircraft building firm, was certainly not high. If they went off active duty while in good standing, the Navy was required by law to give them a bonus of $1,500 as a grubstake and, if they did well in some civilian billet, promotion was likely to be much more rapid than appeared probable in the Navy. Altogether, the pull to stay in uniform was growing steadily weaker.

All this was fully recognized by the Bureau of Aeronautics, and Cook had already made strong recommendations for new legislation. He contended that if these "splendid youngsters" were not fairly treated by the Navy, they could hardly be reproached for seizing the first opportunity to return to civil life or for accepting commissions—with promotion—as fliers with the Army, at that moment very much on the watch to snap up just such promising men, to form "a reservoir of trained, seasoned military pilots." Cook's view was fully supported by King, at sea as Commander Aircraft, Battle Force, and he urged, as one way to encourage the cadets,

their being given commissions when they finished training, without
serving for several years afloat. Adm. E. C. Kalbfus, at that time
commanding the Battle Force, commented that the term "cadet"
was "neither fitting nor, in any sense, descriptive of the duties performed in the Fleet by individuals of this group." He approved
King's recommendation and also that of the Commander Battleships, Vice Adm. John W. Greenslade, asking that the cadets be
given more training in the general duties of officers. Admiral Bloch,
Commander in Chief, did not go quite as far as these high-ranking
subordinates but he did consider that one year at sea, before commissioning, would be ample. Even with all this backing, however,
the Chief of the Bureau of Navigation unfortunately decided that
the current session of Congress was "an inopportune moment" to
ask for remedial legislation, and since such a step was distinctly
his to take, the whole matter marked time. The chairman of the
House Naval Affairs Committee nevertheless suggested to Cook
that he prepare a plan which would do the cadets justice, and what
Cook accordingly submitted eventually led to appropriate provisions in the Naval Aviation Reserve Act of 1939.

Such an act was considerably overdue, especially because the
shortage of aviators in the regular Navy made it imperative to
keep the cadets on active duty instead of returning them, as
originally planned, to the Reserve. Moreover, congressional appropriations for reserve training had been very small during the
years immediately preceding, thus slowing up the recruiting program, besides lowering the general efficiency of those who were enrolled. In September, 1938, the Fleet Aviation Reserve, composed
of men from the regular Navy whose length of service permitted
them to transfer to it, numbered only 222 officers with about 1,000
men for ground duties. Theoretically this reserve, paid a nominal
sum for a stipulated number of drills and given full pay for 15
days' yearly active duty, was considered trained and ready for
service.

Actually, considering the rapidity of technical advances, this
could not be true, but the Fleet Reserve was much better trained
than the Volunteer Aviation Reserve which at the same moment
numbered only 127 officers and a few hundred men. These volunteers, divided into the two categories of those for general service
and those for technical specialties, got their training when and as
they could, wholly without compensation even for their time.
Among them, to be sure, were a number of men who were eligible, by

reason of previous naval service, for the Fleet Reserve but who were living either in an area where the quota was already filled or at some point that made it impossible for them to travel the necessary distance to attend drills. Taking both together, these units could not be considered in any sense adequate to the need but they represented almost all the help then in sight.

The Plans Division of the Bureau of Aeronautics had long been disturbed by the situation and had expressed its conviction that victory in any war—with Japan, for example—would depend more upon the production of enough pilots than upon the production of enough planes. The matter had also been studied by the Federal Aviation Commission, and its report of January, 1935, contained the comment that both Army and Navy appeared to be handling reserves upon a scale so small "as scarcely to constitute more than a working model." This commission, however, praised the paper organization prepared in the Bureau of Aeronautics to provide for 31 reserve squadrons with 251 pilots, "to fly as a unit for some 45 hours a year and to undergo substantial periods of supplementary training." For this unit, and for other steps in reserve training, the commission recommended that more funds be appropriated and that the personnel be at least doubled. Up to this time the funds available had been barely enough to train reserves already enrolled, and for an increase to a strength of 7,500, then estimated as necessary to carry out all aviation duties, much more money was needed.

A little help in training had been obtained when numerous officers of the Fleet Aviation Reserve were called to active duty as instructors of cadets, because the 15-day period of active duty to which these officers would otherwise have been entitled could be assigned, instead, to officers of the Volunteer Reserve. On the other hand, this had meant that Fleet Reserve—or, as it was soon to be christened, Organized Reserve—had only 138 officers not on active duty; a mere handful to meet a call for mobilization. By the spring of 1939 the enrollment of reserve aviators amounted to only about 12 per cent of the contemplated strength, and after cuts by the Navy's own budget officer and by the Bureau of the Budget, training funds for the Volunteer Reserve were reduced until they provided for the training of only one officer out of every 25. Capt. Felix Gygax of the Bureau of Navigation, in a report that should stand high among understatements, suggested that two weeks' training every 25 years might fairly be called inadequate. It should be noted, however, that this lack of funds could not with justice be attributed to Congress, but rather to those who had cut the Navy's original requests and estimates before they ever reached Capitol Hill.

Some other help was in sight as a result of the establishment, under the Civil Aeronautics Authority, of the Civilian Pilot Training Program announced by President Roosevelt at the end of December, 1938. The ostensible purpose of the program was the encouragement of general civilian flying, but behind this lay the hope of providing men who could quickly develop into military pilots. With $100,000 allotted from the National Youth Administration, experimental classes were organized at 13 educational institutions from New York to California, and these were so successful that broader plans designed to provide for training 20,000 pilots a year were drawn. This matter, like those already mentioned, was one that would be taken up in the new naval reserve act.

This was the general situation at the end of Cook's administration. With the help of all hands he had presented the needs of Naval Aviation at the congressional hearings, but before the resulting bill reached final action it became time for him to go to sea again.

CHAPTER XXVIII

Aviation Meets the Test

TWO weeks before the Naval Reserve Act of 1939 became law Cook was succeeded as Chief of the Bureau of Aeronautics by Rear Adm. John Towers. For Towers this landing at the top came after a long flight because, since Ellyson's death in 1928, he had been the Navy's most experienced flier, the oldest living graduate of the school established by Glenn Curtiss in 1911. He could vividly recall the days when primitive engines, mounted in "orange-crate" planes, might stall or fly apart at any moment; when to stay in the air for half an hour was to be a redoubtable pilot; when a night landing on the water, in the glare of flaming gas torches, was both dramatic and epoch making. More thoroughly than any of his predecessors in office he knew the heavy odds against which Chambers, Richardson, Westervelt, Hunsaker, Taylor, Craven, and many others had struggled to bring dependable planes and proper administration into Naval Aviation, while Smith, Bellinger, Mustin, Geiger, Chevalier, Byrd, and dozens like them lifted aircraft to their proper level as an arm of the Fleet. Escaping his own death in the air by a miracle of coolness and strength, he had been the shipmate of all those, from Billingsley through Floyd Bennett to Moffett, who had given their lives to an idea. Word for word, he knew the chapters of bitter disappointment, the chapters of brilliant achievement written into the record of a generation. Having had much to do with the pages that covered the Navy's flying in World War I, he was well fitted for a leading part in the writing of far more important pages in World War II.

Within three months after Towers took office the outbreak of war in Europe emphasized, to military and naval minds, the general unpreparedness of the United States for what was dangerously apt to follow. Once again the Navy, particularly Naval Aviation, realized the vital truth of that old pronouncement of Horatio Nelson's on "the relatively far greater importance of personnel, compared with that of its weapons." To meet war, planes and more planes certainly would be needed, but the chief essential would be a tremendous increase in the number of trained men. It was therefore encouraging that the new reserve act set the minimum strength of aviation officers of the Naval Reserve at 6,000 and also, by improving the position of the aviation cadets, offered inducements to those who might wish to enroll with them. Commissioning at the end of their training period was authorized, and after three years of active duty they would be eligible, after examination, for promotion. They would be required to serve at least four years, after which they could leave the Navy with a bonus of $500 or, at their own request, serve another three years. All cadets with the Fleet on the day the act became effective were to be commissioned immediately as ensigns, with the option of accepting the pay of that grade and the new bonus, or continuing at the pay rate and bonus provided by the act of 1935 described earlier. That the cadets responded well to these changes is proved by the quality of their later performance.

Under a clause in the new law directing the Secretary of the Navy to appoint a board to "investigate . . . the regular and reserve personnel of the Navy and Marine Corps," such a board was convened under Rear Adm. (later Adm.) Frederick J. Horne, soon to be prominent as the Vice Chief of Naval Operations, right hand of Admiral King in keeping the fleets up to fighting strength. In its report this board reaffirmed opposition to anything like a separate flying corps, the stated reason being that such a corps would tend to "disrupt that unity of thought so essential in Naval Operations," and "seriously reduce the present high efficiency." In the board's view, anything likely to "divorce Naval Aviation from the line of the Navy . . . might bring disaster in time of war"; on the contrary, there must be forged an even closer bond between airman and seaman, in order that each might fully understand what the other planned to do and recognize what the other was about when he began to do it. Anyone who reads the story of the Navy's war in two oceans can see how this bond was destined to become stronger with each passing day.

Based on the authorization of 3,000 planes by 1945, the Horne Board estimated aviation personnel requirements by that date at 4,300 pilots, 980 ground officers, and 35,000 enlisted men. To meet such numbers of officers, the original plan for 1,050 regulars by 1939 would have to be amended to 1,730, a figure which, after allowing for training periods and for attrition, could be reached only by the assignment of 450 regulars to aviation each year. Since but

85 at the most could be obtained from each class graduating at the Naval Academy, such a total of assignments was out of the question ; even halving the allowance of pilots from the regular Navy to planes and thus setting the total at 225 would not produce enough. The only recourse was to the reserves, and to make this possible the board urged immediate legislation to permit calling them back to active duty. Under such new laws officers of the Reserve should be given, while on active duty, the full pay and allowances of regular officers of the same rank. Ensigns who had served three years should be eligible for promotion to lieutenant, junior grade, and the latter, at the end of four years, should become eligible for lieutenant. In peacetime any officer who had served at least four years and wished to return to inactive status should be permitted to do so, with a bonus of $500 for each year of service up to eight. He should be urged to continue periodic training with a Reserve unit, and to make this possible there should be a great increase in appropriations for that training as well as for reserve air stations.

Another recommendation strongly advocated continuing the assignment of warrant officers to aviation, urging an increase in the number annually assigned to 30, particularly in the grades of boatswain, gunner, and radio electrician; all to be regarded as permanent and not subject to arbitrary shifts to other duties. A third recommendation proposed dropping the class of partially trained fliers known as "observers." A fourth suggested a sliding scale of physical requirements for pilots on the ground that men of 40 or more, while fully able to fly under ordinary conditions, should not be expected to equal the running, jumping, and weight lifting, the practically unlimited endurance to be found in youths of 20. All these recommendations were made in much greater detail as to officers because the board found that existing laws and procedures governing enlisted men were good, leaving appropriate expansion in numbers as the only requisite. Although the board did include a statement of estimated mobilization requirements, its report as a whole should be regarded as a program for orderly peacetime expansion, rather than one for overnight mushrooming in time of war. Its ideas, however, were quite constructive enough to furnish Congress with a basis for action.

The time for action was at hand. Although the average American, clinging to his wishful belief that his country would manage to keep out of a world war, apparently failed to see that theoretical neutrality was fast becoming belligerency, those on the inside could no longer have many doubts. Within a few days after Europe began shooting, the Atlantic Squadron had been ordered to establish air and surface patrols—called, to be sure, neutrality patrols—over areas extending as far east as the 65th meridian, as far south as Trinidad. The squadron commander was Rear Adm. Alfred W. Johnson, long prominent in aviation but at the moment flying his flag over a few battleships, cruisers, and destroyers, all of old types, with some 80 aircraft. The battleships and cruisers had 25 planes between them, while the squadrons from Patrol Wings 3 and 5 mustered 54 all told. There were a few planes operating in the Canal Zone, but except for these and the groups in training for the *Ranger* and the *Wasp* every other element of aviation was in the Pacific. Stretching that small force to its utmost, Johnson carried out his orders through the winter, but probably he would have found the task impossible had not the war in Europe, after Germany's attack on Poland, moved into the "phony" stage, with little action anywhere. The coming of spring made the task stiffer, for in April the Nazis seized Denmark and Norway; in May they began moving through Holland and Belgium, to make the fall of France only a question of days. What the Navy was doing in the Atlantic was not publicly described as war but whatever the United States could do to make the going harder for the U-boats was done, lest the war be lost to the Allies. Meantime, many astonished Americans awoke to the realization that between them and a conquering Germany lay only Great Britain, whose ability to hold out was seriously debatable. Suddenly, over clubs, shops, and street corners in the United States there loomed the black shadow of Hitler's mighty air force.

On May 16, 1940, President Roosevelt suddenly demanded that the aircraft of the Army and the Navy be increased to 50,000 and that building capacity be expanded to provide for that same number each year. Civilians were stunned by this pronouncement and so, too, were soldiers and sailors, for they had been accustomed to estimate in tens and twenties rather than in thousands. The airplane industry, its production methods not much advanced in some respects beyond the handicraft stage, was staggered because it was still thinking of the Navy's order for 200 Catalinas in one year as enormous. Moreover, military men and industrialists alike could recognize that any such expansion in the air would almost certainly be accompanied by a similar expansion in ships and shore stations, all involving the manufacture of unheard-of quantities of equip-

ment of every conceivable kind. Whereas the common expectation
had been that there would be a gradual strengthening of forces
afloat and ashore, with a corresponding increase in available resources, to be followed by mobilization and a declaration of war,
this sudden ballooning seemed to presage a headlong plunge into
the fighting. Under such circumstances it was fortunate that the
President could invoke a World War I statute, never repealed, to
re-establish the National Defense Advisory Commission, with members drawn from every business and profession, to study the complicated problems certain to arise. Fortunately, too, American
industry was led by men not to be long daunted by anything in the
way of organizing and supervising stupendous enterprises. Most
fortunately, the ordinary citizen had an extraordinary faculty,
the ability to doze under his blankets until emergency thundered
at his bedroom door and then leap, like a fireman, into his overalls
and boots. Between them all, they manned innumerable offices,
agencies, and plants to create a production fabulous in conception,
record breaking in accomplishment.

In the Bureau of Aeronautics there came, of necessity, a violent
readjustment in thinking. After years of being pinned down by
economies, the bureau had to learn how to spend uncounted dollars. Since the facilities of the contractors with whom it had been
accustomed to deal were wholly inadequate, it must seek new ones,
often only to find these already overloaded with orders from the
War Department or from the British; forced to look still further,
it frequently found those who had little to offer until they could
adjust themselves to the crisis. As procurement and production
daily grew more complicated, it became impossible for the bureau
to make all the decisions upon what to do and then supervise what
was done, a situation which was saved by the re-creation in 1941
of the office of Assistant Secretary of the Navy for Air, abolished
in 1932 to save money. To fill this post the President appointed a
man whose brilliant record as a flier with the Yale Unit in 1917 had
been supplemented by years of broad experience in finance and industry, Artemus L. Gates. He shouldered the responsibility for
coordinating the expansion programs—men, aircraft, bases, and
ships—and, by surrounding himself with men of similar ability
and experience, he solved innumerable problems. In the great number of these problems that bore heavily upon army procurement
and production activities, Gates was very fortunate in having, as

his opposite number in the War Department, another member of the old Yale Unit, Robert A. Lovett.

In June, 1940, under the 3,000-plane program, Naval Aviation had had 1,741 aircraft and 2,965 pilots. That it was then still optimistic over what might be accomplished in war by this small force is shown by the uncertainty of its early recommendations. On the 14th of the month Congress authorized 4,500 planes, next day raising the number to 10,000. When the fall of France and the German attacks on Britain encouraged the Japanese war party to increase pressure in the Far East, the Navy went back to Capitol Hill and this time the ceiling rose to 15,000. In addition, this latest legislation provided that if in the judgment of the Secretary of the Navy the total number of aircraft was insufficient for national defense, he might, with the approval of the President, make such plans for additional procurement as proved necessary. It was with this wholly unprecedented latitude that most of the wartime increases were made. Problems were many and solutions were often complex, but it is not within the scope of these pages to recount these nor to retell the many stories told by others of what was accomplished with the huge store of planes and equipment finally assembled during four years of war. Here it is possible only to suggest what was acquired, to hint at what was done with it, as these two subjects appear to have followed logically from what has been discussed in earlier chapters. In the designs of planes, the Bureau of Aeronautics soon discovered that its 20 years of research, in collaboration with industry, had produced valuable results. In 1940 the F2A or Brewster Buffalo and the F4F or Grumman Wildcat were in production, while the F4U or Corsair, by Chance Vought, and the F6F or Grumman Hellcat were well along in the design stage. Other carrier types, already generally accepted, included two from Douglas, the SBD or Dauntless dive bomber and the TBD or Devastator torpedo plane, both to prove useful until the former was replaced by the SB2C or Curtiss-Wright Helldiver, the latter, after the battle of Midway, by the TBF or Grumman Avenger. The big flying boats for patrol duty included two from Consolidated, the two-engined PBY or Catalina and the giant four-engined PB2Y or Coronado, with one from Martin, the PBM or Mariner. For cruisers and battleships, to spot and to patrol close aboard, the Curtiss biplane, Seahawk, more familiarly known from its designating letters as the "SOC," was gradually being super-

seded by Chance Vought's OS2U, the Kingfisher. All these were
supported by numerous training, utility, and transport planes, designed through the years and still very useful, and by a few blimps.

It is to the credit of the Bureau of Aeronautics and of the aircraft industry that so many of the original naval types remained
appropriate for service through most of the war, but this does not
mean that no improvements in these types were found desirable.
Many such improvements were introduced and one or two types
were dropped because they could not accommodate new equipment
developed as practice and experience in war came to the help of
designers. That most of the original designs were sound, however,
was shown by planes like the Wildcat, which came out of the war
carrying additions including armor for the pilot, self-sealing fuel
tanks, more powerful engines, increased fire power, radar, and innumerable gadgets, yet remained essentially a Wildcat.

The one real lack in designs was a land-based plane suitable for
naval use, a lack naturally resulting from that earlier division of
air responsibility which left the use of this type to the Army. During the winter of 1940–41 naval operations in northern waters
demonstrated the difficulty of getting seaplanes off the surface in
cold weather, and this led to a modification of the Catalina which
made it amphibious but left it still unable to meet all that would be
required of it. Late in 1941 the Army supplied a number of Lock-
heed Hudson landplanes, first of several types, like the PV-1 or
Vega Ventura and the PB4Y-1 or Consolidated Liberator, used
with excellent results in reconnaissance, patrol, and antisubmarine
attacks. For strictly naval purposes however, all these required
many changes, at a cost in labor nearly equal to one half that represented by original building; an obvious waste of time and money,
with results never wholly satisfactory. Later in the war the
PB4Y-2 or Consolidated Privateer, an army design modified to
meet the Navy's needs, began coming off the assembly lines, but it
was not until after hostilities had ceased that a landplane designed
from the start for the Navy was adopted.

To keep pace with plane building, work was pushed, as funds
became available, on those essentials of a fighting air force, bases
and ships. Among the former were the big training stations which
began to grow up at Corpus Christi, Texas, and Jacksonville,
Florida, and the smaller ones at Quonset Point, Rhode Island, and
Alameda, California. All the old bases, including those assigned to
the reserve units, were considerably improved, and a program of

building fields got underway on Pacific and Caribbean islands owned by the United States. As much advantage as possible was taken of the opportunity to cover the approaches to the Atlantic coast with "foreign" bases acquired in the historic exchange with Great Britain which gave her 50 World War I American destroyers.

As to ships to support aircraft, there came an unforeseen slant to the program for building these. The Royal Navy, in its fight against the U-boats, very soon learned the importance of aircraft and then realized the inability of land-based planes to cover all the oceans. What was needed was a small carrier with enough speed to make her useful in the protection of merchant convoys. When this was brought to the attention of President Roosevelt, he asked the Navy Department to study the possibility of converting merchantmen, already afloat and in service, into makeshift carriers. By a coincidence, this request reached the Navy Department at the same time as a similar one, made for a different reason by Rear Adm. (later Fleet Adm.) W. F. Halsey, Jr. Halsey, then Commander Aircraft, Battle Force, foresaw that fighting a war would mean using all existing carriers in operations against the enemy, leaving none available for the demands of training pilots or for transporting aircraft overseas. His recommendation that merchant ships be converted to these auxiliary purposes, with favorable endorsements from both Adm. J. O. Richardson and the latter's successor as Commander in Chief, Adm. H. E. Kimmel, got to Washington in time to suggest that the solution of the convoys' problem and the Fleet's problem might be the same. On March 4, 1941, the cargo ship *Mormacmail* began a conversion from which, in just under three months, she emerged as U.S.S. *Long Island*, first of more than 100 CVE or escort carriers converted or built in American shipyards for the United States and Britain. The essential difference between the *Long Island* and earlier designs for light carriers lay in the idea that she would be noncombatant—an idea which would very soon go overboard as escort carriers found themselves in some of the hottest actions of the war.

With planes, carriers, ships, and bases coming into being, where were the men to be found and how were they to be trained? In the days when Naval Aviation had been small, it had been a comparatively simple matter to take a graduate of the Naval Academy, already thoroughly grounded in the regulations and customs of the Navy, send him to Pensacola and from there to the Fleet to become a combat pilot. On the new scale, thousands of physically fit young Americans must be found and then, in the absolute minimum of time, taught both how to fly and how to be naval officers; a very large order indeed. To fill it the Navy, like the Army, reread its Kipling and turned to the "playing fields" of the colleges for the generation whose fathers had made their fine showing in World War I. To get these youths trained some requirements were dropped, for example the one demanding that every pilot must be able to fly every type of plane. Each man concentrated upon one combat type, and instead of spending a long training period in the Fleet, which was fully occupied with other and more pressing duties, he went to an operational training squadron to get his final polishing in group and squadron tactics. From the start all training was guided by the understanding that these youngsters were going into war, not preparing for a lifelong career, but as the war progressed and as the pilot shortage became rather less acute, it proved advisable to extend the one-year training period to two years, with obviously good results. Even so, the system was a very rigorous one, as indeed it must be to produce men to do their job.

What that job was likely to be was evident even before the system was firmly established. As Johnson's neutrality patrol took on broader duties, it became necessary to move more and more ships around from the Pacific. Many new ships built on the Atlantic side remained there, partly because of the patrol, partly because many in high places believed that the coming war would be fought chiefly in the Atlantic. All this made reorganization imperative and on February 1, 1941, the United States Atlantic Fleet was reborn with Adm. Ernest King as its Commander in Chief. His organization was of the "type-command" variety which, as to aviation, continued the distinction between patrol planes and carrier planes but made it clear that there would be plenty of work for both. It needed only a few weeks to prove that, for in March came the Lend Lease Act, in July came the garrisoning of Iceland by the United States, both steps which took the Navy into still wider areas of activity. This was not even yet officially called war, but it gave the units involved an experience far more realistic than anything ever afforded by Fleet exercises.

Through these events, and through the efforts made to meet events that were likely to follow, a few of the clouds of confusion were blown away, a few others were becoming thinner. At least some of the innumerable elements of preparedness had been acquired, while some others had been provided for, even though true preparedness was still not much more than a blueprint hope. The number of air craft available by December, 1941, was 5,260, and the number of pilots, including those in the Coast Guard and the Marine Corps, had reached 6,750. Added to these were 1,874 ground officers and a total of 21,678 enlisted men. The carriers, beginning with the little *Long Island* and ending with the *Saratoga* and *Lexington*, numbered eight. Even aircraft tenders, for which Moffett had so persistently fought, had increased to 34: nine of them, to be sure, still the old "bird-class" mine sweepers; one that converted veteran, the *Langley*, and 14 partially converted destroyers of World War I, but five large and five small tenders really designed and built specifically for that purpose. Material and equipment were slowly assembling at all points and this fact, together with the figures just given, might suggest that Naval Aviation was prepared to stand the test of war. Actually, what had been got together represented, by comparison with what would be needed, hardly more than a "sergeant's guard" with half-filled bandoliers and haversacks.

When the worst came at Pearl Harbor, it had but one redeeming feature. The damage to the battleships removed all possibility of what might otherwise have been expected, a demand by the American people that the Fleet at once attack Japan. With the pitifully inadequate protection in the air, this must inevitably have spelled disaster and probably a much longer war. As it was, through the lucky circumstance that the Japanese did not destroy the shops at Pearl, it became possible to rebuild the battleships to be much more powerful than they had been before they were damaged. In the end, protected by adequate aircraft, the Fleet was vastly stronger for the task it had to do.

During those months of repairs the Navy fought delaying actions when and where it could in the Pacific. While a handful of cruisers, destroyers, and submarines did their best to be in half a dozen places at once, the five Pacific carriers, in seven months, steamed 180,000 miles to make raids on targets that ranged from New Guinea to Japan itself. In the four days that began on May 4, 1942, the enemy was stopped in the Coral Sea even though the opposing surface forces never sighted one another. A month later, between June 3 and 6, the enemy was decisively beaten from the air above Midway, and it was these two successes that led to the first limited counteroffensive against the Solomon Islands, an operation supported by both carrier-based and land-based planes of the Navy and Marine Corps. During that first year of the Pacific war four of the six carriers engaged were lost and the other two were badly damaged, but they held the front in the air. They made it possible, without losing the war in the interim, to gain time enough to create a fleet in which all units were adequate for their several parts, and it should be noted that the battleships of that fleet had been designed to win World War II, not necessarily to win some future war when aircraft might have become both invulnerable and wholly self-supporting.

In the early stages, aircraft of all types found themselves doing almost anything at any given time, often a job for which they had not been specifically designed. In all the theaters of action harassed commanders frequently broke through theoretical lines of division between what the Army's planes or the Navy's planes were supposed to do; to reach some immediate objective they used anything able to take the air at the moment. In 1942 and in 1943 army planes did valiant service in the Atlantic antisubmarine efforts while the Navy's planes flew many army missions from their Pacific bases.

On distinctly naval missions, the Catalina and Mariner flying boats carried out endless reconnaissance, accompanied invasion forces, and on numerous occasions began their operations from occupied islands before landing fields had even been taken, much less reconditioned. They attacked enemy merchant shipping, handled much of the sea-rescue work, and evacuated large numbers of the wounded. It was only their slow speed and their great vulnerability that led to their being replaced, for antisubmarine and reconnaissance work, by landplanes.

As has been noted, it was the inability of land-based planes to cover enough of the ocean that led to the creation of the small escort carriers and this type very soon made a name for itself. Since larger carriers could not be withdrawn from the Pacific, it was the little ones with the help of the *Ranger*, that covered the North African and the southern France landings when these were made, doing the aerial spotting for the preliminary naval bombardments which did so much to clear the way for these landings. This was not to the neglect of their original mission, the protection of convoys, for their planes had a large part in the 83 sinkings credited to aircraft among the 174 losses counted against the U-boats. Conspicuous among them were the *Bogue* and later the *Guadalcanal*, which fought one U-boat practically hand to hand. After the war Grand Admiral Doenitz declared that his submarines, originally designed to proceed on the surface and dive only to make an attack or to escape one, had been beaten by aircraft equipped with radar. Certainly it was the effectiveness of planes which first drove the wolf pack out into mid-ocean and then forced the Germans to design a submarine able to remain submerged indefinitely and to make high speed underwater.

Out in the Pacific the effect of building became greater week by week. By the middle of 1943, when the total number of planes had risen to 16,691, the pilots to 26,651, ground officers to 23,377, and enlisted men in aviation ratings to 156,836, the increase in carriers was impressive. There were then 12 large ones including the 27,000-ton *Essex* class and the 10,000-ton *Independence* class. Incidentally, the latter class went back to a size rejected in 1925 and used, for its hulls, the designs made for the *Cleveland* class of cruiser. By this same period there were 17 of the escort carriers available, with as many more due to be commissioned within another six months. Their increasing usefulness was evident as soon as they began to appear in the Pacific as the only available carrier defense against enemy carriers in the Solomons; later they were almost everywhere. Towers, relieved by McCain as Chief of the Bureau of Aeronautics and put in command of the Air Force, Pacific Fleet, used the carriers in the Gilbert landings, and their success at Tarawa and Makin resulted in their continuous use for landings after that. They could defend themselves, just as had been predicted by the board studying the bombing tests of 1921, when naval observers declared that the best defense against aircraft was to operate better aircraft. Their planes, with navy or marine pilots, achieved a great degree of accuracy in pin-pointing revetments, pillboxes, and gun emplacements that were opposing a landing, an accuracy directly traceable to training methods developed from exercises in amphibious landings conducted years before and especially by the marines. To be sure, the little escort carriers supporting these planes were themselves extremely vulnerable, but since only five were lost in the Pacific it appears that they were not often hit, even though they were present at all the landings from the Gilberts through the Philippines to Iwo Jima and Okinawa.

Between the day in 1929 when Admiral Pratt had sent the *Saratoga* on her lone-hand "bombing" of the Panama Canal, and the Marshall Island strike in February, 1942, Naval Aviation had moved a long way. Yet, even then, it was still held that carriers should act independently, to evade the enemy, and that even as many as two carriers in company represented a great risk. Only a month later, however, the *Lexington* and the *Yorktown* together raided Salamau and Lae in New Guinea, and the effectiveness of their coordinated attack was not lost upon such observers as Capt. (later Vice Adm.) Frederick Sherman, commanding the *Lexington*. His reports and recommendations combined with others to produce a revision of carrier tactics. By the fall of 1943, when the carrier numbers had increased to those given above, a fair-sized fleet of them was assembled for the Gilbert landings; 11 carriers, in four groups, all under the command of Rear Adm. C. A. Pownall, at this writing the Governor of Guam. As a matter of history, those ships formed the first actual Fast Carrier Task Force, each group with its own screen of battleships, cruisers, and destroyers. With planes and heavy gunfire to protect them, it was these task forces which later, under Mitscher and McCain, led the way across the Pacific. Their dive bombers, equipped with self-sealing tanks and with armor, proved far less vulnerable than had been expected, while their accuracy became proverbial. Torpedo planes justified Fiske's old prediction—luckily while he was still alive to see the day—for, although they had to be protected by fighter squadrons, they too built up an impressive record of hits.

These were the planes that became famous, but behind them those of the Utility Wings and the Naval Air Transport Service were doing everything that an aircraft is mechanically able to do or a pilot humanly able to think of doing. At one time or another they flew anything anywhere. To keep them in the air without neglecting the fighting planes had been, from the very first, a most important factor in the Fleet's ever-growing problem of logistics. Personnel must be where it was needed, fuel and oil must be instantly available, and not a plane must be idle for lack of upkeep and repair.

As early as February, 1942, Admiral Nimitz had reorganized the Pacific Command, abolishing the titles Battle Force and Scouting Force, but at that time he had left the planes divided into Patrol Wings, Utility Wings, and Carriers, each organized separately, as was the Fleet Marine Force, with its planes dependent upon supplies from the Navy's sources. After the battle of Midway, however, he saw that it was impossible to continue dealing with two supply offices in San Diego and two more at Pearl Harbor, while at least three aviation commands had a hand in logistics; the only possible course was the creation of what had been proposed as long before as 1928, a single type command for all aircraft. In September, 1942, this became the Air Force, United States Pacific Fleet, at first commanded by Vice Adm. A. W. Fitch and later, as noted above, by Towers. It was this command which organized pilots and ground officers, airmen and ground crews into operating units where they could be trained for combat, and at the same time supervised the distribution of all aviation personnel as well as the maintenance and repair of all planes and all ships in aviation. Under the two commanders named, the force became so efficient that it was copied in the Atlantic in 1943, the force on that side being successively commanded by two veteran fliers, Rear Adm. A. D. Bernhard and Bellinger, by this time a vice admiral. Something of what this type command had to do may be inferred from the size of the Fleet's aviation forces by the end of 1944, when there were 36,721 planes, 55,956 pilots, 32,707 ground officers, and 312,146 enlisted ratings, with 25 larger or CV and CVL carriers and 65 of the CVE or escort types.

It goes without saying that among so many officers and men many who had joined the Navy, as their fathers had done in 1917, to fight in the air never had a chance to do it. Instead, they found themselves at some rear-area base or at a desk in Washington, Chicago, or San Francisco, at the everlasting job of administration. Since 1921 aviation had spoken through the Bureau of Aeronautics or, when there was one, through the Assistant Secretary of the Navy for Air. Twenty years later, with a war to be won, these offices could not adequately handle, for the Chief of Naval Operations, aviation's share of logistics; new offices became essential.

In August, 1943, Admiral King was furnished with a Deputy Chief of Naval Operations for Air under whom were presently grouped all divisions of King's office concerned with aviation as well as those divisions in the Bureau of Aeronautics concerned with planning, training, flight, and distribution of personnel, all of which had become too big for the bureau itself. Vice Admiral McCain, who had been Chief of the Bureau of Aeronautics since October, 1942, turned that post over to Rear Adm. (now Adm.) D. C. Ramsey, and moved up to the new one. From it he and his successors could speak directly in the name of Admiral King and thus deal far more effectively with every element of logistics.

The office spread through numerous subordinates. During its

first year a special board headed by Rear Admiral Radford produced the so-called Integrated Aeronautic Program for Maintenance, Material, and Supply under which it became possible to
deliver fully equipped planes just where they were needed, use
them for a stated period, then dispose of those unfit for combat and
bring the rest back to be repaired and used for training. Later,
turning its attention to bases, the deputy's office found ways to save
taxpayers' money by transferring equipment from a base which
the course of the war made unnecessary to a base that was still
active. Similarly, the three types of training, primary, advanced,
and operational, were finally grouped under a Chief of Naval Air
Training, who later also administered the Technical Training
Command. Personnel, for the obvious reason that no one could
guess how long the war might last and how many men might be
needed to win it, remained a problem, but another board under
Rear Adm. (later Vice Adm.) H. B. Sallada by the summer of
1945 completed a plan to meet such problems as the one created
by testing young men, enrolling them, and then weakening their
morale by bidding them await a call to active duty. All these were
intricate matters since, by that time, the figures had again expanded. Naval Aviation came to V-J Day with 41,272 planes,
60,747 pilots, 32,827 ground officers, and 344,424 enlisted men.
Afloat, there were 28 larger, 71 smaller carriers.

There it stood when thousands of young men must be de-
mobilized, when tons of equipment must be sold or scrapped, old
plane models destroyed, and new ones, along with the carriers, laid
up not in lavender but in cellophane. That was almost half a century after Theodore Roosevelt had listened to the story of Langley
and then, without even Towers looking over his shoulder, written
his historic memorandum. Theodore Roosevelt was dead and so,
too, was Franklin Roosevelt, another who had been Assistant Secretary of the Navy and then President. Congressmen such as Frederick Hicks of New York and others too numerous to name, who had
authorized the Bureau of Aeronautics and voted money to sustain
it, were long gone. Administrators like Chambers, Bristol, and,
above all, Moffett, had not lived to see what they had built stand
the test. Ellyson and Rodgers, Bronson, Saufley, Chevalier, and
all the honored men of two wars, had paid for their devotion with
their lives, leaving only a handful who had known the beginnings.
Only they could know the long road from the moment when it had
been suggested that the Navy try the machine "on a scale to be of

use in war." All could know, however, that this war, like every important war in history, had been won by sea power, but this time with a difference. Sea power could no longer be effective by controlling the waters of the earth on and under their surface. It must henceforth have one mighty arm reaching high into the air.

Sources

DOCUMENTARY COLLECTIONS

1. National Archives, Navy Section. These collections are of basic importance and include: (a) Bureau of Aeronautics. When this bureau was created in 1921, as many documents bearing on aviation as could be drawn from other bureaus and offices were combined with Aeronautics' own files. These treat every phase of development.

(b) Records of the Bureau of Navigation (now Naval Personnel), the Bureau of Ordnance, and the combination of Construction and Repair with Steam Engineering, now known as the Bureau of Ships. All these deal with Naval Aviation in the branches with which they were directly concerned.

(c) Files of the offices of the Secretary of the Navy and of the Chief of Naval Operations. These deal with policy, fleet organization and training, and annual exercises.

(d) Files of the Office of Naval Records and Library. These are operational records through the year 1937 and are of particular importance on World War I, because they include the reports, dispatches, and letters of Sims, Benson, Cone, Irwin, etc.

2. The Library of Congress. The Manuscript Division contains the papers of many officers and others connected with Naval Aviation, notably those of the late Rear Adm. Mark L. Bristol.

3. The General Board, Navy Department. This board keeps its own records, with much material on policy, building programs, ship construction, bases, and the military characteristics of aircraft. The records of hearings before the board are very informative.

4. The Office of Naval Records and History. The files include those of the former Office of Naval Records and Library (1[d] above) after 1937.

5. The papers of Capt. Washington I. Chambers. A large collection of these is in the possession of Mr. Frederick J. Schmitt, Patent Counsel of the Bureau of Aeronautics. Combining a personal interest in history with his profession, Mr. Schmitt has preserved much that would otherwise have disappeared.

MANUSCRIPT HISTORIES

1. The National Archives, through transfer from the Office of Naval Records and History, has numerous reports and narratives originally pre-

pared for a history of World War I which was never published. Since many
of these are in rough draft, their statements should be subjected to checking. The following are particularly useful:

C. E. Mathews, Lt. (jg), USNRF,   "Patrolling and Patrol Stations on
                                   the Western Atlantic."

C. E. Mathews, Lt. (jg), USNRF,   "Training in America."

D. G. Copeland, Civil Engineer,   "Lessons Learned from the Con-
USN,   struction of United States Naval
                                   Air Stations, Ireland."

T. T. Craven, Capt., USN,   "History of the French Air Sta-
                                   tions."

T. T. Craven, Capt., USN,   "Introduction by the Aid for Avia-
                                   tion." A sketch to be used as intro-
                                   duction to a history of naval air ac-
                                   tivities—France.

[K. R.] Ellington, Lt. (jg)   "Naval Aviation Activities During
[USNRF],   the War." Deals largely with ord-
                                   nance matters.

F. R. McCrary, Comdr., USN,   "History of the Irish Bases, 1917–
                                   1918."

K. Whiting, Lt. Comdr., USN,   "History of the First Aeronautic
                                   Detachment, United States Navy."

Anon.,   "Aviation Activities of the Navy in
                                   Europe . . ."

Anon.,   "History of Naval Aviation, For-
                                   eign Service, French Unit, 1917 and
                                   1918."

Anon.,   "History of United States Naval
                                   Aviation in Italy."

Anon.,   "Memorandum on Aviation in Amer-
                                   ica."

Anon.,   "Northern Bombing Group, United
                                   States Naval Aviation Forces in
                                   France."

Anon.,   "Preliminary Preparations." Deals
                                   with preparations for a European
                                   program.

Anon.,   "Shore Facilities for Aviation."

Anon.,   "United States Naval Aviation in
                                   France." Covers period June 5,
                                   1917 to November 1, 1918.

Anon.,   "Historical Sketches of Certain
                                   Bases and Units."

These files also contain the draft of Capt. (now Vice Adm.) T. T. Craven's "History of Aviation in the United States Navy" from the beginning to the spring of 1920. This is full of information but unfortunately it includes certain inaccuracies which have crept in print elsewhere.

Numerous brief studies, prepared by Comdr. J. C. Hunsaker in 1923, deal with events and developments with which he was familiar. These are reliable and of great value on technical points.

Lt. Comdr. J. J. White (MC) USN, contributed a "Brief History of the Fleet Patrol Plane Squadrons" from the organization of the first one in 1919 to the organization existing in 1933.

Another study of importance, by Rear Adm. H. E. Lackey, USN, is a history of the evolution of "The Shore Station Development Board."

"The Chronology of United States Naval Aviation," from its beginning to January 1936, prepared for Rear Adm. A. B. Cook when he became Chief of the Bureau of Aeronautics in that year, is not strictly history but it is informative.

2. The Office of Naval Records and History. In these files will be found the four bound volumes forming the documented draft of the research by Clifford L. Lord from which the present volume is drawn.

Also in this office are copies of many narratives, monographs, and historical summaries prepared by the Aviation History Unit under the program for World War II. Certain of these are still under "Security Classification" but it is hoped that all will be generally available before long. Included are:

J. Grimes, Lieut., USNR,	"Aviation in the Fleet Exercises, 1911–1939."
R. W. Dittmer, Lt. (jg), USNR,	"Naval Aviation Planning in World War II."
I. D. Spencer, Lieut., USNR, and D. M. Foerster, Lieut., USNR,	"Aviation Shore Establishments, 1911–1945."
C. L. Lord, Lt. Comdr., USNR, and G. M. Fennemore, Lt. (jg), USNR,	"Aviation Training, 1911–1939."
A. O. Van Wyen, Lieut., USNR,	"The Civil Aeronautics Authority War Training Service."
W. O. Shanahan, Lt. Comdr., USNR, D. A. Bergmark, Lieut., USNR, A. R. Buchanan, Lieut., USNR, and H. W. Lynn,	"Aviation Procurement, 1939–1945, Part I."
G. T. Tobias, Lieut., USNR, W. O. Shanahan, Lt. Comdr., USNR, and A. R. Buchanan, Lieut., USNR,	"Aviation Procurement, 1939–1945, Part II."
R. M. Carrigan, Lt. Comdr., USNR, R. C. Weems, Lt. Comdr., USNR, and T. A. Miller, Lieut., USNR,	"Aviation Personnel, 1911–1939."

C. F. Stanwood, Lt. Comdr., USNR,	"Financial and Legislative Planning, 1911–1945."
G. M. Fennemore, Lt. (jg), USNR, M. B. Chambers, Lt. Comdr., USNR, and A. F. Vaupel, 2nd Lt., USMCR-W	"Aspects of Aviation Training, 1939–1945."
W. O. Shanahan, Lt. Comdr., USNR,	"Procurement of Naval Aircraft, 1907–1939."
E. L. Smith, Capt. USMCR-W	"Aviation Organization in the United States Marine Corps, 1912–1945."

BOARDS AND HEARINGS

The reports of all naval boards mentioned in the text, often including voluminous testimony, are in the files of the Navy Department.

Among the customarily printed records of hearings before regular committees of the Congress, the most pertinent are those of the Senate and House committees on naval affairs. Hearings by certain special boards or committees created to investigate aviation are also important.

No story would be complete without consulting the following:

House of Representatives, 68th Congress, *Inquiry into Operations of the United States Air Services,* Hearings before the Select Committee of Inquiry [Lampert Committee] (Washington, Government Printing Office, 1925), 4 vols.

Senate Document No. 18, 69th Congress, 1st Session, *Aircraft in National Defense,* Report of the board, appointed by the President of the United States on September 12, 1925, to make a study of the best means of developing and applying aircraft in National Defense [Morrow Board] (Washington, Government Printing Office, 1925).

House of Representatives, Committee on Interstate and Foreign Commerce, 69th Congress, *Aircraft,* Hearings before the President's Aircraft Board [Morrow Board] (Washington, Government Printing Office, 1925), 4 vols.

Senate Document No. 15, 74th Congress, 1st Session, *Report of the Federal Aviation Commission* (Washington, Government Printing Office, 1935).

Also of significance are:

House Document No. 1946, 64th Congress, 2nd Session, *United States Navy—Commission on Navy Yards and Naval Stations* (Washington, Government Printing Office, 1917–1918), 4 parts. These are the six reports of the so-called "Helm Board," headed by Rear Adm. J. M. Helm, USN. It made a number of recommendations regarding aviation school and patrol base sites.

House Document No. 132, 71st Congress, 2nd Session, *Letter from the Secretary of the Navy transmitting Report covering Selection of Locations Deemed most Suitable for a Naval Airship Base* [Report of the Moffett Board] (Washington, Government Printing Office, 1929).

United States Navy—Special Board on Shore Establishments, *Report of Special Board on Shore Establishments. Approved January 13, 1923* (Washington, Government Printing Office, 1923). The important "Rodman Board" report, which laid down the basic pattern for the shore establishment for the period 1923–1938, i.e., until the Hepburn report.

United States Senate—Committee on Naval Affairs, 66th Congress, 2nd Session, *Naval Investigation,* Hearings before the Subcommittee of the Committee on Naval Affairs (Washington, Government Printing Office, 1920), 2 vols. These are the hearings in the investigations respecting Admiral Sims and the conduct of naval operations in World War I. Pp. 1719–1746 are especially useful for aviation history.

House Document No. 65, 76th Congress, 1st Session, *Report on Need of Additional Air Bases to Defend the Coasts of the United States, its Territories, and Possessions. December 23, 1938* (Washington, Government Printing Office, 1939). This is the report of the Hepburn Board.

BIBLIOGRAPHIES

Among its many contributions to research, the National Advisory Committee for Aeronautics in 1921 issued its *Bibliography of Aeronautics, 1909–1916.* This volume was followed annually by others until with the volume for 1932, appearing in 1936, the series was suspended. Included are all features of aviation development, both technical and historical, with lists of articles, books, and official publications.

In G. H. Fuller, *Expansion of the United States Navy, 1931–1939,* (Washington, 1939), there is a useful bibliography of documents published officially.

OTHER PRINTED SOURCES

The *Annual Report of the Secretary of the Navy.* Through fiscal 1933, the reports of the various Chiefs of Bureau, the Commandant of the Marine Corps, etc. were also printed, most important being the *Annual Report of the Chief of the Bureau of Aeronautics.* For later years, the bureau reports were issued in mimeograph.

Navy Department General Orders have been printed as they appeared.
A. O. Van Wyen, *Aeronautical Board, 1916–1947* (Washington, 1947),
includes many documents in the appendices.

The Statutes at Large should be consulted, as should *Laws Relating to
the Navy, Annotated,* a compilation prepared in the Office of the Judge
Advocate General, Navy Department.

PERIODICALS AND NEWSPAPERS

The Proceedings of the Naval Institute, 1874 to date, contain many informative notes and articles.

While scholarly historical publications generally have not given much
space to aviation, the review issued by the American Military Institute
since 1937 has done so. This has been successively titled the *American
Military Historical Foundation,* the *Journal of the American Military Institute,* and finally *Military Affairs.*

Air Affairs, 1946 to the present; the *Journal of the Society of Automotive
Engineers;* and the *Journal of the American Society of Naval Engineers*
are also available.

For the early days, such periodicals as *Flying, Aeronautics,* etc. give
interesting information on aircraft, flights, and other minutiae. Newspapers
have been little used for this book, but *The New York Times, The Washington Post,* and *The Army and Navy Register* have been consulted on
specific points.

PUBLISHED BOOKS

Older histories of the Navy deal chiefly with general policy or with
operations. Among these, the following are informative as background for
Naval Aviation: D. W. Knox, *History of the United States Navy* (rev. ed.,
New York, 1948); A. Westcott, *American Sea Power Since 1775* (New
York, 1947); H. and M. Sprout, *The Rise of American Naval Power, 1776–
1918* (rev. ed., Princeton, 1942), and *Toward A New Order of Sea Power*
(Princeton, 1940); G. T. Davis, *A Navy Second to None* (New York,
1940); B. Brodie, *Sea Power in the Machine Age* (Princeton, 1941); and
W. D. Puleston, *Mahan* (New Haven, 1939). The only effort at synthesis,
D. W. Mitchell, *History of the Modern American Navy* (New York, 1946),
contains a good many errors and is far from complete. It is to be hoped that
the works on which Dr. R. G. Albion is engaged will fill this gap.

Valuable information on the early days of aviation may be found in
B. A. Fiske, *From Midshipman to Rear Admiral* (New York, 1919);
M. A. DeWolfe Howe, *George Von Lengerke Meyer* (New York, 1920);
C. Studer, *Sky Storming Yankee, the Life of Glenn Curtiss* (New York,
1937); A. Hatch, *Glenn Curtiss* (New York, 1942); G. Loening, *Our*

Wings Grew Fast (New York, 1935). An interesting comparison with the
Navy's experience of the early days may be found in C. Chandler and F.
P. Lahm, *How Our Army Grew Wings* (New York, 1943).

There are a few books specifically dealing with aviation before World
War I. No early aviator has set down his recollections, but it is hoped that
those recently retired from active duty may do so.

Among general books on the subject are H. B. Miller, *Navy Wings*
(New York, 1943), a dependable, anecdotal account with emphasis on
personalities and feats of early flying; Henry Woodhouse, *Textbook of
Naval Aeronautics* (New York, 1917), the work of a promoter with many
sections written by the participants; W. H. Sitz, "A History of U. S.
Naval Aviation," Bureau of Aeronautics, *Technical Note No. 18* (Washington, 1930), which is full of minor errors; and C. E. Rosendahl, *Up Ship*
(New York, 1932), a study of lighter-than-air craft development by one
of the Navy's experts.

In the great amount of literature on World War I, the following have
been found particularly useful: U.S. Navy Department, Bureau of Yards
and Docks, *Activities of the Bureau of Yards and Docks, 1917–1918*
(Washington, 1921); U. S. Navy Department, Office of Navy Intelligence,
Historical Section, *The American Naval Planning Section* (London, Washington, 1923), prepared by D. W. Knox, Capt., USN; J. Daniels, *The
Wilson Era* (Chapel Hill, 1944–1946), 2 vols.; J. Daniels, *Our Navy at
War* (New York, 1922); W. S. Sims, *Victory at Sea* (New York, 1920);
E. E. Morison, *Admiral Sims and the Modern American Navy* (Boston,
1942); Sir W. Raleigh and H. A. Jones, *The War in the Air*, (London,
1937), 6 vols.; B. M. Baruch, *American Industry in the War, a Report of
the War Industries Board* (Washington, 1921); and G. B. Clarkson, *Industrial America in the World War* (New York, 1923).

Although General Mitchell set forth his theories in numerous writings,
they can most conveniently be found in *Our Air Force* (New York, 1921),
and *Winged Defense* (New York, 1925). Their impact on army aviators
is sympathetically dealt with in J. L. Cate and W. F. Craven, eds., *Army
Air Forces in World War II* (Chicago, 1948), Vol. I. The best biography
is A. Gauareau and L. Cohen, *Billy Mitchell* (New York, 1942).

Although the history of World War II is still being written, the following give an idea of the part played by Naval Aviation: E. J. King, *U. S.
Navy at War, Official Reports to the Secretary of the Navy* (Washington, 1946); A. R. Buchanan, ed., *The Navy's Air War* (New York,
1946); and Office of the Chief of Naval Operations, *U. S. Naval Aviation in the Pacific* (Washington, 1947). Anyone interested should also
consult the publications of the United States Strategic Bombing Survey,
particularly, *Summary Report, Pacific War* (Washington, 1946), *Cam-
paigns of the Pacific War* (Washington, 1946), and *Interrogations of
Japanese Officials* (Washington, 1946), 2 vols. Begun during the war, the

series of volumes entitled *Battle Report,* prepared by W. Karig and others, gives a generally accurate account of the naval war, in a popular vein. More scholarly and authoritative but equally well written is S. E. Morison's, *History of United States Naval Operations in World War II,* the volumes of which are currently appearing.

Index

ACOSTA, BERT, 262
Act of July 2, 1926, 257
Act of May 21, 1926, 257
Aerial photography, 41, 72, 214, 234–235, 262, 288
Aerial scouting, 45, 62, 81
Aerial spotting, 53, 60, 62, 81
Aerial warfare: amphibious operation, 303; Army-Navy Board (1898), 1–2; assignment of functions, 76, 179–180, 184, 252, 278; Beachey's tests, 21; Bristol, 79–80; carrier group, 272; carriers, 214–215; Curtiss' prophecy, 6; defense of Grand Fleet, 81; defense of Philippines, 16; defense of shore establishment, 64–65; Eberle Board, 243 ff.; experience of Royal Naval Flying Service, 81; Fast Carrier Task Force, 319–320; General Board considers, 25, 62–64; group tactics, 88; importance, 155; mine detection, 38; Naval War College, 209; Pratt-MacArthur agreement, 278 ff.; role in naval operations, 200; tests with Fleet, 60; value of LTA, 281; see also Fleet exercises
Aero Club, 32, 93–94
Aerology, 103, 268, 288
Aeromarine Plane and Motor Co., 109, 115
Aeronautical Board, 76, 181; see also Cognizance Board, Joint Aeronautical Board, Joint Army and Navy Board on Aeronautic Cognizance
Aeronautical laboratory, 16–17
Aeronautical Society of New York, 16
Air bases, naval. See Air stations
Aircraft: acceptance tests, 66; appropriation requested, 9; Army buys one, 5; Army trials (1908), 4; Bolling Commission, 112–114; British, 153; Chambers' policy, 8; Deperdussin control, 56–57; development of types, 63; first landing aboard ship, 12; first shipboard launching, 10–11; inadequate number, 58, 60; increasing naval interest, 7–8; Langley, 1–3; multiple purpose type, 260; naval experi-

ments (1911), 20; Navy investigates, 4–5; on hand (1913), 29, (1917), 96, (1941), 317, (1943), 319, (1944), 321, (1945), 322; report on (1911), 14; Rheims aviation meet (1909), 6; tractor type, 67; types for naval use, 154; World War II models, 313–314; Wright brothers, 3
Aircraft industry: allocation of plants, 109; automobile companies, 83; code of conduct, 242–243; condition (1916), 82–83; cross-licensing agreements, 116; foreign orders, 46; government factory, 47; grievances, 240 ff.; lighter-than-air, 84; Morrow Board, 251 ff.; Naval Aircraft Factory, 116–117; Navy's good relations, 252; outbreak World War I, 106–107; problems of expansion, 311 ff.; spruce for, 118; subcontracting, 117; survey (1915), 55–56
Aircraft procurement: abroad, 112; Aircraft Production Board, 108 ff.; Chambers' policy, 15; cooperation with Army, 179–180; facilities preempted by Army, 107; first purchases, 17; France for U. S., 113; from Italy, 128; no corruption, 243; orders (1916), 83; policy, 240–241, 257, 277, 287–288; price and contract policy, 117–118; problems of expansion, 311 ff.
Aircraft production, raw materials for foreign plants, 113
Aircraft Production Board, 108, 109, 111, 113, 174; see also Aircraft industry, Aircraft procurement
Aircraft programs: Chambers' Board, 33; five-year program, 208–209, 227, 257, 259–260, 276–278; flying boats, World War I, 115; General Board (1916), 73–74; Lampert Committee, 293; not less than 3,000, 300; postwar, 155; U. S. 50,000-plane program, 311; Vinson-Trammell Act, 285; World War I difficulty, 110; World War I record, 147; World War II, 313
Air Force, U. S. Pacific Fleet, 321

Literature and History of Aviation

AN ARNO PRESS COLLECTION

Arnold, H[enry] H.
Global Mission. 1949.

Bordeaux, Henry.
Georges Guynemer: Knight of the Air. Translated by Louise Morgan Sill. 1918.

Boyington, "Pappy" (Col. Gregory Boyington).
Baa Baa Black Sheep. 1958.

Buckley, Harold.
Squadron 95. 1933.

Caidin, Martin.
Golden Wings. 1960.

"Contact" (Capt. Alan Bott).
Cavalry of the Clouds. 1917.

Crossfield, A. Scott and Clay Blair, Jr.
Always Another Dawn. 1960.

Fokker, Anthony H. G. and Bruce Gould.
Flying Dutchman: The Life of Anthony Fokker. 1931.

Gibson, Guy.
Enemy Coast Ahead. 1946.

Goldberg, Alfred, editor.
A History of the United States Air Force 1907-1957. 1957.

Gurney, Gene.
Five Down and Glory. Edited by Mark P. Friedlander, Jr. 1958.

Hall, Norman S.
The Balloon Buster: Frank Luke of Arizona. 1928.

Josephson, Matthew.
Empire of the Air: Juan Trippe and the Struggle for World Airways. 1944.

Kelly, Charles J., Jr.
The Sky's the Limit: The History of the Airlines. 1963.
  New Introduction by Charles J. Kelly, Jr.

Kelly, Fred C., editor.
Miracle at Kitty Hawk. 1951.

La Farge, Oliver.
The Eagle in the Egg. 1949.

Levine, Isaac Don.
Mitchell: Pioneer of Air Power. 1943.

Lougheed, Victor.
Vehicles of the Air. 1909.

McFarland, Marvin W., editor.
The Papers of Wilbur and Orville Wright. 2 volumes. 1953.

McKee, Alexander.
Strike From the Sky: The Story of the Battle of Britain. 1960.

Macmillan, Norman.
Into the Blue. 1969.

Magoun, F. Alexander and Eric Hodgins.
A History of Aircraft. 1931.

Parsons, Edwin C.
I Flew with the Lafayette Escadrille. 1963.

Penrose, Harald.
No Echo in the Sky. 1958.

Reynolds, Quentin.
The Amazing Mr. Doolittle. 1953.

Saunders, Hilary St. George.
Per Ardua: The Rise of British Air Power 1911-1939. 1945.

Stilwell, Hart and Slats Rodgers.
Old Soggy No. 1. 1954.

Studer, Clara.
Sky Storming Yankee: The Life of Glenn Curtiss. 1937.

Turnbull, Archibald D. and Clifford L. Lord.
History of United States Naval Aviation. 1949.

Turner, C. C.
The Old Flying Days. 1927.

Von Richthofen, Manfred F.
The Red Air Fighter. 1918.

Werner, Johannes.
Knight of Germany: Oswald Boelcke, German Ace. Translated by
  Claud W. Sykes. 1933.

Wise, John.
Through the Air. 1873.

Wolff, Leon.
Low Level Mission. 1957.

Yakovlev, Alexander.
Notes of an Aircraft Designer. Translated by Albert Zdornykh. n.d.